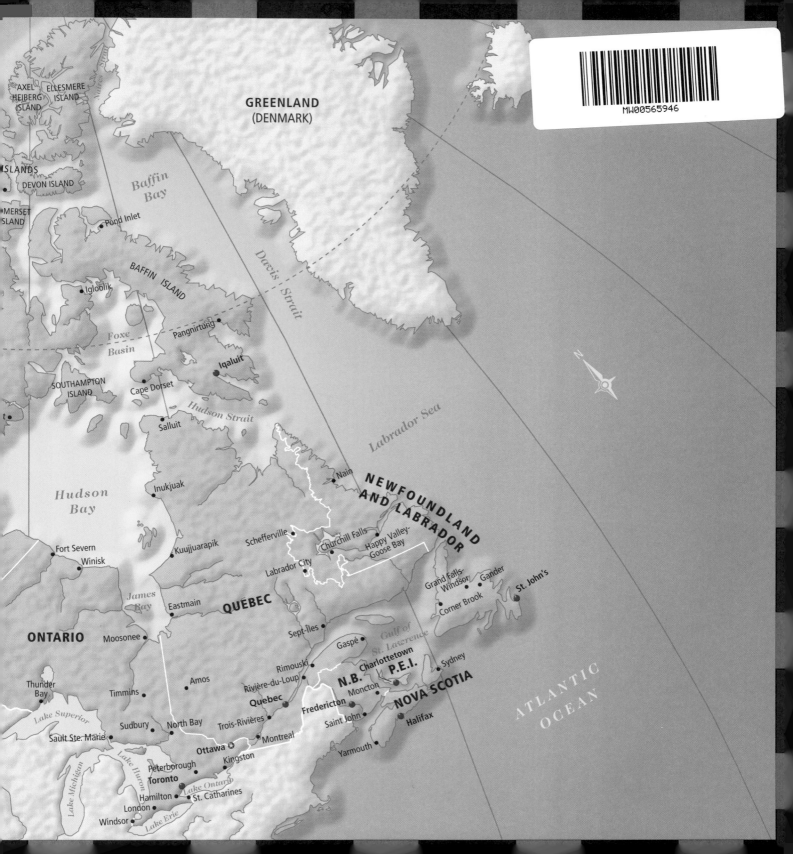

Continuity and Change

Canada

NEW EDITION

A HISTORY
OF CANADA
SINCE 1914

Don Bogle
Eugene D'Orazio
Don Quinlan

Fitzhenry & Whiteside
Markham, Ontario

Canada, Continuity and Change
New Edition

© 2006 Fitzhenry & Whiteside Limited
195 Allstate Parkway, Markham, Ontario L3R 4T8

Watch for this icon within *Canada, Continuity and Change*. It identifies pertinent moments in Canadian history, as dramatized on the Historica Minutes DVD.

Every reasonable effort has been made to find copyright holders of illustrations and quotations. The publishers would be pleased to have any errors or omissions brought to their attention

Senior Editor/Consultant: Douglas O. Baldwin, *Aboriginal Studies Consultant:* J. Peter Hill
Reading Consultant: Deborah Kekewich, *Project Coordinator:* Kate Revington
Production Editors: Amy Hingston, Morgan Grady-Smith
Design: Wycliffe Smith Design Inc., *Cartographer:* Deborah Crowle, *Illustrator:* Steven Hutchings

Cover images: Aboriginal Woman, Glenbow Archives NC-7-852; Women's Ice Hockey Team, 2002 © Kim Kulish/Corbis; David Suzuki, CP PHOTO/Larry MacDougal; Supreme Court Judges, © POOL/Reuters/Corbis; Michaelle Jean, CP PHOTO/Fred Chartrand; Canadian Soldier, CP PHOTO/Hans Deryk; PM Trudeau, CP PHOTO/Peter Bregg; partial reproduction of Ozias Leduc's "L'Enfant au Pain" © Estate of Ozias Leduc/SODRAC, 2000.

Fitzhenry & Whiteside acknowledges with thanks the support of the Government of Canada through its Book Publishing Industry Development Program in the publication of this title.

Library and Archives Canada Cataloguing in Publication
Bogle, Don
Canada, continuity and change: a history of Canada since 1914 /
Don Bogle, Eugene D'Orazio and Don Quinlan. — 2nd rev, and updated.

Includes index.
Target audience: For use in grade 10.
ISBN 1-55041-581-6

1. Canada—History—20th century. 2. Canada—History—21st century.
I. D'Orazio, Eugene II. Quinlan, Don, 1947- III. Title.

FC600.B63 2006   971.06   C2006-901964-9

Printed in Canada

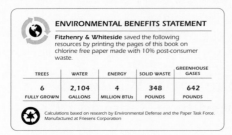

FSC
Mixed Sources
Product group from well-managed forests, controlled sources and recycled wood or fibre
Cert no. SW-COC-1271
www.fsc.org
© 1996 Forest Stewardship Council

ENVIRONMENTAL BENEFITS STATEMENT
Fitzhenry & Whiteside saved the following resources by printing the pages of this book on chlorine free paper made with 10% post-consumer waste.

TREES	WATER	ENERGY	SOLID WASTE	GREENHOUSE GASES
6	2,104	4	348	642
FULLY GROWN	GALLONS	MILLION BTUs	POUNDS	POUNDS

Calculations based on research by Environmental Defense and the Paper Task Force. Manufactured at Friesens Corporation

Contents

Students often ask, "Why do we have to study Canadian history?"

That question could be answered in many ways. The study of a country's history has often been compared to the examination of a person's memory. Imagine how empty you might feel without some knowledge of your own past. You could not enjoy your achievements, remember your struggles, or learn from your mistakes. If you did not know or could not remember what had happened before, it would be harder for you to make wise decisions today. In the same way, citizens cannot make wise decisions unless they know something of their nation's past.

This book explores the central events and experiences that have shaped the development of Canada's identity as a nation since the First World War. Its purpose is to expand your knowledge of important developments in Canada's history. *Canada: Continuity and Change*, New Edition, will make you aware of issues, tensions, questions, and achievements that have emerged over time.

You will be able to review the changes in our population, our society, our laws, and our way of life that have contributed to present-day Canadian society. It is hoped that you will come to better appreciate the hard struggles and great achievements of Canadians who came before you. You may better understand the strengths and challenges of the Canada in which you live today. Perhaps you will be inspired to help apply those strengths and deal with those challenges.

An intelligent citizen needs not only knowledge of the past, but also the skills to act upon that knowledge. Your course and this book will let you develop your abilities to communicate—by writing, by discussing, and by making oral presentations. You will be able to go beyond this text to develop your research skills. You will be invited to think, to analyse, to compare, and to evaluate the ideas of the past. You will also be asked to join classmates in co-operative learning activities, to solve problems, and to present solutions. All of these skills are necessary not only in a student, but in a successful citizen.

Finally, learn about Canadian history since the First World War because you may find it fascinating. We hope this book helps you see that studying Canadian history can be useful, enjoyable, and challenging. After all, the next pages in this nation's history will be written by you and your peers.

REMEMBRANCE

AIR FORCES • FORCES AÉRIENNES

CANADA

SOPWITH F.1 CAMEL

46

CANADA POSTAGE POSTES

In Flanders Fields
—
In Flanders fields the poppies blow
Between the crosses, row on row,

5

JOHN McCRAE
1872-1918

During the First World War, Canadians flocked to join the British air force. By war's end, one in four Royal Air Force officers was Canadian. More than 1600 Canadian airmen gave their lives. The Sopwith F.1 Camel shown here was piloted by Major William George Barker (1894–1930), who earned the prestigious Victoria Cross for single-handedly taking on 60 German aircraft on 27 October 1918. *Why do you think some young men would rather fight in the air than on the ground?*

Why are McCrae and his poem better known than Barker and his Victoria Cross?

HISTOR!CA
Minutes

Chapter One
War and Recognition

Expectations

Overall Expectations:

By the end of this chapter, you will be able to

- describe some of the major local, national, and global forces and events that have influenced Canada's policies and Canadian identity since 1914
- explain the significance of key individuals and events in the evolution of French–English relations in Canada since 1914

Specific Expectations:

By the end of this chapter, you will be able to

- identify the major groups of immigrants to Canada since 1914 and describe the push and pull factors that led to their immigration
- identify the causes of the First World War and explain how Canada became involved
- describe some of the contributions Canada and Canadians made to the overseas and at-home war efforts during the First World War
- summarize the key contributions of women to the war at home and on the battlefield
- explain how some key technological innovations in military and other fields (e.g., gas warfare) changed the way war was planned and fought, and describe their impact on combatants and civilians
- assess key instances in which the Canadian government chose to restrict citizens' rights and freedoms in wartime
- explain why conscription was controversial and how it divided English Canada and Quebec during the First World War
- evaluate Canada's participation in the war

Word List

Armistice	Canadian Expeditionary
Censored	Force
Convoy	Conscription
Dogfights	Eastern Front
Enemy aliens	Internment camps
No man's land	Over the top
Pacifist	Profiteering
Propaganda	Royal Canadian Legion
Self-determination	Shell shock
Treaty of Versailles	Triple Alliance
Triple Entente	Ultimatum
War Measures Act	Western Front

❶

❶ The early 1900s were a time of growth for Canada. Many people farmed, but factories were also being built. People lived in towns, but cities were also growing. Immigrants were settling in Canada. Times were peaceful.

A busy Canadian city in the early 1900s.

❷ In 1914, Europe was not as peaceful. War broke out, with Germany and Britain on opposite sides. Canada was part of the British Empire. Suddenly Canada was at war, too. Many Canadians volunteered to go to war.

Many Canadians were eager to join the fight.

❸ Soldiers dug trenches on the battlefields. They lived and fought in these trenches. The war was brutal. Many soldiers were killed, but many battles were won. Canadians gained a new pride in their country.

4 Early in the war, planes were used only to spy on the enemy. Later, machine guns were mounted on the planes. The

Airplane factory during the First World War.

age of air warfare had begun. Canadian pilots were among the best fighter pilots in the war.

6 Canada's factories produced machinery and weapons needed for the war. Men, who normally worked in these factories, were fighting in Europe. Women went to work in their place. They were happy to help with the war effort. They also wanted to vote in federal elections. Some got the right.

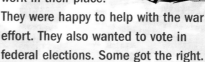

7 By 1917, many soldiers had been killed. Volunteers were too few to replace them. Canada introduced conscription. This forced young men to join the army. French Canadians did not feel close to Britain. They did not want to go to war. The unity of Canada was threatened.

5 Many ships carrying troops, food, and weapons gathered in Halifax harbour. They then set out together for Europe. This gave them more protection. In 1917, two ships in the harbour collided. One carried high explosives. In the explosion, many people were killed and the city was destroyed.

8 The war ended on 11 November 1918. Britain and its allies won. It was a day of both happiness and sadness. Not all soldiers returned home safely. Over 66 000 Canadians lost their lives in the war. In all, more than 9 million soldiers were killed.

Canada Before the War

The People

What was Canadian life like before the First World War? Try to place yourself back in time. Your life would have been quite different from what it is today. As you read this section, consider whether life at the turn of the 20th century was better or worse than life today. Try to notice the major differences and similarities. Would you consider changing places with a young Canadian in 1900?

In 1914, most Canadians lived on farms. Few young people went to high school. In the country, they were needed on the farm. In the city, their wages helped pay for the family's food and rent. Work was hard and the hours long. People married young and began raising families early. Adult responsibilities came quickly.

As well, many new immigrants to Canada chose to settle and develop the vast stretches of the fertile land in the West. Canada's Aboriginal peoples faced new challenges. They struggled to hold on to their identity, lands, and rights in a world dominated by European arrivals. Canadian women began to claim new roles. They found new respect in Canada's changing society. The turn of the century was a new beginning for Canada and Canadians.

A Rural Society

By 1900 the population of Canada was 5 200 000. Montreal,

CANADA BEFORE THE WAR

This map shows Canada's provinces and territories in 1905. How is it different today?

Toronto, and Halifax were the largest cities. Vancouver was the boomtown of the West Coast, but not many people lived west of Winnipeg. Regina, Calgary and Edmonton were small but growing pioneer cities.

Most people earned their living by work-

A "caboose" takes children to school one wintry morning in the early 20th century.

ing hard. The hours were long, salaries poor, and conditions difficult. Farming was the main occupation in 1900. Fishing was an important occupation in the Maritime provinces. Still other people worked in construction. Railways, roads, sewers, and buildings were all being constructed in the new cities. Women worked in factories, as servants for the rich, as teachers, nurses, and store clerks, and on their own farms and in their own homes.

Living Close to Home

Most people depended on the horse and buggy for local travel and the train for long journeys. By 1885, Canada was linked from sea to sea by railroads. Automobiles were so rare that people did not have driving licences. There were no speed limits, no stop signs, and no traffic lights. People usually spent their lives close to home. Life revolved around such institutions as the town band, the local baseball, lacrosse, or hockey team, and the church. There were few telephones, no supermarkets, no radios and no television. Newspapers were common, but international news was always slow to arrive. The age of the professional singer, comedian, or athlete was still to come. Most people provided their own entertainment. Singsongs around the family piano or dancing to a treasured violin or accordion were high points of any family gathering. A night out meant watching local talent in a play or a concert at the church hall. Opera and music halls were very popular in some parts of the country.

A New Century

The 1800s had been a period of gradual change. In 1900, most Canadians expected that the 20th century would continue in the same way. This was not to be. Canada would take part in two world wars and several regional wars. Canadian scientists and inventors would make dramatic strides forward in technology, communications, transportation, and medicine. Our population would grow with the arrival of new immigrants. The country would be known for its rich, multicultural diversity by the start of the 21st century. Aboriginal peoples would make great advances in **self-determination** and land rights. French Canadians would struggle to control their own destiny. Canadian astronauts would fly into space. Natural resources would play a vital role in the country's economic and social growth. Canada would develop its unique national character and heritage.

Prime Minister Wilfrid Laurier once said: "The nineteenth century has been the century of the United States…. The twentieth century shall be the century of Canada." Perhaps this century did not develop quite as he expected. Canada at the end of the 20th century was a very different place from the Canada that Laurier knew.

John Ware was one of Canada's greatest cowboys. Born a slave in 1845 in Texas, he arrived in Canada in 1882. He worked as a cowhand and bronco rider until 1888, when he bought his own ranch. He was famous for his remarkable horsemanship. There was not a horse "running on the Prairie which John could not ride." Ware died in 1905 after a tragic riding accident.

Women's hockey has deep roots in Canadian society. These women stitched buckshot into the hems of their skirts to keep them down. How important is hockey in your community?

The Ukrainians Ukrainians were among the many groups attracted to the Canadian West in the first years of the 20th century. This community has played an important role in the development of Canada. It has also maintained close ties with its homeland and traditions. Most Ukrainians were subjects of the Russian Czar or the Emperor of Austria-Hungary at the turn of the century. Here, they suffered political oppression and economic hardship. Crop failures, overpopulation, and the threat of war made life hard. They wanted a better future. Canadian agents in Europe offered 64 hectares of land per person for $10. Along with that came religious and political freedom. Earlier Ukrainian visitors, such as Dr. Joseph Oleskow, described the Canadian West as a land of golden opportunity.

From 1891 to 1914, about 170 000 Ukrainian farmers came to Canada. They were eager to take on the challenge of building a new life. They were poor and

Many people immigrated to Canada looking for freedom and to give their children a better life. Today, the Ukrainian community thrives in such urban centres as Edmonton, Winnipeg, and Toronto. Well-known members of the community include former governor general Ray Hnatyshyn and comedian Luba Goy.

unskilled in modern farming techniques, but worked hard. The settlers established communities in Alberta, Saskatchewan, and Manitoba.

During the First World War, Canadian authorities treated Ukrainians as **enemy aliens**. This happened because they came from Austria-Hungary, with whom Canada was at war. Many Canadians turned on the same settlers they had first welcomed and treated them with hatred and prejudice. Thousands of Ukrainian men were rounded up, some with their families, and sent to **internment camps** in remote areas of the country. Authorities admitted later that these people had done nothing wrong.
What factors "pushed" Ukrainians from Europe to Canada? What factors "pulled" Ukrainians to settle in Canada?

FOCUS

1. List at least 10 ways in which living in Canada in 1900 was different from today.
2. Select three ways in which life was better in 1900, and three ways in which it is better today. Explain the reasons behind the choices you made.
3. Why did so many people come to Canada before the First World War? Why do people come today?

The Road to War

In August 1914, most major European countries became involved in the First World War. From the end of the Napoleonic wars in 1815 to the outbreak of the First World War, there had been no major strife. All this ended in 1914.

A number of causes led to the outbreak of war in 1914:

1 – Emergence of Germany as a Major Power

By 1871, the German Chancellor (Prime Minister), Otto von Bismarck, had united most German-speaking people. They were a strong new nation that wished to be recognized as a major power of Europe. German leaders increased Germany's power by expanding its army and navy.

2 – Clash of Empires

Britain, France, Spain, and Portugal had large empires. They had colonies in Asia and Africa. By the 1890s, German leaders demanded that Germany also get colonies. These would be sources of raw materials for German industries and markets for manufactured goods. Most accessible lands had already been conquered. To get land, Germany would have to deal with Britain and France.

3 – Naval and Arms Race

In the early 1900s, the British navy was the largest in the world. Its main duty was to protect Britain's global empire. If Germany were to have a colonial empire, it, too, would require a large navy. Germany began to build a powerful, modern navy. Britain saw this as a challenge. The two countries got into a race to see who could build the biggest and strongest navy. Germany also competed with France and Russia to build the largest and best-equipped army. The naval and arms races increased tension and hostility in Europe. The world was drifting towards war.

4 – Nationalism

Countries that prize national interests over anything else often cause wars. The period before the First World War reflects this. European countries wanted to assert themselves and their national identity.

5 – Alliance System

Rivalries in Europe forced each country to make defensive alliances. Allies were needed for protection. Two alliances were established. In the **Triple Alliance**, Germany, Austria-Hungary, and Italy agreed to support each other if attacked by France, Britain, or Russia. In the **Triple Entente**, France, Russia, and Britain agreed to support each other if attacked by Germany, Italy, or Austria-Hungary. By 1914, Europe was divided into two heavily armed and hostile camps. All that was needed to cause an explosion was a spark.

The Technical Edge

One of the new century's most impressive weapons was a battleship called the dreadnought. It was heavily armoured, speedy, and loaded with huge 30 cm guns. These guns could fire 400 kg shells a distance of 6000 m. The dreadnought made all existing wooden warships almost obsolete. Both Germany and Britain engaged in a furious race to build these powerful ships.

Machine guns and tanks were also major new weapons that played key roles during the war. The machine gun, firing 600 rounds per minute, made it almost impossible for attacking armies to overrun an enemy's position. A bloody stalemate would result.

The tank helped to end the stalemate. It could ram through enemy lines. The tank was particularly effective during the final year of the war (1918).

The arrival of the dreadnought meant the days of wooden battleships were over. Here, a British dreadnought heaves in her anchor.

New powerful weapons made war more deadly than ever. Why would dreadnoughts and tanks be such effective weapons of war?

The Spark

A Serbian terrorist group, the Black Hand, assassinated Archduke Franz Ferdinand, the heir to the Austrian throne, on 28 June 1914 in Sarajevo, Bosnia-Herzegovina. This was a state within the Austro-Hungarian Empire. The Austrians sent Serbia an **ultimatum**. The Serbs refused. Austria invaded. Russia came to the aid of its Serbian allies.

Within one month, most members of the rival alliances were drawn into the conflict. Germany and Austria-Hungary fought against France, Russia, and Britain. Italy left the Triple Alliance with Germany and Austria, and later came into the war on the side of France and Britain. Japan also fought against Germany in the First World War. It captured German colonies in China. Canada was a member of the British Empire. If Britain went to war, that meant Canada was at war, too. Most Canadians were enthusiastic in their support for Britain.

TIMELINE

The First World War had both long- and short-term causes. The short-term events are listed here.

THE STEPS TO WAR—SUMMER OF 1914

28 June	Archduke Ferdinand is assassinated at Sarajevo.
23 July	Austria sends ultimatum (a list of far-reaching demands) to Serbia.
25 July	Serbia replies, rejecting one term.
28 July	Austria invades Serbia.
29 July	Russia mobilizes army along borders with Austria and Germany. Germany declares war on Russia.
3 August	France mobilizes forces to assist Russia. Germany declares war on France.
4 August	Germany invades Belgium, whose neutrality is guaranteed by Britain. Britain declares war on Germany.
5 August	Canada and the rest of the British Empire are at war.

Given the events, do you think the war could have been avoided? Explain.

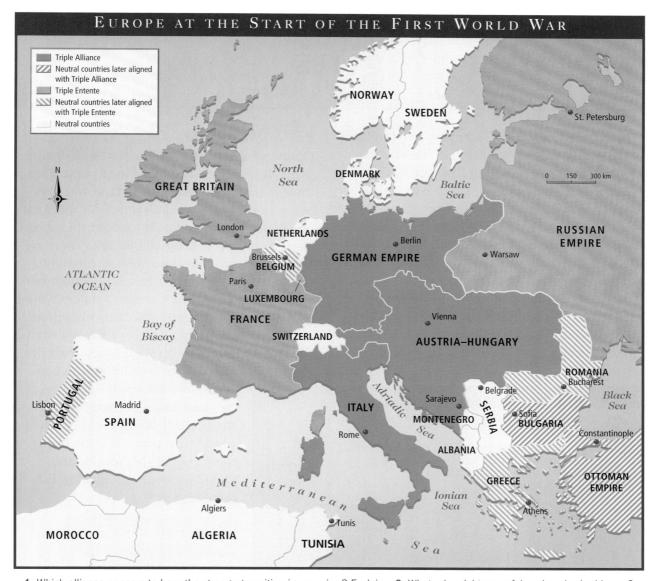

EUROPE AT THE START OF THE FIRST WORLD WAR

Triple Alliance
Neutral countries later aligned with Triple Alliance
Triple Entente
Neutral countries later aligned with Triple Entente
Neutral countries

N

NORWAY
SWEDEN
St. Petersburg
DENMARK
North Sea
Baltic Sea
GREAT BRITAIN
London
NETHERLANDS
Berlin
RUSSIAN EMPIRE
Warsaw
Brussels
BELGIUM
GERMAN EMPIRE
ATLANTIC OCEAN
Paris
LUXEMBOURG
FRANCE
Vienna
Bay of Biscay
SWITZERLAND
AUSTRIA–HUNGARY
ROMANIA
Bucharest
Belgrade
Sarajevo
Black Sea
PORTUGAL
Lisbon
Madrid
SPAIN
ITALY
MONTENEGRO
SERBIA
Sofia
BULGARIA
Constantinople
Rome
ALBANIA
Adriatic Sea
GREECE
OTTOMAN EMPIRE
Mediterranean
Algiers
Ionian Sea
Athens
Tunis
MOROCCO
ALGERIA
TUNISIA
Sea

0   150   300 km

1. Which alliance appears to have the strongest position in your view? Explain. 2. What role might powerful navies play in this war?
3. How might Canada participate in a war so far from its shores?

FOCUS

1. **Briefly describe the major long-term causes of the First World War.**
2. **What were the major short-term causes?**
3. **Why was Canada involved in the war?**

World War Begins

During the late 1800s, Germany tried to keep on friendly terms with Russia. The German Kaiser (Emperor) and the Russian Tsar (Emperor) were cousins. If war came, Germany expected it to be with France, not Russia. This would mean battles to the west, or a **Western Front**. If Russia joined France against Germany, it would mean more battles to the east, or an **Eastern Front**.

When Germany allied with Austria in 1879, Russia's friendship was lost. Russia then became France's ally. How could Germany avoid a war on two fronts at once?

THE SCHLIEFFEN PLAN

- - - The Western Front, 1914–15
→ The Schlieffen Plan
→ German Army, 1914

The failure of the Schlieffen Plan led to a bloody stalemate on the Western Front.

The Schlieffen Plan

German General Von Schlieffen developed a plan. He expected the Russians to take a long time to mobilize their army. He would first move rapidly against the French on the Western Front. Doing so would mislead their army as to the origin of the main attack. The French army would then concentrate along the southern part of the Franco-German border, believing that the German soldiers would cross over into France from their homeland.

Schlieffen's plan called for the majority of the German army to invade France from the north. They would then sweep across the flat lands of neutral Belgium and northern France to the English Channel. Then, they would turn towards Paris from the west. All this would take about six weeks, Schlieffen estimated.

The French would be knocked out of the war, and the Germans could then turn their attention to the Russians on the Eastern Front.

Why the Schlieffen Plan Failed

Schlieffen based his plan on a gamble. About 70 years earlier, France, Germany, and Britain had signed a treaty guaranteeing that Belgium should be neutral.

Germany wrongly assumed that Britain would not object to the invasion of tiny Belgium. But Britain did object. It used the invasion as a reason to enter the war. General Von Schlieffen died in 1913. The new German generals continued with his plan, but made a few changes. While approaching Paris from the west, they were forced to turn south too soon. This meant the French army at the French-German border could now reach them. The Germans were also attacked by French troops moving out from Paris and British troops from the Channel ports.

The German advance was halted on

A group of Aboriginal soldiers have their picture taken before joining the Canadian Expeditionary Force. Despite discrimination against Blacks and Aboriginals, these Canadians enlisted and served with distinction.

One last embrace before going off to war. Most men expected the war to be over by Christmas.

the Marne River. Both sides "dug in" and built extensive trench systems. These trenches were protected by artillery, barbed wire, and machine guns. The Schlieffen Plan failed. Instead of knocking France out of the war, the Germans found themselves trapped on the Western Front. They faced the combined armies of France, Britain, and the members of their empires, including Canada. Russia threatened on the Eastern Front. Instead of a short, swift campaign, Germany's attack on France became a long, costly, war. Four years of trench warfare had begun.

Canada Responds

At the start of the war, Canadian Liberal Party leader, Wilfrid Laurier, stated, "When the call comes, our answer goes at once, and it goes in the classical language of the British answer to the call of duty: 'Ready, aye, ready.'"

Volunteers are recruited for the war.

even before the British asked for one.

In 1914, Canada's armed forces consisted of an army of 3100, a militia of some 60 000, and a navy of one light and one heavy cruiser. After enlistments, the army swelled to 250 000 in 1915, and to 500 000 the next year. By war's end, over 600 000 men had

Why might this poster encourage people to join the army?

Most regions of Canada were quickly caught up in war fever. Young men rushed to join the armed forces. Many worried the war would be over before they got there! Some men enlisted for glory, excitement, and medals. Others joined for free room and board and $1 a day pay. Outside Quebec, few questioned whether Canada should take part. Canadian citizens rushed along the road to war. Although Canada was at war when Britain was at war, Canada was able to determine how much it would participate. Canadians were so keen to fight that a **Canadian Expeditionary Force** was prepared

In Uxbridge, Ontario, men march through town before joining the battle overseas.

joined the army, with an additional 8000 each for the navy and the air force. About 2500 women served as nursing sisters overseas. The brutality of the next four years, however, would test Canada's enthusiasm and unity.

Sir Sam Hughes

BORN: 1853, Darlington, Ontario

DIED: 1921, Lindsay, Ontario

SIGNIFICANCE: Hughes organized the Canadian Expeditionary Force in a matter of weeks. He stubbornly fought to maintain it as an independent Canadian unit.

BRIEF BIOGRAPHY: Hughes was a teacher and newspaper owner–editor before he entered politics. He was appointed minister of Militia and Defence in Robert Borden's new Conservative government in 1911. Hughes was one of the most energetic supporters of the war effort. He pushed for rapid expansion of Canada's armed forces. Within months, the army had 100 000 volunteers. With just two months of training, its first contingent of 3000 left Canada for Britain. When British officers attempted to blend Canadian soldiers into British units, Hughes furiously refused. Hughes was energetic and tireless in his defence of Canada. He also behaved rashly, made many enemies, and created many foolish schemes. He was not liked in French Canada because of his anti-Roman Catholic attitude. Eventually, Borden asked for his resignation. Interestingly, Hughes's niece, Laura, was a peace activist and an outspoken critic of the war. **In your view, what were the major strengths and weaknesses of Sir Sam Hughes?**

CANADIAN LIVES

FOCUS

1. What was the main aim of the Schlieffen Plan?
2. Why did the plan fail?
3. Why did Britain declare war on Germany?
4. Who was Sir Sam Hughes? What was his job?
5. How did most Canadians respond to the outbreak of war? Would you have volunteered for the armed forces? Explain.

War in the Trenches

Mud. Barbed wire. Lice. Hardtack and bully beef. Rain, sleet and snow. Mud. Rats. Shell holes full of stagnant water. Bodies. Machine-gun bullets. Sandbags. More mud.

Digging In

The Schlieffen Plan had failed. The Germans could not advance. The French and the British could not drive them back. Both sides set about digging-in to fortify their positions on the Western Front.

They dug trenches (ditches) to protect their troops. Each trench was about 2 m deep and topped with sandbags. Soldiers could stand in the trench without being seen by the enemy. A narrow strip, called **no man's land**, lay between the Allies and their enemies. The opposing trenches were sometimes so close that rifle and machine gun fire spattered across no man's land whenever a soldier detected movement in enemy territory. Shells flew from the artillery behind the front lines, spraying shrapnel everywhere.

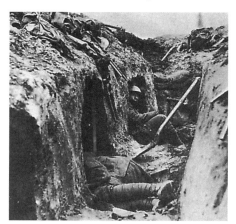

Trench life was cramped, dirty and uncomfortable. Soldiers suffered from "trench mouth" and "trench foot."

These soldiers are going "over the top" in a dangerous, costly, and often futile attempt to gain some distance in no man's land.

Over the Top

Officers would sometimes order an advance, which meant going **over the top** of the trench and across no man's land fully exposed to enemy fire. Occasionally, the troops managed to capture the enemy's front line. The enemy then retired to its reserve trenches a short distance away. Barbed wire stretched across the new patch of no man's land. A few metres of land had been lost or won. Hundreds of thousands of soldiers were often killed in the process. Then the whole bloody business started all over again.

Soldiers fought, died, ate, and slept in the trenches. Eventually, they were relieved for a few days by fresh troops. In winter, they froze in the snow and sleet. Spring rains filled the trenches with water. In summer, rich farmlands turned to mud.

In Their Own Words

"We are filthy. Our bodies are the color of the earth we have been living in these past months. We are alive with vermin and sit picking at ourselves like baboons. It is months since we have been out of our clothes."

Source: Charles Yale Harrison, *Generals Die in Bed* (Hamilton: Potlatch Publications, 1974).

ment went over the top. It was an almost suicidal attack against German machine guns. The regiment was torn to pieces within minutes. Ninety-one percent of the Newfoundland Regiment died that day. Of the 840 who left their trenches, only 79 were able to answer roll call the following morning. The war settled into a long slaughter of the Western world's youth.

Battle of the Somme—Beaumont Hamel

The Battle of the Somme was one of the bloodiest, most wasteful battles of the war. On its first day, 57 540 casualties were recorded. On that terrible day, 1 July 1916, the young men of the Newfoundland Regi-

Trench warfare meant injury and death for millions.

The war turned rich farmland into a wasteland of mud and death.

Two Letters Home

One of the best sources of information about the brutal reality of trench warfare is the letters of soldiers from the front lines. Read these two letters. **What are the major differences in their view of the war? Why?**

Before heavy action:
24 March 1915

"We have been put in the trenches for a week with British troops. Then we'll be taken back for further training. Then we will be in the trenches for 5 weeks, and then we get a rest.

Our German friends opposite have a sense of humour. One day they stuck a toy horse up above their trench. Our chaps shot it down. They put it up again with a bandage round its neck.

They call out things like 'We no shoot, you no shoot.'

'If you come halfway, we'll give you cigarettes.'

'Hello B.C., how'd you like to be walking down Hastings Street?'

Our men are so light-hearted—full of life and ginger. Somebody is going to be badly hurt when these boys let loose."

After heavy action:
15 May 1915

"We were called out from Ypres about 5 o'clock. The sky was a hell of bursting shrapnel. We lay in reserve until nearly midnight. Then they told us to take the wood. We charged across 500 m of open country. We lost many men during that charge. I saw poor Charlie go down and stopped to help him, but he urged us on. Then Andy fell, shot right through the head. When we got to the edge of the wood we found a trench just dug by the Germans. This is when the hell began. They had 2 machine guns, and the fire was like hailstones on a tin roof. Somehow they missed a few of us, but the other fellows were cut in half by the stream of lead.

I have often wanted to see a fight. Never again. I remember the next morning, all the dead and dying lying around in twisted shapes. War is hell.

We are going back to the base to be reorganized. We had 26 officers before, and 2 after, so you can see it was pretty bad. I shall try to transfer, as most of my nerve has gone."

FOCUS

1. Carefully describe the reality of trench warfare.
2. Imagine you are a soldier fighting in the trenches. Write a letter home describing your experiences.
3. Could you have survived these events? Explain fully.
4. What do the first-hand accounts in this chapter reveal about the war?

A Tale of Two Battles

The first Canadian troops arrived in England in October 1914. British officers said sneeringly, "These 'colonials' were sloppy. They couldn't even salute properly. The only way to lick them into shape would be to divide them among British units. They would be no use in their own regiment."

The Canadian minister of militia, Sam Hughes, was furious. He refused to let the Canadians be broken up. As a result, Canada had its own army. The Canadian Corps soon proved its worth.

Ypres

The Canadians arrived in France in March 1915, after four months of training in Britain. They were sent to Ypres, a city near the Belgium coast, in order to stop the Germans from breaking through to the English Channel. Since the failure of the Schlieffen Plan the year before, there had been little fighting here.

The Germans wanted to break the stalemate. They decided to use a new weapon—poisonous chlorine gas. On April 22, a gentle breeze blew towards the Allied lines. It was perfect weather for a gas attack.

The Canadians had been assigned a section of the front-line trenches.

A bleak landscape.

Soldiers injured in gas warfare.

To the left were troops from the French colony of Algeria. The Algerians saw a green cloud drifting across no man's land. As it reached the trenches, they found themselves choking and gasping for breath. Those who were not suffocated fled.

Although people had talked about gas warfare, the Allied commanders did not think it would be used, so they sent the Canadian soldiers to the front without gas masks. When the Germans used chlorine gas, the soldiers had no protection. All they could do was soak

War and Recognition

The once splendid 500-year-old Cloth Hall and Cathedral in Ypres, destroyed by war.

cotton pads in urine and hold them over their faces. The acid in the urine neutralized the chlorine. The soldiers then moved into the gap to prevent a German breakthrough. They somehow held on for two whole days. Finally, British relief troops took over. The Canadians had proved themselves. Nobody sneered at them after the Battle of Ypres or "Wipers," as Canadian and British soldiers pronounced the name.

Gas was feared as a weapon during the war, so men and beasts wore masks.

Vimy Ridge

"Zero hour will be 5:30 a.m."

The word spread through the Canadian Army on Easter Sunday, 1917. Every soldier was aware that Vimy Ridge was the key to the German lines. If the Allies were to break the stalemate of the war, Vimy Ridge would have to be taken. In two years of tough fighting, Canadians had done well. The dubious honour of storming Vimy Ridge would fall to them.

HISTOR!CA
Minutes

The soldiers looked across no man's land. About 100 m away lay the German trenches. It would be sheer hell to get across. That night they enjoyed one last hot meal and a shot of rum to heat their stomachs and give them courage.

For the past two weeks the artillery had been firing shells into enemy lines. Easter Monday dawned cold, with sleet and snow falling. At 5:30 a.m., the command was given to go over the top. Covered by more shellfire, 15 000 soldiers moved in the first wave of attack. They valiantly struggled across the mud and through what barbed wire remained. The return fire from German machine guns and artillery was murderous, but the Canadians wiped out the German front line—the soldiers had passed it in the snow without knowing. They surprised the second line of defence. Some Germans fled. Others surrendered. Despite massive losses, by midmorning the Canadians had seized the heights. Vimy Ridge was in Allied hands.

The pride felt after such an accomplishment was dampened by the cost. In just a few hours, Canada had suffered 10 000 casualties with 3600 dead.

Canadian and German wounded help each other through the mud at the terrible Battle of Passchendaele.

In Their Own Words

Vimy Ridge was the first great Allied victory since the beginning of the war. Canadian pride received a great boost that cold morning in northern France. As one participant noted:

"From dugouts, shell holes and trenches men sprang into action, fell into artillery formations and advanced to the ridge, every division of the Corps moved forward together. It was Canada from the Atlantic to the Pacific on parade. I thought then and I think today, that in those few minutes I witnessed the birth of a nation."

Source: Brigadier General Alex Ross

Canadian Vision

The Power of Words

The First World War generated more poetry than any war before or since. By 1918, more than 3000 volumes of war-related poetry had been published, mostly by amateurs. Perhaps the most popular and enduring poem is John McCrae's "In Flanders Fields." McCrae, an army surgeon from Guelph, Ontario, published the poem anonymously in the winter of 1915. He died a few weeks afterwards. His poem, however, became the most successful recruitment incentive of the war. The power of his words brought the war home to Canadians. McCrae's vision of the devastation of war has become a key element in most Canadian Remembrance Day services.

HISTOR!CA
Minutes

In Flanders Fields

In Flanders Fields the poppies blow
Between the crosses, row on row,
That mark our place; and in the sky,
The larks, still bravely singing, fly
Scarce heard amid the guns below.

We are the Dead. Short days ago
We lived, felt dawn, saw sunset glow,
Loved, and were loved, and now we lie
In Flanders Fields.

Take up our quarrel with the foe:
To you from failing hands we throw
The torch; be yours to hold it high.
If ye break faith with us who die
We shall not sleep, though poppies grow
In Flanders Fields.

Which lines are the most moving in your opinion? Why? To what extent does the third verse differ from the first two verses?

FOCUS

1. Explain the important role played by Canadians at Ypres and Vimy Ridge.
2. Identify all the first-hand sources presented in this chapter.

The War in the Air

The Wright brothers flew the first successful airplane at Kitty Hawk, North Carolina, in 1903. Six years later, John McCurdy flew the Silver Dart—designed by McCurdy and Alexander Graham Bell—at Baddeck, Nova Scotia. Airplanes were regarded as a luxury;

Canadian officers, Royal Flying Corps, Reading, England, 1916.

therefore, at the outbreak of the First World War, Canada had no planes and no pilots.

Many young Canadians who wished to be pilots went to Britain to join the Royal Flying Corps (later the Royal Air Force). They were among the best fighter pilots of the war.

Dogfights

Meetings between warring aircraft often became deadly **dogfights**. Pilots tried to tailgate enemy planes so that the enemies could not return the gunfire. Being shot down usually meant instant death. Pilots were not allowed to carry parachutes because, if they did, they might bail out. Their officers wanted them to try to save planes instead. The average lifespan of a pilot was only three weeks long. They called their planes "flying coffins."

One of the leading "aces" of the Royal Flying Corps was a Canadian, Billy Bishop. He reportedly shot down 72 enemy planes. The greatest flying ace of the war was Germany's Manfred von Richthofen, the famous "Red Baron." He shot down 80 planes.

War and Recognition

The Red Baron's Last Flight

One day in April 1918, Richthofen took his pilots on their usual daily patrol. They were met by a British squadron led by Roy Brown of Carleton Place, Ontario. Soon the two groups were in a fierce dogfight.

Wilfrid "Wop" May was on his first combat flight. The young Canadian realized his guns were jammed and drifted out of the battle. The Red Baron moved onto his tail.

Preparing for the kill, he did not notice that Roy Brown had flown behind him. Brown got the German ace in his gun sights and shot him out of the sky. A Canadian had downed the legendary Red Baron!

Recently, some Australian soldiers have disputed this claim. They maintain that they shot down the Red Baron when his plane flew close to the ground chasing Brown's plane. Germany went into national mourning after the death of their hero.

Wilfrid May lived to become one of Canada's leading bush pilots and a pioneer in search and rescue techniques.

Billy Bishop

BORN: 1894, Owen Sound, Ontario

DIED: 1956, Palm Beach, Florida

SIGNIFICANCE: With 72 recorded "kills," Billy Bishop was Canada's greatest flying hero in the First World War and the greatest ace in the British Empire. He earned the Victoria Cross, the highest award for bravery under fire.

BRIEF BIOGRAPHY: Billy was a charming, rambunctious youth. He did not do well at school, but was an excellent marksman. Bishop entered the war as a cavalry officer. He soon saw that flying was where the action was. He became a gunner-observer and then a pilot. Bishop was a rebel who often found himself in trouble with authorities. He was also a brave and gifted fighter pilot. The average lifespan of a rookie pilot in combat was 11 days. Bishop was a natural pilot. In his first month at the front, he downed 17 enemy aircraft. He duelled with the Red Baron, and both men limped home in shot-up aircraft.

Bishop shot down 5 enemy aircraft in one battle alone. He won the Victoria Cross for his daring solo attack on a German aerodrome, which resulted in three "kills." He was recalled to Canada to inspire recruiting and the sale of Victory Bonds. These bonds were a means of raising funds to support the war.

After the war, Bishop flew in air shows, gave lectures, and dabbled in business. When the Second World War began in 1939, Bishop was made an Air Marshal to spur recruitment to the RCAF. For more information, visit www.billybishop.org. **Why is Billy Bishop considered a hero?**

The Technical Edge

Warplanes Aircraft design had not advanced greatly prior to the First World War. Most planes flew at about 150 km/h. They had open, single-seat cockpits. Planes were used mainly to observe enemy troop movements, a big advance over the use of balloons. The thrill of flying united all pilots. British, German, and French fighters waved to one another as their planes passed above the battlefields. Soon, some pilots started to bring rifles into the cockpit. They shot at enemy planes in order to stop information reaching enemy generals. The friendly camaraderie was over.

A young Lester B. Pearson, future prime minister of Canada.

Airplane factory during the First World War.

Next, machine guns were mounted on the planes. A major problem with this new design was that the bullets often hit the plane's propellers. One British design mounted the gun behind the pilot. The French placed it above the propeller, on the top wing of the biplane. The Germans had a gun timed to fire through the propeller without hitting the blades. When the British tried this system, it did not always work perfectly. These guns had fixed mounts. The only way to aim the gun was to point the plane directly at the target. By war's end, many new designs had been built. Bombers, zeppelins, and fighters were a regular feature in the skies above the trenches. Aircraft now had a central role in modern warfare.

How were airplanes used in the war?

FOCUS

1. Define the words "dogfights" and "flying coffins."
2. Who was the Red Baron?

The War at Sea

When the war began, Canada had only two mid-sized cruisers in its navy. One was the H.M.S. *Niobe* in Halifax and the other was the H.M.S. *Rainbow* in Vancouver. By the end of the war, the Royal Canadian Navy had grown to about 100 ships. Most were small coastal vessels. Only one warship was lost at sea during the war.

Atlantic Convoys

Canada's main role in the war at sea was in shipping Canadian troops, food, and munitions to Europe. The German navy wanted to stop goods reaching Britain. They declared a war zone in the waters around the British Isles.

The Germans used submarines to attack ships on their way to Britain. A German submarine sank the *Lusitania*, a British passenger liner, in 1915. Over 1000 people died, including 128 Americans. The *Lusitania* tragedy contributed to anti-German feelings in the United States.

The British started to put ships into large groups called convoys. **Convoys** sailed together from Quebec, Halifax or St. John's. They were protected from submarines by warships. The convoy system greatly reduced the number of ships sunk. Halifax had a large harbour and an excellent location. It soon became the major assembly point for convoys to England.

The Halifax Explosion

Throughout the war, the Halifax harbour was crowded with convoys of ships. They were loaded with war supplies of food, munitions and troops ready for the voyage to Europe with heavily-armed warships as escorts. Neutral vessels anchored in the harbour,

their crews forbidden to land for fear any might supply information to the enemy. New railway lines and terminals were almost completed, made necessary to handle the extra pressure of traffic. The population was swollen with troops, and people who had come to benefit from the plentiful employment.

Thursday, 6 December 1917, dawned clear and mild in Halifax. At 7:30 a.m., the *Mont Blanc*, a French freighter, started to move through the Narrows to Bedford Basin, the city's inner harbour. It was loaded with

In the city, factory workers were already at their jobs. Children were assembling in school playgrounds. Offices and stores were getting ready for the day's business. As the *Mont Blanc* and the *Imo* drew close to each other, they signalled their intentions. Suddenly, the *Mont Blanc* sailed directly across

The Halifax Explosion destroyed Halifax, leaving 10 000 people homeless in the middle of the winter.

benzene, picric acid, and TNT. It had come from New York to join the next convoy across the Atlantic. At about 8:00, the *Imo*, a Norwegian tramp steamer carrying relief supplies for Belgium, headed out through the Narrows.

the *Imo*'s bow. At 8:43 the *Imo* rammed the *Mont Blanc*. The two ships drifted apart. People in the city enjoying the winter sunshine watched as a wisp of smoke rose from the harbour. At 9:06, the *Mont Blanc*'s cargo of high explosives blew up.

Schools, factories, stores, and houses in a 5 km area were completely destroyed. Part of the two-ton anchor of the *Mont Blanc* was found 4 km away. Over 2000 people died and another 9000 were injured. That night, with 10 000 people homeless, the temperature plunged to -8°C and a blizzard was on the way.

Within days, relief supplies began to pour in from other parts of Canada, and as far away as Jamaica and New Zealand. The state of Massachusetts sent a relief committee, for which reason Halifax still sends a Christmas tree annually to the city of Boston.

The 1917 Halifax Explosion was the biggest man-made explosion in history until the dropping of the atomic bomb on Hiroshima in 1945.

Haligonians pay tribute to those killed by the explosion.

HISTOR!CA
Minutes

This is what Halifax looked like after the explosion. Many people thought the explosion was due to German sabotage. What needs would the survivors have? *For more information, visit* www.cbc.ca/halifaxexplosion.

The Canadian Red Cross Society

The Society was founded in 1876. When the First World War began in 1914, it had 156 local branches across Canada. By the end of the war, there were 1303 branches. They were staffed almost entirely by female volunteers. The Society made clothes, raised money, bought medical supplies and packaged food. They sent these items overseas to Canadian soldiers in army hospitals. At Christmas, these soldiers were surprised to find stockings hanging by their beds. The Red Cross had provided them. They contained clothes, food, candy, and cigarettes. All of these things were hard to get in Europe. After the Second Battle of Ypres, when 1500 Canadians were taken prisoner, the Red Cross set up a Prisoners of War Department. The department prepared parcels to be sent to the men in the P.O.W. camps. Nearly all of the one-half million parcels sent safely arrived. The Halifax Explosion stretched the resources of many Canadian volunteer organizations. Canadians gratefully accepted donations from other countries.

Red Cross supplies stand ready to be sent to Canadian forces in Europe.

Why was the Red Cross an important body during the war? To learn more about this important Canadian organization, visit the Canadian Red Cross Web site at www.redcross.ca.

FOCUS

1. **What important role did the Canadian navy play during the First World War?**
2. **How did the Halifax Explosion bring the horror of the war home to Canadians?**

Women at War

By 1900, women composed one-quarter of the manufacturing workforce in Canada. The largest number of women worked as domestic servants. Three of every four teachers were women. Female teachers were paid less than males, could not become principals, and

Women took skilled factory jobs to help meet the demands of war.

were largely confined to elementary schools. Before the war, some women began breaking out of traditional roles. By 1900, almost 1 in 10 university students was a woman. Still, women were pushed into arts programs and steered away from science courses. In 1895, Clara Brett Martin became Canada's first woman law graduate, although she had a difficult time practising her profession. In medicine, Emily Howard Stowe and Jennie Trout were forced to train as physicians in the United States because no Canadian medical school would admit women. Cora Hind in Winnipeg and Kit Coleman in Toronto proved that women could be excellent journalists. But these were special cases. It was still almost impossible for women to get hired for many jobs. They still could not vote. The war dramatically changed the lives of Canadian women.

The Needs of Industry

The wartime industrial boom created a problem. Male factory workers enlisted in the army. Women filled the gap by working in the war factories. Over 20 000 women were employed making guns, shells, and aircraft. These were skilled jobs. Before the war, women had done only unskilled work in the factories. Skilled jobs had been for men.

Women also replaced men in many civilian jobs. They became streetcar drivers, secretaries, and office managers. More than anything else, they worked farms to help plant and harvest the crops.

Women without paying jobs also did their part. They knitted socks for soldiers, sent letters and care packages, and visited the families of men who had been killed.

Women supported the Canadian Red Cross and other volunteer organizations.

In Their Own Words

"When you're young, you do what everybody's doing.... Everybody wanted to be there; you were in the swim of things; everything was war, war, war. I think a lot of the girls.... they were a wonderful bunch, and I see so many of them to this day. They enriched my life so.

There was everybody, every single class.... In meeting these people that we had never had the opportunity to meet before, and finding they were just the same as we were, but they hadn't had the chances that we'd had for education and that kind of thing, we began to realize that we were all sisters under the skins.

Wars do bring every class together and I think we need to do a little bit more of that without war if we can."

From Daphne Read, ed. *The Great War and Canadian Society: An Oral History* (Toronto: New Hogtown Press, 1978).

How was the war a positive experience for some women?

The Army Medical Corps

Wounded soldiers on the Western Front needed medical care. Over 3000 women became army nurses and ambulance drivers. They were called "Bluebirds" because they wore blue cloaks. Most of them served overseas. They willingly shared the dangers of warfare with Canadian men.

As the war continued, field hospitals and hospital ships became German targets. Forty-six "Bluebirds" lost their lives, some from German bombs and torpedoes.

Pacifists

Some Canadian women and men were **pacifists** and worked for peace. They tried to start a peace movement. They were tired of seeing the brutality of war and the total misery it brought everyone. Laura Hughes was niece of Sir Sam Hughes. She was a leading spokesperson for the Canadian Women's Peace Party. The peace movement gained strength after the full horrors of the First World War were revealed.

The Right to Vote

Prime Minister Borden passed the Wartime Elections Act shortly before the 1917 election took place. This Act took the vote away from citizens who had emigrated from "enemy" countries. It was feared that they might vote against **conscription**. It gave the vote to women—but not all women. Only army nurses and close relatives of soldiers were allowed to vote, since they would probably support conscription, or compulsory service.

Burial of Canadian nurses killed in a German air raid, May 1918.

This Act was unfair to other women. In 1918, all women were given the vote, but they still could not be elected to Parliament. That right did not come until 1920. In 1921, Agnes Macphail became the first woman elected to the House of Commons. The first steps had been taken, but the long struggle for real equality had just begun.

Silver Cross mothers, like this one, were women who had lost sons in battle.

TIMELINE—Gaining the Vote, 1916–1922

Canadian women faced a long, uphill struggle to win political equality with men in the 20th century. One of the most important victories was gaining the right to vote. Here is a list of key dates:

1916 Women in the Western provinces of Manitoba, Saskatchewan, and Alberta won the right to vote in provincial elections.

1917 The Military Voters Act granted the vote in federal elections to Canadian nurses serving in the war. The Wartime Elections Act gave the vote in federal elections to close female relatives of soldiers. Women in British Columbia and Ontario won the right to vote in provincial elections.

1918 Prime Minister Borden's Union government gave the vote to Canadian women over 21 for federal elections.

1919 Women in New Brunswick won the right to vote in provincial elections.

1920 Canadian women earned the right to run in federal elections and become members of Parliament.

1922 Women in P.E.I. won the right to vote in provincial elections.

FOCUS

1. What new and important roles did Canadian women play during the First World War?
2. Why were women given the right to vote?
3. Why might immigrants from "enemy" countries vote against conscription? Why would women whose husbands, fathers, sons, or brothers were fighting in the war vote for conscription?

The War on the Home Front

Wars have traditionally been fought by soldiers. The First World War was the first war to involve all sections of society. It was a total war. In Canada, far from the battle lines, people made their contributions. The war put great stress and strain on Canadian society.

Women served on the battlefront and on the home front in this "total" war.

Farming

The war disrupted farming in Europe, which caused major shortages of food. More than three-fifths of the soldiers fighting in Europe came from farms. Canadian farmers had to fill a large part of the food shortages during the war. By the end of the war, "sod busters" in the West had doubled the land used for wheat farming. Cheese exports tripled. Pork and beef exports shot sky high.

Industry

Canadian business found new markets. Before the war, factories produced goods solely for the Canadian market. Few tried to compete outside the country. Most of the exports were raw materials—to be processed elsewhere.

Business people now saw new opportunities. Canadian companies started to make armaments for the Allied forces. Steel companies turned out shell cases. Others made fuses and explosives. By 1917, Canada was making one-third of the shells used by Britain during the war. This increased the demand for nickel and copper in northern mines and further boosted the economy.

Canadians made guns, airplane parts, submarines, and ships. Aluminum, nickel, railway tracks, and timber were all sent to Europe. Uniforms, equipment, and medical supplies were made for the Canadian Army.

Most Canadians worked hard to help the war effort. City workers gave up their free time to help farmers harvest the crops. Women entered the workforce to keep the soldiers supplied with essentials. Children worked in fields and created Victory gardens. Some bought "Victory stamps" to help pay for the war effort. Business people and government officials worked long hours without extra pay. All this activity created great opportunities for profit.

Profiteering

Most business people were content to take a fair mark-up, but some tried to "corner the market" on a product. A few engaged in what is known as **profiteering**. They would not sell until they could get the best price. Others used cheap materials and did sloppy work. The boots the first Canadian troops were given wore out in less than two months. Canned meat for soldiers sometimes came from diseased animals. Some industrialists used bribery to get government contracts.

Many women worked in factories as part of the war effort. Note the lack of safety precautions.

The War Measures Act

At the outset of the war, some Canadians were suspicious of those who had recently entered Canada from enemy countries. The same people who were asked by Clifford Sifton and his agents to come to Canada were now seen as security risks. Borden's government passed the **War Measures Act**. This Act had the power to take away freedoms and to arrest and detain "enemy aliens."

During the war, over 8000 men were sent to toil in remote camps across Canada. Ukrainian Canadians were a targeted group because many had come from lands controlled by Austria. Ukrainians were often denied work. The government **censored** or closed down their newspapers. No evidence was ever found that any of these people posed a threat to their adopted country.

Religious communities such as Hutterites and Mennonites who believed in nonviolence faced restrictions and harassment. Democracy and freedom also became victims of the war.

Victory Bonds

War is expensive. Canadians paid no tax on income or profit in the early 20th century. How could the government pay for the war?

To raise money, Canada issued Victory Bonds. Canadi-

ans were urged to buy bonds to help the war effort. After the war, they could cash in their bonds and get their money back with interest. Banks and large companies purchased most of the bonds, but ordinary citizens did their part as well.

Two new "temporary" taxes were introduced. The first was a business profits tax (now called Corporate Tax). The second was an income tax. Canadians still pay these taxes.

Victory Bonds were a necessary part of the war effort. These advertisements used **propaganda** to attract support. Which of these posters is most effective? Why?

Tommy Ricketts

BORN: 1901, Middle Arm, Newfoundland

DIED: 1967, St. John's, Newfoundland

SIGNIFICANCE: At only 17, he fought in the Battle of Beaumont-Hamel and became the youngest winner of a Victoria Cross for bravery.

BRIEF BIOGRAPHY: Newfoundland was a British colony during the First World War. It did not join Confederation until 1949. The rugged Islanders were quick to volunteer alongside Canadians to stand beside Britain. The soldiers of the Royal Newfoundland Regiment took part in some of the war's bloodiest battles. They were almost annihilated at the Battle of Beaumont-Hamel in 1916. One of their young fighters became famous because of his courageous actions during the terrible battles of Europe. Ricketts lied about his age and enlisted in the Newfoundland Regiment when he was only 14. He soon saw action and was wounded in 1917. In 1918, under heavy fire, Ricketts displayed uncommon courage. He raced, unarmed, across no man's land, to gather ammunition for his unit. He then led an attack against a German battery with no artillery support. This action resulted in the capture of German field and machine guns and eight prisoners.

After the war, Ricketts returned to Newfoundland, where he studied pharmacy at Memorial University in St. John's. When he died in 1967, he received a state funeral. **Why is Tommy Ricketts considered a hero?**

CANADIAN LIVES

FOCUS

1. How did Canadian farmers, women and businesses help in the war effort?
2. How and why did Ukrainian Canadians become victims of the war?
3. What is profiteering?
4. How did young people help in the war effort?

Wartime Issues

Conscription

The Canadian army relied on volunteers for most of the war. Many young men were excited at the idea of fighting for their country. They rushed to volunteer to go overseas.

The horrors of the trenches soon changed that. Canadian soldiers earned a reputation for courage. They were often chosen for the toughest, most dangerous missions. They fought at Vimy Ridge in April 1917. That month more than 10 000 Canadian soldiers died, but fewer than 5000 men enlisted. The volunteer system was not recruiting enough soldiers to replace the losses.

Prime Minister Borden had promised that his government would not introduce conscription. Now he had to break that promise. He called an election to win approval for conscription. This campaign was one of the fiercest in Canadian history.

People Against Conscription

The largest group against conscription was French Canadian. When the war started, many French Canadians volunteered to enter the army. The Royal 22nd Regiment, the "VanDoos" (from vingt-deux), was a French-speaking unit. It had a great fighting record throughout the war.

The minister of militia at the war's beginning was Sam Hughes, an Irish Protestant. Hughes did not understand the French Canadians. He disliked Roman Catholics. He sent Protestant clergymen as recruiting officers to Quebec. He insisted the French soldiers be trained in English. Borden fired Hughes in 1916, but it was too late to save the situation in Quebec.

French Canadians felt that they were being asked to defend Britain, not Canada. Former prime minister Wilfrid Laurier, leader of the Opposition during the war, did not feel this way. He urged French Canadians to join the army, but did not think they should be forced to do so.

In Their Own Words

"When the war broke out, the country went mad. People were singing in the streets. Everybody wanted to go to war. We hadn't had a war since the Boer War in 1899. Everybody was going to be a hero, and I wanted to be a hero too. But I wasn't big enough. I was only 150 cm tall and weighed 40 kg. I was 19 but looked 15. Finally a drill sergeant said, 'We need buglers!' So I joined the army as a bugler."

Bert Remington of Montreal,
who had emigrated from Britain in 1910.

"Me? I was probably as patriotic as most, but I was mainly restless. I joined up because it was a chance to see the world."

Robert Swan, Yarmouth, N.S.

Are young people today as likely to want to go far away to fight a war? Explain.

This poster says: Forward! For the King. For the Fatherland. For France. Your blood for humanity and freedom. To Arms! Sons of Montcalm [Battle of Quebec] and Chateauguay [A battle in the War of 1812 in which French Canadians defeated the invading Americans]. How does this poster try to stir up war fever among French Canadians? Is this an effective poster? Explain.

In the West, many settlers objected to conscription. They had moved to Canada to get away from European wars and conscription. They thought they had escaped that way of life. Now it seemed to be coming to Canada.

PATTERNS

By 1917, the war had grown even more desperate and bloody. People at home read the casualty lists. The wounded soldiers who returned home were often maimed and disfigured. Some were in baskets because they had no limbs. Few people now believed the war was glorious or that it would end soon. It became more difficult to find volunteers willing to risk their lives and future for a long, brutal struggle in a foreign land. Examine these statistics on enlistment and casualty figures.

MONTH	ENLISTMENTS	CASUALTIES
January	9 194	4 396
February	6 809	1 250
March	6 640	6 161
April (Vimy Ridge)	5 530	13 477
May	6 407	13 457
June	6 348	7 931
July	3 882	7 906
August (Hill 70)	3 117	13 232
September	3 588	10 990
October	4 884	5 929
November (Passchendaele)	4 019	30 741
December	3 921	7 476

What pattern seemed to be emerging? What was happening to the Canadian army? Why might these figures suggest a crisis?

Canada's Aboriginal Fighters

Many Canadian communities supported Canada's efforts in the First World War. Canada's First Nations were particularly eager. At first, officials discouraged the recruitment of Aboriginal Canadians. Some held racist views. Others felt that the Aboriginals might be mistreated if captured. However, the need for men was great. Aboriginal Canadians persisted in their attempts to volunteer. About 4000 Aboriginal Canadians fought in the war. They were greatly valued as scouts and snipers. These were two of the most dangerous and important combat positions.

Scouts penetrated enemy positions and reported back to headquarters. As well, they created confusion behind enemy lines.

Snipers were crack shots. They could camouflage themselves and fire into the ranks of the enemy. Canada's best snipers were Aboriginal Canadians.

Tom Longboat, one of Canada's most famous Aboriginal athletes, set aside a running career to serve with distinction as a dispatch carrier with the 107th Pioneer Battalion in France. Here, he is shown buying a newspaper in France. What contributions to the war did Canada's Aboriginal soldiers make?

Francis "Peg" Pegahmagabow, an Ojibway from Parry Sound, Ontario, is credited with numerous hits on enemy soldiers. Henry "Ducky" Norwest, a Cree, had the best sharp-shooting record in the British forces. He had 115 observed "kills." A Métis relative of Louis Riel, Patrick Riel, was also a skilled marksman with 38 "kills."

After the war, these soldiers returned to a Canada slow to recognize their efforts. Only recently has the Canadian government created a special war memorial in Ottawa. It is dedicated to the memory and contributions of Canada's Aboriginal fighters.

Many farmers objected to conscription. Their part in the war effort was to provide much-needed food. Who would work with them if their sons were taken away?

What the Government Did

Prime Minister Borden was convinced that conscription was necessary. He had to win the election to justify breaking his earlier promise. First, Borden asked Laurier to join him in a coalition or union government. Laurier could not do this. Although he supported the war effort, he was against conscription. He knew Quebec would be bitterly opposed. Borden then approached English-speaking Liberals. Some of them were for conscription. Several Liberals joined the Conservatives in a new party. They called it the Union Party.

The Election of 1917

The Union Party won the election with 153 seats; the Liberals had 82. Only 20 of those 82 seats came from outside Quebec. The results did not show the true feelings of the people. Many English-speaking Canadians did not want conscription, either.

The conscription issue aroused many bitter feelings. In Quebec, there were bloody riots. Canadians were divided as they had not been since the execution of Louis Riel in 1885. Borden's wartime victory cost the nation dearly. Few conscripted men made it to the battlefields before the war ended.

A CLOSER LOOK AT PACIFISM

Canada is home to several religious communities for whom war is a mortal sin. These peoples were persecuted in other countries before immigrating to Canada. They were promised religious freedom in Canada. Mennonites from Russia and Holland settled the Canadian prairies in the late 19th and early 20th centuries. Doukhobors from Russia settled first in Saskatchewan, and then in southern British Columbia in 1908. The first Quaker immigrants to this country fled the violence of the American Revolution. They had refused to join in military service. All of these communities are pacifist. They oppose war or any kind of military activity. They believe that violence is immoral and that the natural state of humankind is peace. Canada had guaranteed all of these communities the right to live according to their belief in nonviolence. Even though many of these people bought war bonds and helped in the factories and farms, they often faced hostility and ridicule. **Are you a pacifist? Why or why not?**

FOCUS

1. What was conscription?
2. Who was opposed to conscription and why?
3. What was the Union Party?
4. What was the result of the 1917 election?

The War Ends

The stalemate on the Western Front in France and Belgium continued into 1918. Neither side was able to win the battle that would bring victory.

Soldiers on all sides wondered why they were still fighting. The fighting offered little hope. For many, it meant certain death.

On the Eastern Front, Russians revolted against Tsar Nicholas II, in 1917. They

The Tower, St. Martin's Cathedral, Ypres, Belgium, damaged by the war.
RIGHT: *A Canadian soldier tends to a tiny victim of the war.*

demanded "Land, Bread, and Peace." Soldiers and sailors in Russia rebelled and refused to fight. Led by Vladimir Lenin, Russian communists seized power. In March

1918, the Russians signed a separate peace treaty with Germany. This was called the Treaty of Brest-Litovsk. Germany then turned all of its armies against the Allies on the Western Front.

The United States Enters the War

When Germany announced unrestricted warfare against neutral shipping in April 1917, the United States entered the war on the side of Britain and France. Germany knew that a large supply of American troops would arrive in France within the year. General Erich Ludendorff decided on a final German offensive before the American forces arrived.

Germany's last offensive began in April 1918. More than 3 million soldiers attacked, supported by massive artillery barrages. The German forces advanced over 60 km. It appeared that a major breakthrough had been achieved.

But, British, French, and Canadian forces pulled back to new defensive lines. The German offensive slowed down.

Reinforcements poured in for a counter-attack. For the first time, these forces included thousands of American troops. The counter-attack began in July 1918. Canadian forces met with great success. This Allied advance forced the German army back. By August, the German army was in total retreat.

In Germany, there were riots because of food shortages and protests against continuing the war. Some members of the German navy mutinied and refused to go to sea. By October, it was obvious that Germany and its allies had lost the war. Negotiations for peace began.

ABOVE: *People line the streets of Mons, Belgium, celebrating the end of the long and brutal war.*

BELOW LEFT: *Army doctors tend to the wounded.*

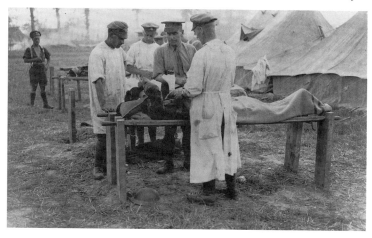

An **armistice** was signed on 11 November 1918. At 11 a.m. on the 11th day of the 11th month, the war came to an end.

Over 9 million soldiers had died. More than 20 million more would live out their lives with wounds, **shell shock**, gassed lungs, and lost limbs, sight, or hearing. An equal number of civilians were also victims of war.

Sir Arthur Currie

BORN: 1875, Napperton, Ontario

DIED: 1933, Montreal, Quebec, while vice-chancellor of McGill University

SIGNIFICANCE: Currie was the first Commander of the Canadian Corps. He successfully led Canadian troops until the end of the war.

BRIEF BIOGRAPHY: Currie was an active member of the militia when the First World War began in 1914. He was appointed Brigade Commander of the 2nd Canadian Infantry Brigade. In 1915, he took over full command of the entire Canadian Division. In 1917, Currie was appointed Commander of the Canadian Corps. He planned the attack at Vimy Ridge. He wanted new tactics. He insisted on careful training of soldiers, close support of artillery, the element of surprise, and rehearsals on mock targets. Under Currie's careful control, Vimy Ridge fell to Canadian forces.

This victory is sometimes viewed as the birth of the Canadian nation. Troops from all over Canada fought as a single unit. Currie was thought of as a modern general with new ideas. British Prime Minister Lloyd George even considered him for Commander of all British forces.

After the war, Currie became the principal and vice-chancellor of McGill University. Though he had no formal post-secondary education himself, Currie was extremely successful at his administrative duties at the university.

HISTOR!CA
Minutes

Why was Currie seen as a "modern general"?

CANADIAN LIVES

This account appeared in a newspaper obituary (death notice) in 1992. It shows that there are other human costs in war, not just death or physical wounding. For some, wars never really end.

"World War I, the Great War, the war to end all wars! What a price was paid in human lives and human misery. It was all so long ago but there are still a few souls left to remind us of those far oft times. My uncle ... was such a one. Perhaps there are those who would say he was fortunate to escape with his life, but I wonder what kind of life it has been for him. Uncle Jim and his brother John were fighting in the trenches in Passchendaele, France, when the call came to pull back. Jim would not leave without his brother and waded through the bodies, wiping the mud from the faces of the wounded and dying soldiers until he saw the face of his brother. He picked him up and carried him back behind the lines. Upon reaching the Red Cross medical tent, Jim placed his brother's wounded body on the table. 'Here,' he said, 'this is my brother, look after him—you have to save him.'

Jim then retreated outside into the darkness and collapsed. When he awoke hours later, he found himself lying on a pile of dead bodies. His brother was saved, but what of Jim? Uncle Jim was sent back home and made an effort to take up a normal semblance of his old life once more, but it was in vain. The ceaseless bombardment and the horror of the senseless slaughter of human lives had taken its toll. He retreated into a world where no war could reach him again.

Unfortunately, he also shut out the rest of the world.

In 1931, Jim was admitted to the Veterans' Hospital where he remained until July 15, 1992. 'Shell shock,' they called it.

No physical injury, just a damaged mind. His days passed in a twilight world where no one could reach him. Yet I must believe that his sacrifice was not in vain, and I also must believe that he is at peace...."

What price did Jim pay for his heroic effort?
What is shell shock?
Do you think that soldiers in modern wars can suffer shell shock? Explain.

FOCUS

1. **How did the following affect the stalemate on the Western Front?**
   (a) the Russian Revolution (b) the entry of the United States into the war
2. **What is the origin of Remembrance Day?**

The Treaty of Versailles

The November 11 Armistice ended the fighting. Germany agreed to withdraw its troops, to surrender its fleet to Great Britain, and to disarm its army.

The victorious powers met in Versailles, France, to draw up a permanent peace treaty. Strong differences of opinion existed among the Allied leaders. Georges Clemenceau, the French premier, wanted Germany to be punished. He demanded a harsh peace treaty.

American President Woodrow Wilson wanted a softer peace settlement. Wilson had previously drawn up the "14 Points" as a basis for a settlement. These included such ideas as "national determination for all peoples," "freedom of the seas," and "open peace treaties rather than secret agreements." One major proposal was for a League of Nations to guarantee world peace.

Germany expected a treaty based on the "14 Points." Instead, the **Treaty of Versailles** included many of the harsher terms of Clemenceau and British Prime Minister Lloyd George.

TERRITORIAL CHANGES IN EUROPE AS OF 1919

Legend:
- Lost by Germany, 1919
- Saar: League of Nations control, 1919–35
- Demilitarized Rhineland, 1919–36
- Austria-Hungary until 1918
- Plebiscite areas
- Former territory of Imperial Russia

Reaction to the Peace Treaty

The French and British considered the treaty to be fair and just. Both sides had lost hundreds of thousands of their youth in the horrible battles on the Western Front. Both were determined that the treaty should do everything possible to prevent the outbreak of another world war.

Most Germans were shocked by what they considered to be the treaty's harsh and unfair terms. The demand that Germany pay for the costs of the war (reparations) would crush their struggling industries. They did not want to lose parts of their country to France, Poland, and Czechoslovakia. They did not like the limits put on their armed forces. The War Guilt Clause offended their sense of justice.

After 1919, the sense of injustice festered like an open wound. A myth developed that Germany had been "stabbed in the back" by civilians (mostly Jews). They had not been defeated on the field of battle. Fourteen years later, Adolf Hitler appeared to be the leader who would help Germany to avenge the Treaty of Versailles.

Adolf Hitler, seen here in the 1920s, blamed the Treaty of Versailles for the economic hardship Germany faced after the war. The First World War was not to be "The War to End All Wars."

TREATY OF VERSAILLES

Geographical Terms
- Germany lost control of all its colonies.
- Alsace-Lorraine was transferred from Germany to France.
- The rich Saar coal region was to be run by France for 15 years.
- Part of eastern Germany was given to Poland.

Reparations
- Germany was to pay money and goods to Great Britain, France, and Belgium to repair damage caused by the war.

Military Controls
- The German Army was restricted to 100 000 people, and was to have no tanks or heavy guns.
- Germany was not to have an air force.
- The German Navy was to include only small ships.

War Guilt Clause (Article 231)
- Germany was forced to sign a statement that it had been the primary cause of the war.

Sir Robert Borden

BORN: 1854, Grand Pré, Nova Scotia

DIED: 1937, Ottawa, Ontario

SIGNIFICANCE: Borden was prime minister 1911–20. He led Canada through the long, difficult years of the First World War. He oversaw Canada's remarkable contribution of people, resources, and finances to the war effort. He encouraged the development of an independent Canadian identity. He won Canada its own place on the world stage.

BRIEF BIOGRAPHY: Robert Borden often disliked serving as PM. He found the work tiring and depressing. Nevertheless, he successfully led Canada through some of the most important and divisive issues the young nation had ever faced.

In 1901, Borden became the Conservative Party leader. In the tough election of 1911, Borden skillfully organized the defeat of Wilfrid Laurier. He worked with both English and French-Canadian nationalists to do this.

During the war, Borden insisted that Canadian soldiers fight as an independent unit.

He demanded and won a larger voice for Canada in the direction of the war. Under his leadership, Canada provided soldiers and vast quantities of war materials. As prime minister, Borden introduced legislation giving the vote to many Canadian women.

During the conscription crisis, Borden proved to be a shrewd, tough leader. He was able to steamroll over the opposition. When the war ended, he successfully insisted that Canada deserved its own place at the peace conference. When the League of Nations was formed, Canada joined on its own, separate from Great Britain.

The toll of the war years wore Borden down. In spite of his successes, Borden knew the country was also divided. French Canada turned away from the Conservative Party. Many workers and farmers thought the war benefited only rich manufacturers.

Other Canadians were troubled by the price Canadians had paid for victory and recognition. Suffering from poor health and political fatigue, Borden resigned in 1920.

In your view, what was Borden's greatest achievement? Why?

CANADIAN LIVES

Canadian Vision

The Canadian War Memorials Fund

One of the most remarkable Canadians of both world wars was Max Aitken. He moved to England after earning a fortune in the Canadian newspaper business. He was named a British peer and took the title Lord Beaverbrook. He was an enthusiastic supporter of the war. Beaverbrook organized a highly effective and secret propaganda effort on behalf of the British government. He created the Canadian War Memorials Fund. This Fund hired artists to record the events of the war. About 800 works of art, many of great power and beauty, resulted. You can see some of these paintings at Canada's War Artists: http://collections.ic.gc.ca/courage/canadaswarartists.html.

The title of F. H. Varley's war painting is "For What?" How would you answer that question? *Varley later gained fame as a member of the Group of Seven.*

FOCUS

1. **What was the Treaty of Versailles?**
2. **In your view, was the treaty fair? Explain.**
3. **How did the treaty help lead to the Second World War?**
4. **What lessons might be learned from the tragedy of the First World War?**
5. **Draft your own treaty and suggest why it is good.**

A Changed Nation

After the victory parades and memorial church services, a different Canada emerged from the war. The war had united Canadians in their grief and in the glory of victories like Vimy. On the world stage, Canada had earned both respect and recognition. Canada had its own seat at the peace conferences that followed the war. When the League of Nations was established, Canada was a member independent of Great Britain. Canadian pride and sense of national purpose had been dearly bought with Canadian blood.

Canada was also a tired, exhausted, and divided nation. Conscription split the country, particularly along language lines. Many average Canadians felt that only a few powerful business leaders had really benefited from the war. Women, who had experienced economic freedom during the war, soon found that the factory doors were closed to them at the end of the war. The feverish war economy was cooling and men were returning to their old jobs. Farmers found that the wartime markets had suddenly closed. Wartime repression had meant controls on freedom of thought and expression. Many Canadians born in foreign lands had been imprisoned or harassed. Soldiers hoping for new prosperity often found poverty, disease, and disappointment. It was a difficult and painful peace.

The site of the most desperate Allied offensive in Belgium, Tyne Cot Cemetery holds 12 000 soldiers, Canadians among them. Seventy percent are unidentified.

Canadians Shot at Dawn

Many thousands of Canadians died during the war, but 23 were deliberately executed by fellow soldiers. Canada followed the traditions of the British Army which executed deserters by a firing squad of their peers. Many of these 23 soldiers were teenagers who had no experience with war. They were executed because they were too afraid to fight, threw their weapons away, or fell asleep on duty. Apparently, one Canadian was shot because he reported late for duty after visiting his French girlfriend.

Arthur-Joseph Lapointe viewed the body of an executed fellow soldier. He noted: "His tunic was splattered with blood, and his head hung down on his chest. His face had such an air of resignation that he seemed to be smiling weakly, even in death. I carry with me such a vivid image of that horrible spectacle that it seems I will never forget it."

Today, most experts agree that this practice was barbaric. In 2001, the Canadian government issued an apology and added the names to the Book of Remembrance on Parliament Hill. Some people continue to ask for a Royal pardon for these Canadians.

Jeremiah Jones distinguished himself at the Battle of Vimy Ridge, but was not awarded a medal.

A White Man's War?

The Canadian armed forces rarely accepted visible minorities. The notion that non-whites had less intelligence caused many Canadians to believe non-whites would make poor soldiers. Some wondered what would happen if Blacks or Asians acquired a taste for killing white men. Others felt uncomfortable fighting next to people unlike themselves. Army commanders argued that their units would not work as well if racial minorities were admitted.

Throughout the war, officials repeatedly insisted that there was no "colour line." When visible minorities offered their services, however, they were turned down. Fifty Blacks from Sydney, Nova Scotia, arrived at the recruitment office to be advised: "This is not for you fellows, this is a white man's war."

Canada's visible minorities volunteered for battle out of a sense of patriotism and a yearning for adventure. They also believed that participation in the war would help improve the status of their people. The crisis in recruitment in 1917 helped crack the wall of racial prejudice. The Canadian military called for an all-Black labour battalion, headquartered in Nova Scotia. In all, more than 1000 African Canadians served in the Canadian forces.

Prejudice did not stop once they enlisted. Units that were made up of visible minorities were likely to be pushed into forestry and construction activities. They were segregated whenever possible from whites. African Canadians were segregated on ships and in camps. They even had to wait for the creation of a separate "coloured" YMCA for their evening entertainment. Their service in the war did not change their status once they returned home. Their efforts were largely forgotten in accounts of the war effort. This racism and discrimination is also part of the legacy of the war.

No. 2 Construction Battalion served honourably in France, providing lumber to maintain trenches on the front lines. Some members went on to serve in combat units. These included Jeremiah Jones who fought bravely at Vimy Ridge. Jones, 56, stormed across the ridge and seized an enemy machine gun nest by himself. "I threw a hand bomb right into the nest and killed about seven of them," he reported. The survivors surrendered to Jones. His commanding officer wanted to award him the Distinguished Conduct Medal, the second highest award for valour, but that did not happen.

A Deadly Epidemic: The Spanish Flu

In 1918–19, a silent killer stalked the world. A form of influenza, called the Spanish flu, killed between 20 and 40 million people, more than twice the number of soldiers who

During the Spanish flu, a simple gauze mask was all the protection people had. Even today, influenza takes about 1000 Canadian lives yearly. In 2003, a new influenza-type virus caused many deaths and much fear. SARS (Severe Acute Respiratory Syndrome) originated in China and caused many casualties in Canada, particularly in Ontario.

died during the war. Soldiers who had somehow survived years of trench warfare died at the hands of this mysterious virus. Its impact was similar to the Black Death that killed so many people in Europe in the 14th century. It arrived in Canada on ships crowded with returning troops. This virus infected 2 of every 9 Canadians. At its height, it killed 1000 Canadians a day. It claimed the lives of 50 000 Canadians.

The Spanish flu was carried on crowded troop ships to Europe where it thrived in the unclean wartime conditions. It returned to North America on ships that were bringing back wounded soldiers. Authorities desperately tried to contain the disease. They quarantined sick people and closed schools, hospitals, churches, theatres, art galleries, dance halls, and more. Even the Stanley Cup playoffs were cancelled. The Spanish flu finally receded in the late spring of 1919. To a world still reeling from the horrific losses of the First World War, it was almost too much. It was not until the 1930s that the virus causing this influenza was identified.

Masked Albertans protecting themselves from the Spanish flu.

In Their Own Words

They shall grow not old,
as we that are left grow old;
Age shall not weary them,
Nor the years condemn.
At the going down of the sun
And in the morning
We will remember them.

These moving words from Laurence Binyon's poem "For the Fallen" are repeated at every meeting of the <u>Royal Canadian Legion</u>. What do you think is the purpose of reciting this verse, known as the Ode? For more information about the Royal Canadian Legion, visit www.legion.ca.

FOCUS

1. **What were the major positive and negative results of the war for Canada?**
2. **What lessons have you learned from your study of the First World War?**

Sharpening Your Skills

Evaluating documents for accuracy and bias

THE SKILL
Recognizing bias and deciphering fact from opinion

THE IMPORTANCE
Separating gossip from fact, and getting the story correct

Detectives examine evidence to reconstruct the crime and discover who committed it and why. Similarly, historians investigate evidence to reconstruct the past and discover what really happened. Both groups rely upon the evidence, the facts, they uncover.

Facts are pieces of information that can be proven to be true—W. L. Mackenzie King was the Canadian prime minister in 1940, or Céline Dion was born in Quebec. Sometimes, what seem like simple facts hide other more complicated facts. For example, the fact that George Brown, editor of the Toronto *Globe* newspaper, was shot and killed by an unhappy employee is really more complicated.

Brown was also the owner of the newspaper. And his wound was only superficial. Brown refused to take the doctor's advice and continued to work. As a result, his wound became infected and he died of gangrene. The above sentence also implies that the motive for the shooting was the fact that the employee was unhappy. But unhappy workers don't usually shoot their bosses. Further research reveals that the worker was drunk. Still, drunk, unhappy employees rarely shoot their bosses. In fact, Brown had fired the worker earlier in the day. Drunk, the employee returned to get his belongings, ran into Brown, got into an argument, and shot Brown.

Simple statements can thus be misleading. They may hide a great deal of information that can put a different interpretation on the "facts."

In deciding what information to include in your report, it is essential to determine its accuracy. Almost every document is filled with opinions, values, feelings, conclusions, and biases. These ideas might be correct, but not necessarily. Before deciding whether to use such information, the historian examines the author's biases.

People are shaped by their environment. Fifty years ago, for example, females were not considered very important. History books were written in sexist language. Statements such as "the pioneers took their wives and children with them to the West," or "inventors and their wives," or "a scientist must devote his every waking hour," excluded women from these roles and gave the impression that science, invention, and pioneering were only male activities.

These authors didn't realize that they were being sexist—almost everyone thought that way. The same was true for racism. Modern-day historians must remember to account for such biases in their sources.

All documents should be viewed with skepticism. Here, at right, are some questions to ask of a document to determine its biases and reliability.

QUESTIONS TO DETERMINE ACCURACY AND BIAS

- **Who created the document?** Did the author's gender, age, political and religious beliefs, income, or ethnicity influence his or her interpretation?
- **Why did the author create the documents?** What motives might the author have, and how would this affect the reporting? Who was the author writing to (or for) and how might this influence what was said?
- **What was the author's relationship to the event?** Was the author in a good position to observe? How did the author learn of the event? Was the author an observer or a participant? Did the author understand the language being spoken?
- **When was the document recorded,** and does this affect its reliability?
- **How good was the author's physical ability to observe and report?** Was the author on drugs? Was he or she tired, sick, or bored? How good was the author's eyesight, hearing, and writing ability?
- **How knowledgeable was the author** on the topic and how reliable are his or her other writings?

Application

What potential problems with bias or accuracy might exist for each type of evidence identified to the right? An autobiography, or personal telling of one's life story, for example, may have these problems: (a) memory lapses because it has been written years after events; (b) a bias because the author is the subject; (c) effects of having many of the people mentioned still alive; (d) an author's focus on leaving a good impression; (e) a bias stemming from the author being a participant.

1) A Canadian soldier's diary of the Battle at Vimy Ridge in the First World War
2) A newspaper reporter's account of this battle, the first battle he observed
3) A German soldier's diary of this battle
4) A Canadian soldier's letter about the battle to his girlfriend
5) The same soldier's letter to his best male friend
6) A radio report of the battle
7) A veteran's account of the battle told 50 years later
8) A Canadian nurse's report of the battle to the Red Cross

Questions and Activities

Questions & Activities

Match the person identified in column A with the description in column B.

A	B
1. Archduke Ferdinand	**a)** opposed conscription for Canada during the First World War
2. General Von Schlieffen	**b)** was the leading German air ace
3. Wilfrid Laurier	**c)** federal minister who insisted that Canadian soldiers fight together in their own army
4. John McCrae	**d)** was assassinated in Sarajevo in an incident that sparked the outbreak of war
5. Sam Hughes	**e)** wrote a poem about soldiers on the Western Front
6. Billy Bishop	**f)** planned the German invasion of France
7. Manfred von Richthofen	**g)** was the leading Canadian air ace

Do Some Research

1. Find out more about the development of one of these weapons.

    a) the fighter plane   **b)** the machine gun
    c) chlorine gas   **d)** the submarine
    e) the tank   **f)** the dreadnought

2. What different kinds of weapons dominate warfare today?

3. Complete further research on the changing role of women during the First World War. Focus on either the home front or the battlefront.

4. Find out more about the causes and effects of the Halifax Explosion. Consider visiting the CBC Digital Archives at www.cbc.ca/archives and look at the file "The Halifax Explosion."

Be Creative

1. Prepare a newspaper on Canada's contribution to fighting the First World War. Your newspaper could include maps, interviews, letters, statistics, pictures, and editorials. Try to cover as many aspects of the war as possible, including recruitment and training, supplies and equipment, volunteer work, and fighting on land, on sea, and in air. Include as much primary source material as you can.

2. What does your school do for Remembrance Day each year? Design a Remembrance Day program for your class or school.

3. With another student, choose a person who played a prominent role at the time of the First World War. Conduct an interview, with one of you playing the interviewer and the other, the historical person. You will need to do further research in order to prepare questions and answers that will highlight the role that person played in the war. You might consider figures such as General Arthur Currie, Billy Bishop, and Prime Minister Borden.

4. Create your own Canadian Lives feature, similar to the one in this book, about someone involved in the war. Include a brief biography and illustration, and indicate why your subject is important. Make sure that you consult primary source material.

5. Organize a debate on one of the following topics related to the First World War:

    a) Conscription or Not   **b)** The Fairness of the Treaty of Versailles
    c) Women and the Vote   **d)** Should Canada Have Participated?

Discuss and Debate

1. What role did the following groups play during the war? Rank these groups in order of importance. Compare your ranking with that of other members of your class.

   a) farming families   b) city families
   c) armament workers   d) soldiers
   e) nurses   f) politicians

2. It has been said that "war brings out the best in people and the worst in people." In small groups, compose two lists: The Best in People and The Worst in People. Compare your lists with those of other groups of students.

3. Here are two different opinions on the Treaty of Versailles. Read them and decide which you agree with most. Discuss the treaty with your classmates, giving reasons for your views.

   I think the Treaty of Versailles was fair. Germany had caused the war. It had invaded Belgium, a neutral country, without excuse. Germany had been trying to expand for 75 years. It had to be punished and it had to be weakened. When the new Soviet government in Russia wanted to withdraw from the war, Germany imposed much harsher terms in the Treaty of Brest-Litovsk than the Western Allies did in the Treaty of Versailles. This kind of treaty was the only way to guarantee that a strong Germany would not cause another war. If the treaty was enforced, it would keep peace in Europe.

   I think the Treaty of Versailles was too harsh. The war had not been caused by Germany alone; much of Europe was just as guilty. Making Germany pay all that money for the war meant its economy could not recover. Germany should not have had its colonies and so much territory taken away. After the war, the Allies and the Germans would have to live together. The treaty was so unfair that the Germans were bound to be resentful. They would look for a chance to get back what they had lost. This might lead to another war.

Web Watch

For more information about the First World War, consider a visit to the following:

Imperial War Museum: www.iwm.org.uk

World Wars Through Canadian Eyes: www.collections.ic.gc.ca

Canadian War Museum: www.warmuseum.ca

Canadian Military Heritage Museum: www.bfree.on.ca

Spartacus Internet Encyclopedia: www.spartacus.schoolnet.co.uk

The Aerodrome (air war): www.aerodrome.com

Veterans Affairs (soldiers, battles, diaries, etc.): www.vac-acc.gc.ca

Trenches on the Web: www.worldwar1.com

SUPERMAN

As classmates, Toronto-born Joe Shuster and Cleveland's Jerry Siegel created the character Superman, which was launched in Action Comics in June 1938. In July 1939 the "Man of Steel" was titled Superman.

HISTOR!CA
Minutes

Why do you think the character is still such a part of popular culture?

Chapter Two
Boom and Bust

Expectations

Overall Expectations:
By the end of this chapter, you will be able to

- explain some major ways in which Canada's population has changed since 1914
- evaluate the impact of some technological developments on Canadians in different periods
- explain changing economic conditions and patterns and how they have affected Canadians
- describe the impact of significant social and political movements on Canadian society
- describe how individual Canadians have contributed to the development of Canada and its emerging sense of identity
- assess the changing role and power of the federal and provincial governments in Canada since 1914
- describe changes in Canada's international status and its role in the world since 1914

Specific Expectations:
By the end of this chapter, you will be able to

- explain some of the ways in which the lives of adolescents, women, and seniors have changed since the First World War as a result of major population shifts, social changes, and technological development
- summarize the key struggles and contributions of the labour and women's movements in Canada during the 1920s and 1930s
- identify changes in Canada's international status since the First World War

Word List

Alberta Five	**Assembly line**
Bootleggers	**Capitalism**
Collective bargaining	**Communism**
Depression	**General strike**
Inflation	**League of Nations**
Prohibition	**Recession**
Socialism	**Specialization of**
Statute of	**labour**
Westminster	

Advance Organizer

❶   ❷   ❸

❶ In the early years of the 20th century, women were not seen as equal to men. They were not encouraged to get jobs or a good education. It was difficult for women to become doctors or lawyers. A group of

women, including Emily Murphy, fought hard for women's rights.

❷ After the war, soldiers returned to find that the price of goods had increased and the number of jobs had decreased. Wages for existing jobs were low. Workers joined together to form unions. Trade unions helped workers demand higher wages.

In the Winnipeg General Strike of 1919, more than 30 000 workers left their jobs.

❸ The "roaring twenties" was a decade of prosperity. There were many jobs and high wages. People could afford homes and cars. Restaurants, theatres, music halls, and dance clubs were popular. Many people put money into the stock market.

Most urban Canadians worked 9 to 10 hours a day, including a half day on Saturdays, but there was still plenty of time for pleasure on weekends.

④   ⑤

④ In 1929, the bottom dropped out of the
stock market. The Great Depression had begun.
The stock market crash affected the whole
world. Workers were laid off, causing
them to search
desperately
for jobs that
did not
exist. Sometimes
they ended up in hobo camps
outside the towns.

⑤ Tough economic times lasted through the
1930s. Canada gained a
greater sense of identity.
The nation was a
respected member of
the world community.
The Depression ended
when the Second World
War began.

By 1933, one in five Canadian
workers had no job. There was
no employment insurance. Two
million people in this country
were on relief.

After the War

The First World War ended on 11 November 1918, after four years of fighting. Canada's nine million people had reason to be proud of the country's war effort.

Many Canadian soldiers, sailors and airmen had not been home in a long time. Now they were returning to take up their lives again. What would they find? How would their nation welcome them back? Troop ships tied up at the government docks in Halifax, and troop trains streamed west, loaded with returning heroes. Cheers greeted them at every station. Family and friends turned out in celebration; the celebrating ended, though, when they tried to get jobs and buy things. Prices all over the country had skyrocketed. The dollar did not buy as much as it had before the war. This **inflation** meant that people's savings and earnings were worth less.

These war veterans are protesting the lack of jobs. Why would they be so unhappy? What other ways might they have protested?

Worker's Unrest

When Canada's war veterans returned home in 1919, after fighting "the war to end all wars," they expected that the country would be grateful, that they would find secure employment and live better lives. Instead, they found widespread worker unrest and frustration. Many ex-soldiers could not even find a job.

The year 1919 began a period of change for Canada. The booming economy ended with the war. Many industries fell into a slump, and factories closed or cut production. Ammunition, weapons, and military equipment were no longer needed. As factories closed, some people lost their jobs. Employers had no new jobs for ex-soldiers. As a result, unemployment increased and many people faced tough times. There was no employment insurance in 1919.

What had happened? Who was to blame? Some people blamed immigrants who had come to Canada before the war. They believed immigrants took jobs away from native-born Canadians. Many soldiers were also angry with some business people who had made much money during the war.

The Canadian government set up a Royal Commission to study the labour problem, but it didn't help much. Unhappy workers wanted answers. The two political parties did not seem to have any.

In the late 1800s, workers had begun to band together to get what they wanted. Workers within the same trade (such as printers) formed trade unions. However, the government and business leaders did not allow them to strike for better conditions or wages. After the First World War, more people joined together to form unions. Each union chose a few people to represent all its members and to bargain with employers. This process is called **collective bargaining**.

CARD OF MEMBERSHIP

ONE BIG UNION

NATIONAL INDUSTRIAL UNION OF THE DOMINION OF CANADA

"Money is the Root of All Evil," saith the Lord.

I. the undersigned, do hereby declare that, by the help of God, I will STRIKE against the use of money at any time I may be called upon.

Name ....

Address ....

Witness ....

Unions become stronger after the First World War.

Robert Boyd Russell

BORN: 1888, Glasgow, Scotland

DIED: 1964, Winnipeg, Manitoba

SIGNIFICANCE: Russell was dedicated to fighting what he saw as the abuse of Canadian workers by rich factory and business owners. Russell spent his life championing the plight of the working class.

BRIEF BIOGRAPHY: Russell became an apprentice machinist in 1900 at the age of 12, and learned how to build machines and engines from engineers' drawings. He immigrated to Canada in 1911. He settled in Winnipeg, and found a job in the Canadian Pacific Railway machine shop. He soon became involved in organizing a union at the CPR. During the First World War, Russell refused to support Canada's participation in the war. He believed that Canadian workers were being unfairly asked to bear the cost of the war on the battle lines, while their bosses sat back and made large profits at home. In 1919, at the close of the war,

Russell became a central player in the One Big Union (OBU) and helped organize the Winnipeg General Strike. He was arrested and spent two years in prison for his role in the Winnipeg General Strike. After serving time, Russell travelled widely in support of the OBU; however, he found that the ideal of a universal union was slowly losing ground. Workers left the OBU to return to their trade unions. In the 1930s, Russell supported the CCF (see page 110). He became the executive secretary of the Winnipeg Branch of the newly organized Canadian Labour Congress in 1956. He retired from political life in 1962 and died a few years later. Winnipeg's R. B. Russell Vocational School was named in his honour in 1967. **Do you think working people in Canada still need champions? How useful are strikes? Explain.**

CANADIAN LIVES

Companies were not always willing to discuss wage and working conditions. Union members could vote to strike or to stop work to put pressure on an employer. Sometimes, workers from many unions voted together to hold a **general strike**. General strikes could disrupt many public and private businesses.

In March 1919, workers met in Calgary to organize the One Big Union, or OBU. The founders planned to unite workers throughout Canada into one union. This one union would have enormous power. E. T. Kingsley and Robert Boyd Russell were two leading OBU organizers.

Organizing the different industrial trades, however, was not easy. OBU leaders returned home to recruit more workers. They wanted to build a strong union, which could call a general strike to help its members get what they wanted.

Many Canadian political and business leaders did not like the OBU. Some believed it was based on **communism**. Others feared union power. They thought collective bargaining was dangerous. Politicians worried about what might happen if the unions got out of control. They wanted to make sure that a workers' revolution—like the one happening in Russia at that time—did not happen in Canada. Americans to the south worried about "The Red Scare."

A CLOSER LOOK AT COMMUNISM

Karl Marx is the father of communism. His ideas were first written in *The Communist Manifesto* (1848). As Marx saw it, **capitalism**, with its constant search for profits, takes advantage of the working class. Marx believed that the only way workers could improve their lives was to overthrow the government and create a new government by the working class. In this new system, everyone would share and benefit equally. Later, communist parties were established in many countries. The Communist Party of Canada was established in Guelph in 1921. At times, it was illegal or banned. Some members became active as union leaders and organizers.

FOCUS

1. How did the war benefit the Canadian economy?
2. What kind of economy did returning soldiers face after the First World War?
3. What was the One Big Union? How did it plan to use the general strike?

The Winnipeg General Strike

In May 1919, 2000 building and metal workers went on strike in Winnipeg. They wanted wages higher than 85 cents an hour and a workweek reduced from 60 to 44 hours. The Metal Trades Council also wanted to be recognized as a union with the right to bargain for its workers.

During the Winnipeg General Strike of 1919, the city ground to a halt. Thousands of workers walked off the job. What made them do so?

When employers refused, the workers asked the Winnipeg Trades and Labour Council for help. The Council asked all unionized workers within the city of Winnipeg to walk off their jobs in support of the metal workers. They believed that if all the workers went on strike, the employers would be forced to give in. Council members voted 11 112 to 524 in favour of a general strike. The strike began on May 15 at 11 a.m. Firefighters, streetcar drivers, telephone operators, sales clerks, garbage collectors, street cleaners and dairy workers all left their jobs. Non-union members left their jobs, too. Within three days, more than 30 000 workers were on strike.

The strikers were led by a strike committee. When the police wanted to strike, the committee asked them to stay on the job to protect property. The committee also asked other essential service workers to return to work so people would be able to have electricity, heat and food. It asked theatres and movie houses to stay open so people would have something to do in their spare time.

A Divided City

Not all Winnipeggers supported the strike. Business people organized the Citizens' Committee of One Thousand to ensure essential city services were maintained. They wanted to make sure no lasting damage to the city's economy occurred. Some citizens feared that the workers wanted more than higher wages and claimed that the strike was part of a communist plot. Some union leaders seemed to speak in the same terms as the Russian communists, which suggested that the strike was the beginning of a revolution in Canada. Feelings against immigrants and foreigners ran high. The Committee of One Thousand urged the federal government to step in.

When Winnipeg employers refused to back down by the middle of June, workers' enthusiasm for the strike began to wane. Many strikers could not afford to stay out any longer. Public opinion began to turn against unions. The strike committee seemed to be running the city. People began to drift back to work; many strikers were disappointed.

Angry workers overturn a streetcar during the strike.

The Arrests

Then, on June 17, the government decided to act. It arrested many of the strike leaders. The men were taken to Stony Mountain Penitentiary and charged with conspiracy and libel before being released on bail. Protests erupted all across Canada. A mass meeting and march were planned for Saturday, June 21. Winnipeg Mayor Gray forbade the rally and read the Riot Act. In protest, a group of ex-soldiers led thousands of people down Main Street. They were met by Mounties swinging clubs and firing pistols. Two people died in the riot that followed. The federal government sent troops into the city to patrol Winnipeg streets with machine guns. "Bloody Saturday" was a day many Canadians would never forget. The strike committee called off the strike a week later.

A Communist Plot?

The strike leaders were not planning a revolution. However, their speeches were filled with revolutionary-like words. The growth of communism in Europe, as well as several violent strikes in the United States, added fuel to some people's worries.

J. S. (James Shaver) Woodsworth

BORN: 1874, Etobicoke, Ontario

DIED: 1942, Vancouver, British Columbia

SIGNIFICANCE: Woodsworth was the first leader of the Co-operative Commonwealth Federation (CCF) in 1933.

BRIEF BIOGRAPHY: Woodsworth was ordained as a minister at the age of 26. He preached what is known as the social gospel. He urged his followers to improve life for people on Earth rather than worry about heaven. In 1904, he moved from his middle-class church to a mission in Winnipeg's slums. He worked tirelessly to help the city's poverty-stricken immigrants. His experiences led him to write *Strangers Within Our Gate*, an analysis of Canada's immigration system. It was highly critical of government policies.

By 1914, Woodsworth had become a supporter of trade unions and pacifism. He was fired from his job as director of Social Research in 1916 because he opposed the First World War and conscription. In 1918, to protest the church's support of the war, he resigned from the ministry. He took a longshoreman's position on the Vancouver docks.

In Winnipeg in 1919, Woodsworth took over the strikers' newspaper after its editor was arrested. His editorial position also caused Woodsworth to be arrested. Charges were dropped when prosecutors realized he had been quoting from the Bible.

In 1921, Woodsworth was elected as an Independent Labour member of Parliament (MP) for Winnipeg. As a politician, he continued his fight against workers' exploitation and the unfair treatment of immigrants. He also supported old age pensions and unemployment insurance.

In 1933, Woodsworth was elected leader of the newly formed Co-operative Commonwealth Federation (CCF). By the outbreak of the Second World War, Woodsworth's belief in pacifism had not changed. He was the only MP to vote against Canada fighting in the Second World War. **Briefly outline your personal opinion of J. S. Woodsworth.**

HISTOR!CA
Minutes

C A N A D I A N   L I V E S

CAPE BRETON MINERS' STRIKE

Winnipeg was not the only place to experience violent strikes. From 1921 to 1925, Cape Breton miners went on strike three times against the Montreal-based British Empire Steel Corporation. They demanded higher wages and better working conditions. Labour unrest lasted four years. More than two million workdays were lost to striking miners.

By far the most violent and bloody battle occurred in 1925, when the miners went on strike for five months. Credit was cut off from company stores, so the miners could not afford groceries and clothing. The company asked provincial police and federal troops to calm the angry workers. During a nasty battle at Waterford Lake, many miners were injured. One miner was killed by police. His death is still mourned

by Cape Bretoners every June 11, on Miners' Memorial Day. In the end, a Royal Commission reprimanded the company, but failed to help the miners.

Seven of the arrested strikers were convicted of conspiracy. They received sentences of up to two years in prison. Five men were never brought to trial. Two strike leaders, Fred Dixon and A. A. Heaps, were acquitted. Charges against J. S. Woodsworth were dropped. Four Slav immigrants who had nothing to do with the strike leadership were deported.

Although the strike had failed, it proved to be a turning point in labour relations. It sparked a political consciousness of the issues. In 1920, several strike leaders were elected to the Manitoba legislature, and the following year, workers had political representation in Ottawa. Workers found other ways to solve their problems, and the public became more aware of these problems and concerns. The Canadian trade union movement gained support, although Manitoba's labour movement would be divided and crippled for many years.

Woodsworth turned to politics and later founded the CCF in 1933 as the first major democratic socialist party in this country.

FOCUS

1. What caused the Trades and Labour Council to call a general strike?
2. What was the goal of the Citizens' Committee of One Thousand?
3. Should government forces be employed to stop strikes? Why or why not?

Women Are Persons Too

Canadian women's positions were changing in the early years of the 20th century. Women were starting to take on different roles in the workplace, in sports, socially, and even at home. Alcohol, poverty, and child welfare became important social issues. Many women's groups believed that the use of liquor was hurting the Canadian way of life. They felt it caused financial problems, crime, and often physical and mental abuse within the family. The Women's Christian Temperance Union, or WCTU (organized in Ontario in 1875) worked hard to ban the sale of liquor in Canada. Thanks to the need for grain for the troops in the First World War, and to Prime Minister Borden's desire to get elected, **Prohibition** began in March 1918.

But Prohibition did not work. People who really wanted to drink alcohol found it. Bootlegging became big business as criminals found ways to make, sell, or import liquor illegally from the United States. By 1924, most provinces decided liquor control was better than Prohibition. Making alcohol legal would force **bootleggers** out of business. The government would be able to control liquor sales and make money from liquor taxes. Legal bars and beverage rooms would replace the illegal places to get liquor. Canada's temperance movement did not succeed, but it did make Canadians aware of alcohol abuse. Canadian alcohol use never again reached the same high levels of the late 19th century.

In 1938, Prime Minister W. L. Mackenzie King unveiled a plaque to honour the Alberta Five. With him (from left to right) are Back row: Senator Iva Campbell Fallis and Senator Cairine Wilson; Front row: Mrs. Muir Edwards (daughter-in-law of Henrietta Muir Edwards), J. C. Kerwood, and Nellie McClung. What is the significance of the two senators in the photo?

Women Are Persons Too

In 1916, the city of Edmonton appointed Emily Murphy as Judge of the Juvenile Court. Within a year, the province of Alberta made her a magistrate. Murphy was the first female judge in Canada. On her first day in court, a male lawyer challenged her appointment. He claimed that only a "qualified person" could sit on the Bench. British law considered only men as persons; women were not even mentioned.

The persons issue did not go away. Canada's constitution (the British North America Act) stated that Canadian senators must be "qualified persons." Were women persons? Did the wording in the BNA Act mean women could not be senators? In 1919, the Montreal Women's Club asked Prime Minister Borden to appoint Emily Murphy to the Canadian Senate. They wanted to test the law.

Borden refused. He claimed it was impossible for him to appoint a female to the Canadian Senate. Women's groups believed Borden's decision discriminated against women.

Murphy had given many years of public service to Canada. She worked for poor people, for new immigrants, for Aboriginal Canadians, for children, for women, and for drug addicts. Murphy's book about the drug trade, *The Black Candle*, was the first of its kind. It had an impact around the world.

Many people felt its author would make an excellent senator.

By 1927, Emily teamed up with Nellie McClung, Louise McKinney, Irene Parlby, and long-time women's rights worker Henrietta Muir Edwards. They

HISTOR!CA
Minutes

Emily Murphy was an important political and social reformer in Canada.

became the **Alberta Five** and they fought the Persons Case in the courts. The government won round one when the Supreme Court ruled women were not persons. The court based its decision on social conditions at the

Agnes Macphail

BORN: 1890, Owen Sound, Ontario

DIED: 1954, Toronto, Ontario

SIGNIFICANCE: In 1921, Macphail became the first woman in Canada to be elected to Parliament. She was responsible for the first equal pay legislation in Canada (1951).

BRIEF BIOGRAPHY: Macphail became an MP for the United Farmers of Ontario in 1921. This was the first year women were able to vote in the province. As the only woman in Parliament, she was seen as a novelty and faced much discrimination. The press paid more attention to what she wore than to what she said. "I was intensely unhappy," she later recalled. "Some members resented my intrusion, other jeered at me ... most of the members made me painfully conscious of my sex." That first year she lost 12 pounds. Rather than be stared at in the Parliamentary dining room, she ate in "greasy spoons."

Macphail fought for equality for women, peaceful solutions to international conflicts, family allowances, old age and disability pensions, and better conditions for workers and prisoners. Macphail was re-elected four times. It wasn't until 1935, though, that another woman MP joined her. Macphail was an ardent spokesperson for female equality and women's rights. She founded the Elizabeth Fry Society of Canada and took an active part in the Woman's International League for Peace and Freedom. She championed the "powerless." Macphail fought tirelessly to improve the lot of farmers, workers, the elderly, and the physically and mentally challenged. Her socialist and pacifist beliefs often led her to support the politics of J. S. Woodsworth and, later, the CCF. **Name a modern Canadian who fights for the powerless. For more about the Elizabeth Fry Society, go to www.elizabethfry.ca.**

Minutes

CANADIAN LIVES

time of Confederation in 1867. At that time no one expected women to hold office. The BNA Act never even considered women when it referred to persons. By 1927 times were different. The women now appealed their case to the Judicial Committee of the Privy Council in England. This was the final court of appeal for all members of the British Empire. The Privy Council ruled on 18 October 1929 that women were indeed

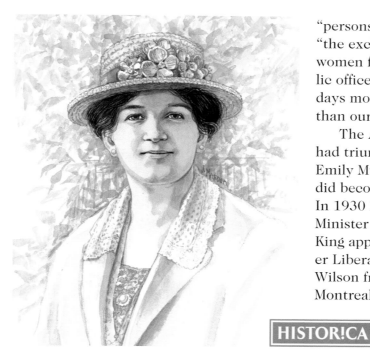

Nellie McClung, reformer and suffragette.

HISTOR!CA

Minutes

"persons," and that "the exclusion of women from all public offices is a relic of days more barbarous than ours."

The Alberta Five had triumphed, but Emily Murphy never did become a senator. In 1930 Liberal Prime Minister Mackenzie King appointed another Liberal, Cairine Wilson from Montreal, to be the first female in the Canadian Senate.

In Their Own Words

Emily Murphy describes her first day in court:
"It was as pleasant an experience as running rapids without a guide. Besides, the lawyers and police officials looked so accustomed and so terribly sophisticated. Indeed, I have never seen brass buttons so bright and menacing as on this particular day. All the men became embarrassed and started to stammer over their manner of addressing me. One said 'Your Worship' and others 'Your Honour'... and the rest said 'Sir.'"

How did Emily Murphy feel on her first day in court? How did the rest of the court feel?

FOCUS

1. Who were the Alberta Five? Why are they important?
2. Who was Emily Murphy?
3. Who was Agnes Macphail? How did she help the "powerless"?
4. Identify some current issues of importance to Canadian women.

New Opportunities for Women

Canadian society in the 1920s had many biases towards both minority groups and women. For instance, it was not proper for a married woman to work. Many employers even fired a woman who got married!

Not many women got university or college degrees. Society thought that if a woman had to work, she should be a cleaning lady, teacher, clerk or nurse. People felt that these were the natural jobs for women. Jobs in medicine, law, and journalism were viewed as natural for men. It was difficult for women who wanted to study and practise in these fields. They faced discrimination, ridicule, financial hardship and loneliness. Only the most determined women were able to succeed.

Sports

Some women found freedom in sports. They played basketball, hockey and baseball, often for company-sponsored teams. Women's basketball games were broadcast on the radio. More than 6000 spectators filled Toronto's Sunnyside Stadium to watch women's baseball games. Crowds for the men's games were often nowhere near as large.

Canadian female athletes began competing at the summer Olympic Games in 1928. Canada's track and field team won medals in nearly every event. Ethel Catherwood, "the Saskatoon lily," won a gold medal in the high jump. Bobbie Rosenfeld won a silver medal in a dead heat in the 100 m race, and led the Canadian women to gold in the 400 m relay.

By the 1930s, though, women were discouraged from active sports. Men and boys became the "real athletes." Company sponsorship of women's teams decreased, and women's teams had trouble getting time in public sports arenas. Some doctors even said that doing sports harmed a woman's ability to have children. This attitude lasted well into the 1950s and beyond.

Sportswriters named Fanny "Bobbie" Rosenfeld the best Canadian female athlete of the first half of the century. She played on championship basketball teams, won the Toronto tennis championship, threw the discus and the javelin, ran the hurdles, and starred in hockey and softball. In 1928, Rosenfeld set three Canadian records which lasted almost 30 years: she long-jumped 18 feet 3 inches; threw the discus 120 feet; and soared 8 feet 1 inch in the standing broad jump.

CANADA'S DREAM TEAM: THE EDMONTON GRADS

Canada's most successful basketball team ever was the Edmonton Grads. They were the Commercial Graduates Basketball Club at McDougall Commercial High School. Coached by Percy Page, the Grads ruled Canadian basketball from 1915 to 1940. They never lost a series in the 23 years they competed in the International Underwood Championships. Indeed, they won that cup so often they were given permanent possession of it in 1940. They won 96 percent of their games and 49 out of a possible 51 Canadian titles. After losing the first North American Championship, the Grads came back with a vengeance—winning the next three years straight. They played in the 1924 Women's Olympics in Paris and were declared World Champions by the Federation Sportive International. In 1928, they won the French and European championships.

During their 25-year career, the Edmonton Grads had only 48 different players on their roster. The turnover rate for this phenomenal dream team was less than two players a year. All team members, with the exception of two, attended McDougall Commercial High School. Playing against both men and women throughout their history, the Edmonton Grads held 108 local, provincial, national and international titles at the time of their retirement. Known simply as the "finest basketball team ever," by basketball's inventor, Canadian James Naismith, the Edmonton dream team played for the love of the sport. No member ever received payment for her skills on the basketball court. **What made the Grads so special in Canadian sports history? For more, see www.collectionscanada.ca/women.**

Clothing

Another aspect of women's lives that changed dramatically in the 1920s was clothing. Skirts barely covered the knees. Bobs and shingled haircuts replaced long hair and hairpins. The "boyish look" was all the rage. The ideal body shape was to be thin, almost mannish. Short, loose dresses emphasized the legs and arms rather than the hips and breasts. Bare, sun-tanned legs replaced stockings. Corsets were replaced by bras and girdles, with their new "two-way stretch" materials of silk, cotton, and rayon. Department stores opened junior sections of "foundation garments" for 12- to 14-year olds, and recommended girdles to prevent their figures from getting larger.

Other freedoms followed. It was not uncommon to see young women smoking—and even drinking—in public.

Elsie MacGill

BORN: 1905, Vancouver, British Columbia

DIED: 1980, Cambridge, Massachusetts

SIGNIFICANCE: MacGill was the first woman to graduate with a degree in electrical engineering. She pioneered in aeronautical research.

BRIEF BIOGRAPHY: MacGill was the daughter of Helen MacGill, women's rights activist and journalist who was appointed a juvenile court judge one year after Emily Murphy's appointment. MacGill was raised in a strongly feminist environment. Excelling at science and mathematics, she enrolled in the University of Toronto's Engineering Department in 1923. Four years later, she became the first woman to graduate with a degree in electrical engineering. She pursued her studies at the University of Michigan. In 1928 she became the first woman to graduate with a degree in aeronautics. Determined to continue her studies, MacGill was accepted by the prestigious Massachusetts Institute of Technology (MIT) in 1933 to continue her work in aeronautical research. From 1934 to 1957, she helped test-fly the first Canadian-designed and -built all-metal aircraft for Fairchild Aircraft Ltd. in Longueuil, Quebec, where she was employed. In 1939, MacGill left this job for another at the Canadian Car and Foundry in Fort William (now Thunder Bay), Ontario. She was in charge of engineering on the Canadian-built Hawker Hurricanes and the U.S. Navy Helldivers, which were launched by catapult from aircraft carriers. In 1946, MacGill helped the International Civil Aviation Organization (ICAO) establish air-worthiness regulations. She married Eric Soulsby, an executive at the firm. She opened her own consulting business, which she ran well into the 1970s. In 1955, she published a biography of her mother entitled *My Mother the Judge*. In 1967, continuing the legacy of her mother, she served on the Royal Commission on the Status of Women. **Why might MacGill make an excellent role model for Canadian women today?**

CANADIAN LIVES

Nurses The first trained nurses who arrived in Quebec in 1639 were members of a Roman Catholic religious order. These nuns served as doctors, helping the sick in and around Quebec. The Sisters of Charity, a non-cloistered order, arrived in 1737 and are thought of as Canada's first public health nurses. Training was mostly on the job. They built hospitals and canoed to remote areas to provide care to the sick. Their first hospital opened in Montreal in 1737.

In 1874, the first school of nursing opened in St. Catharines, Ontario. Nursing programs next opened in hospitals in Toronto in 1881 and in Montreal in 1890. Nurses in these programs did little more than make the hospitals look nice. They had no professional status. Their training was decided by the doctors who ran the hospital. Working hours were from 12 to 20 hours a day with half a day off every week. Working conditions were cramped and crude. Most graduates left the hospital for private nursing in the homes of the wealthy.

The Victorian Order of Nurses (VON) was established in 1897 by Lady Aberdeen. She wanted to close the gap between the nursing care that the rich could afford and that which the poor received in the hospitals. The VON built and operated over 40 hospitals. During the early years of the 20th century, a group of nurses tried to get professional status for nurses. They wanted to improve the education of nurses and protect the title of nurse. The Canadian National Association of Nurses was formed in 1907, as a result of their action. The University of British Columbia began a university degree program for nurses in 1919, but most nursing schools remained under the control of the hospitals. It was not until the 1960s that nurses gained control of their education. At last, professional degrees were widely available to those entering the profession. Today, there are more than 250 000 registered nurses in Canada. **For more information about this community, visit the Canadian Association of Nurses at www.cnc-nurses.ca.**

FOCUS

1. What gains did women make in the 1920s in employment and recreation?
2. How did the change in fashion mirror a change in social attitudes towards women?
3. In your opinion, what is Elsie MacGill's most important achievement?

The Roaring Twenties

The Age of Radio

In 1923 there were 10 000 radios in Canada. Six years later, there were 300 000. By 1931, about one-third of Canadian households owned a radio. The average North American household listened to the radio three to four hours a day.

Evenings in many homes were spent around the kitchen table listening to homemade crystal radio sets. Crystal sets did not have amplification so listeners had to wear earphones. Montreal's CFCF was Canada's first commercial radio station. By 1929, all the major cities had radio stations. Big electric radios in fancy wooden cabinets became a major source of family entertainment. Farmers and small towns were no longer isolated from the

Canadian Reginald Fessenden is credited with making the first radio broadcast in the world in 1906. He is known as "the Father of Radio."

cities. Businesses could advertise their products. Politicians could speak instantly to the public. The first radio broadcasts were live. Performers, dressed in tuxedos or long gowns, would sing or play their instruments right in the studio. Listeners often heard the broadcast unedited, complete with mistakes.

Technology and Canadian Life in the 1920s

Today, Canadians take many things for granted. We flip a

In Their Own Words

"I'll always remember the first time I listened to a radio. I was fourteen years old, so that would have been 1924…. Trembling with excitement I put the earphones on. Like magic, from the very air around, I heard the song 'Oranges and Lemons.' The music was in my ears, clear and melodic, as if the singers were actually in the room. How could they possibly be a hundred miles away? In a trance I listened, wishing I could listen forever…. Papa tapped me on the shoulder when it was time for Esther and Thora to listen. I took off the earphones and returned to reality. The music was gone. But I could see it now in my sisters' smiles and in their faraway, unfocused eyes."

Source: Irene Morck, *Five Pennies*
(Calgary: Fifth House, 1999)

The Technical Edge

Batteryless Radios In 1912, at the age of 13, Edward Rogers won a prize for making the best amateur radio in Ontario. He won an American contest seven years later. This next prize was for low-power broadcasts sent across the Atlantic Ocean. Rogers quit his job at the Independent Telephone Company in 1925 and worked on the world's first alternating current (AC) radio tube. This invention allowed radios to run on a regular 110-volt household current. Up until that time, radios were run on acid-filled batteries that needed to be recharged. The noise from these receivers was often louder than the radio signals. Roger's new invention eliminated this problem.

In 1929, Rogers and his father founded Rogers Majestic Radio Company to sell batteryless radios. The following year, he established several broadcasting companies, including 9RB (named for Rogers Batteryless). This station later became CFRB, which is still on the air today. In 1931, Rogers was awarded one of Canada's first television licences. He died in 1939 at the age of 38. His son Edward Jr. later founded Rogers Radio Broadcasting. This company pioneered FM broadcasting in 1962 with Toronto radio station CHFI. Now, Rogers Communications has interests in cable television, telephones, wireless communications, and the Internet.

switch and turn on our lights, our TV, and our appliances. Many homes have central heating and air conditioning. Compact discs have digital sound, and computers provide multi-media and satellite communication. Life was not always so. An era of invention in the early 1900s gave the lifestyle we know today. Electricity became part of everyday life in the 1920s. People could buy electric stoves, washing machines, irons, vacuum cleaners and toasters. These appliances may not have looked like those we use today, but they helped make housework and cooking easier.

Improvements in technology made the telephone more common in Canadian homes. By 1928, over 1 million Canadian homes had telephones—an average of 12.79 telephones per 100 people. New international lines in 1927 made it possible for Canadians to phone relatives in Great Britain. Overseas calls were not cheap. There was a charge of $75 for 3 minutes and $25 for any additional minute. In 1928, rates were reduced to $45 for the first three minutes plus $15 per extra minute.

This radio studio was a dynamic exhibit at the 1934 Canadian National Exhibition in Toronto. Curious crowds gathered to see live broadcasts behind clear glass.

Leisure Time Entertainment

Most urban Canadians worked long hours. They toiled 9 to 10 hours a day, including a half-day on Saturdays. When they finished working they wanted to relax. As a result, the entertainment industry boomed. People looking for something to do had lots of choice.

Many Canadian cities and towns had theatres, which had been built during the early 1900s. Travelling theatre companies performed the latest plays from London or New York. Live variety shows for the whole family, known as vaudeville, were popular. So were burlesque shows where, in between the stand-up comics and the skits, audiences watched the ladies in the chorus line, or the exotic dancers, or even the strip-tease artists.

Many young people flocked to nightclubs, where they listened to jazz music. Others went dancing, doing the tango, Charleston, black bottom, and more. Live orchestras in the dance halls played the latest tunes.

But the most popular entertainment of all was the movies. In the beginning, motion pictures had no sound. Live music from an orchestra, subtitles, and sound effects were used instead. There were movie houses in every city and town across the country. Many people felt a week was not complete without time spent laughing and crying with Charlie Chaplin, falling in love with Rudolf Valentino, or watching Douglas Fairbanks rescue a beautiful woman from certain death.

In 1927, the first talking motion picture, *The Jazz Singer*, starring Al Jolson, was made. It ended the era of silent films.

Consumerism

Canadians learned to be "buy now, pay later" consumers. People could buy a car with a small down payment, and pay the balance (with interest) over a two- to five-year period. Consumer spending rose rapidly as prosperity grew. People wanted to buy more and more products. Canada had entered a new era of consumerism as large department stores, such as Eaton's and Simpsons, carried the many items consumers wanted. Increased world demand forced the price of Canadian wheat up in 1924. Canada exported $352 million worth of wheat by 1928. Many Canadian farmers on the prairies took advantage of the boom to buy expensive new equipment. Most borrowed the money from banks or bought the machinery on credit. Farmers organized into wheat pools or co-operatives, which allowed them to sell their product for the highest possible price. Farm co-op stores allowed farmers to buy their supplies and materials for the lowest possible price.

Not everyone in Canada thrived. The economy of the Maritime provinces remained poor. Life was hard for immigrants in the cities. They often did not speak English, and had few job skills. Employers paid them as little as possible. Women were paid much less than men for doing the same work. Wages for most factory workers stayed low. A company might be making huge profits, but workers did not share in them. Business owners priced goods as high as possible. Often, the workers could not afford to buy the very

goods they helped produce. As a result, unsold merchandise began to pile up in warehouses and stores.

Most people thought the booming twenties would last forever, but some people saw danger signals. They did not like the unequal

The twenties were sometimes referred to as "The Jazz Age."

distribution of wealth. The rich got richer, while workers, immigrants, and some farmers did not have enough money to buy their share of the goods.

FOCUS

1. How did radio change Canadian life during the early twenties?
2. What new inventions changed Canadian lives?
3. How did consumerism change the way Canadians purchased goods?
4. Why did many (a) immigrants, (b) women, and (c) factory workers not share in the prosperity of the 1920s?

Easy Street

Cars in Canada

The automobile began life at the turn of the century as a motorized cart. One early design was a large tricycle with a small motor. Henry Ford brought cars to North Americans. He invented the **assembly line**. In this manufacturing system, each piece was installed by a separate worker as the car moved gradually from worker to worker. One group of workers added wheels, another the motor, others the gas tank, and still others the radiator. Each worker or group did a single job on many cars. This was called **specialization of labour**. Ford's assembly line could produce cars cheaply. In 1917, the "Tin Lizzie" cost $495. By 1925, so many cars were rolling off Ford's Canadian assembly line in Windsor that the price had dropped to $424.

By 1919 more than 13 000 workers (mostly in Ontario) had jobs making cars.

Thousands more made tires or spare parts, or repaired cars. Thousands of workers and engineers worked on roads. Many new occu-

Gas stations soon appeared all over the country. Gas was relatively cheap.

pations emerged or increased in numbers because of the automobile. These included service station attendants, motel operators, traffic policemen, camping ground owners, sign makers, and travelling salespeople.

Mud was a problem for cars in the 1920s. Few roads were paved.

The car allowed people to travel. This ability promoted the growth of tourism, which added more than $300 million to the Canadian economy by 1929. About 94 percent of the tourists came from the United States.

Industrial concentration began during this time. Big companies swallowed up small companies. This was certainly the case in the automobile industry. At one time, about 70 companies, many of them Canadian, sold cars in Canada. By 1926, there were only 14 such firms left. Ford, General Motors, and Chrysler made 75 percent of all cars sold in Canada. The last Canadian car firm, Brooks Automobile Company, went out of business in 1927. From that date on, most of the cars made in Canada were from plants owned by American companies.

Cars changed the way Canadians lived. Families could drive up to 40 km to visit friends and still be home by dark. Weekend outings became popular. Farmers had faster access to markets.

Soon the car became a status symbol. Exotic makes like the Auburn, Cadillac, Lincoln, and Cord, many with 16 cylinder engines, could reach speeds of 160 km per hour. These expensive models shared the roads with lower priced Model Ts and Chevrolets.

The car opened Canada's vast wilderness. Camping became accessible to more people.

The number of new cars grew from 838 672 in 1926 to 945 672 in 1927. Of the 9832 km of new roads constructed in 1927, 4043 km were dirt roads, 4481 km gravel, 388 km asphalt, and 240 km concrete. The car was not much use in winter. Even if it started, roads were often too dangerous to travel. Many people put their cars up on blocks until the spring.

Driving during the other seasons could be risky, too. Many farmers made extra money by lending their horses to pull vehicles out of the mud. The Canadian Motor Vehicles Act of 1903 set speed limits of 16 km per hour in the cities and 22 km per hour in the country (speeds raised to 30 km and 40 km in 1919). The limit on Ontario roads was 10 km per

Frederick Banting

BORN: 1891, Alliston, Ontario

DIED: 1941, in a plane crash

SIGNIFICANCE: He discovered insulin.

BRIEF BIOGRAPHY: Banting graduated from medical school in 1916. He joined the army in France as a doctor. In 1921, he began research on diabetes with Charles Best at the University of Toronto. Banting and Best knew that diabetes was a result of pancreatic malfunction. While experimenting with diabetic dogs, they found that an extract of the pancreas (later called insulin) controlled sugar buildup in the blood. The only known treatment for diabetes at the time was starvation. If the body did not get food, it would slow the blood sugar buildup.

In 1922, Banting tested insulin on Leonard Thompson, a 14-year-old diabetic who had lost so much weight he was close to death. Within a few weeks, the boy had regained normal health. Banting sold the insulin patent to the University of Toronto for one dollar, as long as any profits went to medical research. In 1923, Banting was awarded the Nobel Prize for Medicine. From 1923 until 1929, Banting served as director of the Banting and Best Department of Medical Research at the University of Toronto, where he supervised work on cancer, lead poisoning and silicosis, among other things.

A good amateur painter, Banting befriended A. Y. Jackson from the Group of Seven. In 1939, he investigated the effects of high altitudes on pilots for the Royal Canadian Air Force. He died in 1941 in a plane crash on route to England while on a "mission of high importance" for the government.

Why is Banting considered to be such a great Canadian? For more information about the discovery, visit CBC Digital Archives at www.cbc.ca/archives and look at the file, "Banting, Best, Macleod, Collip: Chasing a Cure for Diabetes."

CANADIAN LIVES

hour whenever a horse-drawn carriage was near. Ontario drivers were not licensed until 1927, and even then, no one had to pass an exam. Anyone who had driven 800 km, who had no physical or mental impairments, and who paid the $1 fee could get a licence.

Investing in Stock

The 1920s was a time of social and economic revolution in North America. More Canadians than ever before were able to afford the comforts of life. One of every two Canadian families owned a car in 1928. By 1929, more than 60 percent of Canadians had electricity in the home.

Many businesses were too large to be owned by one person or family. When these companies needed money, they financed themselves by selling shares of company stock to the public through the stock market. Share prices were set by supply and demand. If the stock was popular, its price rose. If more people wanted to sell shares than buy, the stock price fell.

Careful investors bought wisely. They investigated a company's prospects before purchasing stock. Stock values increased dramatically during the 1920s, and the stock market rose. As the excitement of buying and selling took over, some people forgot what the whole business was about. Many people borrowed money to invest. Shares were traded at higher and higher prices. Investors made huge profits, at least on paper. However, the price of a company's shares often bore no relation to the real value of its earnings and profit.

Taking Risks

Compared to the general population, the number of investors was small, but everyone bought into the "get rich quick" philosophy of the time. Daring investors took big risks. They bought on margin (with borrowed money) paying the stockbroker 10 to 15 percent of the price of the shares. If the value of the stock rose, the shares would pay for themselves. Investors could sell, pay the broker what was owed, and still make a profit. Of course, if the stock fell, the broker could ask for his money and the investor would have to pay all the money owed. But no one worried about this. The stock market was rising too fast to worry. This "boom" mentality would not last forever.

FOCUS

1. **What are the advantages of producing goods on an assembly line?**
2. **In what ways has the automobile changed our lives?**
3. **What was dangerous about investing in the twenties?**

The Dirty Thirties

The Stock Market Crash

Nobody knew on 3 September 1929 that the stock market had finally reached its peak. Prices began to slip, but they had slipped before. Most investors expected a turnaround soon. None came. Prices continued to plunge and brokers wanted their money. Investors could not pay up.

Winnipeg Grain Exchange. What are the men in the upper half of the picture doing?

On Thursday, 24 October 1929, thousands of stock shares bought on margin were dumped onto the stock market. There were no buyers, however, so prices took a nosedive. When the news hit the newspapers, other investors panicked. Five days later, things were even worse. This day is known as Black Tuesday. Small investors began dumping stock, rushing to sell out before they lost everything. The stock market bubble had finally burst. Within days, stocks that were once valuable became worthless. Within months it became obvious that the economic downturn, or **recession**, had turned into a worldwide **depression**. The price of raw materials collapsed: pulp dropped from $29.57 per ton in 1929 to $19.65 per ton in 1932; copper prices fell from $19.75 to $7.02. Investors lost everything.

The Great Depression

The panic that caused the stock market crash of 1929 began in the United States. It spread quickly to Canada and to all other countries involved in trade. The stock market crash triggered the Great Depression of the 1930s. Canada suffered greatly while the whole world was in an economic slump. At first, many Canadians did not realize the seriousness of the problem. Mackenzie King's Liberal government believed the economy would correct itself naturally. Many small investors thought they could survive the crash. After all, they still had jobs. Many more Canadians had never invested in the market at all. Why should its crash affect them?

The Downward Spiral

Canada's economy was resource based and Canadian prosperity depended on the export of raw materials. Our natural resources— wheat, lumber, fish and minerals—were sold to other countries, particularly the United States and Europe. After the crash, these countries bought much less and the decrease

THE ECONOMIC CYCLE

PROSPERITY ▶	RECESSION ▶	DEPRESSION ▶	RECOVERY
• many jobs • money to spend • much production • much business expansion • high profits • more jobs & spending	• fewer sales/jobs • business cuts • low profits • unemployment • bankruptcies • more job cuts	• very low sales • high unemployment • business closings • very low wages • low demand for goods • more unemployed	• jobs increase • production increases • demand increases • jobs are added • more money to spend • business expands

What phase in the economic cycle is Canada in at present? Explain.

in demand resulted in lower prices. Canadian farmers were unable to sell their wheat. Mining companies were left with unsold coal, iron ore and copper. Lumbering companies lacked buyers for their pulp and logs. In the meantime, they were unable to keep up payments for equipment bought on credit. Many companies went bankrupt.

The Depression spread around the world. Other countries that normally bought our wheat, fish, wood, and other goods could no longer afford to buy them. Eighty percent of the products of our farms, forests, and mines were sold abroad. To help their own people, many countries reduced Canadian imports by putting a tax (tariff) on them. The United States, for example, taxed Canadian cattle and dairy products. When Spain, Portugal, and Italy taxed Canadian dried cod and fresh fish, it crippled the Atlantic fishery.

Canada's manufacturing industry fared no better. Many Canadian businesses had too much unsold inventory. They had been overproducing, churning out new products as fast as they could to meet consumer demand. Now, no one could afford to buy cars, boats, appliances, or even clothing. Factories and businesses closed down, or laid off workers until the backlog of goods was sold. Companies that stayed in business often made workers take pay cuts. Companies were forced to lower their prices to survive. Banks called in their loans. Many businesses and people could not repay their loans, so they went bankrupt.

People no longer had money to buy luxuries like radios and vacuum cleaners. Workers who made these products were laid off. Then the people who supplied the raw materials to build these products lost their jobs. Soon, many Canadians could not afford to buy coats, dresses, or even shoes. Most consumers who had bought goods on the "buy now, pay later" plan could no longer make the payments. People lost their furniture, their cars and even their homes.

By 1933, one in five Canadian workers were unemployed. There was no employment insurance. Two million people in this country were on government relief. The area hardest hit was Canada's four western provinces. Canada's Atlantic provinces never had a chance to recover from the economic depression that hit them in the 1920s, but they were partially sustained by fishing and farm-

into the office with tears in their eyes suffering humiliation at being forced to apply for assistance."

Women seeking well-paying jobs were frowned on because men "needed the jobs more." Many women accepted lower wages, and they sometimes found jobs when men could not. Every day that wives, sisters, and mothers went out to work, their husbands, brothers, and sons lost a little more self-respect.

To ensure that only people who

Soup kitchens seemed to appear overnight in the Depression. Does Canada have similar places today? Explain.

ing. Canada's young people, small business people, and farmers were the true victims of the Depression. Many large businesses, property owners, and people with jobs actually made money during this period.

Learning to Survive

Perhaps the worst part of living through the Depression was the shame of being out of work. People had been taught that if they were poor, it was their own fault. Only lazy people failed. Every time Canada's homeless, hungry, and unemployed lined up at a soup kitchen or accepted vouchers to exchange for goods, their despair grew. One Edmonton relief officer noted: "I have seen men come

"deserved" help received it, the government often forced people to work for food. Some people were required to cut fire wood, others pulled dandelions beside the road, or dug a hole one day and filled it in the next.

Who got relief and who didn't depended on the province, the town, and the person in charge. A relief officer refused to give one newly married couple relief because he thought that people who married during such hard times should not expect any sympathy or help. People who received relief could not drink alcohol, or own a phone, a radio, jewellery, or a car. Individuals seen drinking, driving a car, or attending a race track lost their relief.

But Canadians did not give up; they made do. People patched old clothes. When the clothes fell apart, they wore flour sacks. Wads of newspaper placed in worn-out shoes made them last longer. Tea leaves, coffee grounds and soup bones were used over and over until there was no flavour left. People bartered services for goods. Many Canadians left the cities to return to the land. When there was nothing left at home on the land, they set off across the country, looking for work.

the next town. A knock on the farmhouse door sometimes got them a meal, but rarely any work. Often, these transients worked for their food. Lines of unemployed gathered at factory gates only to find "No Help Wanted" signs and no work.

In summer, people slept beside open fires in hobo jungles on the edge of town. In winter, they might be allowed to sleep on a jailhouse floor, or in barns or church basements. For many Canadians, this way of life went on for 10 years. These were the Dirty Thirties.

Top: *Sleeping on the street became a way of life for many in the thirties.*
Bottom: *Riding the rails was one way to find work.*

Riding the Rails

With money scarce, some people rode in empty freight cars or rode on top of them. Others hitchhiked along the highways.

Perhaps there would be work on the next farm or in

AVERAGE ANNUAL INCOME PER PERSON (in dollars)		
	1928	**1933**
Saskatchewan	480	140
Alberta	550	210
Manitoba	470	240
British Columbia	590	310
P.E.I.	280	150
Ontario	550	310
Quebec	390	220
New Brunswick	290	180
Nova Scotia	320	210
CANADA	**470**	**250**

Source: John Herd Thompson and Allen Seager. *Canada, 1922–1939: Decades of Discord* (Toronto: McClelland & Stewart, 1985), page 351.

FOCUS

1. Explain what happened to cause the stock market crash of October 1929.
2. Compare the upward economic spiral of the 1920s with the downward spiral of the 1930s.
3. How did people survive during the Dirty Thirties?
4. How do poor people cope with their situation today?

The Drought and the Dustbowl

The worst place to be during the Depression was on the Prairies. In 1929, wheat sold for $1.60 a bushel. By 1932, farmers could hardly get rid of their crop at $ .38. World economic conditions improved slightly in 1933. Some factories in central Canada hired more workers. Mines started to reopen. For farmers in Manitoba and Saskatchewan, however, the real trouble was just beginning. The world's supply of grain was much higher than the demand, and wheat prices remained low. Workers on the Prairies had no jobs, and many farmers abandoned their homes and their land. The weather brought more trouble.

Although parts of the Prairies had been experiencing droughts as early as 1927, 1931 was a particularly dry summer. Drought returned in 1933. It would be another five long years before Prairie farmers would see real rain again.

Crops grow in soil or topsoil on the land's surface. Topsoil contains the moisture and nutrients plants need to develop.

Subsoil contains no real nourishment. The 1930s drought caused topsoil in the prairies to dry up and turn to dust. Strong winds whipped the dust into black

It is hard to imagine that this is Canada. Years of drought turned fertile soil into dust.

blizzards, piling it high against fences and barns. Farmers stood by, watching helplessly as the land that fed them blew away. They watched as their once fertile farms turned to rocks and clay, and the few remaining wheat plants to survive the wind shriveled and died in the parched subsoil. Canadian wheat production decreased from 440 million bushels in 1927 to a low of 219 million bushels in 1936.

Then the grasshoppers came. They hatched by the millions in the prairie desert.

Grasshoppers thrive under drought conditions. Farmers would look up to see dark

Dust storms darkened prairie skies during the drought and depression of the 1930s.

In Their Own Words

SASKATCHEWAN
Saskatchewan the land of snow,
Where winds are always on the blow,
Where people sit with frozen toes,
And why we stay here no one knows.

Our pigs are dyin' on their feet
Because they have no feed to eat,
Our horses, though of bronco race,
Starvation stares them in the face.

The milk from cows has ceased to flow,
We've had to ship 'em East, you know,
Our Hens are old and lay no eggs,
Our turkeys eat grasshopper legs.

But still we love Saskatchewan,
We're proud to say we're native ones,
So count your blessings drop by drop,
Next year we'll have a bumper crop.
                                            Bill Smith

clouds of these insects blotting out the sun. Little was left alive after the grasshoppers passed. One farmer reported that they had even stripped the bristles from his broom—only the metal band and a chewed handle remained. During the 1930s, grasshopper damage to Saskatchewan wheat crops rose as high as 40 percent and up to 80 percent to other cereal crops.

Saskatchewan produced 8 750 000 tonnes of wheat or 1.6 tonnes per hectare in 1928. In 1937, the worst year of the thirties, production was only 920 000 tonnes or .2 tonnes per hectare. It was no wonder that the average Saskatchewan farmer was in debt $9771 in 1936.

Hit by the double blows of the Depression and the Dustbowl, families went barefoot, dressed in flour bags and burned wheat instead of wood because it was cheaper. They ate gopher stew. Farmers did without telephones, newspapers, and cars. They fell behind on their mortgage payments and were forced off their land when the banks foreclosed. Some farmers moved to parkland areas north of Prince Albert where rain fell. Others gave up and headed for the cities of Ontario or west to British Columbia. Over one-quarter of wheat farms on the Prairies were abandoned during the thirties.

Most families just hung on, hoping that the rains would come next year. Even if the crop was good, the price they were paid for it did not cover the growing costs. The rains came again in 1938. So did the grasshoppers and hailstorms.

It was not until 1939 that farmers on the Canadian Prairies began to recover. It took the Second World War to bring farming back to a profitable level.

In Their Own Words

"Every year of the Depression was worse than the one before it. We were all short of money…. One day, a neighbour came into [the] store for his mail. 'Oh good,' he said, 'this must be the cheque from the cattle I shipped to market last week. I sure need it. Me and my family are just plumb out of money.'

'Bet that cheque will hardly be worth cashing,' said one of the farmers, 'the way the price of cattle has been falling.'

'Yeah. You might get a couple of dollars per steer, or something ridiculous like that,' said another.

'Anything is better than nothing,' said the man, opening the envelope. His smile vanished, to be replaced by a look of horror. 'I don't believe it. This can't be true.'

'What's wrong?' We all rushed over to him. 'A bill. They say I owe them money.'
'For what?'
'For freight.' He looked ill. 'They say it cost more for the railway freight charges to ship my cattle than what they sold for at the market! Where am I going to get the money to pay this bill?'

In the weeks to come many more farmers had the same horrible experience, having to pay a bill when they sold cattle. Soon no farmer dared send livestock away to sell. What family could take that chance?"

Source: Irene Morck, *Five Pennies* (Calgary: Fifth House, 1999)

Food for Thought In our nutrition-conscious age, we often forget that it was not always easy to find healthy food. In the early 1900s, people ate what was available. In the summer they ate fresh garden vegetables. In the winter they ate vegetables, such as rutabaga, carrots, and potatoes, that could be easily stored. Childhood diseases were common. Thousands of Canadian children died before reaching their fourth birthdays. Two Canadian discoveries helped change all this.

Fish was not a popular food for most Canadians, because there was

Hungry prairie farmers line up for food.

no way to transport it without losing freshness. Dr. Archibald Huntsman worked at the Biological Board in Halifax in 1926. He proved that if fish was frozen at the height of its freshness, it would keep both its flavour and nutritional value. After three years in the lab, Huntsman finally had a product that people would buy. His frozen fish packages were called "Ice Fillets." They went on sale in Hamilton, Ontario, in January 1929. Today,

millions of Canadians enjoy the benefits of eating fish without having to live near an ocean.

In the early 1900s, Canada's infant death rate was a serious problem. Doctors were seeing many childhood sicknesses that they believed were 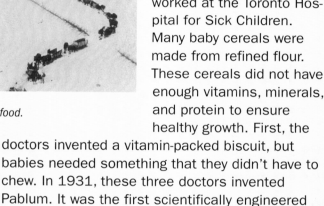 caused by poor nutrition. Dr. Frederick Tisdall, Dr. Alan Brown, and Dr. T. G. H. Blake were pediatricians, or children's doctors. They worked at the Toronto Hospital for Sick Children. Many baby cereals were made from refined flour. These cereals did not have enough vitamins, minerals, and protein to ensure healthy growth. First, the doctors invented a vitamin-packed biscuit, but babies needed something that they didn't have to chew. In 1931, these three doctors invented Pablum. It was the first scientifically engineered baby food. Instead of using refined flour, Pablum is made up of wheat meal, oatmeal, cornmeal, wheat germ, bone meal, brewer's yeast and alfalfa. It became an instant hit around the world. Now, all children could be given a healthy meal.

FOCUS

1. **Give three reasons why the Prairies were the worst place to be during the Depression.**
2. **How did families survive during this great economic slump?**
3. **What Canadian inventions improved health for Canadians?**
4. **How would you survive an economic depression? Explain.**

The On-to-Ottawa Trek

The Depression was probably hardest on young, single men. When employers were forced to cut staff, they let the young and single go first, assuming that older, married employees were more dependent on the work. Young women were often unemployed, but it was considered natural that their families would support them.

These men are at a relief camp in Ontario. What were the problems with relief camps?

Canada's young men set off to look for work in other cities across the country. Usually, there were no jobs anywhere. City relief officers worried about these drifters. Relief monies and goods were already being used up in support of regular city residents. There was nothing left for the newcomers. The young men were asked to move on. There was no place to go. The drifters were desperate for food, for shelter, and for work.

Authorities had many fears. What if the men turned violent? What if they organized together with the help of communist agitators? Canada could find itself in the middle of a revolution, just as Russia had in 1917. Canadian city officials demanded action from Ottawa.

Relief Camps

The federal government decided to stop a possible revolution before it started. It set up Unemployment Relief Camps in remote areas of the country. It wanted to move the growing crowds of drifters off the roads, out of the cities, out of trouble, and to places where they could easily be controlled. Canada's relief camps were run by the Department of National Defence.

Camp inmates worked 8 hours a day, 6 days a week. They built roads, dug ditches, and planted trees. In return, each worker received clothes, a bed, food, and 20 cents a day. Most men were unhappy. They felt that they were living in a mixture of army and prison camps. They were cut off from the world, without a future. They were bored—there was nothing to do after work. One bunkhouse measured 24 m by 7.3 m, and had no windows. The 88 men who lived there slept 2 to a bunk.

Reaction

In April 1935, 1500 men from British Columbia's relief camps went on strike.

They made their way to Vancouver and took over the city library and the Hudson's Bay Company store. On May Day, 20 000 striking men and their supporters paraded through the city.

Men boarded trains during the On-to-Ottawa Trek. Why might the Trek make government leaders nervous?

Vancouver could not help them. It had little relief money. Still, the strikers remained in the city for two months. When organizer Arthur "Slim" Evans of the Worker's Unity League (WUL) suggested that the men travel to Ottawa to carry their message directly to Prime Minister Bennett, the response was enthusiastic. The On-to-Ottawa Trek was born.

The Trekkers had no money. They would have to ride the rails to Ottawa. On June 3, 1000 strikers climbed on top of the boxcars of an eastbound CPR freight train. First stop was Kamloops, after a long overnight ride through the mountains. Next came Golden, then Calgary after the terrifying trip through the long Connaught tunnel. Most Trekkers thought they would die from the black engine smoke. Then it was on to Medicine Hat, Swift Current, and Moose Jaw. The Trekkers were met by crowds bearing food and good wishes at every stop. There were Tag Sales to raise money. Other unemployed people joined the Trek. Even the train crews co-operated.

Bennett's government was terrified. It had set up the relief camps to avoid trouble. It had forbidden camp workers to form committees, and still a mass movement had begun. Crowds of workers waited in Winnipeg, Thunder Bay, and Toronto to join the strikers. The On-to-Ottawa Trek had to be stopped. When 2000 Trekkers arrived in Regina, Bennett ordered the railroads to refuse further transport. The Trekkers were rounded up and taken to the Regina Exhibition grounds. Eight leaders, including Evans, were allowed to continue to Ottawa for a meeting with the prime minister on June 22.

ON-TO-OTTAWA TREKKERS ARRESTED ON JULY 1st, 1935

FOR YOUTH AND DEMOCRACY

SECTION 98

The Trek came to a violent end in Regina. What additional information do these photos supply?

The meeting was a failure. Both sides were angry. Bennett refused to listen to the Trekkers' demands. He believed the strikers were trying to start a revolution. Bennett called Evans a criminal, and Evans called Bennett a liar. The delegates returned to Regina determined that the Trek would continue. Bennett was equally determined it would not.

The Regina Riots

On July 1, Dominion Day, Trekkers and their supporters held a meeting in Regina's Market Square. They needed to raise money to continue. The government was worried that the crowd would get out of control and planned to arrest the strike leaders. It stationed troops in large furniture vans at each of the four corners of the square. At the sound of a whistle, the van doors opened, and out poured RCMP and city police waving batons.

"We took it for a few minutes, and then we let go against them," one Trekker recalled. The riot lasted until late evening. One person was killed, several people injured and 130 were arrested. The On-to-Ottawa Trek was over. The Trekkers disbanded. Many of them returned to Vancouver by train at government expense. The government would shut down the relief camps within a year, but the problems of the unemployed remained.

Depression Across Canada

If one worker in five was out of a job, four people were still working. The hardship was great, but the country survived. Everybody suffered to some degree, but those who produced goods for export had particular problems.

The factories of southern Ontario and Quebec produced goods that were sold mainly in Canada. These products were protected by high tariffs. This kept foreign-made goods out of the country, but made these goods more expensive. Some factories remained in production, but produced much less than before.

Farmers in Central Canada and the Maritimes had mixed farms. They planted wheat, corn, and other vegetables, and they raised cattle and poultry. They traded or bartered their produce when they could not sell it. Local storekeepers knew their customers had no cash. A few dozen eggs and a barrel of apples could be traded for a pair of shoes. Maritimers were used to hardship. They had missed out on the boom of the 1920s, and although depression conditions were worse, they knew how to survive.

TOTAL EXPENDITURE ON RELIEF 1930–1937*
* in millions of dollars

Year	All Governments	Federal Governments
1930	18	4
1931	97	38
1932	95	37
1933	98	36
1934	159	61
1935	173	79
1936	159	81
1937	165	89

What year saw the greatest increase in government spending on relief?

British Columbia was almost entirely dependent upon exports. Lumbering, mining, and salmon fishing were the major industries. There were no markets and no jobs.

Prairie farmers were the hardest hit. First, they could not sell their wheat. Second, the Dustbowl meant they could not even grow it.

FOCUS

1. What caused the government to set up relief camps?
2. What caused the On-to-Ottawa Trek?
3. Describe the Regina Riots.
4. How did people cope with the Depression?

Bennett and King

Except for a few months, William Lyon Mackenzie King was prime minister from 1921 until 1930. As a teenager, King had written in his diary, "Surely I have some great work to accomplish before I die." He believed he was marked for greatness.

R. B. Bennett was prime minister from 1930 to 1935. Although he tried, Bennett failed to solve the Depression in Canada.

But during the hard economic times of 1929 and 1930, Canadians lost faith in his leadership. They became worried and wanted solutions to the problems of the Depression. Canadians wanted to get back to work. Prime Minister King and his Liberals had no answers. "Prosperity is just around the corner," they said. The Liberals thought it best to let the Depression run its course. When the provinces (most of which had Conservative governments) asked for unemployment relief, King refused. He would not give "a five-cent piece" to any Conservative. King said each province needed to provide for itself. Voters did not like this answer. The Liberals lost the 1930 election to Richard Bedford (R. B.) Bennett and the Conservatives.

Bennett was from New Brunswick. His first job was as a teacher. He saved his money and used it to pay for university law courses. He worked hard and invested his money in real estate. He also inherited a fortune. Bennett became leader of the Conservative Party in 1927 and three years later became the prime minister. Bennett promised dynamic action to solve the nation's problems.

Bennett moved to protect Canadian factory jobs. He did this by placing high tariffs on imported goods. Canadians would then buy more products made in Canada. Next, he introduced the Unemployment Relief Act. This gave $20 million in relief aid to the provinces during its first year. He also worked to develop a trading group with countries that were part of the British Commonwealth. Most Canadians, however, felt little effect from these policies. They were still out of work. The lines outside the soup kitchens grew longer.

In 1933 the American President, Franklin Delano Roosevelt, announced his New Deal to the people of the United States. Roosevelt had decided that the Depression would not cure itself. He brought the government into the economy by spending money and creating jobs. Slowly, things began to improve in the United States.

R. B. Bennett introduced his Canadian version of the New Deal in 1935, just before the federal election. Bennett proposed an 8-hour workday, a minimum wage, unemployment insurance, and price controls.

"King or Chaos"

Mackenzie King scorned Bennett's plans. The Liberals campaigned on the slogan "King or Chaos." Canadian voters wanted to know why the Conservatives took five long years to do something while Canadians starved?

Mackenzie King was a clever politician who returned to power in 1935.

Letters to Prime Minister Bennett

R. B. Bennett was a rich man, but he could not solve the problems caused by the Depression from his private fortune. He received many letters from desperate Canadians, and often responded with gifts of clothing or money. Which of these letters is the most moving in your opinion? Why?

Chichester, Quebec
March 13, 1935
Dear Mr. Bennett:

I am a little boy 11 years old I live in a very back wood place and I am very poor there is a bunch of us I am going to school My little Sister and I we have three miles to go and break our own path but we don't mind that if we were only able to buy our books, the Quebec books are very expensive so I just thought I would write you maybe you would give us enough to buy our books if you don't I guess we will have to stop and try and earn a little money to help out our father please excuse paper and pencil as I have no better. Hoping to hear from you real soon I am

> Yours Loving Friend
> Albert Drummond
> Please answer soon soon soon

Murray Harbour, P.E.I.
March 24, 1935
Dear Sir:

I am writing you to see if their is any help I could get. As I have a baby thirteen days old that only weighs One Pound and I have to keep it in Cotton Wool & Olive Oil, and I haven't the money to buy it, the people bought it so far and fed me when I was in Bed. if their is any help I could get I would like to get it as soon as possible. their is five of a family. Counting the baby. their will be two votes for you next Election. Hoping too hear from you soon

> Yours Truly
> Mrs. Jack O'Hannon

Calgary
June 18, 1935
Dear Mr. Bennett,

Do please raise the Old Age Pension to at least thirty dollar per month. So many of your very old friends, myself included, have really not enough to exist on.

> Very best wishes for your good health,
> Sincerely, Alma Ward

Sudbury
May 20, 1931
Mr. Bennette

Since you have been elected, work has been impossible to get. We have decided that in a month from this date, if thing's are the same, We'll skin you alive, the first chance we get

> Starving Unemployed

Regina, Sask.
May 24, 1935
Dear Sir:

You will. no doubt be surpriced to recived this requaist.

I thought that you would have second hand clothing that would not be suitable for you to wear. as I am strapped for clothes fit to wear to Church I desided to write to you.

My best suit is over 8 years old and pretty well frayed.

Judging you by your picture I beleve you are about the same size as myself.

I might say my people and I have allways been stunch Conservatives I wouldn't ask a Liberal part if I had to go naked.

I was 69 years of age May 22/35.

I voted as a farmer's son when I was 18 years old for Sir John A McDonald's Government and Im still on the list

> I am yours respectfuly
> J. A. Graydon

Bennett's New Deal sounded like an election ploy to get votes.

King and the Liberals swept to victory in 1935. They didn't offer many new ideas, but Canadians were tired of Bennett. Everyone now believed that government action was needed to help people out of the Depression. The situation was also confused by disagreements between federal and provincial politicians. The federal government could raise money through taxes, but social action, such as unemployment relief, had to be paid for by the provinces. It seemed to be an impossible situation.

In 1937, King set up a Royal Commission on Dominion–Provincial Relations. This Rowell–Sirois Commission supported important changes in the tax system. These changes helped federal–provincial co-operation. The Commission suggested giving more federal money (equalization payments) to the less wealthy provinces than to the wealthier provinces. It argued that the federal government should be responsible for employment insurance.

The Rowell–Sirois Commission's report was not released until 1940. By that time, the Depression was over. The Second World War had begun. Neither the policies of Bennett nor those of King ended the Great Depression—it was ended by the Second World War.

In Their Own Words

"Though Depression and prairie drought had generated massive unemployment and widespread penury, there was no federal welfare department. Old age pensions of $20 a month were paid by the provincial government to paupers over 70, and to those pensions the federal treasury made a 75-percent contribution. The total federal budget was a half a billion dollars a year, including grants to provincial governments to assist in the relief of the unemployed and of destitute farmers in the Prairies."

Source: J. W. Pickersgill, *Seeing Canada Whole: A Memoir* (Toronto: Fitzhenry & Whiteside, 1994)

On 10 September 1939, Canada declared war on Nazi Germany. Canada's unemployed went to work in the army and in the arms factories. The country was ready for another war-related economic boom.

FOCUS

1. Why was King defeated in 1930?
2. What was Bennett's New Deal?
3. Why did voters elect King in 1935?
4. Would governments today do more to help their citizens? Explain.
5. What event ended the Great Depression?

The New Politics

Canada's Liberal and Conservative parties first believed that the government should not direct the economy. They felt that economic problems would solve themselves. Other people disagreed. They wanted the government to help. These people formed new political

The first Co-operative Commonwealth Federation (CCF) convention was in Regina in 1933. The CCF later became the New Democratic Party (NDP).

parties and movements to try to get their ideas heard.

With the Depression came new political ideas. In Alberta, William Aberhart blamed the Depression on Toronto and Montreal bankers. Why, he asked, were stores filled with goods that no one could afford to buy? The Co-operative Commonwealth Federation (CCF) believed that capitalism was to blame. Fascist parties blamed the Depression on minority groups, like the Jews, and used the fear of communism to attract supporters.

(See Chapter 3.) Communists wanted to overthrow the government and replace it with a government by the workers.

The First World War had a major effect on Canadian politics. Prime Minister Robert Borden's decision to conscript soldiers to fight in the war angered most French Canadians. It would be another 41 years before Quebec would vote for a federal Conservative party. The war also angered many Western Canadian farmers. They believed that business people and politicians in Ontario and Quebec controlled the economy for their own benefit. When the economy did poorly after the war, Western Canadians formed their own political party in 1919—the Progressive Party. It was the first successful third party in Canadian history. It was based in Alberta, Manitoba, Saskatchewan, and the rural areas of Ontario. The Progressive Party took 65 seats in the 1921 election—more than the Conservative Party. Five years later, however, better economic times brought an end to the Progressive Party. The fragments of the party would later form the nucleus of the CCF.

Co-operative Commonwealth Federation

The Co-operative Commonwealth Federation (CCF) was founded in 1932 in Calgary. Progressives, Labour Party members, middle-class intellectuals, labour leaders and supporters of the British socialist movement joined together to form it. The CCF platform, known as the Regina Manifesto, was drawn up in 1933. The CCF believed in socialism. It wanted the government to control business and industry for the good of everyone.

The CCF believed that private enterprise and greed had thrown the country into the Great Depression.

THE REGINA MANIFESTO – Program of the CCF

1. **The people (the government) should own all the banks and financial institutions.**

2. **The people should own key industries such as railways, mines, lumbering, telephone systems, and hydroelectric companies.**

3. **There should be a large-scale program of public works (housing, roads, public buildings) to provide jobs for the unemployed.**

4. **Laws should guarantee minimum living standards for all through programs such as unemployment insurance, family allowances, old age pensions.**

5. **Farmers' land should be protected from mortgage foreclosures.**

6. **There should be a guaranteed minimum wage.**

Which of the above do you support? Why? Which do you reject? Why?

Many Canadians confused the socialist CCF with the Communist Party. There were big differences. Communists believed that change could come about only through violent revolution. The CCF believed that change should be made democratically. Communists did not feel individual rights and freedoms were as important as the welfare of the group. The welfare of the state, which represented all, mattered most. The CCF upheld the individual's civil rights. People must be allowed to vote freely. The CCF elected J. S. Woodsworth as its first leader. Woodsworth had worked hard to help immigrants, the elderly, and trade unions. He was highly respected by all political parties.

William "Bible Bill" Aberhart became premier in Alberta in 1935. His Social Credit Party remained in power until 1971.

Poverty in the Midst of Plenty

Alberta stores were stocked with clothes, radios, and tractors, but people had no money to buy them. Farmers had wheat but when and if they sold it, the price they got was often less than the cost of sowing and harvesting it. It was a vicious circle.

William Aberhart was famous in Alberta. To some he was known as Bible Bill, the radio preacher of the Calgary Prophetic Bible Institute. In 1932, this high school principal began to talk about a new political idea. He called it Social Credit. He believed the main problem with the Depression was that people did not have enough money to buy the goods being produced. If people had more money, they could buy more goods. If more goods were bought, more would need to be made. More people would have jobs, and they would earn more money. The Depression would be over and the prosperity cycle would return. Aberhart's Social Credit Party proposed to give each Alberta citizen a monthly cheque of $25. People could use the money to buy what they needed.

This idea made great sense to the farmers and workers of Alberta. They trusted Bible Bill Aberhart. In the 1935 provincial election, Social Credit won 56 of 63 seats and Aberhart became premier.

The federal government ruled that issuing money was a federal power. Aberhart's government had no right to print money. Many Albertans felt that this showed how the Liberal and Conservative parties favoured Ontario and Quebec. It seemed that these parties were more interested in talking about laws than helping people in need.

New parties and new politics sprang up all over Canada during the Depression. In British Columbia, Liberal Premier Thomas Pattullo tried to assist the economy with a "work and wages" program. Maurice Duplessis swept to power in Quebec in 1936 as the leader of the new Union Nationale party. Mitch Hepburn, Liberal premier of Ontario, adopted ideas from the Progressives, including auctioning government limousines.

In Their Own Words

"You can strip down the appeal of Social Credit to the $25 a month. All of us farmers were in desperate straits. Here was William Aberhart promising $25 a month, and he was a Minister of the Gospel. I asked him about that $25 after one of his meetings, and he told me I must have faith."

A farmer from central Alberta

FOCUS

1. Summarize the main ideas of the Regina Manifesto.
2. Would you have voted for the CCF or the Social Credit Party during the Depression? Explain.
3. What did Aberhart believe was the main cause of the Depression?
4. How did his Social Credit Party propose to end it?

On the Sunny Side of the Street

Life in the thirties was not always dull and drab. People had fun in many ways. If they could not afford to travel, they could still get together with friends and neighbours. They could go to the beach or have a picnic. Communities co-operated to help the needy. Parties held at a poor person's home deliberately broke up early, leaving enough left-over food for the rest of the week. Neighbours got together to help one another with planting, harvesting, or barn building.

On Saturdays, there were often concerts in the bandstand at the local park. Amos and Andy, Eddie Cantor, Bing Crosby, Fanny Brice, and Jack Benny were popular entertainers of the thirties. Once you owned a radio, your pleasure was free. Soap operas could be heard every day. People could hardly wait to hear of the loves, fears, disasters and joys of Helen Trent, Our Gal Sunday, or Ma Perkins. Monday evenings, the Lux Radio Theatre presented radio versions of the latest movies. Other nights, people pushed aside the furniture and danced to the music of the big

Radio announcer at KUKU. What might be considered unusual about his clothing?

bands. Guy Lombardo and His Royal Canadians was one of the best known. Every year, millions of North Americans welcomed in the New Year by listening to the Royal Canadians play "Auld Lang Syne."

The Canadian Radio Broadcasting Corporation was established by the government in 1932. By 1936, when the CRBC became the CBC, it had 8 stations and 14 private affiliates. The first French station was added in 1937. Canadians from coast to coast could now listen to entertainment provided by Canadian talent. CBC listeners laughed at the antics of Vancouver's Stag Party, or hummed along with the music of Toronto's Happy Gang. On Sunday mornings, boys and girls listened to the stories of "Just Mary" from the Maritimes.

At Christmas, families gathered around the radio for the King's Message. Farm news first appeared on the French station, and the programs were so popular that English farm broadcasts began shortly after. CBC's first "on-the-spot" news report was of the Moose

River Mine disaster in Nova Scotia. J. Frank Willis reported the news. When Ontario Premier Mitch Hepburn confronted striking auto workers at Oshawa's General Motors plant, Canadians heard about it on the CBC. Canadians learned about the British royalty on the radio. Saturday night was Hockey Night in Canada. Everyone sat around the radio waiting for Foster Hewitt's welcome, "Hello Canada and hockey fans in the United States and Newfoundland," and his famous cry, "He shoots. He scores!"

Many towns had their own movie house. On Saturday afternoon children watched cartoons, the latest episode of *The Shadow* or *Tom Mix*, a full-length movie for 10 cents. They could buy a chocolate bar or jellybeans for just a nickel more. Sometimes they even got a free comic book. A generation grew up on "cowboy and Indian" movies. These movies painted an unreal picture of the Aboriginal struggle for survival. Today, Aboriginal peoples are still fighting the warped attitudes these movies created.

Canadians wanted to escape real life during the Depression. The movies were a perfect way to do this. Comedians Charlie Chaplin, the Marx Brothers, Laurel and Hardy, and W. C. Fields were all popular. Hollywood made many movies about Canada. Although these movies painted a strange picture of the country, this did not seem to bother anyone. Jeanette MacDonald's *Rose Marie* and Shirley Temple's *Susannah of the Mounties* were two popular movies said to be set in Canada. Hollywood producers seemed to think that if they added snow, birch bark canoes, handsome lumberjacks and "wicked" French Canadians to mountains and Mounties, the Canadian picture was complete.

HIT SONGS OF THE 1930s

The music of the thirties reflected the spirit of the time. Some tunes reflected the struggles people faced. Others were more upbeat and hopeful. **Which of the following song titles best reflects the Great Depression?**

- I can't give you anything but love
- On the sunny side of the street
- Brother, can you spare a dime?
- I'm getting sentimental over you
- Smoke gets in your eyes
- Blue moon
- I've got you under my skin
- What a difference a day makes
- The lady is a tramp
- Pennies from heaven
- They can't take that away from me
- Moonlight serenade
- My prayer
- I'll never smile again
- Happy days are here again

The car was very popular by the 1930s. Automobiles now had curved fenders with lots of chrome. Ford made a powerful V-8 engine in 1932. Cadillac introduced its second V-16 engine in 1938.

Chrysler produced a curved one-piece windshield. Automatic transmissions and power brakes were offered for the first time. Canada's roads had also improved. Ontario's Queen Elizabeth Way opened in 1939. It was the first four-lane highway in North America. Canadians could drive between Toronto and Hamilton with ease.

Sport

Professional sports became popular during the 1930s. The Montreal Royals and the Toronto Maple Leafs baseball teams played against American teams. Football was beginning to attract attention. Each year the best Western team travelled east to play the Eastern champions for the Grey Cup. Each year, the west lost the game. Finally in 1935, Fritz Hanson, and several other American imports, led the Winnipeg 'Pegs (later Blue Bombers) to victory. Serious rivalry for the Grey Cup had begun (and still continues).

Then, as now, hockey was the Canadian sport. The excitement was carried across the country by the radio. Children who had never seen the Montreal Canadiens or the Toronto Maple Leafs play knew everything about the latest game. If they missed it on radio, they read the story on the sports page of the newspaper the next day.

Hard times resulted in the NHL (National Hockey League) becoming more American. Some teams folded; other clubs moved to larger cities. In 1930, the Canadian Division included the Montreal Maroons, the Montreal Canadiens, the Toronto Maple Leafs, the Ottawa Senators, and the New York Americans. The Boston Bruins, the Chicago Black Hawks, the New York Rangers, the Detroit Falcons, and the Pittsburgh Pirates composed the American Division. After the Montreal Maroons collapsed in 1938, the NHL was reduced to seven teams playing in only one division.

MAPLE LEAF GARDENS

Maple Leaf Gardens, home of the Toronto Maple Leafs, opened on 12 November 1931. The Toronto Maple Leafs played the Chicago Black Hawks in front of 15 000 spectators. Toronto lost the game 2-1, but would go on to win the Stanley Cup that year. Maple Leafs' owner Conn Smythe took a risk trying to finance such a huge building in the middle of the Depression. Construction workers helped out by taking 20 percent of their salaries in Maple Leaf stock. The Gardens was finished in five months. It would be home to the Maple Leafs until 13 February 1999.

Table-top Hockey During the Depression Don Munro was one of many Canadians out of work. Munro did not have money to spend on toys, so he decided to create a game for his children. Using regular household items and recycling old materials, Munro created table-top hockey. The first version had a four-man team of wooden players. One lever on the board controlled the goalie and another moved the other three men. The steel ball was kept moving by a slight bump in the centre of the board. Munro's children were so happy with their new toy that Munro patented his invention.

He also paid a visit to the toy buyer at the local Eaton's store. The buyer was worried about buying something new during a period of such widespread economic uncertainty. Yet, he was intrigued with the game so he bought one to see how things would go. He sold that game before Munro had returned home. Within hours he was on the phone ordering another six games. Before long, the Munro family business became Munro Games Ltd., and table-top hockey became a major part of growing up in Canada.

Is table-top hockey still popular among Canadians?

The Dionne Quintuplets

The most publicized event of the thirties was the birth of the Dionne Quintuplets in 1934. The five sisters were born to a poor Franco-Ontarian family near North Bay, Ontario. They were the first quints in the world to survive. This miracle-baby story captured the hearts and minds of many people. The Ontario government took the girls away from their family and put them in a special hospital. Tourists paid to watch the girls (behind glass) during three daily visiting times. The quints made millions of dollars for the government during the nine years they were on display. They were used in movies and in baby food advertisements. They had no family life. Finally, in 1998, after a long legal battle, the Ontario government agreed to pay the three surviving sisters $4 million for the suffering it had caused all of the quints for so many years.

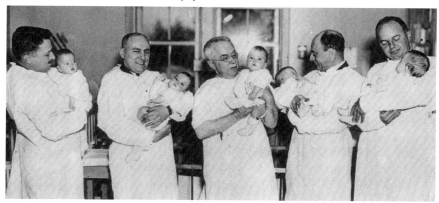

The Dionne Quintuplets, born in 1934, were Canada's sweethearts during the dark days of the Depression. For more, visit www.quintland.com.

FOCUS

1. What types of radio programs did Canadians enjoy?
2. Describe an afternoon at the movies during the 1930s.
3. How did sports fans find out about the achievements of their favourite teams?

Towards a
Canadian Identity

Canada became a nation in 1867. Britain, however, still made foreign policy decisions for Canada and the rest of the British Empire. For example, in the First World War, Canada did not declare war on Germany. Britain declared it, and Canada was automatically at war when Britain went to war. Several important events after 1914 helped Canada achieve full independence from Britain.

The First World War made Canada a more mature nation. Canada and the other Dominions of the British Empire became more important countries and took part in making wartime decisions. At the end of the war, they all sat as separate nations during the Paris Peace Conference. Later, Canada was an active, independent member of the new League of Nations.

In 1923, Canadians and Americans agreed on a treaty to protect halibut on the Northwest coast. Canada announced that its own minister of fisheries would sign the treaty. This was the first time that Canada, with its new independence, signed a treaty on its own.

The British Commonwealth of Nations

The new relationship of countries within the British Empire had to be worked out. At the Imperial Conference of 1926, Canadian Prime Minister Mackenzie King was responsible for the Balfour Report. This report stated that the Dominions were free and equal. It still agreed that they were united by the Crown as members of the British Commonwealth of Nations. In 1931, the British Parliament passed the **Statute of Westminster**. This Act declared that the British Parliament had no power over the laws of the Dominions. Canada began to open its own embassies in cities such as Paris, Tokyo, and Washington.

Canada's Constitution, the British North America Act, was an act of the British Parliament. When the Statute of Westminster was passed, Canadians had not yet worked out how they would make changes to the constitution. Britain kept the power to amend the BNA Act until 1981. When Canada decided to go to war in 1939, it did so on its own, as an independent nation, not as a colony of Great Britain.

A Changing Identity

The Canadian government established the National Research Council (NRC) in 1917. Its job was to "create, acquire and promote the application of scientific and engineering knowledge to meet Canadian needs for economic, regional and social development." The NRC's national laboratory in Ottawa was founded in the late 1920s. It later played a crucial role in war research. NRC scientists researched in many areas. These included weapons development, fuels, packaging, aeronautics, mechanical engineering, medicine, food, energy, and the biological sciences. By 1939, 300 men and women worked at the laboratory.

As British traditions faded and American influences on Canadian life became stronger, the federal government helped people have a sense of their own country. Many people believed that it was important for Canadians to have this. The CBC helped develop a sense of Canadian identity. It provided news, entertainment, and education services. It also informed Canadians about local and international events from a Canadian point of view.

In 1939, the King government created the National Film Board (NFB). The Board helped to make films for Canadians. These films also informed the rest of the world about Canada. British documentary filmmaker John Grierson was Canada's first Government Film Commissioner. By 1945, the NFB employed more than 700 people. It was one of the largest film studios in the world.

First passengers on a Trans-Canada Airlines flight. Passengers tended to dress up for air travel.

Transport by Air

The CPR and CNR helped open the Canadian west in the late 19th and early 20th centuries. They thus helped in unifying Canada. In the 1920s and 1930s, airplanes opened up Canada's north. First World War aces, such as Punch Dickens and Wilfrid May, became bush pilots. They flew under harsh conditions into the Northwest and Yukon Territories. The planes brought food, supplies, mail and medical assistance to Canadians in these remote areas. They also brought prospectors searching for gold and silver. Airline companies were small. They often had only one or two single-engine planes. Passenger service was beginning and no company was able to serve the whole country.

The federal government made the Trans-Canada Airlines a Crown corporation in 1937 (it later became Air Canada). Within two years, the company had 15 ten-passenger aircraft. Former bush pilots became airline pilots. In the early days, flight attendants were also nurses in case a passenger needed medical help.

Canadian Vision

The Group of Seven

Perhaps best known of all Canada's artists, the Group of Seven came together in 1920 as an organization of "modern" painters. The original members included Frank Carmichael, Lawren Harris, A. Y. Jackson, Franz Johnston, Arthur Lismer, J. E. H. MacDonald, and F. H. Varley. They were greatly influenced by Tom Thomson, who painted daring portraits of the land in and around Georgian Bay. His work encouraged the Group of Seven to think about painting landscapes differently. Thomson died in 1917.

"Thomson's Rapids, Magnetawan River," by J. E. H. MacDonald, reflects the painter's love of the land north of Lake Superior. The Rockies was another favourite painting place.

The Group of Seven was best known as landscape painters. Traditional landscape painters of the time painted a realistic likeness of their environment. The Group of Seven's art was an expression of their feelings about nature. Rather than depict what a scene looked like, they wanted to show how it made them feel. They used bold, striking colours and brush strokes to capture the beauty and ruggedness of Canada's land, especially in the Ontario north.

People were critical of their style and paintings at first, but eventually the Group of Seven became very popular. Franz Johnston retired from the Group in 1926 to pursue other interests, and A. J. Casson took his place. The Group disbanded in the early 1930s, but by then, they were famous in Europe, the United States, and at home. Most members became art teachers, influencing the next generation of Canadian artists.

Canadian Vision

Governor General's Literary Awards

In 1937 the Canadian Authors Association initiated the Governor General's Literary Awards. Writers were judged for their works of fiction, nonfiction and drama or poetry. Stephen Leacock won the 1937 nonfiction award for his book *My Discovery of the West*. He was thought to be one of the best comedy authors in the English language. The Canada Council now selects the winners of the Governor General's Awards with the help of two juries—one French speaking, the other English speaking. Each jury has nine members who are experienced writers, academics, and literary critics. Awards have been given to some of Canada's best authors, Margaret Atwood, Dionne Brand, and Rohinton Mistry among them. To review present and recent winners, visit **www.canadacouncil.ca**.

Achievements

Canada was no longer a colony, but an independent nation. It was proud of its citizens and their achievements.

Canadian researchers gave much to the field of medicine. Doctors Frederick Banting and Charles Best discovered insulin. It changed the life of diabetics. In 1934, the Quebec government, in conjunction with the Rockefeller Institute, established the Montreal Neurological Hospital under the direction of Canadian surgeon Wilder Penfield. It would become world famous as an institution devoted to the teaching, research, and

treatment of nervous system diseases such as epilepsy. Medical missionary Wilfred Grenfell worked for years with the deep-sea fishers, permanent settlers, and Inuit of Newfoundland and Labrador. In 1928, he opened a modern hospital at St. Anthony, Newfoundland.

Literary and visual arts in Canada flourished between the world wars. The Group of Seven, painters of Canada's rugged north, were active from 1920–1933. Emily Carr's striking paintings of West coast scenery and Aboriginal life added a new dimension to the Canadian character. Miller Brittain, Carl Schaefer, and Jack Humphrey contributed realistic paintings.

FOCUS

1. How did the Statute of Westminster of 1931 describe Canada's position within the Commonwealth?
2. Name three organizations in Canada established by government.
3. List major Canadian achievements in art, medicine, and literature.

Sharpening Your Skills

History Is Interpretation

THE SKILL
Understanding that "interpretation" is at the heart of all historical writing

THE IMPORTANCE
Not taking everything written in history books as accurate

1) History is **everything** that happened in the past.

2) History is the **remaining record** of what was said and done in the past.

3) History is the **study of the evidence** that remains of what happened in the past.

Note the major difference between the first and second definitions—everything that happened versus what remains of everything that happened. Think of what you did today. When you are long dead, what records will there be of everything you did, heard, or saw today? Historians have only this remaining memory of the past to examine. This means that there may easily be a difference between what really happened and the written record of what happened.

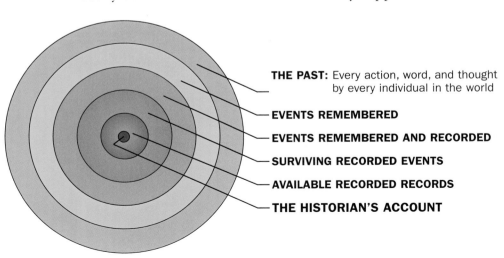

THE PAST: Every action, word, and thought by every individual in the world

EVENTS REMEMBERED

EVENTS REMEMBERED AND RECORDED

SURVIVING RECORDED EVENTS

AVAILABLE RECORDED RECORDS

THE HISTORIAN'S ACCOUNT

If a tree falls in the forest and no one heard it fall, did it make a sound? Relate this cartoon to the three definitions of history.

Historians face several major problems. First, they have too much information. Let's pretend that you become a famous brain surgeon. It is 50 years after your death and Professor Wrong wants to write your biography. If it is to be a complete history of your life, the professor must include everything you said, thought, saw, heard, read, and did throughout your life. Imagine writing down everything you said, saw, and did in just one day—it would fill an entire book. As a result, the final biography of your life is so big it fills an entire classroom.

No one will publish the biography—or read it. Professor Wrong will have to reduce the 500 volumes into one book. The professor must decide what information to include and what to leave out of the biography.

Naturally, not everyone would agree on what to include, what the important influences on your life were. Should the biography include what you learned in this class, your favourite music, your taste in clothing, what pictures you hung on your wall, or who you dated? There is not space for everything. What is significant and what is not?

The final biography is Professor Wrong's interpretation of your life. Other historians would no doubt include different information and arrive at different conclusions.

The other major problem in writing your biography is that there is not enough information. Many of your actions and most of your thoughts, for example, were never recorded. Perhaps you can think of several topics that you have never told anyone. Professor Wrong must fill in the blanks with educated guesses. Why did you decide to become a brain surgeon? Was it because you read about several interesting Canadian doctors in this textbook?

Because there was both too much information and too little, Professor Wrong's biography will differ from the real past. It will be the professor's interpretation of what was important in your life. This task is more like that of the painter than of the photographer. The result is a likeness rather than an exact duplication. Perhaps this is why Napoleon suggested, "History is a trick played by the living upon the dead."

Written history is thus interpretation. What is written down and what is left out of the story is based upon the author's choices.

Application

Take one topic in this chapter. What information have the authors left out about this topic? You can do this assignment by using your imagination, by comparing this text to another book, by consulting other people, or by going on the Internet. Now, try to imagine why the authors of this book did not include the additional information.

Questions and Activities

Match the items in column A with the descriptions in column B.

A	B
1. One Big Union (OBU)	**a)** states the original program of the CCF.
2. Social Credit Party	**b)** granted Canada full independence within the Commonwealth.
3. Regina Manifesto	**c)** fought for women to be legally recognized as persons.
4. Alberta Five	**d)** wanted to give each citizen $25 a month.
5. Statute of Westminster	**e)** wanted better bargaining power by uniting all workers.

Discuss and Debate

1. If a general strike like the one in Winnipeg was organized in your community, what industries and services would be closed down? How would you be affected? Do you think workers should have the right to organize general strikes? Why or why not?

2. Summarize some of the main advances in rights and freedoms made by women between 1919 and 1930. What issues remain today for women in Canada?

3. Discuss the impact of the automobile on
 a) shopping patterns   **b)** city and community planning
 c) jobs and industry   **d)** travel and vacations
 e) convenience and leisure   **f)** social life

4. During the 1930s, the government set up work camps for unemployed young men. Some people suggest that a similar system, but with more freedom, should be established for the unemployed today. There would be a choice of
 a) working in local parks, public buildings, etc.
 b) helping the aged or handicapped
 c) replanting forest land
 d) joining the armed forces
 What do you think?

5. How involved should the government be in running industries and providing services? Here is a list of organizations started by the federal government. What does each one do? Why did the government become involved in these areas? Which are no longer run by the government?
 a) NRC   **b)** CBC
 c) NFB   **d)** TCA (Trans-Canada Airlines)
 List other industries and services run by the federal, provincial or municipal government. Do you think the government should continue to be involved in these areas? Are there other industries or services that you think the government should run? Why or why not?

6. Do you think that Canada is likely to suffer another depression at this time? Explain.

Do Some Research

1. Do any members of your family belong to a trade union? Compile a list of unions that people in your community belong to. Name other unions in Canada today. What are their objectives? How have union aims changed since the Winnipeg General Strike? How have they remained the same?

2. Find out more about one of the following and complete your own Canadian Lives feature:

    a) R. B. Bennett   **b)** William Lyon Mackenzie King

    c) Emily Carr   **d)** Charles Best

    e) The Alberta Five   **f)** one member of the Group of Seven

    g) Ethel Catherwood   **h)** Bobbie Rosenfeld

3. Write a report about an outstanding woman in Canada today in one of the following areas: (a) industry and commerce, (b) sports, (c) politics and law, (d) entertainment, (e) science and technology.

4. After further reading about the causes of the Great Depression, write a paragraph noting which cause you feel is the most important and why.

5. During the interwar years, many Canadians made a major impact or contribution to Canadian and world events. Research the importance of any one of these Canadians:

David Milne   Mazo de la Roche
Jimmy McLarnin   Ralph Connor
L. M. Montgomery   Sinclair Ross
W. O. Mitchell   Frederick Philip Grove
Ada Mackenzie   Morley Callaghan
Guy Lombardo   Mary Pickford
Leslie McFarlane   Morse Robb
Norman Bethune

6. Do some research on automobiles of the 1920s. Describe the basic features and options that were available. How have automobiles changed since the 1920s? What features have disappeared? What new features have been introduced? What "options" of the 1920s are now standard features?

7. Find out more about one of the following: (a) movies of the 1920s, (b) the early days of radio, (c) movies of the 1930s, (d) records and record players. Write a paragraph describing their main features and importance.

8. Find out more about the success of Canadians during the 1928 Olympics. Compare their record to that of Canadian athletes in more recent Olympics. Can you draw any conclusions from this comparison?

9. The Edmonton Grads were one of the most successful sports teams ever. Do further research on the Grads or another Canadian sports team of the 1920s and 1930s. Your report should have some information under the following headings:

    a) Beginnings   **b)** Coaches

    c) Star Players   **d)** Win-and-Loss Records

Be Creative

1. Write a letter from a soldier who has just returned home at the end of the war. Your opening might be: "I'm so pleased to see my family and friends again, but the town sure has changed."

2. With a group of other students, prepare a folder on the role of women from 1914 to 1930. Your folder should include
   a) a poster advertising a women's rights rally
   b) a speech by a supporter of women's rights
   c) a picture of women's fashions and hairstyles during the 1920s with an explanation of how these gave women new freedom
   d) an editorial favouring or opposing the right of women to be senators
   e) a letter to the editor disagreeing with the editorial

3. Design an advertisement for a product or appliance that became available during the 1920s. Let your ad explain how buying the item will make life easier, more convenient, or more entertaining. As a class, compile a brochure called "Advertisements of the Roaring Twenties."

4. Make a mural or picture map of Canada showing industries across the country in the 1920s.

5. Write a letter to Prime Minister Bennett asking for help for you and your family. Write Bennett's reply.

6. Prepare an edition of a newspaper in your community for a specific date in the 1920s or 1930s. Your newspaper should include
   a) reports on local, provincial, national and international events
   b) entertainment and sports news
   c) information on new inventions and scientific discoveries
   d) human interest stories
   e) editorials
   f) letters to the editor
   g) political cartoons
   h) business news on local industries and job opportunities
   i) advertisements for new products
   j) fashion news
   k) Want ads

For some items you will need to do additional research beyond this textbook.

An image of postwar spending and prosperity.

Web Watch

For more information about some of the topics in this chapter, consider a visit to these sites:

The Canadian Encyclopedia: www.thecanadianencyclopedia.com

Canadian Labour Congress: www.clc-ctc.ca/index.php./history (History of Canadian Labour)

CBC Digital Archives: www.cbc.ca/archives—review some of the following files:

"Fair Game: Pioneering Canadian Women in Sports," "Electing Dynasties: Alberta Campaigns 1935–2001," "Group of Seven: Painters in the Wilderness," "Mackenzie King: Public Life, Private Man."

http://www.edmontongrads.com/ (Edmonton Grads)
http://www.ontoottawa.ca/index1.html (On-to-Ottawa Trek)
http://www.nationmaster.com/encyclopedia/R.-B.-Bennett (R. B. Bennett)
http://www.city.north-bay.on.ca/quints/digitize/dqdpe.htm (Dionne Quints)
http://www.geocities.com/CapitolHill/5202/win1919.htm (Winnipeg General Strike)

An image of the Great Depression.

These 1942 stamps are part of a series featuring Canadian contributions to war work. Top: A 25-pound gun being inspected at a munitions factory; Below: A corvette ready to be launched at a smaller shipyard— corvettes were used to transport men and supplies to war fronts.

What do these stamps say about Canada's effort to fight the Second World War?

Chapter Three
The World on Trial

Expectations

Overall Expectations:

By the end of this chapter, you will be able to

- understand how outside forces and events shaped Canada's involvement in the Second World War
- evaluate Canada's participation in the war
- appreciate the impact of the war on Canadians
- describe changes in Canada's international status and its role in the world since 1914

Specific Expectations:

By the end of this chapter, you will be able to

- identify the causes of the Second World War and of Canada's involvement
- explain changes made in Canada's international policy because of the war
- describe how Canada contributed to the war effort and how the war affected life on the home front
- explain how some key technological developments changed the way war was planned and fought
- identify the role played by the Canadian government during the war
- assess key instances in which the Canadian government restricted citizens' rights and freedoms
- describe the events leading up to the Holocaust and aspects of its impact on Canada

Word List

Anti-Semitic	**Black market**
Blitzkrieg	**Concentration camps**
Death camps	**Dictator**
Fascism	**Gestapo**
Ghettos	**Gulag**
Holocaust	**"Juno"**
Kristallnacht	**Nazi**
Order of Canada	**Pogrom**
Ration book	**Wolf packs**

Advance Organizer

1 Life in Europe was not easy after the First World War. The war had destroyed everyday life in many countries.

It was easy for dictators to gain control. They offered simple solutions and promised better times. They silenced those who spoke against them.

2 The most dangerous dictator of all was Adolph Hitler. He blamed Germany's social and economic problems on unfair treatment after the First World War. He began building up the military. Hitler kept Germans living in fear with raids by his secret police force. People who disagreed with him began to disappear.

3 Some nations agreed that Germany had been treated harshly after the First World War. They thought if Hitler took back a little land, he would be satisfied. They did not realize he wanted to create a master race. They did not understand that he wanted all of Europe under German rule.

All German soldiers swore an oath of personal loyalty to Hitler. Under Hitler, the army expanded rapidly.

❶ ❷ ❸ ❹ ❺

Rationing was an important part of the war effort.

❺ Canadians helped the war effort in non-military ways. Canadian factories produced planes, ships, and weapons. Food and gas were rationed so more could go to the troops overseas. Children ploughed up their schoolyards to plant Victory gardens.

❹ Canadians played many roles during the war. In Europe, Canadians fought bravely in the air, on the land, and on the sea. At home, the Royal Canadian Navy organized convoys to send men, food, and weapons to Britain.

Ships waiting for a convoy in Bedford Basin, Nova Scotia.

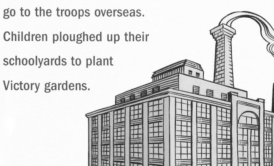

Dictators in a Changing World

Most people in Europe experienced change, insecurity, and frustration through the 1920s. They had expected the Treaty of Versailles to undo the chaos caused by the First World War. Instead, it created as many problems as it solved. The losers of the war felt

EUROPE AFTER THE TREATY

— Borders 1914
— Borders after the 1919 peace treaties
▨ Territory lost by Germany
▨ Territory lost by Austro-Hungary
▨ Territory lost by Bulgaria
▨ Territory lost by U.S.S.R.
▨ Demilitarized zones

FINLAND
NORWAY
SWEDEN
ESTONIA
LATVIA
DENMARK
Baltic Sea
LITHUANIA
North Sea
UNITED KINGDOM
EAST PRUSSIA
NETHERLANDS
GERMANY
POLAND
U.S.S.R.
BELGIUM
Rhineland
LUXEMBOURG
CZECHOSLOVAKIA
FRANCE
SWITZERLAND
AUSTRIA
HUNGARY
BESSARABIA
0 150 300 km
ROMANIA
YUGOSLAVIA
SPAIN
ITALY
Montenegro
BULGARIA
Black Sea
Adriatic Sea
Mediterranean Sea
ALBANIA
Tyrrhenian Sea
GREECE
TURKEY

The First World War changed Europe's borders. The demilitarized zone shown to the left of Germany is known as the Rhineland.

unfairly treated. The winners believed that they had gained nothing. Everyone felt cheated. Who was to blame?

A New Map of Europe

The conference in Versailles decided that every national group should have its own country. As a result, they gave lands that had been part of Germany back to Poland and France (Alsace and Lorraine had been in French territory before 1870). They divided the Turkish and Austrian empires into a number of different countries. They could not, however, draw a neat line and put all Germans or Slavs on one side, and all Poles or Italians on the other. Many minority groups remained within the new borders. They resented being part of these countries. Majority groups feared the smaller nationalities might cause trouble.

Rise of Fascist Dictators

Most countries in Europe had elected national bodies, or assemblies, before the First World War. These assemblies rarely had much power. Princes, kings, emperors, and their advisers made most of the important decisions. After the war, Europeans lost faith in their old leaders. They had led Europe into a tragic war. Under the leadership of American President Woodrow Wilson, diplomats at Versailles tried to set up democratic governments for the "new" countries. Since few people knew how to run a country in a democratic way, voters had difficulty judging the new politicians.

Then came the Depression of the 1930s. It caused social, economic, and political problems in stable democracies like Canada, the United States, and Britain. In an unsettled Europe, the effects were disastrous.

People wanted a way out of the hopelessness, the frustration, and the insecurity. They were ready to follow any leader who promised them better things. They wanted to be told that their country was great. They wanted to believe that their problems were somebody else's fault. They blamed foreigners, communists, democrats, and Jews. **Fascism** appealed to people living in these conditions. Fascist leaders Benito Mussolini, Adolf Hitler, and Francisco Franco rose to power in the midst of hopelessness, fear, poverty, and hatred.

In Turkey, Poland, and Iran, military officers assumed control. Yugoslavia, Romania, and Albania established monarchical dictatorships. Dictatorships also emerged in Bulgaria, Hungary, Greece, Austria, the three Baltic states, Portugal, and Spain.

Fascism in Italy

Benito Mussolini formed the Fascist Party. His goal was to fight communism

Benito Mussolini and Adolf Hitler (centre) formed a powerful alliance. What image do these officers seem to present?

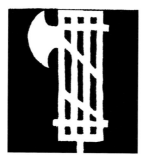

The term fascism came from ancient Rome, where government authority was symbolized by the fasces, a bundle of rods bound together (representing popular unity), with an axe head (symbolizing leadership) sticking out.

and democratic socialism in Italy. Fascists in black shirts gathered to listen to their leader. These "Blackshirts" broke up trade union meetings and communist rallies with clubs and fists. They waged a campaign of terror against their opponents.

There was much poverty and unemployment in Italy after the First World War. Workers formed unions and called for a general strike in 1922. Mussolini said that if the government didn't stop the strike, the Fascists would. Fascists from all over Italy marched on Rome. In a panic, the king asked Mussolini to form a new government. Soon, Mussolini was the **dictator** of Italy. He allowed only fellow fascists to run for office.

The Soviet Union of Lenin and Stalin

By 1917, Russia had seen more than 10 years of civil unrest. The new Bolshevik party led by Vladimir Lenin staged a revolution. The Russian emperor, Nicholas II, was overthrown. Lenin's communist government started to make reforms. Lenin meant to turn the Soviet Union into a classless society. Lenin died in 1924 before achieving many of his goals.

The hammer and sickle symbol represented Soviet communism.

Joseph Stalin came after Lenin and was far more brutal in his methods. He was an able, but ruthless dictator. Under a series of five-year plans, Stalin dramatically changed Soviet society. He wanted to make the Soviet Union a stronger country. He used the army, the secret police, and labour camps called "gulags" against anyone who opposed his plans. Millions of Soviet citizens died as he drove the Soviet Union towards greater power.

The Army in Japan

Meanwhile, Japan was also changing. Modern methods of manufacturing began in the late 1800s. Japan made gains as a result of the First World War. It developed a strong relationship with both the United States and China. In the late 1920s, a group of young army officers, dreaming of a vast empire, took control of the armed forces. Businessmen who wanted raw materials and markets for Japanese industry supported them. The civilian government was weak and divided. Those who opposed the army were often killed. By the 1930s, the Japanese military had control over the government. They dictated Japanese policies.

The Spanish Civil War

In 1936, General Francisco Franco led a military revolt against the elected government of Spain. He wanted to stamp out communism. The Spanish government

Spanish fascists used this symbol.

was made up of many political groups. The Communist Party was one of these groups. Franco got support from the army, rich landowners, the Roman Catholic Church, and the Falange (the Spanish Fascist Party). Hitler and Mussolini sent military and financial aid to Franco. Stalin sided with the government. The world looked the other way as Franco brutally destroyed Spain's democratic government. The Spanish Civil War lasted three years. It left a million dead. By 1939, another fascist was in power in Europe.

Fascism in Canada

Canada was not immune to fascism. Several small parties copied the racism and brutality of Mussolini and Hitler. The most successful of the Canadian fascists was Adrien Arcand. He was a racist who hated Jews and anyone who was not English or French. Arcand organized a private army. Members dressed in navy blue uniforms and displayed the Nazi swastika alongside the maple leaf. Arcand wrote many papers and brochures. He said he had 80 000 followers, but many believe he had only a few thousand. As Hitler and Mussolini became more aggressive and the world drifted towards yet another war, Arcand lost support. Canadian authorities became more active in restraining him. When the Second World War broke out, the RCMP arrested Arcand and other fascists. They were interned until 1944.

The Mac-Paps in Spain

Not all Canadians stood by while fascist dictators took control over much of Europe. When the Spanish Civil War exploded in 1936, people from all over the world volunteered to fight the fascists. These "International Brigades" numbered 40 000. About 1500 Canadians went to Spain to fight for the Republic. They formed the Mackenzie–Papineau Battalion (named after the leaders of the 1837 Rebellions). They were nicknamed the Mac-Paps. Half never returned. They were outgunned and outnumbered. Canadian Prime Minister Mackenzie King did not want to anger Hitler and Mussolini. In 1937, he refused to allow any more volunteers to leave for Spain. The punishment for doing so was two years in jail.

Canadian Nazis joined the National Unity Party. Here, members of Adrien Arcand's party salute at a 1939 meeting held in Montreal. Arcand and other fascists were interned during the Second World War.

The Canadian government disowned the volunteers for two reasons: First, some of them had been active in the On-to-Ottawa Trek of 1935; second, Canada wanted to avoid another terrible world war. However, thousands of Canadians lined up to see them return, even in defeat. These civilian soldiers were right to worry about fascists gaining strength in Europe. Soon, regular soldiers would head to Europe to fight in a long, bloody war.

FOCUS

1. Why did many people not accept the new national boundaries of Europe?
2. Why were so many people attracted to dictators?
3. Who took power in the Soviet Union, Italy, Japan, and Spain?
4. What did the fascist leaders have in common?
5. How did Canadians respond to the rise of European fascism?

Adolf Hitler

In Germany, the leader of the National Socialist German Workers' Party (**Nazi** for short) watched Mussolini's rise to power with admiration. Adolf Hitler was born in Austria in 1889. After an unhappy childhood, he became a homeless drifter. At the outbreak of the First World War, Hitler eagerly joined the German army. He was a good soldier, even though he never rose above the rank of corporal.

When Germany surrendered in 1918, soldiers everywhere cheered because the war was over. Hitler, on the other hand, cried because Germany had been beaten. He swore revenge on the "socialists and Jewish traitors who," he later claimed, "had stabbed Germany in the back." He formed the Nazi Party. Its aim was to rebuild Germany and defeat its enemies.

Hitler made being a Nazi exciting. He

Before the Second World War began, many world leaders were impressed by Hitler. Here, Canadian Prime Minister Mackenzie King (centre) is on a state visit to the "new Germany."

organized the party along military lines. It had its own salute, uniform, songs, and symbol—the swastika. The Nazis listened to stirring speeches from their leader. They marched through the streets of German towns. The brown-shirted "storm troopers" broke up Communist Party meetings, attacked the homes and businesses of Jews, and struck terror into the hearts of other "traitors," anyone who did not view the world as they did.

By 1933, the Nazis were the largest party in the German parliament, although they had never won a majority in a free election. As leader, Hitler was asked to be chancellor of Germany. He accepted on condition that he be given dictatorial powers. That evening, the Nazis held torchlight parades. Swept along by excitement, the crowds roared, "Sieg Heil! SIEG HEIL!" (Hail victory).

German soldiers swore an oath of personal loyalty to Hitler. Under Hitler, the German armed forces expanded rapidly.

Why Germans Supported Hitler
Even people who had not voted for Hitler were glad to see a strong leader in charge. They thought he would solve the country's problems. Few realized his real intentions, even though he had written of them in his book, *Mein Kampf* (*My Struggle*).

Many saw Hitler as an inspiring leader. He was certainly a brilliant and hypnotizing speaker. Nazi rallies were full of colourful parades and rousing marching songs. People who attended felt they were part of a great movement. Paul Joseph Goebbels, Hitler's propaganda minister, used these rallies to spread hatred, especially against Jews.

Hitler Youth clubs were quickly established, and in 1935, only those people who had participated in such clubs were eligible to enter the civil service. The following speech was read when young people joined a youth club.

Dear boy!/Dear girl!
This hour in which you are to be received into the great community of the Hitler Youth is a very happy one and at the same time will introduce you into a new period of your lives. Today for the first time you swear allegiance to the Führer which will bind you to him for all time.

And every one of you, my young comrades, enters at this moment into the community of all German boys and girls. With your vow and your commitment you now become a bearer of German spirit and German honour. Every one, every single one, now becomes the foundation for an eternal Reich of all Germans.

When you, too, now march in step with the youngest soldiers, then bear in mind that this march is to train you to be a National Socialist, conscious of the future and faithful to his duty.

And the Führer demands of you and of us that we train ourselves to a life of service and duty, of loyalty and comradeship. You, ten-year-old cub, and you, lass, are not too young nor too small to practice obedience and discipline, to integrate yourself into the community and show yourself to be a comrade. Like you, millions of young Germans are today swearing allegiance to the Führer and it is a proud picture of unity which German youth today presents to the whole world. So today you make a vow to your Führer and here, before your parents, the Party and your comrades, we now receive you into our great community of loyalty. Your motto will always be:

"Führer, command—we follow!"
(The cubs are asked to rise.) Now say after me: "I promise always to do my duty in the Hitler Youth in love and loyalty to the Führer and to our flag."

Source: Quoted in George L. Mosse, *Nazi Culture* (New York: Grosset & Dunlop, 1968), page 357.

The Depression hit Germany hard. By the 1930s, Germany's economy was in ruins. Unemployment rose from 1.4 million in 1929, to 3.1 million in 1930, and finally to 6 million in 1932. Many other people had only part-time work. Millions of Germans were without food.

Many Germans blamed the new democratic government for the economic hardships. Perhaps the Nazis could put Germans back to work. Hitler promised a strong government. His private army of storm troopers paraded through the streets. They broke up the meetings of other political parties. Many people supported the Nazis out of fear.

Hitler gave the Germans targets to blame for all their problems. His favourite scapegoats were communists and Jews. The Nazis preached "racial purity." They claimed that Germans were the "master race." Jews, Slavs, Blacks, Asians, and other minorities were to be regarded as "impure aliens."

Hitler blamed Germany's troubles on the Treaty of Versailles. The treaty demanded that Germany pay for the First World War with money and goods. As a result, life was difficult for Germans during the 1920s. With the treaty's controversial war guilt clause, they were forced to accept full responsibility for causing the First World War. One day Hitler tore the treaty to shreds before cheering crowds.

Once in power, Hitler delivered on his promises. Germans were put back to work. New roads and bridges were built all over the country. Guns, tanks, warships, and planes— all forbidden by the Treaty of Versailles— started to pour from German factories. Young men flocked to the army and, in 1936, rode the new tanks down the new highways, across the new bridges and into the Rhineland. Under the Treaty of Versailles, this part of Germany was to be demilitarized. Hitler was prepared to challenge the terms of this treaty. The Allies protested mildly, but did nothing to stop Hitler.

Meanwhile, all traces of democracy in Germany were removed. Socialists, democrats, communists, religious leaders, teachers, and scientists—anyone who spoke out against the Nazis—found themselves in **concentration camps**. Jews lost their jobs and were persecuted in many ways. Nazi propaganda poured out of the newspapers and radios. Unions, schools, churches, and the army were under Nazi control. The **Gestapo**, Hitler's secret police, was everywhere.

FOCUS

1. List five reasons why many Germans supported Hitler.
2. What actions did Hitler take once in power?
3. Why might young people have been attracted to Hitler?
4. Would a character like Hitler be attractive to people today? Explain.

The Gathering Storm

Shortly after the First World War, many countries formed the League of Nations. Their plan was to prevent any future wars. The League was to settle international arguments through diplomacy. As a result of a dispute between President Wilson and the U.S. Senate, the United States did not join, which created a serious weakness in the League. During the 1920s, the League managed to settle some disputes between nations, but by the 1930s things were not working as well. Some countries had learned they could defy the League and get away with it.

Manchuria

In 1931, the Japanese army invaded the northern Chinese province of Manchuria. Within weeks, Manchuria was torn from China. The League of Nations was not prepared to act. Asia seemed so far away. All the League did to support China was to refuse to recognize the new government of Manchuria. In defiance, Japan simply withdrew from the League. Japan set out to conquer the rest of China and to build its empire in the Pacific. In a sense, by 1937, the Second World War had already begun in Asia.

In 1936 in Geneva, Switzerland, the emperor of Ethiopia, Haile Selassie (standing), pleaded with the League of Nations to step in and protect his country. Mussolini's armies had invaded it in late 1935. The League listened, but did not act.

Ethiopia and the Rhineland

Mussolini's economic program was not working in Italy. To take people's minds off the problems of the Depression, Mussolini chose to go to war. He wanted to rebuild the Roman Empire. He saw himself as Italy's "Duce," a leader greater than Julius Caesar.

All through the summer of 1935, Italian troops gathered on the borders of the ancient African kingdom of Ethiopia. In October, they attacked. The Ethiopians fought bravely, but spears and old guns were no match for modern machine guns, planes, tanks, and poison gas.

Haile Selassie, the emperor of Ethiopia, appealed to the League of Nations. The League members agreed that Italy was wrong. They said they would cut off Italy's oil supplies. "Oil means war!" replied Mussolini. The League backed down. In any case, it was more worried about Hitler's march into the Rhineland. Would France declare war? France, at the urging of Britain, decided it would not.

With the failure of the League to stop

them, Hitler and Mussolini realized they served each other well. They had kept the League from acting against either of them. In 1936, with the military rulers in Japan, they formed the Rome-Tokyo-Berlin Axis. They made the Anti-Comintern Pact. Under this Pact, they agreed to support one another against communist U.S.S.R. Now Hitler had allies. He was ready to gamble that the leaders of Europe would agree to anything to avoid war.

The Appeasement of Germany

In Hitler's vision of the future, Germans everywhere would be united. In 1938, he announced that Austria, which was mostly German speaking, was to be part of Germany. Austria had no way of defending itself against the German army. France and Britain did nothing. Seven million Austrians were soon under German control. Hitler had his next target almost surrounded.

The rich industrialized Sudetenland area of Czechoslovakia was home to 3 million German-speaking Czechs. Hitler claimed that they were oppressed and threatened to take over the area. France, Britain, and the Soviet Union promised to stand by the Czechs. The leaders of Britain, France, Italy, and

---

TIMELINE

These military events led up to the Second World War.

1931	Japan invades Manchuria in northern China.
1933	Hitler comes to power in Germany.
	Germany begins to rearm.
1935	Italy invades Ethiopia.
1936	The Spanish Civil War gets under way.
	Hitler sends German troops into the Rhineland on the French border.
	Japan, Italy, and Germany sign a treaty of mutual protection.
1937	Japan invades China.
1938	Germany takes over Austria.
	Germany takes part of Czechoslovakia.
	Germany takes the rest of Czechoslovakia.
1939	August: Hitler and Stalin in Russia agree not to fight each other.
	September 1: Germany invades Poland.
	Soviet Union also invades Poland and Finland.
	September 3: Great Britain and France declare war on Germany.
	September 10: Canada declares war on Germany.

Refer to the map at the beginning of this chapter. How would it look by the end of this Timeline? In your opinion, what is the most important event noted?

Germany met at Munich. The British and French leaders gave in to Hitler's demands because they wanted to avoid another war. They also believed Hitler when he said that this was his last demand. British Prime Minister Neville Chamberlain went home to cheering crowds claiming he had achieved "peace with honour, peace in our time." Many people in Canada and elsewhere heaved a sigh of relief. Others, such as Britain's future prime minister, Winston Churchill, warned of greater threats to come.

Dr. Norman Bethune

BORN: 1890, Gravenhurst, Ontario

DIED: 1939, China

SIGNIFICANCE: Bethune established the world's first mobile blood transfusion unit to aid injured soldiers.

BRIEF BIOGRAPHY: Bethune entered the University of Toronto in 1909. He interrupted his studies to take a teaching position with Frontier College. He returned to university in 1911, where he enrolled in medical school. His education was once again interrupted, this time by the war in 1914. Bethune joined the Royal Canadian Army Corps and served as a stretcher-bearer during the First World War. After returning to Canada in 1915, he finally completed his medical degree. Bethune contracted tuberculosis (TB) in 1926. While ill, he forced his doctor to perform a radical and dangerous surgery to help cure the disease. Between 1929 and 1936, Bethune devoted himself to other TB victims and to thoracic (lung) surgery. During this time, he invented 12 medical/surgical instruments.

Bethune became very disillusioned with the medical establishment and with the social and economic aspects of the disease—poor people tended to contract TB. He joined the Communist Party. In 1936, he went to Spain with the Mac-Paps to fight in the Spanish Civil War. While there, he organized the world's first mobile blood-transfusion service on the front lines. Bethune returned to Canada in 1937.

Bethune was soon interested in China's struggle against Japan. He went to China in 1938 to join the Army in Shanxi-Hobei. "That is where I can be most useful," he wrote. In China, he established a hospital to treat the wounded and to train doctors and nurses. When the Japanese destroyed this hospital, Bethune stayed close to the troops and performed operations near the fighting. Because there were only five qualified doctors, he worked 18-hour days. The following year, he contracted blood poisoning while performing surgical duties on the front. He died a hero to millions of Chinese. Canadian authorities declared him a national hero in 1971. **In your opinion, does Bethune deserve "hero" status? Explain. For more information about Bethune, visit www.cbc.ca/ archives and view the file "Comrade Bethune: A Controversial Hero."**

CANADIAN LIVES

Within months, the German army swallowed up the rest of Czechoslovakia.

Hitler next turned to the German-speaking areas of Poland. The leaders of France and Britain realized that they must take a stand. They declared that they would guarantee Poland's borders.

The Soviet Union had decided it could not rely on the Western democracies for help against Hitler. It noted what had happened to Austria and Czechoslovakia. So, the Soviet Union and Germany signed a non-aggression pact in August 1939. They agreed they would not fight each other. A secret agreement was also made to divide Poland between them. With the Soviet Union out of his way, Hitler was now ready.

Canada and Aggression

Most Canadians did not want to force another war by standing up to Hitler and Mussolini. When the Canadian ambassador to the League of Nations spoke out against Mussolini's invasion of Ethiopia, his government said he did not speak for Canada.

Canada's prime minister, Mackenzie King, had met Hitler. He felt that Hitler was not a threat to world peace. He even had an autographed photo of the dictator. Canadians were still clawing their way out of the Depression and had sad memories of the last war. They feared that another war would

One last good-bye before Canadian soldiers left for war. Many never returned.

again divide English and French Canadians.

On 1 September 1939, German tanks thundered across the Polish border and bombers flattened the great city of Warsaw. On September 3, France and Britain declared war against Germany. King was still in favour of appeasing Hitler. One week later, however, the Canadian Parliament voted to declare war on Germany. The first Canadian victim of the Second World War was a 10-year-old, Margaret Hayworth of Hamilton, Ontario. She died when a German submarine torpedoed the *Athenia*, an unarmed passenger ship, on the first day of war. Hayworth's state funeral encouraged Canadians to fight.

FOCUS

1. Why did the League of Nations fail to act against Japan, Italy, and Germany?
2. Why were nations eager to give in to Germany's demands?
3. What was Canada's reaction to German aggression?

Blitzkrieg

Nazi armies crushed Poland in less than a month. By October 19, the Polish armed forces collapsed under the relentless attack by German tanks and Stuka dive-bombers. Hitler taught the world a new word—**blitzkrieg** (lightning war). After the defeat of

Germany struck again during the spring of 1940. Denmark fell in 1 day; Norway in 2. The Netherlands was smashed in 5 days; Belgium took 18. Even mighty France was shattered in six weeks.

Britain stood alone in Europe. The new prime minister, Winston Churchill, promised nothing but "blood, toil, tears, and sweat." It seemed that the war would soon be over. German forces began preparing for the invasion of Britain.

EUROPEAN BATTLEGROUNDS

Unconquered
Non-belligerent
Neutral

The German Reich 1942
The Front at the end of Oct. 1942
The German Reich
Territory administered by Germany
Territory occupied by Axis troops
Axis satellite states
Vichy (unoccupied) France
Territory administered by Italy

The Miracle at Dunkirk

As the advancing German army swung south into France from the Netherlands, British and French troops were pinned against the English Channel near the tiny French port of Dunkirk. If British ships could reach Dunkirk in time, the soldiers could be rescued. But the navy had few ships to spare. Instead, English fishers, weekend sailors, and ferry captains took their boats across the

Poland came a lull in the fighting. Some people called this the "phony war" or "sitzkrieg." It was a time of careful preparation before the bloody struggles to come. While the Allies scrambled to mobilize their armed forces, Germany moved its forces from defeated Poland to staging areas for its next invasion.

channel. Canal boats and river tugs towed rowboats and empty coal barges out to sea to rescue Allied soldiers. This volunteer fleet brought back 350 000

Fighter planes ready for take-off.

men—10 times what the government had hoped to save. The Germans had not been able to get to Dunkirk in time to prevent this

heroic rescue.

In the distant port of Halifax, Nova Scotia, ships were assembling in convoys to cross the Atlantic. They carried the food, weapons, and soldiers needed for one of the most important and critical battles in the war—the Battle of Britain.

Ships wait in Bedford Basin, Nova Scotia, to sail together as a convoy.

Max Aitken, Lord Beaverbrook

BORN: 1879, Maple, Ontario

DIED: 1964, United Kingdom

SIGNIFICANCE: Canadian Max Aitken had a varied career as a millionaire businessman, British politician, and successful author. A member of the British House of Lords, Lord Beaverbrook was a key figure in the Allied successes in both world wars.

BRIEF BIOGRAPHY: Aitken was born to poor parents and left school early. Nevertheless, this energetic and clever Canadian achieved great success in business. He was a millionaire before he was 30. He was behind the creation of the Stelco and Canada Cement companies. While on his honeymoon, he even found time to buy a hydroelectric company and a streetcar company.

Beaverbrook moved to England to pursue business interests. He soon became part of the social and political upper class. He was elected as a member of Parliament and later appointed to the House of Lords.

Between the wars, Beaverbrook returned to business and built a publishing empire. His papers regularly warned readers of the rise of Hitler in Germany. When the Second World War broke out, Prime Minister Churchill called on his friend to oversee the production of aircraft so vital to Britain's survival. He was ruthlessly efficient and boosted production from 183 to 471 aircraft per month. As Minister of Supply, Beaverbrook worked closely with Allies such as the U.S.S.R. (after 1941) and the United States. Winston Churchill said of his superb effort: "He did not fail. This was his hour."

After the war, Beaverbrook returned to his business interests and wrote several best-selling books. Near the end of his life, he spent more time in his native land, Canada. He gave millions of dollars to establish an art gallery in Fredericton, N.B. **In your view, what was Beaverbrook's greatest achievement? Why? If you wish to visit the Beaverbrook Gallery, go to www. beaverbrookgallery.org**.

C A N A D I A N   L I V E S

The Battle of Britain

The British navy and air force controlled the 50 km of water—the English Channel—separating Britain from Europe. Germany needed to control the skies over the Channel before its invasion fleet could sail.

The German air force, or Luftwaffe, set out to destroy the Royal Air Force (RAF). On 10 July 1940, wave after wave of German Messerschmitts and Heinkels streamed across the channel. They spread out over Britain to their bombing targets—radar stations, airfields, ports and factories. Slowly the RAF planes were wiped out. At one point, every fighter plane Britain owned was in the air. Had the Germans launched another attack, no planes would have been available to respond.

Suddenly, the German tactics changed. In August, the RAF made a surprise bombing raid on Berlin. The commander of the German air force, Herman Goering, was furious because he had promised Germans that no Allied plane would ever bomb a German city. The Germans decided to "blitz" British cities in revenge. They planned to terrorize the civilian population into surrender, but the plan backfired. Bombs rained on London, night and day. Londoners moved into air-raid shelters and subway stations. Each day they set about repairing homes, reopening stores—carrying on. British resistance grew stronger, not weaker.

The German raids on London enabled the few remaining RAF Spitfires and Hurricanes to regroup. Newly trained pilots joined those who had been flying almost constantly since the battles began. New planes came off the assembly lines at the rate of almost 500 a month.

On September 15, German planes almost blackened the skies, but the RAF was ready for them. When the day was over, the Luftwaffe was decidedly beaten. Hitler called off the attack two days later. If he could not beat Britain, he would turn against the Soviet Union.

The Battle of Britain was won by a few hundred pilots. They included 80 Canadians as well as Britons, Poles, Australians, New Zealanders, and South Africans. The Luftwaffe lost 1722 planes, the RAF 915. Canadian pilots accounted for 60 definite and 50 probable "kills."

FOCUS

1. What is the meaning of the term *blitzkrieg*?
2. Why was Dunkirk so important to Britain?
3. How did Canadians help win the Battle of Britain?
4. What was Lord Beaverbrook's contribution to the British and Allied war effort?

Battle of the Atlantic

At the outbreak of the Second World War, Canada had a navy of 3500 men and women, and 10 warships. By the end of the war, the Royal Canadian Navy (RCN) had 100 000 sailors and 341 fighting ships. It was the world's third largest navy.

The merchant navy was the "fourth branch" of Canada's military force. It carried military personnel, food, fuel, and weapons to Britain and the Soviet Union. In crossing the Atlantic, it lost 72 ships and more than 1600 merchant seamen. More than 25 000 merchant ship crossings took place during the war.

In 1941, when Germany pushed its U-boat, or submarine, attacks farther into the Atlantic, St. John's became the home of the Newfoundland Escort Force (NEF). The NEF escorted convoys between North America and Ireland. Convoys sometimes sailed as far north as Greenland; however, German U-boats still found and sank many vessels. Hunting in **wolf packs**, they zeroed in on lone ships.

Anchor Memorial, Windsor, Ontario, is dedicated to members of the Canadian Navy and Merchant Navy who lost their lives in the wars. Make a list of street names, parks, and memorials that are war related in your neighbourhood.

The RCN played a major role in the NEF. Canadian warships (destroyers and corvettes) sought to find and sink U-boats before they found and sank ships in the convoys. Twenty-four Canadian warships were lost, mostly from submarine attacks.

The Battle of the Atlantic came closest to Canadian shores. Eyewitnesses sometimes saw explosions of merchant ships as soon as they left the safety of Halifax's Bedford Basin. German wolf packs had hunted them down. In January 1942, German U-boats sank a naval vessel just 15 km from St. John's. U-boat attacks also occurred in Placentia Bay and at Bell's Island. In October 1942 a German submarine torpedoed the SS *Caribou*, a ferryboat between Cape Breton and Newfoundland—137 of the 237 people aboard were killed.

British Prime Minister Winston Churchill felt that the Battle of the Atlantic was a fight for Britain's very survival. "The only thing that ever really frightened me during the war," he said, "was the U-boat peril."

The battle was the longest of the war. As Canadian Rear Admiral Leonard Murray saw it, it was "won by the courage, fortitude and determination of the British and Allied Merchant Navy." The dangerous trip they made over and over again was called the North Atlantic Run. By mid-1943, sonar equipment and shore-based aircraft helped put U-boats in retreat. It was a turning point in the war, one in which Canada had played a key role.

The Technical Edge

Tribal Class Destroyer Her Majesty's Canadian Ship (HMCS) *Haida* was called "the fightingest ship in the Royal Canadian Navy." She became famous by destroying nine enemy vessels. No other RCN ship destroyed as many. HMCS *Haida* was one of 27 Tribal Class destroyers built between 1937 and 1945. She was one of the most advanced fighting ships of the Second World War era. HMCS *Haida* saw much action in the second half of the war. She escorted convoys to Russia and helped Allied forces during the D-Day invasion. A sister ship, HMCS *Athabaskan*, was sunk in 1944 with the loss of 128 lives.

HMCS *Haida* also saw action during the Korean War (1950–1953). As the last Tribal Class destroyer in the world, the proud ship was decommissioned in 1963.

Today, the HMCS Haida sits in Hamilton Harbour and is designated as a National Historic Site. From 1965 to 2003, she was docked in Toronto and was a popular tourist attraction.

FOCUS

1. **Describe Canada's role in the war at sea.**
2. **Why was the Battle of the Atlantic so important?**

Dieppe

As France fell to Hitler's armies, Italy joined the war on Germany's side. By 1941, nearly all of Europe was under German or Italian control. British and Australian troops were desperately fighting Germans and Italians in North Africa. On 22 June 1941, Germany

This Canadian soldier patiently waits for action. Dieppe meant a bloody end to inactivity for Canadian forces.

attacked the Soviet Union. In December 1941, Japan attacked American and British positions in the Pacific. It swiftly captured Hong Kong (imprisoning several hundred Canadians), the Philippines, Malaya, Singapore, and Sumatra.

Reasons for a Raid

By the fall of 1941, the Soviet Union was bearing almost the full weight of German attack. Stalin urged his Western allies to open a second front. If they would attack German-held France, the Soviet Union might get relief.

The British knew they were not ready to start a second front. But the whole Commonwealth was angry about the fall of Hong Kong. The Americans, Britain's new allies, wanted action. Canadian soldiers were also restless. They had been waiting in Britain for three years. A large raid might satisfy the Soviets, the Americans, and the Canadians. It might be useful too. It could test German coastal defences.

A raid could help plan a full-scale invasion. It might

HISTOR!CA

Minutes

also deceive Germany as to the site of the ultimate invasion

of German-held Europe in the future.

The Dieppe Raid

On the morning of 19 August 1942, nearly 5000 Canadian soldiers, 1000 British commandos, and some American and French soldiers crouched in landing crafts off the heavily fortified French port of Dieppe. They intended to seize the town, destroy the port facilities and airport, take prisoners and return to England. The key to victory was surprise.

When the first Canadians hit the beach, the Germans were ready and waiting. They had spotted the enemy ships during the night. Some Allied ships had gone off course and arrived late. The raid did not start until daylight. The element of surprise was lost.

The Canadians found themselves on a boulder beach in front of a town that was fortified with cannons, barbed wire, tanks, traps, and mines. Many landing craft were blown right out of the water. In a boat of 80 men, 40 were killed and 20 wounded within minutes of landing. One regiment had 96 percent casualties. Only a few soldiers ever reached the town.

The slaughter and chaos that was Dieppe is revealed in this painting by war artist Charles Comfort.

When the smoke cleared, 900 men were dead. Nearly 2000 were taken prisoner. The men from Winnipeg, Hamilton, Montreal, Calgary, Windsor, Regina, and Toronto had been savagely defeated.

A British military committee examined the causes of the failure. It noted two problems: (1) It was foolish to attack a fortified beach in broad daylight; (2) The enemy should have been pulverized by aerial and naval bombardment before landing. The report concluded that the results of the Dieppe raid were disappointing and the heavy casualties regrettable. The operation could be seen as worthwhile, however, if its lessons were applied carefully when the time came to re-enter France on a larger scale.

The Dieppe tragedy taught the Allies that much stronger military forces were required to break through the German coastal defences. As well, a much higher proportion of military forces should be held in reserve until the progress of the initial assault was known. Unless this was done, there was no guarantee that any of the beaches would be secured. The D-Day invasion date was now moved from 1943 to 1944.

The next time the Allied forces landed in Europe, they were ready. D-Day occurred on 6 June 1944, the day Allied forces invaded Europe. Many of the disastrous errors of the Dieppe raid were avoided. The sacrifices made by Canadian and other soldiers on the beaches of Dieppe in 1942 reduced the casualties of Canadian, British, and American forces in 1944.

In Their Own Words

Those who fought on the Dieppe beaches left disturbing accounts.

"First thing I remember after I left the boat, I got hit in the eye. I got to the wall, and then again I was hit in the leg. And after that—all hell had let loose, of course—I put the bandage on my leg. And my eye, it was gone. And I got hit in the head when I was trying to fix up my eye. Shrapnel in the eye and the head, and a bullet in the leg."

> Source: Private Peter Macleod, Royal Regiment of Canada, quoted in *In Enemy Hands*, by Daniel G. Dancocks (Toronto: McClelland & Stewart, 1990).

"The landing craft I was in was hit as we were coming in about a quarter mile off shore.... I was shot in the eye at that point, and later, the eye completely closed up, but there was so much to do in a situation like that, you don't really notice these things. It wasn't until later in the action, around 11:00 in the morning, that I realized I was badly wounded and that my eye was gone. When there's so much excitement around you though, you have a tendency to keep going.

I think that everyone who landed on that beach that day deserved credit for doing the best possible job that could be done. I don't believe in medals, but if there has to be such a thing, they should be awarded to anyone and everyone who was there.

No doubt Dieppe did teach the military planners a lot of lessons, but I think those lessons could have been learned without such a great loss of life ..."

> Source: Ed Bennett, quoted in *Voices of a War Remembered*, by Bill McNeil (Toronto: Doubleday Canada Ltd., 1991), page 271.

Do you agree that all who were at Dieppe deserved a medal? Explain.

Canadian Vision

Into the Breach

This Was My Brother

(For Lt-Col. Howard McTavish, killed in action at Dieppe)

This was my brother
At Dieppe
Quietly a hero
Who gave his life like a gift,
Withholding nothing.

His youth, his love,
His enjoyment of being alive,
His future, like a book
With half the pages still uncut—

This was my brother
At Dieppe,
The one who built me a doll house
When I was seven,
Complete to the last small picture frame,
Nothing forgotten.

Corpses on Dieppe beach next to a Churchill tank.

He was awfully good at fixing things,
At stepping into the breach when he was needed.

That's what he did at Dieppe;
He was needed.
And even Death must have been a little shamed
By his eagerness.

By Mona McTavish Gould, poet and broadcaster. *Tasting the Earth* (Toronto: Macmillan, 1943)

What is the message of this poem? Is the sister for or against the raid? Explain.

FOCUS

1. How did the war expand in 1941?
2. Provide three reasons for the raid on Dieppe.
3. What were the results of the raid?
4. In your view, was the lesson learned at Dieppe worth the cost of the lives? Explain.

Canada at War

There is more to war than sending soldiers to the battlefield. How could Canadians and Canadian resources best be used to fight the Second World War?

The War Plan

The Canadian government drew up a war plan. It included what was most important to Canadians, and the areas where Canada could make the biggest contribution to the Allied war effort. The Canadian government carefully co-ordinated its plan with the war plans of other countries. The plan included

- the defence and security of Canada
- the production of food supplies for Britain
- the production of weapons and ammunition for Allied forces
- the training of Allied pilots
- development of the Royal Canadian Air Force (RCAF) for home defence and overseas duty
- development of the Royal Canadian Navy (RCN) for home defence and convoy duty
- development of the Canadian Army for home defence and overseas duty
- development of the Merchant Marine to transport troops and war materials overseas

How effective do you think Canadians would find this wartime poster?

Weapons of War

Under C. D. Howe, the minister of Munitions and Supply, war products poured from Canadian factories.

One thousand ships, 15 000 aircraft, 700 000 trucks, countless guns, bombs, and bullets were produced. Howe wanted to avoid the profiteering that had occurred during the First World War. A Wartime Prices Trade Board limited prices to "cost plus 10%." Even with these controls, the government paid close to $65 million a week for war supplies. War was serious business.

The federal government borrowed heavily by selling Victory Bonds to people. By buying bonds, Canadians helped to finance the war effort.

Rationing

If people had any money left after paying taxes and buying bonds, there was little to spend it on. In 1942, all Canadians received a **ration book**. When they bought sugar, butter, meat, tea or coffee, they had to hand over coupons from their book. When their coupons were gone they couldn't buy any rationed items—except on the **black market**. If they were caught shopping on the black market, they had to pay stiff fines.

Gas was rationed. Canadians could fill up once a month. They could not buy a new car because the last car was produced in 1942.

Anything Canadians could spare went to the war effort. The butter and cheese they didn't eat went to Britain, where rationing was much more severe. The steel that had once made washing machines now made bombers. Even the five cent nickel

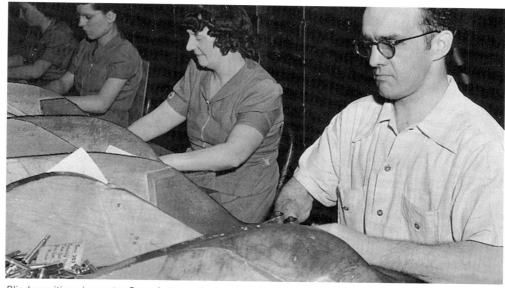

Blind munitions inspector Omer Auger works in a war plant.

Rationing was one way all Canadians helped in the war effort.

changed—it was made of zinc instead. Nickel was needed for armour coating on tanks.

The government encouraged Canadians to conserve for the war effort. Women were asked to check store shelf prices against the government set prices. Families kept Victory gardens and saved metals, rags, papers, rubber, and glass. Bacon fat and bones were saved for explosives. Local clubs canvassed house to house to collect donations. Clothing regulations were brought in to save material. Only a few items could have frills, furs, cuffs, ruffles, or double-breasted jackets.

Canada and the United States: A Growing Partnership

One of the most important and long-lasting results of the Second World War was the new partnership between Canada and the United States. Prime Minister King and President Franklin Roosevelt were on

In 1943 in Quebec, Prime Minister King hosted a conference between American President Franklin Roosevelt and British Prime Minister Winston Churchill. King did not attend the meeting, though. He was reluctant to be directly involved in Allied war decisions.

close personal terms. At one point, Roosevelt pledged American help if Canada was "threatened by any other empire."

The President even took his summer holidays at Campobello Island in New Brunswick.

During the war Canadian and American co-operation grew rapidly. The Alaska Highway, mostly built by Americans, went through Canadian territory. (See Chapter 4.) The 1940 Ogdensburg Agreement created a Permanent Joint Board of Defence. It bound Canada to a continental system of defence.

The Lend-Lease Act and the Hyde Park Declaration made for closer military and economic relations among Great Britain, Canada, and the United States. They also bound Canada more firmly to the American economy.

During the war, the Canadian economy boomed because the United States and Britain purchased war materials. By the end of war, one-tenth of Canadians worked in war plants. They produced 900 000 rifles, 800 000 military vehicles, 244 000 machine guns, 16 000 airplanes, 6500 tanks and 4000 boats. The war effort turned Canada into a modern industrialized nation ready to expand and prosper after the war.

LEND-LEASE ACT AND HYDE PARK DECLARATION

The U.S. Congress passed the Lend-Lease Act just before the Americans entered the war. The Act let the United States help Britain and its Allies without getting directly involved. It gave Americans permission to send military supplies, including ships and weapons, to any country that was vital to U.S. economic and military stability. It allowed countries receiving American goods to postpone payment. It also gave the United States permission to use some British-owned military bases.

The Lend-Lease Act, while it helped Britain, did not help Canada's economic stability. Britain could now buy war materials from the United States. Prime Minister King met with U.S. President Roosevelt. The two leaders amended the act. The Hyde Park Declaration, as it was called, allowed Britain to spend Lend-Lease money on goods manufactured in Canada and the United States to buy more military goods from Canada.

The Children's War Effort

Children collected paper, metal, rags, rubber, and bones. They saved string and the foil from cigarette and candy wrappers. Contests were held to see who could make the biggest ball of aluminum foil. All these items could be recycled into war materials. Students knitted during lunch hour, making socks and scarves for soldiers. They wrote letters to lonely prisoners of war. Children planted Victory gardens in school baseball diamonds to produce food for the war. Boys drilled as cadets. Teenagers were let off school to help bring in the harvest.

Canadian students were prepared for gas attacks.

Volunteers and Spirit of Unity

Canadians volunteered to be air-raid wardens. They patrolled the coasts to guard against an invasion that never came. They studied aircraft to serve as "spotters" in a bombing raid. They built public air-raid shelters. Wealthy Canadians, such as E. P. Taylor, worked for the government for a dollar a year. The war drew Canadians together in a spirit of unity.

FOCUS

1. In your view, what was the most important part of the Canadian war plan? Why?
2. Describe five ways in which ordinary Canadians helped the war effort.
3. How did the war affect Canadian–American relations?

Pilots, Secret Agents, and Seamen

The British Commonwealth Air Training Plan

Strong air power was vital during the Second World War. Crews needed to be trained before they could go into action but, to do this, they needed a safe place to train. Canada provided

The British Commonwealth Air Training Plan trained thousands of pilots.

the bases for the British Commonwealth Air Training Plan.

Trainees came from all over the Commonwealth—from Australia, South Africa, Britain, the West Indies and New Zealand. Volunteers who had escaped when Poland, France, and Norway fell to the Germans also trained in Canada.

The courses were short and often inadequate. The rush to get pilots and service crews ready to fight caused many accidents. In one month, 500 aircraft were put out of service by inexperienced fliers. All told, there were 850 deaths during training. On the other hand, 130 000 graduates, over half of them Canadian, went on to fight the battle of the skies.

The Secret War

On the shores of Lake Ontario near Whitby was Camp X. Few knew it existed. Those who did, said nothing. William Stephenson, a Canadian master spy, was in charge of Camp X. It was a top-secret training post for spies, secret agents, and sabotage experts. Agents from Camp X were dropped behind enemy lines to spy and report back by radio. They worked with underground movements in enemy-occupied countries to disrupt enemy activities. Interestingly, Ian Fleming, the creator of James Bond, trained at Camp X.

Station M was a vital part of Camp X. It was staffed by forgers, safecrackers, chemists, movie set designers, and costume experts. Station M provided agents with false passports and money, battered suitcases and shabby suits, and European-style toothpaste and underwear. Everything an agent carried had to look right to enemy eyes.

Canadian Agents

"Set Europe ablaze," Churchill told the special agents who parachuted into enemy territory. Of the 28 Canadian agents sent into Europe, 8 died. Even today, little is known of what they did.

Guy Bieler was born in Montreal. His spine was badly injured when he parachuted into France. Even so, he organized a sabotage group. They derailed and blew up trains carrying troops and arms. In the end, Bieler was captured and shot.

Joe Gelleny was trained as an espionage agent and parachuted into Nazi-held Yugoslavia. Later, in Hungary, Gelleny was captured and tortured. He lost 77 kg of weight, but finally escaped. While hiding out in Budapest, he forged travel documents for other spies and for Jews facing Nazi persecution. When the Russians arrived, they took him into custody, but he was eventually freed. He felt he had aged 20 years in his two years as a secret agent.

Henry Fung was a 19-year-old Chinese Canadian who parachuted into Malaya. He helped destroy Japanese communications and transportation systems. When the war ended, Fung accepted the surrender of Japanese forces in their jungle garrisons.

Frank Pickersgill of Winnipeg was captured when he landed in France. Nazi double agents had given him away. He refused to

One of the remaining buildings from Camp X near Whitby, Ontario.

break under brutal questioning. When his captors switched from threats to bribery, he broke a bottle on his interrogator's desk, slashed the throat of an SS guard, and jumped out of a second floor window before being stopped by four bullets. In prison camp, he organized resistance, helping prisoners regain lost pride. The Nazis finally executed Pickersgill and 15 other agents by hanging them from meat hooks in 1944.

Canada's Merchant Navy

During the Second World War, Canada had the fourth-largest merchant navy in the world. Most of its ships were built in Canadian shipyards. Wartime spending in the ship building industry was even greater than in

William Stephenson

BORN: 1896, Winnipeg, Manitoba

DIED: 1989, Bermuda

SIGNIFICANCE: Stephenson was a First World War aviation ace, an inventor, and a Second World War intelligence agent known as "Intrepid."

BRIEF BIOGRAPHY: Stephenson showed an early skill for the world of spying. As a teenager he developed his own secret "Morse Code." He fought in the First World War and barely survived two gas attacks. Later, he faked his medical records and joined the Royal Flying Corps. He quickly became an ace. He recorded 26 "kills," including the brother of the Red Baron. He was later shot down and captured, but he escaped. He was a decorated Canadian hero at the end of the war.

Back in Canada, he invented a new process for transmitting pictures without telephone or telegraph wires.

He moved to Britain to earn his fortune. There, he helped organize the British Broadcasting Corporation and set up a film studio. He explored ideas such as laser beams and splitting the atom.

Stephenson took part in intelligence work during the 1930s. Then, for the war, he ran British Security Co-ordination in the Western Hemisphere. He was based in New York and his code-name was Intrepid.

He led an army of code-breakers, spies, robbers, assassins, and sabotage experts. For his efforts in the "secret war," he was decorated by King George VI of Britain. In 1979 he was made a Companion of the **Order of Canada**, the country's highest civilian honour. Although some historians believe Stephenson's legendary exploits are partly "hype," he remains one of Canada's most creative and exciting figures. **What qualities made Stephenson such a hero?**

CANADIAN LIVES

the aircraft industry. Park Company, Canada's major supplier, was producing almost two 10-tonne ships a week by 1944.

The 12 000 seamen in Canada's merchant navy transported cargo and soldiers between Canada and Europe. Their contribution to victory was critical.

Until recently, though, the importance of the merchant navy was largely ignored. This is because they were civilians, not official sailors in the Royal Canadian Navy. During the Second World War, official casualty lists did not include merchant seamen; however, their losses were high—one in eight merchant sailors died. A total of 1629 Canadians and Newfoundland merchant sailors perished keeping the sea open. Eight Canadian women, serving as stewardesses or radio operators, died in the service of the merchant navy. Between 1942 and 1945, more than 4500 Allied merchant seamen were held in the German prisoner of war camp Milag Nord, near Bremen.

Since the Second World War, civilian sailors in Canada's merchant navy have struggled to receive the same benefits and

An example of a naval convoy. This one had 24 merchant ships.

recognition as those who served in the Royal Canadian Navy. In 1992, pensions and benefits were finally awarded to the sailors of the merchant navy. Some continued to fight for benefits not received from 1945 to 1992. Most of these claims were finally recognized and honoured by the federal government in 1999.

FOCUS

1. **How did Canada contribute to the war in the air and on the sea?**
2. **What was the "secret war"?**
3. **Who was "Intrepid," and what did he do?**
4. **What was the role of Canada's merchant navy?**

Japanese Canadians

In 1937, Japan invaded China. In what has become known as the Nanking Massacre, about 300 000 Chinese soldiers and civilians were killed. Atrocities were committed.

When France fell to the Germans in 1940, Japan moved into the French colony of

The attack on Pearl Harbor.

Indochina. Once Hitler attacked the Soviet Union, the Japanese knew they had nothing to fear from Europe. They attacked Hong Kong, Indonesia, and Malaya, and swept through the islands of the Pacific.

Pearl Harbor

It was a pleasant Sunday morning on 7 December 1941. At the American naval base of Pearl Harbor, Hawaii, sailors slept in their bunks. Most looked forward to a lazy day off. Suddenly, waves of Japanese bombers and fighter planes came out of the western skies. In just two hours, much of the American Pacific fleet lay at the bottom of the harbour. The United States had been brought into the war.

Japan's entry into the war caused near panic for many Canadians. To Canada's east, Hitler ruled in Europe. Now Japan was sweeping through Asia to the west. The fall of Hong Kong (including the imprisonment of 1600 Canadian soldiers) and the attack on Pearl Harbor caused fear. Many Canadians worried that British Columbia might be the next target. The Japanese were rumoured to be planning an invasion assisted by Japanese-Canadian citizens. Racists spread these rumours and demanded that all Japanese Canadians be interned.

Canadian or Japanese?

Canadians had not welcomed Asian immigrants. Few Asians were allowed to enter the country after 1913. By 1942, more than half of the 23 000 "Japanese" living in Canada had been born here. They were Canadian citizens. They did not want Japan to take over the Pacific. Many had fought for Canada during the First World War.

Some Canadians paid no attention to these facts. They decided that Japanese Canadians were dangerous. They might be spies who would help Japan attack North America. After Pearl Harbor, Canada declared war on Japan. Japanese-born citizens automatically became "enemy aliens." Thirty-eight Japanese nationals were immediately arrested. Japanese-language schools and newspapers were closed. More than 1200 fishing boats were impounded. In 1942, the government ordered that Japanese-born citizens be moved from the coastal regions of British Columbia. They were sent to isolated camps in the B.C. interior. Some families were separated. Men were sent to

NOTICE TO ALL JAPANESE PERSONS AND PERSONS OF JAPANESE RACIAL ORIGIN

TAKE NOTICE that under Orders Nos. 21, 22, 23 and 24 of the British Columbia Security Commission, the following areas were made prohibited areas to all persons of the Japanese race:—

LULU ISLAND (including Steveston)	SAPPERTON
SEA ISLAND	BURQUITLAM
EBURNE	PORT MOODY
MARPOLE	IOCO
DISTRICT OF QUEENSBOROUGH	PORT COQUITLAM
CITY OF NEW WESTMINSTER	MAILLARDVILLE
	FRASER MILLS

AND FURTHER TAKE NOTICE that any person of the Japanese race found within any of the said prohibited areas without a written permit from the British Columbia Security Commission or the Royal Canadian Mounted Police shall be liable to the penalties provided under Order in Council P.C. 1665.

AUSTIN C. TAYLOR, Chairman, British Columbia Security Commission

In Their Own Words

These excerpts describe life in internment camps.

"Nothing affects me much just now except rather distractedly. Everything is like a bad dream. I keep telling myself to wake up. There's no sadness when friends of long standing disappear overnight—either to camp or to somewhere in the Interior. No farewells—no promise of future meetings or correspondence—or anything. We just disperse. It's as if we never existed. We're hit so many ways at one time that if I wasn't past feeling I think I would crumble.

This curfew business is horrible. At sundown we scuttle into our holes like furtive creatures. We look in the papers for the time of next morning's sunrise when we may venture forth."
Source: Joy Kogawa, *Obasan* (Toronto: Penguin Books, 1981).

"I was in that camp for four years. When it got cold the temperature went down to as much as 60 below. We lived in huts with no insulation. Even if we had the stove burning the inside of the windows would all be frosted up and white, really white. I had to lie in bed with everything on that I had … at one time there were 720 people there."
Source: Gilchnist Wright, *The Japanese Canadians: A Dream of Riches* (Vancouver, 1978).

How do the authors respond to the internment of Japanese Canadians? How would you feel if your family was treated like that?

David Suzuki

BORN: 1936, Vancouver, B.C.

SIGNIFICANCE: David Suzuki is Canada's best-known science broadcaster. His work on television has raised concerns for the environment. He is a passionate fighter against racism and discrimination.

BRIEF BIOGRAPHY: Although of Japanese descent, Suzuki's parents were born in Canada. They spoke English at home. Suzuki and his family were rounded up during the Second World War and placed in an internment camp near Slocan, B.C. Japanese-Canadian kids jeered at him because he spoke no Japanese. Non-Japanese children treated him as an "enemy." After the war, his family moved to Leamington, Ontario, where his father told him: "You have to be ten times better than a white, because if you are just as good as a white, you'll lose out every time." His father encouraged his lifelong interest in the environment.

Suzuki was a brilliant student, winning scholarships to pay for his education. He had a promising career as a teacher of genetics. In the 1970s, however, Suzuki left the academic world to popularize science on radio and television. His television productions are seen all over the world. Suzuki's concern for the planet's environment has made him a powerful spokesperson against pollution. Although best known as a defender of the environment, Suzuki continues to speak out against racism and discrimination. **How did internment affect David Suzuki? For more information about David Suzuki's work, visit www. davidsuzuki.org. For more about the internment camps, visit the CBC Digital Archives at www.cbc.ca/archives and view the file "Relocation to Redress: The Internment of the Japanese Canadians."**

CANADIAN LIVES

one camp, women and children to another. Some men were sent as labourers to farms on the prairies and in Ontario.

The government held auctions to sell these people's personal possessions, homes, and businesses. Although many made their living by fishing, their boats were taken and sold. These were great bargains for the buyers. Japanese Canadians never received a fair price. There was not a single proven case of any Japanese Canadian acting as a spy for Japan. Despite this, the Canadian government refused any compensation for their losses.

These children's faces reveal the fear and pain of forced evacuation.

Partial Compensation for Japanese Canadians

Finally, in September 1988, Prime Minister Brian Mulroney announced that his government would partially repay Japanese-Canadian survivors for their losses.

These were the terms established:
- a public apology for past injustices against Japanese Canadians, their families, and their heritage
- $21 000 for each surviving Japanese Canadian born before 1949
- $24 million to establish a Canadian Race Relations Foundation
- $12 million to the Japanese-Canadian Association for low-cost housing for elderly Japanese Canadians

FOCUS

1. How did Japanese aggression affect Canada and the United States?
2. What led the Canadian government to act against Japanese Canadians?
3. What specific measures were taken against Japanese Canadians?
4. Do you support the 1988 policy to compensate Japanese Canadians for their losses during the Second World War? Explain.
5. Should civil rights ever be restricted in wartime? Explain.

Hong Kong

The first Canadian military engagement of the war took place in the British Crown colony of Hong Kong. In the fall of 1941, most people were not thinking about a war with Japan. Nearly 2000 Canadian troops from the Royal Rifles of Canada and the

also laid siege to the British colony of Hong Kong. The inexperienced, outnumbered troops fought bravely alongside British forces. After 17 hopeless days of battle, Hong Kong surrendered on Christmas Day, 1941.

The survivors spent the rest of the war in

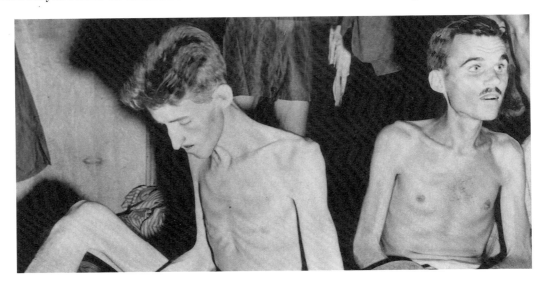

Only half of Canadian troops in Hong Kong survived. These POWs are among them.

Winnipeg Grenadiers were stationed in Hong Kong. They were on non-combat (garrison) duty. Most of them had little military training. Some of the soldiers had never fired their rifles. Some didn't even know how to throw a grenade. There was virtually no air or naval support for these troops.

On 8 December 1941, Japan attacked without warning in Northern Malaysia, the Philippines, Guam and Wake Islands. They

Japanese prison camps. Of the 1975 soldiers from Canada who went to Hong Kong, 290 perished in its defence. Another 267 died in the brutal Japanese prisoner of war camps. One-half of the Canadians who went to Hong Kong were either killed or wounded. This was one of the highest casualty rates for a Canadian theatre of action during all of the Second World War.

1915 1920 1925 1930 1935 1940 1945 1950

In Their Own Words

"In Japan, ... they took their venom out on the prisoners of war for the least misdemeanor or the least error that was made, you received a beating. Which again was hard to take, you had to stand there, and be punched in the face and in the body and without fighting back. The work, it was slave labour. If you can imagine carrying 90 kilos of soybeans on your shoulders.

Governments never take responsibility for anything. We feel Mackenzie King and his government sent us into something ... Well, they claim they didn't know what was going to happen. The Department of Defence knew what was going to happen because they knew that there was likely to be a war with Japan in the very near future.

The Canadian POW cemetery in Japan.

December 7 every year always grips Hong Kong Veterans because the first thing you hear on the news media is Pearl Harbor. There is nothing ever mentioned of what happened to those 1900-odd Canadians on December 7, 1941."

Source: 1986 interview with Harry Atkinson, one of the Canadian Hong Kong survivors. www.hkvca.ca/ accounts/HarryAtkinson .htm

Minutes

Do you feel that Atkinson makes a good argument about how the whole Hong Kong campaign has been treated by the media, books, and the Canadian public? Explain.

FOCUS

1. **Why were Canadian soldiers sent to Hong Kong?**
2. **How well prepared to fight were they?**
3. **Why was Hong Kong such a bitter defeat for Canadians?**

Women Go to War

Firefighting demonstration by members of the Canadian Women's Army Corps, 1943.

Canadian women were eager to defend their country. Initially, Canadian leaders saw little room for women in the war effort. As more and more men left for the battlefront, though, the roles women could play became more obvious.

Industrial strength was the key to success in the war, and Canada had vast resources. Canada's women put their brains and muscles to work. They turned raw materials into tanks, planes, and ships. Over one million women were working in Canadian industry by 1943.

Managers had to change some ideas about workers and how to run a factory. Daycare centres were set up in many plants. Production rose as workers donated free time to produce another tank or bomber. Men were often outnumbered. They sometimes had to endure female wolf whistles, just as women previously had endured male taunts. They learned that, in the right circumstances, women could swear as well as men.

In rural Canada, women took over the farming jobs vacated by men who went overseas. The food supply, at home and abroad, had to be maintained. Women handled the added responsibilities to assist in the overall war effort.

Women volunteered to visit wounded soldiers. They sent packages to prisoners of war. They made dressings for the wounded. The family garbage shrank as housewives saved paper, scraps, fat, and bones for recycling.

These women in the CWAC aided the war effort in Halifax. What roles did women play in the military?

Women in Uniform

Society had initially wanted to keep women out of the factories. Now it was determined to keep them out of the armed forces. When women couldn't register with the armed forces, they set up their own volunteer units such as the CATS (Canadian Auxiliary Territorial Service), which provided technical and first-aid training to women.

CANADA'S SERVICEWOMEN	TOTAL	POSTED OVERSEAS
Canadian Women's Army Corps (CWAC)	21 624	2 900
RCAF Women's Division (WDs)	17 018	1 400
Women's Royal Canadian Naval Service (WRENS)	6 781	1 000
Nursing Sisters	4 172	4 172

Molly Lamb's "Gas Drill" reveals some of the preparations for war. Is chemical warfare still a concern today?

Molly Lamb Bobak: First female official war artist.

Gudrun Bjening: War propaganda filmmaker for the National Film Board of Canada.

Fern Blodgett: First female wireless operator on a wartime ship. She crossed the Atlantic 78 times during the war.

Margaret Brooke: While crossing on the ferry from Nova Scotia to Newfoundland, the ship was torpedoed by a U-boat in Canadian waters. She supported nurse Agnes Wilkie in the icy water all night. At dawn, a giant breaker forced them apart. Wilkie drowned, but Brooke, now unconscious, was rescued.

Kathleen Christie and Maye Waters: These two nurses aided the troops during the battle for Hong Kong and imprisonment.

Marion Orr: One of Canada's first female bush pilots, Orr ferried military aircraft from factories to military bases overseas.

Helen-Marie Stevens: An army nurse who was the heroine at a bombing raid during the London "blitz." She worked for hours aiding customers in a bombed-out restaurant, using champagne as an anesthetic. "I did what any Canadian nurse would do," she said.

Mona Wilson: A public health nurse who took charge of the Canadian Red Cross in Newfoundland. She ministered to the needs of shipwrecked soldiers and sailors in the Battle of the Atlantic. For this work she earned the nickname "the Florence Nightingale of St. John's."

By 1941, the armed forces were in desperate need of recruits. Women were finally allowed to enlist. One young woman walked 30 km to a recruiting station. Eventually, Canada had 45 000 servicewomen. They served in a wide variety of non-combat roles, such as radar operators, truck and ambulance drivers, nurses, secretaries, and mechanics.

Some of these women often found themselves in the heat of battle. They were bombed, shelled, and torpedoed. Some were made prisoners of war. Two hundred and forty-four women won medals for bravery. Sadly, 73 were killed and 19 wounded.

Women Prove Themselves

During the war, women succeeded in a society dominated by men. Initially, many men had doubted their worth. Now, women gained freedom and self-respect. They knew the satisfaction of earning their own money. They also knew the unfairness of getting less pay than a man for doing the same work.

As a result of their work, pants became fashionable. The department of munitions issued a message stating, "Please don't stare at my pants. Would you like to know why I

Some women like this young soldier in the CWAC were expert shooters.

wear trousers like the men when I go about the streets? Because I'm doing a man's job for my country's sake. My coveralls are my working clothes. I wear them for my safety's sake. They are less likely to become entangled in the machinery. I work in a munitions plant. Every piece of war material I help to produce helps to keep the enemy away from our shores."

After the war, many women returned to more traditional roles. For the young couples who had postponed marriage and babies during the war, peace meant that it was time to start a family. It was not until the 1960s and 1970s that women returned to the gains they had made during wartime.

FOCUS

1. List five ways in which women contributed to the war effort.
2. In your opinion, were women treated equally? Explain.
3. How did the Second World War affect women's lives?

Conscription—Again

Should a person be forced to fight during war? This question almost split the country during the First World War. Prime Minister King did not want that to happen again. He promised that his government would not introduce conscription for overseas service.

The conscription referendum split the nation. Which side do these people seem to support?

In October 1939, Quebec's premier, Maurice Duplessis, called a provincial election. Duplessis believed that the federal government wanted to use the war to take power away from Quebec. If Canada was to remain united through the war, Duplessis's Union Nationale party had to be defeated.

The federal Liberals supported the provincial Liberal Party in the election. Three Quebec federal Cabinet ministers campaigned against Duplessis. They told the Quebec people that the federal government would not introduce conscription for overseas service. They said that they would resign if Duplessis was re-elected. This would leave Quebec without any influence in the federal Cabinet. The Liberals were swept into office in Quebec.

Meanwhile, Premier Mitch Hepburn of Ontario thought more Canadians should go to war. He accused his fellow Liberal, Prime Minister King, of being weak on the issue of conscription. King called a federal election in the early part of 1940. The Liberals won an overwhelming victory in all regions of Canada. Hepburn's political career was over.

Home Defence

Volunteers filled Canada's fighting forces overseas. Many people felt this might not be enough. In 1940, Parliament approved conscription for home defence only. Men drafted into this army were often jeered at because they hadn't volunteered to go overseas. They were later called "zombies" by those who thought every young man should want to fight.

Conscription, If Necessary

King had promised not to introduce conscription but, in 1942, he asked the country to release him from his pledge. At that time, it did not look as if the government would need to force men into the armed services. The

1915 1920 1925 1930 1935 1940 1945 1950

Canadian army in Britain was not yet fighting, but King knew the situation might change. If it did, he wanted to be ready.

The government organized a vote on the question. Across the country, 65 percent voted to let the government decide. Ontario, Manitoba, and British Columbia were 80 percent in favour of conscription. In Quebec, 72 percent were against. Many French Canadians felt they had been betrayed. King tried to reduce tensions. He used the slogan "Conscription if necessary, but not necessarily conscription."

The War Heats Up

As long as the Canadian army stayed in Britain, there was no need for conscription. Two years later, after the Italian campaign and the invasion of France, things changed. The battle for Europe had begun and the losses were high. The Canadian government tried its best to recruit men voluntarily. Only a few enlisted. In November 1944, King ordered 16 000 of the soldiers conscripted for Home Defence to go overseas.

There was an uproar. One Quebec Cabinet minister resigned, but most other French-Canadian leaders stood by King. Louis St. Laurent, King's "Quebec lieutenant," told Quebecers that the decision was necessary.

Fortunately, the war ended soon after. Only 2500 conscripts actually fought. Unlike the conscription crisis of 1917, Canadian unity was strained, but not broken.

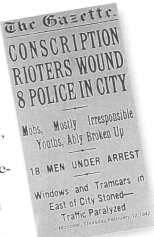

The Gazette.
CONSCRIPTION RIOTERS WOUND 8 POLICE IN CITY

Mobs, Mostly Irresponsible Youths, Ably Broken Up

18 MEN UNDER ARREST

Windows and Tramcars in East of City Stoned— Traffic Paralyzed
—Montreal, Thursday, February 12, 1942

FOCUS

1. What is conscription?
2. Why was it a sensitive issue in Canada?
3. How well did Prime Minister King handle the conscription issue? Explain.
4. Would you have supported or rejected conscription? Why?

The Italian Campaign

The Tide Turns

The tide of war began to turn in favour of the Allies in 1942. British and American troops drove back Italian and German forces in North Africa. Field Marshal Rommel, "the Desert Fox," led these enemy soldiers.

In the freezing Russian winter, German troops faced disaster. The decisive battle was fought at Stalingrad. In February 1943, the once-proud German Sixth Army surrendered. The Russians took 90 000 prisoners. Soviet forces now turned towards Berlin. They had suffered starvation, torture, and atrocities at the hands of German troops. The Soviet forces wanted to take revenge on the German people.

The Americans recovered quickly after Pearl Harbor. They repaired most of the ships sunk on that fateful December morning and put them back into action. In June, American aircraft carriers defeated the Japanese navy at Midway Island. Island by island, American troops moved closer to Japan. In China, communist and nationalist armies fought against the Japanese invaders. British and Commonwealth forces began to drive the Japanese from Southeast Asia.

Even close to enemy fire, Allied soldiers sat down for a Christmas dinner on 25 December 1943. What do you think they thought about?

The Invasion of Sicily

Canadian soldiers had not seen any action since the disastrous raid on Dieppe. Now the 1st Canadian Division took part in the invasion of Sicily under General Montgomery. The battle for Sicily was fought under the blazing July sun. Within 38 days, the victorious Allied troops prepared to invade the Italian mainland. Mussolini's dream of

a new Roman Empire was shattered. His own people rebelled and threw him out of power in 1943. Hitler swiftly moved German troops into Italy. He would not let Italy's surrender hold him back.

The Liberation of Italy

The Italian campaign was long and difficult. Ninety-one thousand Canadians fought in

Italy. More than 30 000 were wounded or killed. The German forces fought hard. A few snipers in the rugged mountains could slow an army to a crawl. Even with the help of Italian partisans, or secret supporters, the Allies paid heavily for every kilometre they won.

For Canadian soldiers, much of the Italian campaign was a street-by-street battle.

In the Battle of Ortona, 1375 Canadian soldiers lost their lives. The Germans turned the battle for the town into a series of house-to-house fights. It took a month to capture Ortona. Canadians became experts at street fighting. They developed the mouse-holing technique.

They used explosive charges to blast a hole from the attic of one house through the adjoining wall into another house. Soldiers, spraying machine-gun fire and tossing grenades, jumped through the hole. They cleared the house of Germans before moving to the next house. Because German forces tried to lure Canadians into houses wired for demolition, the end result was a town in rubble. The Germans developed such a high opinion of Canadian soldiers that they put their best troops against them whenever possible.

On 4 June 1944, the Allied armies entered Rome. Canadian soldiers marched with their British, American, New Zealand, Indian, South African, French, and Polish comrades to the cheers of the Italian people.

The Battle of Ortona was gruelling. It took the Allies a month of tough fighting to win the town.

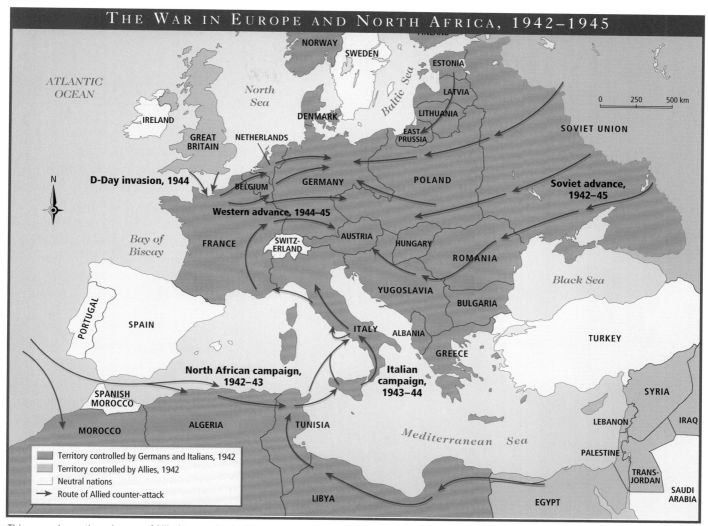

THE WAR IN EUROPE AND NORTH AFRICA, 1942–1945

D-Day invasion, 1944

Western advance, 1944–45

Soviet advance, 1942–45

North African campaign, 1942–43

Italian campaign, 1943–44

Territory controlled by Germans and Italians, 1942
Territory controlled by Allies, 1942
Neutral nations
Route of Allied counter-attack

This map shows the advance of Allied troops in the West. Russian forces were also moving in from the East.

Two days later came D-Day—the long awaited Allied invasion of France. In February 1945, Canadian troops in Italy transferred to Europe to join the Canadian army fighting to free Holland.

FOCUS

1. In what way did the tide turn in 1942?
2. What made the battle for Italy so difficult?
3. What reputation did the Canadians earn for their fighting in Ortona?

D-Day to V-E Day

Everything had been carefully planned. The tide was right. The moon was right. But would the weather be right for D-Day, the big invasion, code-named Operation Overlord, planned for 5 June 1944? Would it have to be put off for a month and kept a secret? The

As Allied soldiers crossed German borders, the end of six years of war was finally in sight.

south of England was one big army camp. Everybody knew that the invasion of France was about to begin, but only a few knew when and where the landings would be made.

On June 4, troops were ordered into the ships. Some ships set out. Suddenly, reports indicated the weather was deteriorating. The landing was postponed and the ships recalled. By next morning, violent winds were battering the coast of northern France. The troops stayed crammed aboard the ships, awaiting further orders. Then, the weather forecasters said there would be a lull in the storm. General Eisenhower, the Supreme Allied Commander, decided that D-Day would be June 6, a day later than planned.

The Normandy Beaches

Across the English Channel, the Germans were waiting at Calais. German pilots returning from bombing raids had reported that the main buildup of troops and equipment was at Dover. What they had really seen were empty tents, dummy ships, plywood gliders, and inflated rubber tanks. One of the greatest hoaxes of all time had succeeded.

The Allies struck 200 km to the southwest on the beaches of Normandy. Bombers pounded the German defences all night long. Just before dawn, paratroopers dropped behind enemy lines. The liberation of Europe had begun.

The Dieppe raid had taught the Allies that the Germans could defend any ports they tried to capture. So, they wouldn't invade a port. Two complete harbours were built in Britain, towed across the English Channel, and assembled in Normandy.

Juno Beach

There were five Allied-coded landing areas: "Utah & Omaha" for the Americans, "Gold and Sword" for the British, and "**Juno**" for the Canadians. Juno Beach was an 8 km beach near four Normandy towns. The Canadian soldiers were supported by 109 ships and 10 000 sailors of the Royal Canadian Navy. The Queen's Own Rifles landed first. They ran a 200 m dash to the cover of a seawall. Then they faced guns that had not been seen on the aerial photographs. These guns wiped out almost an entire platoon before being destroyed. It was a very hard-fought day of battle, but the Canadian troops got farther inland than the other Allied forces. However, 340 were killed and 574 wounded on that "longest day." Another 13 000 were wounded. Two nearby cemeteries contain nearly 5000 Canadians killed during the entire Normandy campaign.

Canadian forces help drive Germans from occupied Europe.

The Push to Berlin

It took 11 months before Western troops met their Soviet allies near the Elbe River in central Germany. Hitler was determined to fight to the end. Canadians were given the task of clearing German forces from the French, Belgian, and Dutch ports during the push towards Berlin. This was slow, dangerous work. Enemy forces fought from behind strong fortifications. Every port taken meant more Allied ships could unload tanks, weapons, and troops.

The ports fell, one by one. On 8 September 1944, Canadian forces entered Dieppe. This time they came by land and as conquerors. The stain of defeat was erased as they marched into the port.

Liberation of Holland

In 1945, the Canadian Army played a major role in liberating the Netherlands. The Germans had opened the dykes that held back the water from the low-lying fields. Canadian troops found

HISTOR!CA
Minutes

HISTOR!CA
Minutes

Garth S. Webb

BORN: 1918, Midland, Ontario

SIGNIFICANCE: This Canadian veteran of the Second World War led the drive to build the Juno Beach Centre in Normandy, France.

BRIEF BIOGRAPHY: Webb served in the Canadian Army and saw action on D-Day. After the war, he returned to civilian life. He graduated from Queen's University in 1947 and became a successful Toronto real estate appraiser.

In 1994, while attending the 50th anniversary ceremonies of D-Day, Webb and Lise Cooper decided to build a Canadian museum in France to honour Canada's Second World War contribution. He stated: "There's a memorial at Vimy for World War I, but there was nothing for World War II." Along with other Canadian war veterans, Webb and Cooper founded the Juno Beach Centre Association. They began the difficult task of fund-raising for the proposed museum. On 6 June 2003, the Juno Beach Centre was formally opened. Prime Minister Jean Chrétien and Garth Webb were key participants. Within two years, more than 100 000 people visited the Centre, including many Canadian school groups.

Webb's contributions to the Juno Beach Centre have not gone unnoticed. In 2002, he received the Gold Jubilee Medal. It is "presented to Canadians in recognition of a significant achievement of distinguished service to their fellow citizens, their community, or to Canada." In 2003, Governor General Adrienne Clarkson presented Webb with the Meritorious Service Cross, along with the following citation: "A veteran of the D-Day landings and of the Battle of Normandy, Garth Webb is the driving force behind the creation of 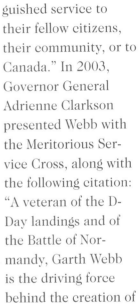 the Juno Beach Centre, an interactive education museum located on the Normandy coast of France. Mr. Webb's dedication and commitment to the Centre preserves the memory of the accomplishments and sacrifices of Canadian soldiers, sailors, and airmen on a critical day in the history of the world, and honours Canada's contribution to the Allied victory in World War II." **What role did Webb play in the Juno Beach Centre? Why is it important for Canadians today to know how earlier Canadians contributed to the Allied victory?**

CANADIAN LIVES

boats and kept moving. As Germans retreated, grateful Dutch families poured out of their homes to welcome their liberators. Even today, Canadians are warmly received in the Netherlands.

This photo, taken in May 2005, shows Governor General Adrienne Clarkson and other dignitaries unveiling a Liberation of the Netherlands commemorative plaque.

The End of the Dictators

On 27 April 1945, Mussolini was captured and shot by his own people. They strung his body upside down on a meat hook and displayed it in Milan. Three days later in his underground bunker, Hitler listened to Soviet guns bombarding Berlin. He placed a revolver in his mouth and pulled the trigger. His body was burned so that it could not be displayed by his enemies. On 8 May 1945, Germany surrendered unconditionally. It was V-E Day—Victory in Europe Day.

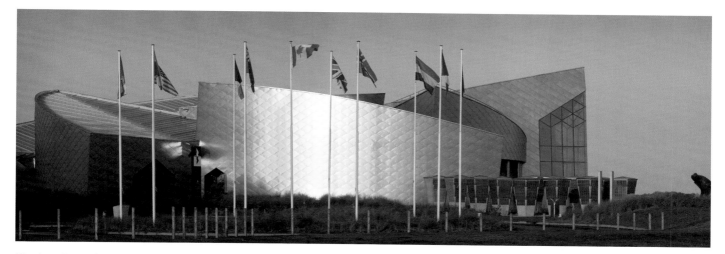

The Juno Beach Centre, in Courseulles-sur-Mer, commemorates Canada's role in the Second World War.

FOCUS

1. Why was the weather such an important factor in the planning of D-Day?
2. What preparations did the Allies make to ensure success for the invasion?
3. What role did the Canadians play after D-Day?

The Holocaust

When Hitler came to power in 1933 he began his war on the Jews. He ordered Germans to boycott Jewish stores. Laws excluded Jews from being teachers, doctors, lawyers, university students, and government employees. To get jobs as civil servants, Germans had to prove that there was no Jewish blood in their veins. Jews lost the right to vote. In many places, they were not

Near the end of the war, a Canadian war artist, Aba Bayefsky, visited Nazi concentration camps. These terrible scenes of human suffering so moved him that he spent the next 40 years of his life trying to capture the tragedy and meaning of the camps. Why does this image remain so powerful today?

allowed to use public parks, swimming pools, or sports fields. Jewish children had to attend schools for Jews only. Western nations made feeble protests against the German treatment of Jews, but took no concrete action. They even attended the 1936 Olympics in Berlin.

In May 1939, the passenger liner *St. Louis* sailed from Hamburg, Germany, with 907 Jews aboard. They were looking for a safe home far from the persecution of Nazi Germany. They tried to land in Cuba, but were turned away. They headed for the United States, but were forbidden to enter. They came north to Canada, but Canadians, too, turned them away. The Canadian prime minister, Mackenzie King, showed a strong **anti-Semitic** attitude at the time. Canada's official response to Jewish refugee applicants was: "At present, Canada is not admitting Jews. Please try some other country." The *St. Louis* returned to Europe where the Dutch, the French, and the British agreed to give its passengers a home. A year later the Germans occupied the Netherlands. The Dutch were powerless to save these and other Jews. Most of the passengers of the *St. Louis* later perished in Nazi **death camps**.

Most countries tried to keep all immigrants out during the Depression years. Many people were particularly prejudiced against Jews. In Canada, over 100 000 people signed a petition to stop Jewish immigration. Attitudes like these kept Jews from escaping Europe during the 1930s. When Hitler overran the continent, they were caught in a death trap.

The World on Trial

Kristallnacht

On 7 November 1938, a Polish-Jewish student, Herschel Grynszpan, shot a German diplomat, Ernst von Rath. When news of Von Rath's death reached Hitler, he ordered his storm troopers to wreak havoc on Jewish communities in revenge. **Pogroms** occurred throughout Germany and Austria during the night of November 9. Ninety-one Jews were killed. Hundreds were seriously injured and many more were terrorized and humiliated.

Almost 7500 businesses were destroyed and about 177 synagogues were burned to the ground. Police were ordered not to interfere. The Gestapo arrested 30 000 wealthy Jews. They were released on the condition that they leave the country and surrender their wealth to the authorities. Insurance payments to owners of businesses destroyed during that night were confiscated by police. **Kristallnacht**—the night of broken glass—marked a major escalation in the Nazi persecution of the Jews.

Concentration Camps

By 1941, the German policy was becoming clear. It wanted the outright extermination of all Jews in areas under German control. It was referred to as the "Final Solution." When Germany conquered parts of the Soviet Union, large numbers of Jews were forced into slave labour camps. The Nazis wanted a more systematic way of killing the Jews. They set up death camps, such as Dachau,

Auschwitz, and Treblinka, to quickly and scientifically kill Jews. Men, women, and children were herded into "showers" and murdered by clouds of poison gas. Later the bodies were burned in huge ovens.

LIFE IN THE GHETTOS

During the Middle Ages, places called **ghettos** were common. The purpose of these areas was to keep Jews together. Usually, ghettos were enclosed within walls or gates, which were kept locked at night. Inside, Jews had complete freedom. They had their own places of worship, schools, courts, and recreation centres. Outside, however, they were in constant danger of being assaulted. Although most ghettos were abolished during the 19th century, the Nazis revived them during the Second World War.

By 1945, over 6 million innocent Jews had died in Nazi death camps—one-third of them children. Several million other enemies of the German government also lost their lives—French, Dutch, Russians, Poles, Romas (gypsies), communists, homosexuals, and Germans who opposed the Nazi regime.

Who Bears the Guilt?

Hitler committed suicide in Berlin in 1945. Many war criminals were hunted down and punished after the war. During the Nuremberg Trials, 174 war criminals were prosecuted. Adolph Eichmann, the person in charge of the "Final Solution," was captured in 1961 in Argentina by Israeli agents. He was tried as a war criminal, found guilty, and executed. The infamous Dr. Josef Mengele, who carried out medical experiments on live Jews, was never captured. He died in South America in 1979. Some Nazis who had been part of the **Holocaust** were given forged identity papers by Allied authorities. They traded information and services for new identities. Some lived with new names in countries such as Canada and the United States.

In 2005, a famous Nazi hunter, Simon Weisenthal died. He was responsible for bringing over 1100 Nazis to justice.

Who bears the guilt?

Was it just Hitler and his fellow Nazis who gave the orders to kill? What of the guards who worked in the camps, the chemical workers who made the poison gas, or the railway workers who carried thousands to the camps? What of the ordinary citizens who watched their neighbours disappear and said or did nothing? What about those who claimed that they were innocent because they simply did what they were told? What of the nations who looked the other way before and during the war; or Canada, which refused to admit Jewish refugees in the 1930s?

Criminals in Canada

In 1987, the Canadian Parliament passed a law allowing the arrest and trial of war criminals living in Canada. Although officials attempt to locate, try, or deport these people, success is difficult to achieve. These crimes are more than 60 years old and it is hard to find witnesses. People change a great deal in more than half a century. Legal proceedings move slowly. Suspects are often too old or sick to be investigated properly.

Canadian Edgar Bronfman has fought long and hard for Jewish families. He has tried to recapture their wealth, which was stolen by the Nazis and hidden in secret Swiss bank accounts. As head of the World Jewish Congress, Bronfman forced the Swiss banks to drop their famous wall of secrecy concerning bank accounts. The Swiss have agreed to search for all that was stolen from European Jews and deposited in their accounts. They have found $300 million so far. The banks are combing the world to find the owners or their heirs. Bronfman has also taken his campaign to other nations holding money originally stolen from the Jewish community. He said, "As long as I draw breath, I will see to it that nobody profits from the ashes of the Holocaust."

The State of Israel

After the war, many Jews who survived the Holocaust wanted to escape from the persecution and destruction of Europe. Some wanted to return to what they believed was their ancestral homeland in Palestine. In the midst of a war with Egypt, Jordan, Syria, Iraq, and Lebanon, the Jewish state of Israel was proclaimed in 1948. The United States and the Soviet Union immediately recognized the new government. The State of Israel was created as a national home for the Jews. Although many survivors moved to Israel, it was not to be the land of peace that they had expected. The creation of the State of Israel greatly offended and hurt the Palestinians and neighbouring Arab countries. The resentment and conflict from this dispute has continued to the present. The progress towards peace has been long and difficult.

In Their Own Words

Some Canadian POWs (prisoners of war) found themselves in the infamous Nazi death camp of Buchenwald rather than a normal POW camp. They spent a few devastating weeks in nightmarish conditions. Here is one moving account of what they saw:

"The trip to Buchenwald was very scary. I didn't know what Buchenwald was. I don't think any of us knew what a concentration camp was at that time. When we arrived at Buchenwald, I don't think we were off the train five seconds when the fellow next to me got hit in the face with a rifle butt. The SS guard hit him because he didn't move fast enough.

First of all, they shaved us, our heads and our whole body. And then they gave us a pair of pants and a shirt and a little tiny hat. And we slept on the bare ground. This is the latter part of August, and Buchenwald is on a mountain, so it gets pretty cold. And we were there for I don't know how many nights. Quite a few, I know, and it was awful cold and uncomfortable.

I think the thing that frightened me most about it was the deaths every day. Because people would die and they would keep them in the huts to get the extra rations. And then the bodies were just thrown out on the street and a wagon came along each morning and they piled the bodies on and took them to a crematorium.... The guards were maniacs. They would think nothing of setting the dogs on a prisoner, and that would be it.

We were suffering from malnutrition, because all we got to eat was a little bowl of soup made from grass or cabbage leaves and an inch of bread and three little potatoes a day."

Source: Pilot Officer Bill Gibson, 419 Squadron, RCAF, quoted in *In Enemy Hands: Canadian Prisoners of War 1939–45* by Daniel G. Dancocks (Toronto: McClelland & Stewart, 1990).

On 10 December 1945, Canada began the first war crimes trial in its history. German General Kurt Meyer was charged with the murders of Canadian POWs. Meyer was later convicted and sentenced to death, but the sentence was never carried out.

JEWISH IMMIGRATION DURING THE 1930s

Country	Jewish Immigrants
United States	150 000
Palestine	100 000
United Kingdom	85 000
Argentina	20 000
Colombia	20 000
Mexico	20 000
Canada	4 000

What do the numbers above reveal about Canada's response to Jewish immigration before the war?

FOCUS

1. **What actions did the Nazis take against the Jews after 1933?**
2. **What is the significance of the *St. Louis*?**
3. **What was the "Final Solution"?**
4. **In your opinion, who was guilty of the mass slaughter of the Holocaust?**
5. **How should Canada deal with war criminals?**

The Mushroom-Shaped Cloud

Devastation was total in the Japanese city of Hiroshima.

On 6 August 1945, a lone American bomber, the *Enola Gay*, flew high over the Japanese city of Hiroshima. The plane dropped a single bomb, nicknamed "Little Boy." For the first time in history, an atomic bomb was unleashed on the world.

Hanging from a small parachute, the bomb drifted over the city. It exploded with a burning white flash "brighter than a thousand suns." Shock waves destroyed buildings.

The Technical Edge

Atomic Bomb The creation of the bomb brought with it great fear and uncertainty. This new technical development threatened the very existence of humankind. Canada has never manufactured or possessed nuclear weapons; however, the bombs that exploded over Japan contained uranium mined in Canada. One of the young scientists involved in the creation of the nuclear bomb was Louis Slotin of Winnipeg. Slotin was an expert at assembling the firing mechanisms for atomic

A model reveals what remained of Hiroshima after the bombing.
Are nuclear bombs still a threat in the world today?

bombs. He completed the assembly of the first test bomb in 1945. Slotin prided himself on his nerves of steel as he finished putting together the firing mechanism by hand. He called this dangerous operation, "tickling the dragon's tail." In 1946, he was going to move to Chicago for a new job. He was performing his procedure one last time when something went wrong. His screwdriver slipped and a deadly chain reaction took place. The lab was flooded in a bluish glow. Fearing an explosion, Slotin separated the materials with his bare hands. He suffered a massive dose of radiation and died within nine days.

Fireballs burned through the streets. Pieces of the city tore through the air. Finally, a huge mushroom-shaped cloud billowed over the city.

People who looked up at the sound of the explosion had their bodies melt from the heat of the blast. Skin turned black and flesh was ripped from bones. By the end of the day, 173 000 people were dead or dying. Those who died at once were lucky. Many more suffered slow, painful deaths from radiation poisoning. Decades later, deformed babies were still being born to the survivors of the Hiroshima bombing.

The United States demanded that the Japanese surrender. There was no reply. Three days later, the same horror was repeated at Nagasaki. Eighty-thousand more people were cremated in a nuclear inferno. Japan surrendered unconditionally on 15 August 1945—V-J Day.

The United Nations

Even before V-E Day, the leaders of the world were looking for a way to maintain peace in the future. The old League of Nations had failed. They would learn from its mistakes and build a better, stronger organization, the United Nations.

It was not going to be easy. The war had created new borders and new hatreds. The "old" world powers—Britain, Germany, France, and Japan—lay shattered and exhausted. Two new rival superpowers—the United States and the Soviet Union—had gained strength and influence.

The Second World War left a bitter, confused, and divided world. The shadow of the atomic bomb and a new arms race lay across it. Could the United Nations keep the peace? What role would Canada play in the new world order?

Robbie Engels moved to Canada after surviving the Holocaust. He was liberated from a Dutch concentration camp by Canadian troops. Engels spent his life ministering to the needy and underprivileged. Here, he is delivering presents for the Toronto Star's Santa Claus Fund. He worked for the Fund for more than 14 years. Why do you think Engels was so keen to "do good" in Canada?

Radar Many people feel that Canada's role in the development of radar (radio detection and ranging) contributed as much to the end of the war as the invention of the atomic bomb. In 1935, A. G. L. McNaughton, an electrical engineer, became president of the National Research Council (NRC). Eleven years earlier, McNaughton and a colleague, W. A. Steel, had patented a cathode ray tube detection finder. The cathode ray tube detection finder detected the position of radio signals. As president of the NRC, McNaughton saw the military potential of his earlier invention. The NRC did not have funding to pursue the development of radar at that time. When Canada entered the war in 1939, however, the army and the RCAF asked the NRC to develop coastal defence and airborne radar. The navy also requested radar. They were concerned about the enemy being in the water close to Halifax. This time, the government allocated substantial funds to the NRC for its research. It formed a secret Crown corporation, Research Enterprises Ltd. (REL), to manufacture any products designed or invented by scientists at the NRC. By 1940, the "Night Watchman," the first operational radar in North America, was installed in Nova Scotia.

Scientists at the NRC made another important contribution to radar development in 1943. They invented a radar unit that worked with wavelengths of 10 cm, rather than the existing 60 m. This new system, called the CDX, was developed by William Crocker Brown. It could identify very small objects. The CDX proved amazing during testing and soon became used for coastal defence. The timing could not have been better. German submarines had become a major threat to Canada's safety by 1943. Indeed, when the CDX radar was being installed on the coast of British Columbia, a submarine periscope was sighted in Canadian waters. The group hastily completed the installation. They turned on the radar unit and, sure enough, a submarine's signal was detected. They quickly alerted the military. After verifying that the submarine was unfriendly, the officers opened fire. The German submarine soon went out of the radar's range of detection. *Why was radar such an important development in the war?*

FOCUS

1. Why is the atomic bomb such a feared weapon?
2. How was Canada connected to the atomic bomb?
3. What was the chief aim of the new United Nations?
4. What new superpowers arose after the Second World War?

Sharpening Your Skills

Analysing Propaganda

THE SKILL
Recognizing and evaluating propaganda

THE IMPORTANCE
We need to be able to evaluate something that we are constantly bombarded with.

Every day we are subjected to propaganda. Advertisements cleverly try to convince Canadians to buy a particular type of shampoo, car, snack, or drink. Teachers emphasize the importance of education and staying in school. Politicians promote their particular political party.

Propaganda may be defined as the organized distribution of information designed to promote a policy, idea, belief, or cause. On a grand scale, it involves the systematic manipulation of public opinion to make people behave in a particular manner.

Wars generate the most propaganda. Each country uses propaganda as part of its military strategy. On the home front, messages are created to instill pride in the country's war effort, to build confidence, and to inspire sacrifice. Other propaganda is designed to boost the soldiers' morale. The best propaganda exploits the power of words and images to appeal to the public's heart and mind. It plays on the peoples' emotions by focusing on such symbols as national flags, families, children, homeland, and the evilness of the enemy.

During the First World War, the Canadian government forbade the publishing of more than 250 publications that it saw as pro-German, anti-British, communist, or negative to the war effort due to gory descriptions of combat. Soldiers' letters home were also subject to censorship.

As the war dragged on, and casualties mounted, Robert Borden's Conservative government began a broad propaganda campaign designed to raise morale and convince Canadians of their responsibility to contribute time, energy, and money to the war effort. Posters, songs, poems, fiction, and cartoons were essential elements in this program.

In 1942, during the Second World War, the Wartime Information Board co-ordinated all Canadian war news and information. It gave guided tours to foreign visitors, gathered and analysed Canadian news, conducted opinion polls, and provided press information. The CBC and the National Film Board were also tools for government propaganda.

To analyse propaganda, ask the questions that appear below and to the right:
- Who produced it?
- When was it produced?
- For whom was it designed (the target audience)?
- What was its purpose (its message)?
- What was the issue or event depicted?
- What symbols were used?
- What emotions were being appealed to?
- What logic was employed?

Application

This exercise is for your artistic side! Analyse the poster presented here and in the first chapter that are designed to recruit soldiers. Then create a suitable poster for either war that contains similar themes. At the bottom of your poster, discuss how it was designed to achieve its goal of encouraging young men to join the army. For additional posters, see: www.civilization.ca/cwm/propaganda.

FIRST WORLD WAR PROPAGANDA POSTER

Questions and Activities

Match the person or item in column A with the description in column B.

A	B
1. Blitzkrieg	**a)** spy training centre near Whitby
2. Little Boy	**b)** Allied retreat from France
3. The Axis	**c)** city in Italy
4. The *St. Louis*	**d)** soldiers conscripted for home defence
5. Pearl Harbor	**e)** an atomic bomb
6. Camp X	**f)** Jewish refugee ship
7. Ortona	**g)** Canadian fascist
8. Adrien Arcand	**h)** alliance led by Germany
9. Dunkirk	**i)** Allied invasion of France
10. Zombies	**j)** lightning war
11. D-Day	**k)** American naval base in Hawaii
12. Holocaust	**l)** the Nazi "war" against the Jews

Who Am I?
Identify the following people from the clues given.

1. I served as British prime minister during the Second World War. I promised the British nothing but "blood, toil, tears, and sweat." Who am I?

2. I am a Canadian scientist of Asian ancestry. My people suffered greatly in Canada during the war. Who am I?

3. I ran a brilliant spy organization during the war. In 1979, I was honoured by the government of Canada. Who am I?

4. I led Canada during the Second World War. I engineeered a solution to the conscription crisis. Who am I?

5. I grew up in Canada, but moved to Britain. I was in charge of British aircraft production during the Battle of Britain. Who am I?

6. I was a Canadian doctor who helped the Chinese in their struggle against invasion by the Japanese. Who am I?

Discuss and Debate

1. The conscription issue divided Canadians during two world wars. Arrange the classroom to look like the House of Commons. Act as a member of Parliament for a certain constituency in Canada. Be prepared to give a speech in favour of, or against, conscription during the Second World War. After the debate, hold a vote on the issue. If your class had been the House of Commons, would conscription have been introduced?

2. The decision to drop the atomic bomb on Japanese cities has often been criticized. Imagine that you are an adviser to Harry Truman, the U.S. president. Write a memo either supporting or attacking the plan to drop the bomb on Hiroshima and Nagasaki. Then hold a meeting of the president's advisers. Be prepared to defend your views.

3. Many Nazi supporters were tried for war crimes at Nuremberg after the war. Hitler, however, had committed suicide and could not be brought to trial. Imagine that Hitler had been captured alive. Organize his trial with judges and defence and prosecution lawyers. Select students to play the parts of witnesses, members of the jury, court reporters, guards, and so on.

Do Some Research

1. Find out about one of the following and write a brief report:

a) a Canadian soldier of the Second World War (perhaps a relative)

b) a famous general of the Second World War

c) some new weapons invented during the Second World War

d) a Canadian winner of the Victoria Cross in the Second World War

e) Aboriginal Canadians during the war

2. Interview someone who remembers the Second World War. Find out about that person's experiences at home in Canada or at the battle fronts of Europe, Africa, or the Pacific. Assemble a class booklet or tape of memories of the Second World War.

3. With a small group, prepare a folder on life on the Canadian home front during the Second World War. Include (a) posters, (b) pictures, (c) songs, (d) slogans, (e) brief biographies, (f) advertisements, (g) wartime regulations, and (h) ration cards.

4. Find out about one of these war figures. Write a "biocard" like the Canadian Lives feature that appears in this book:
   a) "Buzz" Beurling   b) Anne Frank
   c) Winston Churchill   d) Oskar Schindler
   e) Tommy Prince   f) other

5. Design a wall chart comparing Canada's involvement in the First World War with that in the Second World War. You may consider some of these items: (a) number of soldiers fighting, (b) number of people killed, (c) important battles, and (d) types of weapons.

6. Complete a report on the search for war criminals in Canada today. For an annual report on this process, www.cbsaasfc.gc.ca/general/enforcement/annual/menu-e.html.

Be Creative

1. Imagine you are a Canadian war correspondent. Give an on-the-spot news report about one of the following:
   a) The fall of Hong Kong
   b) The Battle of Britain
   c) The Battle of Ortona
   d) Juno Beach on D-Day
   e) The liberation of the Netherlands
   Make your report as authentic as possible. You could present it as a newspaper article, a radio report, or a news film that will be shown in a movie theatre before the main feature.

2. In a group of four or five, prepare a brief play showing a scene from the life of some Japanese Canadians during the war. Present your play to the class and watch the plays of the other groups. Discuss your reactions to the plays. You might also read *Obasan* by Joy Kogawa.

3. Make a model or draw a diagram of a ship or plane used in the Second World War. Write a brief paragraph on its role in the war.

Web Watch

Juno Beach Centre: www.junobeach.org
Department of National Defence: www.dnd.org
Japanese-Canadian Internment: www.lib.washington.edu/subject/canadian/internment/
United States Holocaust Museum: www.ushmn.org
Dieppe Raid Gallery: www.harrypalmergallery.ab.ca
Imperial War Museum: www.iwm.org.uk
CBC Digital Archives: www.cbc.ca/archives

The Digital Archives are an excellent source of audiovisual stories about the war. Consider these story files: "Life After Auschwitz," "The Italian Campaign," "Shadows of Hiroshima," "Canada's Forgotten POW Camps," "D-Day: Canadians Target Juno Beach," "1939–1945: A Soldier's War," "Fleeing Justice: War Criminals in Canada," and "Victory! The End of the War in Europe."

VINCENT MASSEY
1887-1967
GOVERNOR GOUVERNEUR
GENERAL GÉNÉRAL
1952-1959

CANADA

Vincent Massey was Canada's first native-born governor general—the 17 before him came from Britain. Massey travelled as far west as Haida villages in the Queen Charlotte Islands and as far east as outports on the Newfoundland coast. When he flew over the North Pole, he wrote: "I found it an experience as humbling as it was fascinating."

How might the role of governor general promote a sense of national community?

Chapter Four
The Baby Boom: 1945–1967

Expectations

Overall Expectations:
By the end of this chapter, you will be able to

- explain some major ways in which Canada's population has changed since 1945
- evaluate the impact of some technological developments on Canadians
- describe the impact of significant social and political movements on Canadian society
- describe how individual Canadians have contributed to the development of Canada and its emerging sense of identity

Specific Expectations:
By the end of this chapter, you will be able to

- identify groups who have come to Canada since 1945 and describe why they immigrated
- explain how the lives of teens, women, and seniors have changed as a result of major demographic shifts and social changes
- explain how some key technological developments and innovations have changed the everyday lives of Canadians since the First World War
- explain why selected social welfare programs were established in Canada
- explain how Canada's population has changed since 1945
- explain how changing economic conditions and patterns have affected Canadians

Word List

Baby Boom	**CANDU**
Capitalism	**Closure**
Cold War	**Commuter age**
Democratic socialism	**Minority government**
Public transit	**Naturalized immigrants**
Nuclear age	**Nuclear arms race**
Referendum	**Refugee**
Suburbia	**Universal welfare**
War bride	**program**

Advance Organizer

1 The war ended Newfoundland's isolation. Its location had made it a vital part of the air and sea war. After the war, Joey Smallwood encouraged union with Canada. In 1949, Newfoundland became Canada's 10th province.

31 March 1949
Smallwood, Canada's last "Father of Confederation," became the first premier of Canada's 10th province.

2 The fifties were prosperous times in Canada. Natural resources were discovered. New industries sprang up. The St. Lawrence Seaway was built. It helped materials and goods move across the Great Lakes.

3 Soldiers returning from the war were ready to get a job, get married, buy a house, and start a family. Over 4 million babies were born in Canada in the 1950s. Many people moved out to newly built suburbs.

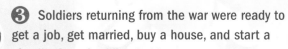

4   **5**   **6**

4 Both Liberals and Conservatives took turns leading the country. The New Democratic Party was formed in 1961. These three parties are still active in Canada today.

5 The sixties were a time of social and political protest. Much of the rebellion was focused on the Vietnam War. The lingering Cold War between the U.S.S.R. and the United States was making people afraid. The country's youth spoke up for tolerance and peace.

6 In 1965, Canada chose a new flag. In 1967, Canada celebrated its 100th birthday. Canada was developing its own unique identity.

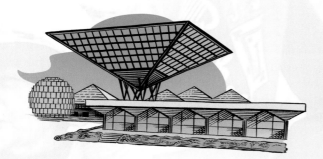

ADVANCE ORGANIZER **197**

An Uneasy Peace

In the fall of 1945, Canada once again faced a period of postwar adjustment. Soldiers, sailors, pilots, nurses, and mechanics returned home from the war. Could the Canadian economy provide jobs for the million people returning to civilian life? Would it make a smooth transition from a war economy to a consumer-based one?

Some people remembered the economic slump after the First World War and the Great Depression of the 1930s. They worried it might happen again.

The end of the Second World War brought the world to the **nuclear age**. The United States had been the first country to develop and use atomic weapons. The Soviet Union was anxious to develop its own nuclear weapons. By end of the decade, the two superpowers were involved in a **nuclear arms race**.

The war also caused friction between the powerful communist Soviet Union and its allies and the equally powerful Western democracies. Each side searched for ways to secure its territory and to extend its political influence. The **Cold War** that resulted caused worldwide fear and tension. The Cold War was not a war with bloody battles. It was a war of words, propaganda, and threats between the Soviet Union and the United States, and their allies.

This underlying insecurity made postwar adjustment challenging. Seeking revenge on Germany was not an issue, though. The Allies agreed that global economic prosperity was necessary for lasting world peace. They thought that a prosperous Europe and Japan would not be tempted by communist ideas. By helping Japan and Europe rebuild their economies,

THE IRON CURTAIN

Soviet Union
Soviet satellites
Iron Curtain

After the war, economic, social, and military barriers arose between Eastern and Western Europe. British statesman Winston Churchill described them as an "Iron Curtain." Countries behind the Iron Curtain were communist. They included East Germany, Hungary, and the Soviet Union. What does this map suggest about world tensions?

After the bombing of Pearl Harbor in 1941, Americans feared a Japanese invasion in Alaska. With Canadian consent, 11 000 American soldiers and about 16 000 Canadian and American citizens built the Alaska Highway from Dawson Creek, B.C., to Fairbanks, Alaska. The 2400 km road cut through five mountain ranges. Finished in eight months, it officially opened in November 1942. The United States paid the total cost and gave the portion built on Canadian soil to Canada in 1946. As this photo suggests, little attention was first paid to road grade. As fear subsided, time was taken to make the road easier for vehicles. Although first opened for military reasons, how might the highway benefit Canada in peaceful times?

they hoped to spread democracy throughout the world. The Soviet Union, however, was just as determined to spread its influence and communist beliefs.

America gave Europe billions of dollars to rebuild after the Second World War. The economic renewal of Europe would also help North America. Europeans would be able to buy North American products. World trade would increase. More jobs would be created.

Canada and the United States became closer during the war years. After the war, American investments in Canada's resources increased.

Canadians shared in the general prosperity. Manufacturing increased. People spent a lot of money on consumer goods. They bought cars, homes, and electric appliances. Overall, most Canadians enjoyed a good life after the war.

The de Havilland Beaver and Otter

The Beaver was an all-purpose bush plane, which first flew on 16 August 1947. The de Havilland plane was a marvel. It was able to take off in only 181 m and could carry six passengers and the pilot. This made it ideal for flights into the Canadian North. As a passenger or cargo plane, the Beaver saw service in the Arctic, the Antarctic, Africa, and the Andes

Mountains. It was popular because it was dependable and versatile. It could be outfitted with floats so that it could land on lakes. It could also be outfitted with skis so that it could land on snow. By 1965, 1600 Beavers were in operation in 63 countries. Its best customer was the United States army, which purchased

more than 900. The de Havilland Beaver and its sister plane, the Otter, are still in use today. De Havilland was a world leader in the development of STOL (Short Take Off and Landing) planes.

Maxwell (Max) William Ward was a bush pilot. He flew both the de Havilland Beaver and the Otter in the 1940s and 1950s. The twin-engine Otter was a newer, bigger plane. Max Ward's Otters played a vital role in opening up Canada's far north. He shuffled prospectors from Yellowknife, Northwest Territories, to remote areas of Arctic Canada. He put skis on his planes for the snowy winters. In the summers, Ward used floats on his planes so he could land on small northern lakes. In this way, his company could serve tourists on fishing vacations as well as mining prospectors.

Eventually, Ward focused on passenger travel. His company, Wardair, became the country's largest charter airline. By the late 1970s and 1980s, Wardair had a fleet of modern jets, including Boeing 747s. Wardair mainly serviced Canada's tour companies. Money problems forced Ward to sell Wardair to Pacific Western Airlines in 1989. ***Why are aircraft so important in a country like Canada?***

William Lyon Mackenzie King

BORN: 1874, Berlin (Kitchener), Ontario

DIED: 1950, Ottawa, Ontario

SIGNIFICANCE: King was prime minister for almost 22 years. He introduced old age pensions, unemployment insurance, and family allowances. He led Canada through the 1920s, half of the 1930s, and during the Second World War.

BRIEF BIOGRAPHY: King was the grandson of William Lyon Mackenzie, who led the 1837 Rebellion in Upper Canada. King graduated from the University of Toronto in 1895. He then studied economics at Harvard University and the University of Chicago. He entered politics shortly thereafter. He became Canada's first deputy minister of labour in 1900. In 1909, he entered Laurier's Liberal Cabinet as minister of labour. When Laurier retired in 1919, King was elected as his successor. King became prime minister in 1921.

During his time as leader of Canada, King's political views changed drastically. At first, he believed that government intervention was bad for the country. As a result, during the Depression he did little to help with people's financial problems. By 1940, however, King's views began to change. He realized that some government action was necessary to keep the country strong and secure. In 1940, he introduced unemployment insurance. After the war, he brought in family allowances.

King never married and had few close friends. Outsiders regarded him as a practical, down-to-earth, ruthless politician. Yet his diary shows that this tough political realist wept for hours over the death of his pet dog. He also believed he received messages from the spirit of his dead mother. When King retired, St. Laurent became the new leader of the Liberal Party and prime minister. **What is your personal view of King as a leader? Explain. For more information about King, visit the CBC Digital Archives at www.cbc.ca/archives and view the file "Mackenzie King: Public Life, Private Man."**

CANADIAN LIVES

FOCUS

1. Define the term *nuclear age*.
2. Explain how the nuclear age threatened world peace.
3. How did the Cold War divide Europe?
4. Give three examples of the booming postwar Canadian economy.

Newfoundland and Labrador Join Canada

Sir John A. Macdonald, the first prime minister of Canada, once said: "Canada cannot be considered complete without Newfoundland. It has the key to our front door."

Canada's land mass is huge. The island of Newfoundland juts out from the east coast of Canada into the Atlantic. Its capital, St. John's, is 5050 km from Victoria, B.C. It is closer to England than to Victoria! Over the centuries, Newfoundlanders remained isolated from mainland Canada. In 1867, only 3.9 percent of Newfoundland's imports and 0.68 percent of its exports involved Central Canada. Newfoundland remained a British colony until 1949.

Fishing for cod is an important part of Newfoundland and Labrador's past.

The people adopted a maritime lifestyle. They developed their own dialect and culture.

For centuries, Newfoundlanders hunted seal and fished for cod. Dried cod was Newfoundland's major export. In 1857, its most important markets were Brazil, Spain, Portugal, Italy, and the British West Indies. Seals also added to the economy. By the 1850s, about one-tenth of the population and up to 350 vessels were involved in the seal hunt. Seals were in demand in Britain for their skins and their fat, which made a fine-quality oil.

A variety of natural resources were found in the island's interior. Lumbering provided most of the wood islanders needed. Later, deposits of iron ore, copper, lead, and zinc created a booming mining industry. These resources were sold to Britain and the West Indies. In return, Newfoundland imported the products that it needed.

The Great Depression and Newfoundland

In 1931 Newfoundland became a Dominion, of equal status within the British Empire as Australia, New Zealand, Canada, and South Africa. The Great Depression hit the Newfoundland economy hard. Economic instability led to political crisis. In 1934 Newfoundland reverted to the status of a Crown colony. A commission to govern the colony was appointed. The commission consisted of six appointed representatives. Three were from Newfoundland and three from Britain. It was responsible solely to Britain, not to Newfoundland.

Strategic Position During the Second World War

During the Second World War, Newfoundland's isolation came to an end. Its location on the Atlantic was ideal. It became a vital part of the sea and air wars against Germany. New airport facilities were built at Goose Bay in Labrador and at Gander on the island. These were important refuelling stations. North American aircraft needed a place to stop on their way to Europe. St. John's became a headquarters for ships on convoy duty.

American military bases were built near Quidi Vidi Lake (Fort Pepperell), Stephenville (Ernest Harmon Field), and at Argentia. These military bases brought economic benefits to many communities on the island. Several military bases remained until the 1990s.

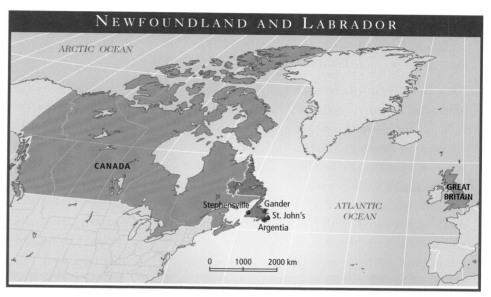

NEWFOUNDLAND AND LABRADOR

This map suggests that joining Canada was a logical choice. Note the strategic position of Gander. On 11 September 2001, the airport there served as an important gateway as it handled redirected flights during the terrorist attacks on New York.

Referendum

After the war, Britain was busy rebuilding its own country and economy. It wanted less responsibility for its colonies. It was time to set up a more democratic form of government in Newfoundland and Labrador. The people who lived there would gain more independence.

Newfoundlanders debated their options. Should they go back to "responsible self-government" and run their own affairs? Should they stay with the appointed commission responsible to Britain? Or, should Newfoundland join Canada?

Joey Smallwood

BORN: 1900, Gambo, Newfoundland

DIED: 1991, St. John's, Newfoundland

SIGNIFICANCE: He brought Newfoundland into Confederation in 1949. He is sometimes referred to as "the last Father of Confederation."

BRIEF BIOGRAPHY: Smallwood began his career as a journalist. He moved to New York City in 1920, where he wrote for a socialist newspaper. When Smallwood returned to Newfoundland in 1925, he continued his socialist activities. He became a union organizer. He also became a radio broadcaster.

In 1946, Smallwood advised the British government on what to do with Newfoundland. The British government wanted to hold a referendum on Newfoundland's political future. Britain wanted suggestions as to what choices should be placed on the referendum. Smallwood favoured Confederation. Newfoundlanders had to vote twice. In 1948, they voted in favour of Confederation. The next year, Smallwood was elected premier in Newfoundland's first provincial election.

Smallwood's government was plagued with problems and embarrassments. His attempt at forced industrialization ended in bankruptcy for most of the manufacturing plants involved. Smallwood lost the 1971 election. He resigned from politics in 1979. He published two volumes of a planned four-volume *Encyclopedia of Newfoundland*. In 1986, he was made a Companion to the Order of Canada. **How would you rate Joey Smallwood as a leader? Explain.**

CANADIAN LIVES

What do these 1943 stamps say about Newfoundland and its economy?

The people of Newfoundland voted on the three options in a referendum. No single option received a majority of the votes. A second **referendum** was held on the two most popular options—responsible government or Confederation with Canada. Pro- and anti-Confederation leaders made passionate speeches to sway voters.

Government workers thought they would lose some of their power if Newfoundland joined Canada. Merchants were afraid Canadians would move in on their markets. Fishery workers, loggers, and miners liked the economic security that Confederation would bring. Joining Canada would give them long-term benefits and stability. They could have unemployment insurance and old age pensions. Joey Smallwood, a popular broadcaster, led the campaign for union with Canada.

When the final votes were tallied, 52 percent were in favour of joining Canada and 48 percent for responsible self-government. Newfoundland and Labrador entered Confederation on 31 March 1949. Joey Smallwood became the first premier of Canada's 10th province. He became known as Canada's last Father of Confederation.

FOCUS

1. Why was Newfoundland isolated before joining Canada?
2. How did this isolation help Newfoundland develop its own culture?
3. On what types of jobs did Newfoundlanders depend?
4. List reasons why Newfoundlanders would join Canada. Suggest reasons why many opposed the union.

The Boom in Resources

The date 13 February 1947 was important in the history of Alberta. On that day, after Imperial Oil had already drilled 133 dry wells and spent $23 million looking for oil, the company finally struck "black gold." Its drilling of Leduc No.1 was the first major hit

This 1948 photo of Leduc No. 1 represents prosperity for Alberta.

in Alberta's oil fields. The discovery of oil changed Alberta's economy. It raised the standard of living of its residents.

Other American oil companies invested money in searching for oil deposits. More fields were discovered in Alberta in Redwater, Pembina, and Joffre. Oil was also discovered in Saskatchewan near Steelman and Weyburn. Natural gas was another important resource found in various areas of the West.

These fuels were used in Canada's factories and transportation systems. They also provided heat for homes, schools, and businesses. More than 20 000 oil and gas wells had been drilled in Canada by 1960. This new petroleum industry created thousands of

Mining in Canada was big business after the war. Here, trucks climb a road from an open pit mine in Sault Ste. Marie.

jobs for Canadians. As well, governments received royalties from oil companies.

Energy and Minerals

Canada also developed huge hydroelectric projects. Canada's rivers were ideal for damming. This meant they could produce hydroelectric power. Several generating stations were built in British Columbia, Labrador, Manitoba, Northern Quebec, and along the St. Lawrence River. Power lines were erected to deliver electric power to remote farming areas and towns. Many Canadians had electricity for the first time.

Prospectors found uranium deposits in several areas of Canada. Research into the peaceful use of atomic energy began. Knowledge about radiation increased. Canada became a world leader in the study of atomic energy.

The booming American economy created a demand for Canadian natural resources. War-torn Europe and Japan were rebuilding their economies. Canadian wood, coal, iron ore, aluminum, and copper were needed.

New towns sprang up in what used to be wilderness. Workers and their families had to be served. Roads, schools, hospitals, airports, and railways were quickly built. The Canadian economy was booming once again.

KEY MINERAL DEPOSITS

This map shows some of Canada's vast mineral resources in the 1950s.

FOCUS

1. **Name three energy resources that helped create an economic boom.**
2. **How does the exploration for natural resources create jobs?**

Canadian Resources and U.S. Investment

The fabulous fifties brought prosperity to some parts of Canada; however, not all Canadians shared in the economic boom. Most of the Atlantic region was barely touched by the new wealth. The Prairies still relied mainly on wheat crops. They were rich one year and poor the next because of climate changes and supply and demand in world markets.

Corporations owned many of the resource developments in Canada. They had headquarters in Toronto, Montreal, and New York. Most of the manufacturing, commercial and financial centres were located in Central Canada. This was the centre of the economic boom.

The Canadian landscape was often treated with little respect. Developers tore the wealth from the earth. They left behind open pit mines and clear-cut logging areas that scarred the land. They polluted the rivers and the air. They did not worry about the environment. Governments and most citizens were not yet concerned about environmental protection.

Prosperity had a price. Americans owned and controlled much of the natural resource industry. By 1956, American companies controlled over half of the manufacturing companies in Canada. Of the 60 largest firms in Canada, fewer than 30 were Canadian owned. The trend was increasing. Were Canadians losing control of their economy?

Pipelines have become as important to the Canadian economy as railroads were in the past.

The Pipeline Debate

Oil and gas had to get from western Canada to Ontario and Quebec. Using the railroad was not a practical way to move large amounts of oil. The best way seemed to be by pipeline. To build a trans-Canada pipeline would be expensive and would take a long time.

The first proposed oil pipeline was routed, in part, through the United States. St. Laurent's Liberal government preferred an all-Canadian route. A Canadian route, however, would be longer and would increase construction costs.

C. D. Howe, minister of Trade and Commerce, agreed to lend money to construction companies to cover the extra costs. The Conservatives and the CCF objected. They claimed that Canadian money was financing American construction companies. An emotional debate followed in Parliament. St. Laurent's Liberal government cut the debate short. It used a controversial procedure known as **closure**, which limited debate in Parliament. In the end, the loan was approved. In 1956, the construction of the Trans-Canada pipeline resumed. By 1960,

The final weld on the Trans-Canada pipeline was made at Kapuskasing, Ontario, October 1958.

the 3600 km pipeline connected Alberta oil fields to Ontario and Quebec consumers.

Conservatives and CCF politicians were concerned about American control of Canada's economy. Canadians, too, were worried about the limit on democratic debate (closure). People saw this as a heavy-handed dictatorial approach. In the 1957 election Canadians voted for change. They voted against the Liberal government and elected John Diefenbaker's Progressive Conservatives.

Nuclear Energy In 1942, the National Research Council (NRC) asked a group of Canadian and British scientists to research peaceful uses of nuclear energy. In 1945, the ZEEP (Zero Energy Experimental Pile) reactor began operation. The reactor was built at Chalk River, Ontario, about 200 km east of Ottawa. Six years later, the reactor laboratories in Chalk River produced the world's first cobalt radiotherapy treatment for cancer. Today, Atomic Energy of Canada Limited (AECL), which took over the Chalk River project in 1952, produces over 80 percent of the world's medical cobalt.

In 1962, a nuclear power demonstration reactor was built in Rolphton, Ontario. By 1967, Ontario's Douglas Point **CANDU** reactor was producing electricity, and by 1971, so was a CANDU reactor in Pickering.

Today, more than 30 CANDU reactors operate in Canada and abroad. AECL has helped build CANDU reactors in India, Pakistan, Romania, Korea, China, and Argentina. This type of reactor needs to be close to water.

AECL continues its nuclear research program at Chalk River Laboratories in Ontario. Until about 1998, it also operated Whiteshell Nuclear Research Establishment in Manitoba. These laboratories specialized in research about storage of used nuclear fuel (waste).

Canada has the expertise and resources needed to build nuclear weapons, but it chooses not to do so. Canada is one of the few industrialized nations that voluntarily does not have such weapons. Canada has signed international agreements against the spread of nuclear weapons.

At left is Canada's first large research reactor, NRX, developed to produce plutonium-239 for nuclear weapons, but turned to peacetime uses; at right is a close up of the powerful MAPLE reactor, which, when finished, will be dedicated to medical isotope production. Both projects have been based at Chalk River.

C. D. Howe

BORN: 1886, Waltham, Massachusetts

DIED: 1960, Montreal, Quebec

SIGNIFICANCE: Clarence Decatur Howe was an American by birth, but a Canadian by choice. He was called the "minister of everything." During the Second World War, Howe mobilized Canada to produce war materials.

BRIEF BIOGRAPHY: Howe graduated from Boston Tech in 1907. He then taught civil engineering at Dalhousie University in Halifax, Nova Scotia. In 1913, he moved to Thunder Bay, Ontario, to build grain elevators. "I've never seen one of these things in my life," he admitted, "but I'll take the job." From 1913 until 1929, Howe built grain elevators all across Canada. When his business collapsed during the Depression, he entered politics. In 1935, Howe was elected as a Liberal. He served as a Cabinet minister under Prime Ministers King and St.

Laurent. He helped set up the CBC and Trans-Canada Airlines.

Howe's most important contribution came during the Second World War. Howe got government, industry, and labour to work together to support the war effort. Under his expert command, tanks, planes and ships rolled out of factories to be used overseas in Europe.

During the Korean War in 1951, he was made minister of defence production. In 1954, Howe determined the route for the Trans-Canada pipeline, which ran from Alberta to central Canada. To get the pipeline construction started, Howe arranged a huge government loan. He forced this through Parliament by using closure. Howe was defeated in the 1957 election mostly over the closure issue. He then retired from politics. **In your view, what was C. D. Howe's major contribution to Canada?**

CANADIAN LIVES

FOCUS

1. **Why was a pipeline necessary?**
2. **Why was it initially built through American territory?**
3. **Explain what closure is. Do you think it should be used in Parliament?**
4. **Why were American companies investing in Canada's resources? Does this continue today?**
5. **Which regions of Canada prospered most? Which prospered least? Why?**

The St. Lawrence Seaway

The St. Lawrence River was swift and rugged. From Jacques Cartier's arrival in 1535 until the 1950s, the Lachine rapids prevented travel upstream from Montreal. The opening of the St. Lawrence Seaway in 1959 changed everything. Ships could now travel from Lake Superior to the Gulf of the St. Lawrence. The Seaway was a vital part of Canada's booming post-war years.

Construction of the St. Lawrence Seaway began in the 1950s. It was an example of economic co-operation between Canada and the United States. The Great Lakes provided water access into the interior of both countries. Grains, minerals, and manufactured products had to find a way to their markets. The Great Lakes were deep enough to take seagoing vessels, but their location provided challenges.

Throughout the 1800s, investors on both sides of the border understood the benefits of canals. Between 1855 and 1900, canals were built between Lake Superior and Lake Huron in the Sault Ste. Marie area. In 1824, construction of the Welland Canal began in Ontario. This 42 km water route connected Lakes Erie and Ontario. It bypassed Niagara Falls. As commerce increased, the canal was rebuilt several times. By 1932, the Welland Canal was large enough to hold ocean-going vessels. It could handle vessels 23 m wide and 225 m long.

Canada needed the seaway. The Prairie provinces had to ship their agricultural products to markets in the east. New mines in Quebec and Labrador needed a way to get their

Ships waiting for the opening of the St. Lawrence Seaway.

minerals to plants in Hamilton, Toronto, and Chicago.

Americans and Canadians had discussed the possibility of a joint venture on several occasions. One agreement to build a seaway was defeated in the American Senate in 1932. The idea was brought up again in 1940. Pressure from American railway and mining companies in the eastern states prevented an agreement.

Canada finally decided to build the seaway on its own. This decision caused the United States to think about the seaway again. An agreement was reached in 1954. Each country would pay for and build sections of the seaway in its territory. Costs of common sections on the St. Lawrence River would be shared.

When they built the seaway, workers required heavy equipment. Planners, therefore, decided to build power-generating stations at the same time. Hydroelectric stations were planned for Ontario and Quebec. They would provide economic and social benefits to Canadians living along the St. Lawrence River.

Rapids made construction difficult. Lands were flooded and 6500 Canadians had to find new places to live. Construction costs were high. Nevertheless, the project was

A construction site of the massive St. Lawrence Seaway project, 1957.

completed. In 1959, Queen Elizabeth II and the American president, Dwight Eisenhower, officially opened the St. Lawrence Seaway.

THE ROLE OF THE SEAWAY

The opening of the 3790 km long St. Lawrence Seaway in 1959 signalled the end of a mammoth engineering and construction effort between Canada and the United States. The Seaway serves the provinces of Ontario and Quebec, and the states of Illinois, Michigan, Ohio, Indiana, Wisconsin, Minnesota, New York, and Pennsylvania. Seaway traffic also travels to and from overseas ports in Europe, the Middle East, and Africa.

The Seaway's economic impact on Canada and the United States is huge. It makes a key contribution to the basic industries of both countries. It makes possible the shipping of bulk commodities at reasonable rates. Earlier, it permitted the iron ore deposits of Quebec and Labrador to be exploited. This development turned Canada from an importer to an exporter of iron ore.

Today, about 50 million tonnes of cargo move through the St. Lawrence section of the Seaway annually. That is more than four times the amount that moved through the Seaway in the late 1950s. Ships sailing the Seaway carry grain, iron ore, coal, and steel, and other cargo or finished goods, such as chemicals and lumber. Many specialized lakers have self-unloading capability at ports.

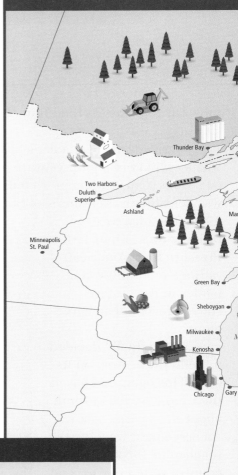

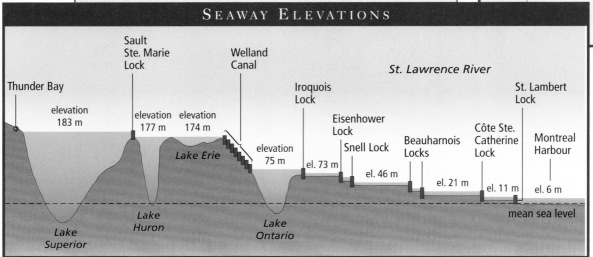

Where would Niagara Falls be located? What is the difference in elevation between Lakes Ontario and Superior?

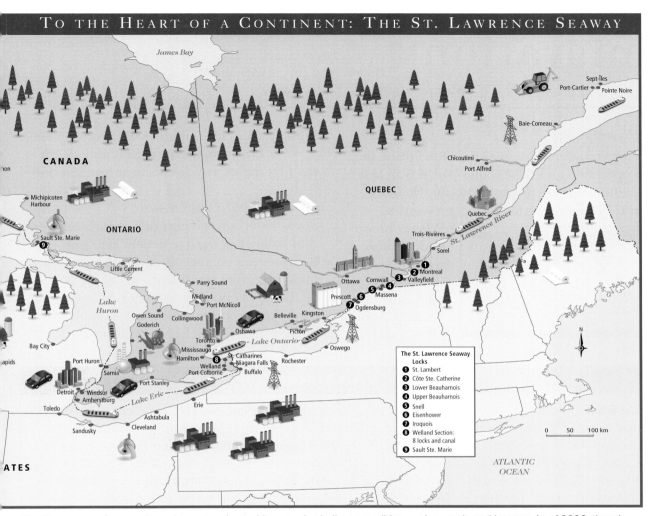

TO THE HEART OF A CONTINENT: THE ST. LAWRENCE SEAWAY

James Bay

Sept-Îles
Port-Cartier   Pointe Noire

Baie-Comeau

CANADA

Chicoutimi
Port Alfred

QUEBEC

Michipicoten
Harbour

Quebec

ONTARIO

Trois-Rivières   St. Lawrence River

Sault Ste. Marie   ❾
Sorel

Little Current
Ottawa   Cornwall   ❶ Montreal
❸ Valleyfield
❷

Parry Sound   ❹
❺ Massena
Midland   Prescott   ❻
Port McNicoll   ❼ Ogdensburg

Owen Sound   Collingwood   Kingston
Goderich   Belleville
Oshawa   Picton

Lake
Huron

Bay City   Toronto
Mississauga   Oswego
Port Huron   Hamilton   ❽ St. Catharines
Sarnia   Welland   Rochester
Niagara Falls
Port Colborne   Buffalo

The St. Lawrence Seaway Locks
❶ St. Lambert
❷ Côte Ste. Catherine
❸ Lower Beauharnois
❹ Upper Beauharnois
❺ Snell
❻ Eisenhower
❼ Iroquois
❽ Welland Section: 8 locks and canal
❾ Sault Ste. Marie

Detroit   Port Stanley
Amherstburg   Erie
apids   Windsor
Toledo   Lake Erie
Ashtabula
Sandusky   Cleveland

N

0   50   100 km

ATES

ATLANTIC
OCEAN

The St. Lawrence Seaway depends most on large ships carrying bulk commodities, such as grain and iron ore. As of 2006, though, plans were under way to encourage smaller container ships, especially from China, to use the Seaway. For example, a large ship could carry about 6000 containers to Halifax; then, smaller ships could carry about 800 containers each upstream to ports such as Toronto and Chicago. The Seaway typically opens in late March.

FOCUS

1. **List three reasons why Canada needed the seaway.**
2. **Suggest reasons why Canadians and Americans could not agree.**
3. **How did Canadians and Americans decide to pay for the seaway's construction?**
4. **How did the seaway change the life of people living in towns along its path?**
5. **What industries make use of the seaway?**

Immigration

War Brides

Few immigrants came to Canada during the Depression and the Second World War. Many soldiers serving in Great Britain, Holland, and Belgium married European women. When the war ended, these **war brides** joined their husbands in Canada. About 48 000 war brides and 21 000 children came to Canada.

War brides and their children made up the first major wave of postwar immigration.

Country	Number of Wives	Number of Children
Great Britain	44 886	21 358
Holland	1 886	428
Belgium	649	131
France	100	15
Other	72	28

Refugees and Immigration

Since 1948, a basic part of Canada's immigration policy has been to accept refugees. Refugees are people who flee their countries to escape cruel treatment.

Some people who immigrated to Canada came from communist countries such as Poland, Yugoslavia, Latvia, and Hungary.

In Their Own Words

A War Bride Remembers

"My husband decided to take me to visit his sister in Saskatchewan. He was hoping to make farming our future, and I was to get a first-hand look.

To me it seemed like the end of the world— great stretches of land and sky, neighbours and towns miles away.

I was scared of the livestock, the outdoor toilet didn't help matters and the quietness was something I wasn't used to. I'd come from Wolverhampton and for the first time I began to miss the things of home: the pubs, the movie shows, big stores, dances and the faster pace of life. The loneliness was unbearable at times and I became very homesick. I was also pregnant and physically ill. But I had to forget my misery and pitch in and help. Harvest was in full swing, and meals had to be prepared and taken out to the fields ...There was no time for self-pity.

We went back to B.C. but were unsettled and decided to move in with the in-laws in central Alberta, the land of mixed farming. I wasn't prepared for the long, cold winter with bitter winds, drifting snowstorms and temperatures of 40 and 50 degrees below zero at times. And living with the in-laws was not that easy. The house was cold and draughty. Water had to be hauled daily, along with wood for the stove and pot-belly heater. At night the heater had to be kept low as a precaution against overheating the pipes. In the morning we'd get up to frozen water pails and ice-cold floors."

What proof is there that the writer is a city woman? How do you know she suffers from loneliness?

Source: From *The War Brides* by Joyce Hibbert (Toronto: Peter Martin Associates), page 101.

They wanted a new life. They felt that Canada, with its new mines and factories, offered opportunity. They brought with them a strong belief in democracy. Gradually, the numbers of immigrants from Italy, Greece, and other parts of Southern Europe increased, too. As a result, the character of cities, such as Toronto and Montreal, changed. Canada began to lose its largely British and French nature. By 1951, only 47 percent of Canadians had their roots in Britain. The multicultural society had arrived.

These Hungarian refugees were among Eastern Europeans who did not want to live under communist rule. They sought a better life in Canada.

Canadian Citizenship Before 1947, there was no such thing as "Canadian citizenship." Native-born Canadians were considered British subjects. **Naturalized immigrants** were those who had lived in Canada for at least five years without criminal records. The Citizenship Act of 1947 gave Canadian citizenship to all Canadian-born residents and naturalized immigrants. Some say that the Citizenship Act helped establish a Canadian identity.

IMMIGRATION TO CANADA BY YEAR

1901	55 747	1906	211 653
1913	400 870	1914	150 484
1919	107 698	1929	164 993
1934	12 476	1942	7 576
1948	125 414	1951	194 391
1957	282 164	1964	112 606
1974	218 465	1980	143 117
1994	216 988	1996	194 451

FOCUS

1. Explain the term *war brides*.
2. What is a refugee?
3. How did postwar immigration change the nature of the Canadian population and society?
4. Turn the table of immigration to Canada into a graph.

The Baby Boom

The Second World War had interrupted life for Canadians. Those who had served overseas were eager to return home, get married, and start a family. As the country's economy began to grow, so did the size of Canadian families. During the **baby boom**, annual births in Canada rose from an estimated 300 000 in 1945 to over 400 000 by

1952. It seemed like babies were everywhere. In 1941, children under 5 made up 9.1 percent of the population. By 1951, they made up 12 percent. By the mid-1960s, more than half of Canada's population was under 25.

When Canadian soldiers returned home from overseas, women were expected to return to the home. They were seen as the natural guardians of the family. During the war, they had taken part in the workforce.

Social attitudes towards women, however, had not really changed. A 1944 Gallup poll indicated that 75 percent of Canadian men and 68 percent of women believed that men should be given preference in employment. Dorise Nielsen, an MP from Saskatchewan, said sarcastically, "Well, girls, you have done a nice job: you looked very cute in your overalls ... but just run along; go home." Married women were once again barred from the civil service. They would not return until 1955.

The new family allowance system was designed to reduce women's need to work outside the home. The federal government ended the daycare programs it had started during the war.

The number of women who worked outside the home dropped from 34 percent in 1944 to 24 percent in 1946. Television shows, such as *The Adventures of Ozzie and Harriet, I Love Lucy,* and *Father Knows Best,* made it clear that good wives and mothers stayed at home. Fashions that now emphasized rounded shoulders, full busts, and willowy waists suggested the same.

Women at home took their job seriously. They worked about 99 hours a week cleaning, cooking, shopping, and looking after their children. Babies became a popular topic of conversation. Child-rearing advice appeared regularly in magazines and newspapers. Discipline was more relaxed.

Play was seen as an important step in a child's physical and intellectual development. Building blocks, dolls, and trucks had an educational as well as a recreational value. Manipulating wooden blocks into castles and buildings helped develop a child's motor coordination. The toy industry boomed. Families spent much more money on children's recreational needs.

During the baby boom, school enrolments soared.

Education

The boom in babies pushed school enrolment levels sky high. School enrolment increased by 668 000 students between 1951 and 1955. By 1961, it had increased another 1.2 million. More and more schools were built. More and more teachers were hired to teach all the children attending those schools.

When the grandparents of these youngsters had attended school, most had stayed in school for an average of six years. Education was a luxury few could afford. Children helped at home or with the crops. In 1951, more than one-half of Canadians had finished nine grades of schooling or less. The baby boomers believed that education was a right. Students began to stay in school longer. High school and university now seemed open to many more people.

FOCUS

1. Explain the term *baby boom*.
2. How did the baby boom change Canada's education system?
3. How did the baby boom change the nature of Canadian society?
4. Why was education becoming more important?

The Coming of Suburbia

By the 1950s, a car was often a necessity.

American influence continued to increase in the 1950s. The American car was the perfect example. Canadian-owned automobile companies did not exist. Automobiles became the focal point of life in North America. Even city planning focused on the car. A national road-building boom took place. Local highways connected suburbs to cities and to new shopping malls. Expressways connected major cities. Road construction created many jobs and contributed to the general prosperity. The Trans-Canada Highway, opened in 1962, helped link the entire country.

The car came to symbolize one's personal space. As freeways grew, North America became a drive-in culture. People drove everywhere. They drove to work, schools, shopping malls, movies, and restaurants. As people travelled more, chain stores became popular. Society became "car friendly" and **public transit** declined in some cities and towns.

The 1950s saw other important changes in Canadian lifestyles. Families moved farther away from downtown areas. As the population increased, new subdivisions were constructed in areas just outside the cities. These areas became known as **suburbia**. The **commuter age** had begun. Residents drove as much as one to two hours to and from work. The suburbs offered single-family homes with more space. Their construction created thousands of jobs. Schools, stores, hospitals, utilities, and recreation facilities had to be provided.

Toronto's subway line provided some commuters with an alternative. Here, Yonge Street is planked to allow traffic on top of the construction.

Canada's first subway system was started in Toronto in 1949. In four years, 7.4 km of subway line stretched south from Eglinton Avenue to Union Station, the train station. Teams of skilled workers and labourers, many of whom were newly arrived immigrants, did the job. The line was later extended north, and an east—west line built.

Although public transit was on the rise in Toronto, most people in the 1950s would likely have preferred a sporty car.

Canadian Vision

Welfare Programs

Canada has government programs to help citizens live better lives. These plans are sometimes called welfare programs. After the war, they expanded greatly.

UI: The Unemployment Insurance Act of 1941 was originally passed to help blue-collar, or factory, workers who were out of work. It gave them money between jobs. By 1971, funds became available to all workers. In 1996, an employment insurance (EI) program came into effect. It places more emphasis on retraining.

BABY BONUS: To calm fears of an economic depression, the government passed the Family Allowance Act in 1944. Family Allowance became better known as the "Baby Bonus." It gave families $5 to $8 monthly for each child under 16. In 1973, the top age was changed to 18, as long as the children were students. The Baby Bonus was Canada's first **universal welfare program**. All families received it, no matter how much money they had. By 1993, it was phased out. The Child Tax Benefit Plan replaced it.

FOCUS

1. Define *suburbia*.
2. What is meant by the "commuter age"?
3. In the 1950s, why did the car become so necessary?
4. In your opinion, which is more important—public transit or the car? Explain.
5. What do you think are the pros and cons of social welfare policies?

Television and Entertainment

After the war, everyone wanted a television. Unlike radio waves, television signals do not follow the curvature of the earth. The higher the transmission tower was, the greater the signal's strength. As a result, television did not penetrate into Canada as well as radio. By

Here, Malcolm X is the "mystery guest" on Front Page Challenge. Why do you think Canadians enjoyed the program?

1948, television sets were expensive, and there were only about 3600 of them. In 1952, fewer than 10 percent of Canadian homes had a television. By 1960, it was 80 percent.

In the 1950s, adults and children spent many hours watching TV. They could now watch variety shows, sports, politics, and news every day. At last, Canadian sports fans could see hockey games. Before TV, they

tuned in to the radio to hear Foster Hewitt tell them what was happening on *Hockey Night in Canada*. In 1952, Foster Hewitt first appeared on television to report on hockey games on CBC. At first, the National Hockey League worried that fans would stay at home to watch the game rather than go to the rink. *Hockey Night in Canada* became the CBC's most popular TV show. The prospect of even greater television revenues prompted the NHL's expansion in 1967.

Programs reflected family values of the times. American shows, such as *I Love Lucy* and *My Three Sons*, attracted millions of viewers. These programs showed ideal, white, middle-class families. Everyone got along and all the problems were worked out. Many programs targeted children. *Howdy Doody*, Disney's *Mickey Mouse Club*, and Saturday morning cartoons were popular. For Canadians, television also represented a cultural threat. Would Canadian children be influenced by American ideas and values?

Content for Canadians

In the 1950s, Canadian television took on a larger role. Some programs produced in that decade were very popular with Canadians. *Front Page Challenge* debuted in 1957 and aired until 1995. Panelists included Pierre Berton, Gordon Sinclair, Betty Kennedy, and

Charles Templeton. Guests ranged from Gordie Howe to Martin Luther King to Sir Edmund Hillary. *La Famille Plouffe*, written by Roger Lemelin in 1948, made its debut on CBC in 1953. It was the first serial show on Canadian TV and was broadcast in English and French.

Another popular show during the 1950s was *Our Pet, Juliette*. This variety show was hosted by Manitoba singer Juliette Augustina Sysak. She was perhaps one of Canada's first superstars. Juliette entertained audiences for over 20 years. *The Nature of Things* first aired on CBC in 1960. Its focus is environmental and scientific issues. More than 40 years later, with David Suzuki the host since 1970, it is still running.

Some Canadian entertainers enjoyed huge success south of the border, too. John Wayne and Frank Shuster met at the University of Toronto. During the Second World War, they wrote and performed comedy for the *Army Show*. The two men continued to perform together after the war, first on radio and later on TV. The comedy duo delighted Canadian and American audiences for years with their zany, slapstick comedy routines.

LEFT: La Famille Plouffe *was a popular CBC family drama.*
ABOVE: *Wayne and Shuster are perhaps Canada's best-remembered comedy duo.*

Wayne and Shuster performed on the popular American *Ed Sullivan Show*. By 1970, they had appeared a record-breaking 67 times.

A *Medium for Advertising*

Television became a powerful advertising medium. Most advertising was aimed at the young. Playdough, Frisbees, and hula hoops became popular with boys and girls. In 1959, the first Barbie doll was sold. Barbie was also popular with Canadian children. Most of these products were made from plastic. It was the new wonder product. Television emphasized the age of consumerism.

The Teenager A new species of person, known as a *teenager*, appeared in the 1950s. In earlier times, a child had gone straight from school to adulthood. The new prosperity meant parents could afford schooling for their children. Students could finish high school and some could go to college or university. This new group of students were certainly not children, but they were not adults, either. About 1.3 million teenagers were in the country by the end of the decade. They created their own culture.

This energetic group soon made its presence felt. Teenage fads in boys' hairstyles ranged from crew-cuts (short and bristly) to duck-tails (long and greasy). Girls wore bobby sox, sweater sets, and ruby red lipstick. Fitting in with the crowd was all-important. A teenager's greatest fear was to be thought "an oddball."

Teenagers danced to a new form of music. Some parents and church ministers did not like it, but rock 'n' roll was here to stay. Each week, teenagers waited to hear which of their idols had tunes in the Top Ten. Would it be Elvis Presley, Connie Francis, or Buddy Holly? Would it be a Canadian star, like Paul Anka or Juliette? Many Canadian teens loved the TV show *American Bandstand*. It broadcast the latest music and dances every day at 3 p.m.

Adults, then as now, did not always understand teenagers. For some, the "generation gap" became a matter of concern. Businesses, though, were quick to recognize that teenagers were becoming an economic force. Marketing executives targeted teens for clothing styles, running shoes, music records, and newly invented portable radios. **What do businesses try to sell to teenagers today? How successful are they?**

Here, teenagers enjoy a rock 'n' roll concert. They might have been listening to Canadian Paul Anka, a 1950s teen idol.

Canadian Vision

Live Theatre in a Tent

Television did not hold sway over all of Canadian society, though. Some citizens wanted more than just TV shows. They wanted live theatre and the best possible.

In 1951, a businessman dreamed of having an annual drama festival and formed a local committee. A year later, Tyrone Guthrie, a leading British director, agreed to serve as artistic director. The businessman was Tom Patterson. His town was Stratford, Ontario.

"The tent must have flowers planted around it. We don't want people to think it's a circus." That's what Guthrie said when what is now the Stratford Shakespearean Festival opened with two plays in a tent. In July 1953, the theatre presented Shakespeare's *Richard III* and *All's Well That Ends Well*. Its season was just six weeks.

The idea caught on. The seasons lengthened. By 1957, the tent was replaced by the Festival Theatre, designed by Canadian architect Robert Fairfield. The shape of the theatre's roof reflects its tent heritage. This theatre now seats about 1800. Directors, such as Michael Langham and Robin Phillips, succeeded Guthrie. Canadian actors, such as Christopher Plummer, Martha Henry, and Douglas Campbell, performed at Stratford. It grew to four theatre spaces; its season runs from May to early November.

But this might not have happened but for another vision for Stratford. In 1913, citizen Frank Orr fought against putting railway tracks along the Avon River. He persuaded enough citizens to protect the town's park system instead. Now, thousands of people come to Stratford to see the plays *and* to enjoy the town's beauty. **How does the story of the Stratford Festival reflect more than one vision?**

HISTOR!CA
Minutes

Sculpture of raising the first tent.

FOCUS

1. List some popular television shows of the 1950s.
2. Compare teen culture in the 1950s with teen culture today.
3. What is meant by the term *generation gap*? What proof is there that it exists today?

Canada and the Cold War

The 1950s offered excitement, but also brought fear. The Cold War between the U.S.S.R. (Union of Soviet Socialist Republics) and the United States made Canadians nervous and edgy. It was a war of words, propaganda, and espionage.

Canadians fought many fierce battles in the Korean War.

After the Second World War, Western democracies became concerned about the military expansion of the Soviet Union. The Soviet Union had been an ally during the war. After the war, the Soviet Union wanted to take advantage of the disruption and poverty in Europe. It hoped to use this condition to expand its control. Western democracies did not want this to happen. The United States felt that Soviet control in eastern Europe would mean a rise in communism. As a capitalist country, it did not want to see this.

The tensions of the Cold War continued throughout the 1950s. Americans and Soviets raced to develop new weapons of mass destruction. Each country was trying to outdo the other. In 1952, the United States exploded the first hydrogen bomb. In 1957, the Soviets successfully launched Sputnik. This was the world's first manned spacecraft to leave the earth's atmosphere. The Americans acted quickly. They developed spacecraft and inter-continental missiles with nuclear warheads. This nuclear arms race left many fearing that the world was on the verge of nuclear war.

Korean War Soviet—American tension was high in 1950. Soviet-controlled North Korea invaded American-supported South Korea. Many believed this was the first step to a world war between communism and capitalism. The Canadian government didn't want to send troops. It remembered the conscription crisis of the Second World War. It eventually sent a brigade to serve with UN forces in Korea. Twenty-two thousand Canadians fought in that war. Of that number, 309 were killed, 1202 injured, and 32 became POWs. The Korean War lasted until 1953.

Espionage was also a real threat. In 1945, a clerk at the Russian Embassy in Ottawa, Igor Gouzenko, proved there were Soviet spies in Canada. This brought the Cold War directly home to Canadians. The Soviets were trying to steal atomic secrets. The Americans arrested and executed Ethel and Julius Rosenberg in 1953 for their espionage activities. They supposedly passed atomic secrets to the Soviet Union. The threat of nuclear war was not taken lightly. Some Canadians even built bomb shelters in their basements. Some cities installed air raid sirens.

COLD WAR ALLIANCES

NATO

In 1949, Canada and the Unites States joined with 10 Western European countries to form the North Atlantic Treaty Organization (NATO). Its purpose was to defend Europe and the North Atlantic from Soviet aggression. In 1955, the Soviet Union formed its own alliance with the Soviet satellite countries in Eastern Europe. It was called the Warsaw Pact. In the event of attack by NATO countries, Warsaw Pact members agreed to come to one another's defence.

NORAD

In 1957, Canada and the United States signed what was first called the North American Air Defence Agreement (NORAD). Its original purpose was to protect North America from a Soviet attack. Everyone was worried about a nuclear war. The NORAD agreement put Canadian and American fighter planes, missile and radar units under a single command centre. This centre is located deep inside a mountain in Colorado. The commander-in-chief is an American general. A Canadian general serves as deputy commander. Both are always in direct contact with the American president and the Canadian prime minister.

Soviet clerk Igor Gouzenko was so fearful for his life that he never revealed his face in public. He defected to Canada and wrote two books. The Fall of a Titan *won the Governor General's Award for fiction in 1954.*

DEW

In 1957, the United States and Canada built a long line of radar warning stations. The stations stretched from Alaska to Baffin Island. These were known as Distant Early Warning (DEW) stations. They were built to monitor airspace activity. If any of the 50 stations detected missiles or aircraft of unknown origin, it sent a message to NORAD headquarters in Colorado.

Louis St. Laurent

BORN: 1882, Compton, Quebec

DIED: 1973, Quebec City, Quebec

SIGNIFICANCE: St. Laurent was Canada's second French-Canadian prime minister. He began construction of the Trans-Canada Highway and the St. Lawrence Seaway. He also led the country through a period of great economic growth.

BRIEF BIOGRAPHY: St. Laurent was born to a French-Canadian father and an Irish mother. The children spoke French to one parent and English to another. When he entered school, St. Laurent realized how unique his bicultural family was. He graduated from Laval University in 1905 with a law degree. In 1941, Prime Minister King asked St. Laurent to become minister of justice in his Liberal government. St. Laurent accepted. He was elected to the House of Commons the following year. He supported King's position on conscription.

He represented Canada at the meeting to establish the United Nations. In 1946, King made St. Laurent secretary of state for external affairs. St. Laurent was a strong believer in Canada's membership in NATO. He felt that Canadians must oppose commu-

nism alongside its allies. In 1948, when King retired from politics, St. Laurent became the new Liberal leader. He won sweeping victories in the 1949 and 1953 elections.

As prime minister, he was responsible for making the Supreme Court of Canada the final court of appeal. Until then that had been the British Privy Council. He made the old age pension universal at age 70. He promoted immigration. He appointed the first Canadian-born governor general, Vincent Massey. He created the Canada Council and CBC TV. He also started construction of the St. Lawrence Seaway and the Trans-Canada Highway. Also, a 1957 Act gave federal money to provinces for hospital insurance programs.

In 1957, however, in response to problems related to the Trans-Canada pipeline, St. Laurent was narrowly defeated by John Diefenbaker's Conservatives. At the age of 74, he retired from politics and returned to law. He died in 1973. For someone who once said, "I know nothing of politics and never had anything to do with politicians," St. Laurent proved to be an able national leader. **In your view, what are St. Laurent's most important accomplishments?**

CANADIAN LIVES

The Diefenbunker In 1959, fear of a nuclear war was high. It prompted the Canadian government to build a massive underground bomb shelter in the town of Carp, near Ottawa. The secret project aroused much interest from local residents and the media because of its size. The government said that it was just a communications centre.

In the event of a nuclear emergency, Canada's prime minister, Cabinet ministers, and the nation's top military officials would be flown to the site by helicopter. These leaders would then communicate to the rest of the country from the safety of the shelter. It was called the Diefenbunker. Named after Prime Minister John Diefenbaker, it took two years to build. The Diefenbunker was a four-storey structure built totally underground. It was surrounded by 1.5 m of shock-absorbing gravel. All machinery in the bunker (from simple fans to huge diesel generators) was positioned on specially designed springs. This was done to cushion it from the concrete floor.

The underground structure did not need heating or air conditioning. An advanced fan and filtered circulation system provided the necessary air. Fresh water was obtained from deep well pipes. Special garburators were designed to crush and compact garbage.

The Diefenbunker could handle 300 to 500 people for 30 plus consecutive days. It had its own hospital, morgue, cafeteria, and bedrooms. The prime minister had a private room with a bath nearby. The CBC had a communication facility to speak to Canadians.

The Diefenbunker was staffed and maintained from 1961 until 1994. It is now a National Historic Site. *Do you think that the threat of nuclear war is still alive today? Explain. You can visit the Diefenbunker Web site at* **www.diefenbunker.ca.**

FOCUS

1. What was the Cold War?
2. What is NATO?
3. What was the purpose of NORAD and the DEW Line?
4. Does Canada still need to be a member of NATO and NORAD? Explain.

The Diefenbaker Years, 1957–1963

It seemed to Canadians that the Liberal Party had been in power forever. From 1935 to 1957, Liberal Prime Ministers King and St. Laurent governed Canada. In 1956, the Conservatives chose a new leader, John Diefenbaker. He was a small-town lawyer from Prince Albert, Saskatchewan. He was nicknamed "The Chief." A fiery speaker and a passionate Canadian, Diefenbaker brought new life to his party. His leadership gained strength as the Liberal Party weakened. The Liberals seemed to be tired and out of ideas. Canadians remembered the Liberals' use of closure during the pipeline debate. It was time for a change.

In the election of 1957, Diefenbaker's Conservatives won 111 seats to the Liberals, 105 seats. The CCF won 25 seats and the Social Credit 19. Shortly after the defeat, St. Laurent resigned. Lester Pearson became the new leader of the Liberal Party.

Since the Conservative Party did not have a majority of the seats in Parliament (111 to 149) it formed a minority government. It was forced to negotiate with the other parties when legislation was proposed. In 1958, Diefenbaker called another election.

John Diefenbaker contributed a bill of rights to Canada.

His speeches energized Canadians and gave the Conservatives a landslide victory. It was the greatest win in Canadian history. The Conservatives won 208 seats, while the Liberals and rest of the opposition had only 57 seats combined.

Diefenbaker tried to accommodate all Canadians. He chose Ellen Fairclough as the first female Cabinet minister (Secretary of State) in 1957. He appointed James Gladstone to the Senate. Gladstone was the Senate's first Aboriginal member.

Bill of Rights

One of Diefenbaker's most lasting contributions to Canadian society was his Bill of Rights. For the first time, the freedoms and rights of Canadians were written into law. They included

- freedom of speech, of religion, and of the press
- protection of the law without discrimination because of race, colour, religion, gender, or national origin
- right of the individual to life, liberty, and security

The Bill, however, had its limitations. It applied to federal law only. As well, the Canadian Parliament had the power to change the Bill of Rights and to override it in times of national security.

Disappointments

As the 1950s came to an end, so did the economic boom. Unemployment increased. Diefenbaker's government tried to fix the economy by devaluing the Canadian dollar to 92.5 cents against the U.S. dollar. This made

Diefendollar

exports cheaper and imports more expensive. Canadians did not favour this move and nicknamed our dollar the "Diefendollar."

More controversy followed in 1959, when Diefenbaker cancelled the Avro Arrow project. The Canadian-owned A. V. Roe Company had developed a new jet fighter, the Arrow. Cancellation cost more than 15 000 jobs in the Toronto area. Many workers were highly skilled engineers. They had specialized in different areas of aviation. Most went to the United States to work for NASA. Some Canadians blamed Diefenbaker for dealing a crippling blow to the Canadian aircraft industry. The loss of engineers to the United States was called a "brain drain."

Avro Arrow In 1949, the Canadian government commissioned the Arrow. Each plane cost $2 million. The threat of Soviet bombers over the Canadian North motivated this decision. The RCAF (Royal Canadian Air Force) was looking for a replacement for its fighter plane. It needed something that would still be used in 10 years time. It needed a design that was years ahead of its time. On 4 October 1957, the first Avro Arrow was shown to the public. When it was test-flown a few months later, the Arrow exceeded everyone's expectations. It was, perhaps, the most advanced twin engine, supersonic jet of its time. The Air Force had asked for a plane capable of Mach 2—twice the speed of sound. The Arrow reached that speed while still climbing and accelerating.

Leading-edge technology is not cheap. Canada had to develop the Arrow's engine, as well as its fire-control and missile systems. The cost rose accordingly. By 1957, each plane cost the government $12.5 million. Orders for the Arrow began to decline. Money problems continued. In 1958, the new Conservative government cut the missile and fire-control parts of the development. By this time, the United States was losing interest in the Arrow. It had just developed the BOMARC missile. The U.S.S.R. had launched the ICBM missile. This suggested that Soviet bomber threats were no longer an issue. In 1959, the Diefenbaker government cancelled all orders. A. V. Roe, the plane's manufacturer, fired 15 000 employees. The government ordered all the planes, plans, drawings, photographs, negatives, and films to be destroyed.

HISTOR!CA

Minutes

Do you think that the Arrow should have been cancelled? For more information, visit the CBC Digital Archives at* www.cbc.ca/archives *and view the file "The Avro Arrow: Canada's Broken Dream."

BOMARC

Enemy missiles could only be stopped by surface-to-air missiles. Canada bought American BOMARC missiles. They were set up in Ontario and Quebec and in Canadian NATO bases in Europe. Diefenbaker and his government couldn't decide whether or not to put nuclear warheads on the BOMARC missiles. The BOMARC missiles were worthless to the military without nuclear warheads. Diefenbaker's own party was split over this issue. Several members left the party. Lester Pearson, the Liberal Party leader, criticized the government. He stressed that Canada was obliged to meet its international duties. Canada had accepted the missiles—it should accept the nuclear warheads. Most Canadians agreed. Pearson came across as a decisive leader. In early 1963, Diefenbaker was forced to call an election over the issue. Pearson won his first election with a minority government.

Not all Canadians were eager to get into an arms race. Some, such as Thérèse Casgrain (pictured here), pushed for a ban on nuclear weapons.

FOCUS

1. Give three reasons why voters chose the Conservatives over the Liberals in the election of 1957.
2. How did Diefenbaker try to protect the rights of all Canadians?
3. What problems led to Diefenbaker's defeat in 1963?

Lester B. Pearson: The Diplomat

Lester Pearson was a successful Canadian diplomat before becoming prime minister. Here, he is speaking at the United Nations in 1957.

Lester Pearson had been a career diplomat. He had represented Canada in several different countries. As Canadian ambassador to the United States, he was involved in the founding of the United Nations. He oversaw Canada's joining of NATO. In 1952, he was head of the United Nations General Assembly.

In 1958, Pearson entered politics and was elected to the House of Commons. He served as St. Laurent's minister of external affairs. He got a lot of attention when he played an important role in ending the Suez Crisis of 1956. He suggested that the United Nations send troops to keep peace in the area. Canadian troops were included in the UN force. Pearson was awarded the Nobel Peace Prize in 1957 for his leadership. His efforts reinforced Canada's role as a peacekeeper and as a "middle power."

Pearson as Prime Minister, 1963–1968

Leading a minority government is not easy. The ruling party must obtain some support from other parties to stay in power.

Pearson did this by supporting some NDP policies. During Pearson's terms in office, Canadians received universal health care and the Canada Pension Plan. His government established the Royal Commission on the Status of Women in 1967. It sought to address women's demands for equality.

The Flag and Canadian Identity

Canadian Confederation in 1867 came about peacefully. Nova Scotia, New Brunswick, and the United Province of Canada asked the British Parliament to pass the British North America Act. The Act became Canada's Constitution. After 1867, Canada was still part of the British Empire. In 1931, the Statute of Westminster made Canada an independent country, but it still kept the British flag.

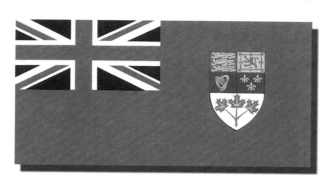

The new Canadian flag (above) replaced the Red Ensign in 1965. Today it is a well-recognized symbol of modern Canada.

The Red Ensign, a British naval flag with Canada's coat of arms, was flown internationally to represent Canada. It was seen at events such as the Olympics, international conferences, and at embassies abroad.

Canadians whose background was not British did not care for the British flag. Many French Canadians did not like the British flag. In a way, the flag divided Canadians instead of uniting them.

In 1964, Pearson announced that Canada would choose a new flag. He created a committee to look at more than 2000 designs. The choice was narrowed to just a few. After 33 days of bitter debate, the red maple leaf design was chosen. Most Canadians quickly identified with the new design. The Red Maple Leaf came to represent Canada's unique identity.

Shadows for the Future

Canadians were worried about French–English relations in Canada. Quebec's demand for more provincial powers in the 1960s created a unity crisis in Canada. The challenge for the Pearson government was to keep the country united.

Pearson established the Royal Commission on Bilingualism and Biculturalism in 1963. Its job was to investigate the relations between French and English Canadians. The Commission listened to the complaints of both. It then made many recommendations

Not all Canadians were happy with the new flag. These supporters of the Red Ensign were protesting on Parliament Hill, 1964.

in its report. Not all the recommendations were adopted. The government agreed to make the federal civil service bilingual. French and English Canadians were to have equal opportunities for promotions in the federal civil service.

Pearson retired in 1968. The Liberal Party then elected a new leader. This leader was Pierre Elliott Trudeau.

Canadian Vision

Ontario Human Rights Code

In 1962, the Government of Ontario passed the Ontario Human Rights Code. This law protected residents of Ontario from discrimination. It brought together and improved existing anti-discrimination laws of the province. The government has amended the Human Rights Code from time to time. It needed to be updated as the times changed. The most important part of the law is to make sure that all Ontarians have equal rights. Everyone has the right to live free from discrimination in such areas as employment and housing. As well, the Code's mandate is to prevent harassment based on race, colour, gender, handicap, or age.

A board of enquiry, separate from the Human Rights Commission, investigates and makes the final decisions on all complaints. Ironically, the Code defines "age" as being between 18 and 65 years. As a result, until 2005, employers in Ontario had the right to force employees to retire at age 65.

Research the Ontario Human Rights Commission at http://www.ohrc.on.ca/.

a. Summarize the types of current issues it has investigated.

b. Report your findings to the class.

Georges Vanier

BORN: 1888, Montreal, Quebec

DIED: 1967, Ottawa, Ontario

SIGNIFICANCE: Georges Vanier was the governor general of Canada from 1959 until 1967. He believed in the importance of the family. He also worked hard to help the poor and the young.

BRIEF BIOGRAPHY: After becoming a lawyer in Quebec, Vanier enlisted in the First World War. Vanier helped found the 22nd Regiment, the famed "Van Doos." He was famous for his acts of bravery and heroism. He was awarded both the Military Cross and the Distinguished Service Order. These are two of Canada's highest military decorations.

After the war, Vanier served in the Canadian diplomatic corps at the League of Nations. He was also the Canadian ambassador to France from 1944 to 1953. In 1959, John Diefenbaker appointed him Canada's first French-Canadian governor general. Vanier served with distinction in his eight years as head of state.

In 1965, Vanier and his wife, Pauline, created the Vanier Institute of the Family. This national charitable organization focuses on issues such as childhood poverty, family, and violence. After Vanier died in 1967, his wife, Pauline, continued with the institute's work until her death in 1991. Their son, Jean, has carried on humanitarian work. He has established homes for the disabled worldwide.

HISTOR!CA
Minutes

What do you think motivates people such as the Vaniers to promote human welfare?

C A N A D I A N   L I V E S

FOCUS

1. Why was Lester B. Pearson awarded the Nobel Peace Prize in 1957?
2. How do you feel when you view the Canadian flag?
3. List Pearson's achievements. Assess whether you think they were positive or negative for Canada.

The New Democratic Party

Capitalism in Canada dates back to the fur trade. The Conservatives and the Liberals have governed Canada since 1867. Both parties supported capitalism. In 1933, the new Co-operative Commonwealth Federation (CCF) offered voters the choice of **democratic socialism**. There is no single definition of democratic socialism. The idea started more than 200 years ago in Europe. Like other political ideas, it has changed over the years. Social democrats believe governments must ensure that profits from natural resources and business benefit all people. The profits should not go just to investors and owners.

Socialism also wants to make sure that all citizens have a minimum standard of living. Setting up pension plans, passing minimum wage laws, and establishing welfare programs for the needy can do this.

Workers' Movements and Labour Unions

In 1956, several unions came together to form the Canadian Labour Congress (CLC). This large group tried to strengthen workers' movements all across Canada. It had much more political and economic influence than a single union.

The 1950s saw a decline in support for the CCF. The Canadian Labour Congress and CCF members got together to revive the social democratic movement. In 1961, the New Democratic Party (NDP) was formed. Canada's labour movement got a political voice. Like the CCF before it, the NDP presented social democratic ideals to Canadians.

The CCF and NDP have always fought for social security programs. Tommy Douglas was

What issue appears to be important at this 1963 NDP rally?

the provincial CCF leader in Saskatchewan from 1944 to 1961. He introduced a government hospital plan and medicare for his province. The Liberal governments of King, Pearson, and Trudeau "borrowed" popular socialist ideas to stay in power. King's Old Age

HISTOR!CA

Minutes

Pension plan of 1927 was set up due to the influence of J. S. Woodsworth. The Pearson Liberals introduced medicare for all Canadians in the 1960s. Later on, in the 1970s, Petro-Canada, the Foreign Investment Review Agency, and the National Energy Program were created because of the NDP influence during minority Trudeau governments.

Today, Canadians are glad they have universal health care, old age pensions, family benefits, workers' compensation, and workplace safety laws. These "social safety net" programs began as social democratic ideas of the CCF and later, the NDP.

Provincial NDP parties have formed governments in several Canadian provinces from the 1970s to the present. On the federal level, though, the NDP has not been as successful. Nevertheless, the party has had considerable influence.

COMMUNITY SNAPSHOT

The Royal Canadian Legion After the First World War, returning soldiers faced economic hardship. Jobs were hard to find and the cost of living had risen while they had been away. The federal government and various lobby groups did not want these problems to happen again. The Canadian Legion of the British Empire Service League was founded in 1926. It was a Canadian veterans' association. It wanted to make sure that soldiers returning from war would get all available government benefits. The Legion lobbied for more financial assistance, educational benefits, insurance, and medical assistance.

The 1930 War Veterans Allowance was one of the Legion's early achievements. Clothing allowances, pensions, job training, and preference in civil service employment are other areas in which the Legion has been active. In the 1940s, the Legion founded the Foster Fathers Program for boys who had lost fathers in the war. The National Poppy Remembrance Campaign commemorates the memory of those Canadians who died in the military, merchant marine, and ferry command services. The Royal Canadian Legion (the name was changed in 1960) has more than 1600 branches in Canada, and contributes millions of dollars annually to community projects across the country.

HISTOR!CA

Minutes

Tommy Douglas

BORN: 1904, Falkirk, Scotland

DIED: 1986, Ottawa, Ontario

SIGNIFICANCE: He was the founder of Canada's "social safety net" and the NDP.

BRIEF BIOGRAPHY: Tommy Douglas moved with his family to Manitoba in 1919. He attended the ministry program at Brandon College. Here, he was introduced to the social gospel. It is a form of Christianity concerned as much with improving life on Earth as with life in the hereafter. He graduated in 1930 as an ordained Baptist preacher. He went to Weyburn, Saskatchewan, just as the Depression hit. Douglas joined the CCF and ran in the 1934 provincial election, but lost. The following year, he ran in the federal election and won. For nine years he was the CCF's agricultural specialist.

Douglas had a funny, sarcastic, and self-mocking style of speaking. He quickly earned a reputation as one of the best speakers in the House of Commons. He returned to Saskatchewan in 1944, where he became the first social democrat premier in Canada. His first budget gave 70 percent to social services. Costs of medical and dental care for old-age pensioners, and of all cancer treatments were covered. In 1947, Douglas introduced universal hospital insurance.

Health care was important to Douglas, because as a child he had suffered from a serious bone disease. Since his family was poor, they could not afford the proper treatment. If not for some lucky coincidences and charitable people, Douglas would have lost a leg to the disease. He did not want others to be dependent on the generosity of strangers. Douglas believed that everyone should have the right to proper medical care. At the time, this was a revolutionary idea to Canadians. In 1960, Douglas decided to put into effect a universal medical care plan that would satisfy both doctors and patients. He resigned as premier shortly before the universal medical bill went into effect to lead the NDP. The federal government made medicare a national program at the end of the decade. Douglas was made a Companion of the Order of Canada in 1980.

In November 2004, CBC Television released results of a nation-wide poll in which Douglas ranked as the greatest Canadian. Why do you think he is held in such high regard? In your view, what was his most important contribution to Canadian life?

HISTOR!CA
Minutes

CANADIAN LIVES

Canadian Vision

Music

Music during the 1950s and 1960s was mainly imported from Britain and the United States. Canada, however, produced a number of major players who earned international fame.

The Guess Who was one of North America's most popular rock bands in the 1960s and 1970s. It was led by Winnipeggers Randy Bachman and Burton Cummings. They had a huge hit with "American Woman." Bachman fronted other groups including Bachman-Turner-Overdrive, whose "Taking Care of Business" is one of North America's most popular songs. The group continues to headline concerts across Canada.

Gordon Lightfoot was perhaps our most popular male vocalist during the 1960s and 1970s. Lightfoot grew up in Orillia. He was a boy soprano and teenage member of a barbershop quartet. Lightfoot also wrote songs for other musicians, including Ian and Sylvia Tyson, Peter, Paul and Mary, Elvis Presley, Bob Dylan, Barbra Streisand, and Harry Belafonte. When he eventually started to sing his own songs, such as "If You Could Read My Mind," his career took off. He won numerous Juno Awards and became a Companion of the Order of Canada in 1971.

Joni Mitchell was born in Macleod, Alberta, in 1943. She has had an influential career in the music industry. Her fourth recording, *Blue*, from 1971, is still considered one of the best of its time. Indeed, it's hard to think of a contemporary female rock star who doesn't have some trace of Mitchell in her music. Alanis Morissette and Sarah McLachlan owe much to this award-winning singer-songwriter.

Neil Young was the son of journalist Scott Young. He was a founding member of the popular 1960s band, Buffalo Springfield. After the band broke up in 1968, Young went solo. He has had an extremely successful career. His many albums and CDs have sold in the millions. He has remained popular for over 30 years. Known as the Godfather of Grunge, Young recorded *Mirror Ball* with Pearl Jam in 1995. "Heart of Gold" is both a popular Young song and title of a documentary about the musician.

FOCUS

1. Which two groups formed the New Democratic Party?
2. What is medicare? Do you think it has been successful in fulfilling its aims?
3. What are some of the NDP's major contributions to Canadian society?
4. Why has the federal government adopted some NDP policies?

The Rebellious 1960s

The 1960s was a time of rebellion, excitement, and creativity. Many North American young people questioned existing values. They rebelled against social and economic inequalities. North American youth supported the American civil rights movement and

Canadian protesters demonstrate against the Vietnam War.

equal opportunities for non-whites. Some organized strikes and sit-ins at schools and universities. Others dropped out and entered the hippie drug culture.

A few turned to communes, sharing living space and possessions, to redefine community and family. The majority went to school, played loud music, and wore new styles of clothing. Both men and women wore shoulder-length hair. Granny glasses, jeans, and sandals replaced the bobby sox, sweater sets, and coiffed hair of the 1950s.

The hippies promoted the more casual look of blue jeans. Television influenced Canadian and American ways of thinking.

The Cuban Missile Crisis in 1962 was the first world crisis to receive widespread TV coverage. People saw the American naval blockade of Cuba. American and Russian viewpoints were reported on the nightly news. Television allowed people to see how close the world came to a nuclear war.

The television coverage of the Vietnam War (1964–75) made it "a real TV war." Nightly news telecasts showed bombs exploding. They showed American soldiers being killed. Americans and Canadians were disturbed by images of bloody faces and body bags. Reporters told disturbing stories about American atrocities against Vietnamese civilians. Many people wanted an end to the war.

It was as if viewers were there. Everyone became a "television witness" to the Vietnam War. Viewers also saw the assassinations of President Kennedy in 1962 and of his brother Robert Kennedy in 1968. The impact of these events was enormous. The baby boom generation had grown up with TV. It had made them more aware of what was going on in the world. Television contributed to the anti-Vietnam War movement of the 1960s and to the general rebelliousness of the time.

The Baby Boom: 1945–1967

1940   1945   1950   1955   1960   1965   1970

Times of Challenge

Canada's Aboriginal peoples fought against racism and neglect. Native and Métis leaders such as Harold Cardinal, Howard Adams, Buffy Sainte-Marie, and Kahn-Tineta Horn called attention to the plight of their people. They demanded justice and equality.

Women from all regions, classes, and ethnic groups began to challenge sexual stereotypes. Betty Friedan's *The Feminine Mystique* (1963) shattered the happy-housewife myth. Some women's groups wanted governments, businesses, and community organizations to involve women equally with men at all levels of decision making. More radical groups claimed that increased female representation was

Marshall McLuhan, a professor of English at the University of Toronto, was a major voice on the effects of mass media, such as television, on how people think and behave. In the 1960s, McLuhan foresaw that the Internet and computers would radically change the way people communicate. It was he who said, "The medium is the message." What do you think he meant?

not enough. They said that institutions themselves had to change, as well as the behaviour of both men and women. The Royal Commission on the Status of Women agreed that changes were necessary.

The women's liberation movement became a powerful force. Women challenged their traditional roles as homemakers. They protested and marched for legalized abortions, simpler divorce laws, and fairer employment practices. More and more women entered the workforce. Some needed the pay cheque. Others wanted a career and a broader role and identity. Most wanted equal opportunity with men and equal pay for work of equal value.

FOCUS

1. Why were the 1960s termed the *rebellious sixties*?
2. To what extent have teenagers changed since the 1960s? In your opinion, are teenagers more rebellious now than then? Are they more political now than then?
3. What concerns did Aboriginal leaders and women raise?

Canada's Centennial: 1967

This Expo picture shows several Canadian pavilions, including Canada's own triangular pavilion (lower right), the teepee-like Indians of Canada pavilion (left), and the tree-topped Pavilion of Western Canada, which follows the topography of the four provinces (centre).

In 1967, Canadians celebrated the 100th birthday of their country. All across the land, they held parades, dances, banquets, and carnivals. They built libraries, schools, concert halls, and stadiums. That year Canadians gloried in being Canadian.

Hosting Expo '67, a world fair held in Montreal, was an important part of Canada's Centennial celebrations. Canada invited the whole world to help celebrate. Expo '67 was held on three islands in the St. Lawrence River. One island was totally man made! The theme of the day was "Man and His World."

Many nations, private corporations, and even provinces sponsored pavilions at the fair. They showed off their latest technologies and achievements. Since the 1956 world fair in Brussels, Belgium, there had been great progress in such fields as film, architecture, and science. Much was shown at Expo '67 for the first time, and the architecture on the Montreal site was much admired.

A nation celebrating its 100th birthday is still young. It was still difficult to define Canadian identity or Canadian character. In a way, Canadians were still trying to figure out who they were and what kind of country they wanted to build. In 1967, Canadians did not control their constitution, but did have their own distinctive flag—the Red Maple Leaf. It was a new symbol of unity, pride, and optimism. Canadians could enjoy their pride in Canada and its place in the world.

The Baby Boom: 1945–1967

ONTARIO

QUEBEC

NOVA SCOTIA

NEW BRUNSWICK

MANITOBA

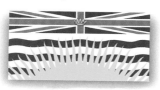

BRITISH COLUMBIA

PRINCE EDWARD ISLAND

SASKATCHEWAN

ALBERTA

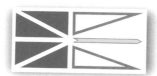

NEWFOUNDLAND AND LABRADOR

NORTHWEST TERRITORIES

YUKON

Canada's provincial flags are as unique as Canada's history. They illustrate a country made up of many different peoples. Ontario's flag, for example, adopts Britain's Union Jack as its major image.

NUNAVUT

Quebec's flag, on the other hand, shows the French fleur-de-lis. Nunavut's flag features the inukshuk, a stone monument that guides people on land and marks sacred places.

FOCUS

1. **What joys did Canada have in 1967?**
2. **What problems did the country still face?**
3. **Suggest a new flag design for your province or territory.**

Sharpening Your Skills

Researching Primary and Secondary Sources

THE SKILL

Finding and distinguishing between primary and secondary sources

THE IMPORTANCE

All decisions should be based on the best information.

Everybody conducts research. To decide which movie to watch, you might read a review in the paper or ask a friend who saw it. Sportsline bettors study the results of previous games before making their choices. Fashion magazines and observation of people around you help in deciding what to wear. What is the best automobile to buy, what is the finest acne cream, diet, or restaurant—all involve research.

Because history involves everything that has been said or done in the past, nothing is safe from the historians' interest:

- Photographs reveal how things really looked.
- Ads indicate what the advertisers thought would convince people to buy their product.
- Paintings illustrate the artists' feelings and ideas.
- Music reflects society's tastes.
- Interviews provide individual feelings and memories.
- Architecture reveals people's ideas about space.
- Wills disclose an individual's wealth and attitudes towards family.
- Newspapers provide day-by-day accounts of politics, sports, entertainment, fashion, humour, and more.
- Tools show how advanced a society was technologically.
- Parliamentary debates indicate what politicians thought was important.
- Credit statements reveal where a person was and what was purchased.
- Laws indicate what society thinks is important.
- Cemeteries illustrate attitudes towards the dead and show how long people lived.
- E-mails and letters provide personal opinions.

Where do historians go to find their sources? Almost anywhere! Libraries provide information on what other historians have discovered. Archives and museums contain old newspapers, photographs, private letters, government reports, diaries, and birth and death records. In addition to public archives, many companies have their own archives that house information on business decisions, profits and losses, personnel problems, and their customers. Schools keep students' records, yearbooks, and class pictures. The Internet and its search engines are also a valuable source of historical information—both primary and secondary.

In general, historians distinguish between primary and secondary sources. A primary source is first-hand evidence. It is information created in the time period that the historian is examining. A secondary source is second-hand evidence. It was created by someone who was not present in the time period the historian is examining. For example, if you were writing a biography of a member of the Group of Seven, your primary sources would include the artist's paintings, personal letters, an interview with him, his high school report cards, his studio, and his books. Secondary sources would include what people have written about him—biographies, obituaries (death notices), books, and newspaper articles.

Primary sources are the historians' basic raw data. Finding and making sense of them is fun, exciting, and challenging. Your arrangement and interpretation of the primary sources is what makes your history unique and important. Once you have written your history, it becomes a secondary source for other historians.

Every day you distinguish between the value of secondary and primary sources. In choosing which movie to attend, you are more likely to listen to someone who saw the movie than to a person who learned about it from someone else.

Application

Examine the short biography of William Lyon Mackenzie King in this chapter. Make a list of possible primary and secondary sources for an extended biography of King. Then, search the Internet for primary and secondary sources.

Questions & Activities

Questions and Activities

Who Am I?

1. I led Newfoundland into Confederation with Canada. I became known as the "last Father of Confederation." Who am I?

2. As prime minister, I gave Canadians their first Bill of Rights. My political supporters knew me as "the Chief." Who am I?

3. I won the Nobel Peace Prize in 1957. I was prime minister when Canadians received their own national flag. Who am I?

4. I was premier of Saskatchewan from 1955 to 1961. I brought medicare to the people of Saskatchewan. Later, I became the first leader of the NDP. Who am I?

5. I was a popular musician during the 1960s. Although I have been in the industry for over 30 years, I have more recently gained popularity as the "Godfather of Grunge." Who am I?

Discuss and Debate

1. What would have happened to Newfoundland if Newfoundlanders had voted not to enter Confederation in 1949? Write your thoughts down in a brief paragraph. Be prepared to read your paragraph aloud during class discussion.

2. List the good and the bad results of the economic boom of the early 1950s. Hold a class debate on the topic: Resolved that the economic boom of the 1950s created more problems than it solved.

3. With a group of students, discuss this statement: Parents rarely understand teenagers and teenagers rarely understand adults.

4. Canada underwent a baby boom in the 1950s. Today, Canadians are having fewer children or none at all.
a) Suggest reasons for this drop in the birth rate.
b) What does the drop mean for the future of Canada? Possible areas of discussion are schools, the labour force, immigration, and support of the elderly.

Do Some Research

1. Visit the library to find out more about Newfoundland and Labrador since it joined Canada in 1949. You might use the following headings: (a) Geography, (b) Culture and Traditions, (c) Transportation, (d) Communities, (e) Political Leaders, and (f) Economic Issues.

2. Research the recent history of a "boomtown" in your area.
- Why was the town established?
- Has the town continued to develop?
- What do you think the town's future will be?

3. Find out more about the cancellation of the Avro Arrow project by the Diefenbaker government. Make a list of the reasons for and against the decision. State your personal conclusions clearly and firmly.

4. Write a brief biocard on a significant Canadian of the 1950s or 1960s. Here are a few suggestions:
a) Paul Anka	**b)** Marshall McLuhan
c) Maurice Richard	**d)** Jacques Plante
e) John Diefenbaker	**f)** Margaret Laurence
g) Marilyn Bell	**h)** Celia Franca

5. Summarize the achievements and changes won by the protest movement of the 1960s.

6. Find out what projects your community undertook to celebrate Canada's 100th birthday. Were these projects a good idea?

7. Research the women's movement of the 1960s. How did it differ from the suffragette movement of the early 1900s? What were women protesting against? How did the women's movement change life for Canadian women? Can you see any changes in your own life that could be attributed to the women's movement?

8. Find out about the civil rights movement in the United States. In terms of racial views, to what extent did Canada differ from the United States?

9. Research the history of Canada's national flag, the Maple Leaf. (Why was a new flag proposed? Why was it so different from the old flag? Why have a maple leaf as national symbol? What other designs were proposed and rejected? Why was its adoption so controversial?)

10. Investigate the origins of one of the provincial and territorial flags and show how the design reflects the heritage of the province or territory.

Be Creative

1. Divide into groups and prepare a time capsule for the 1950s or 1960s. Include photo records, magazines, records, souvenirs, fashions, and news statements. You might celebrate the end of your project with a theme party.

2. Compare the hit songs of the 1950s and 1960s with each other, and the hit songs of today. Identify what differences the songs reveal about (a) values, (b) technology, (c) teenagers, and (d) love.

3. What role did folk music play during the baby boom? Find examples of popular songs and make a presentation to your peers.

Web Watch

For more information about topics in this chapter, be sure to check out these sources:

http://www.ggower.com/dief/ (For Diefenbaker)

http://particle.physics.ucdavis.edu/bios/Pearson.html (For Pearson)

http://collections.ic.gc.ca/heirloom_series/volume5/volume5.htm
(For biographies of famous Canadians, listed by topic
and alphabetically)

St. Lawrence Seaway: www.seaway.ca
The Baby Boom: www.babyboomers.org
The Diefenbunker: www.diefenbunker.ca
Innu Nation: www.innu.ca
Avro Arrow Alliance: www.arrow-alliance.com
Canadian Labour Congress: www.clc-ctc.ca
The Royal Canadian Legion: www.legion.ca
CBC Digital Archives: www.cbc.ca/archives

Consider reviewing the following audiovisual files: "The Gouzenko Affair," "Seeking Sanctuary: Draft Dodgers," "Gordon Lightfoot, Canada's Folk Laureate," "Has Confederation Been Good for Newfoundland?" "Mackenzie King: Public Life, Private Man," "Tommy Douglas and the NDP," "The Birth of Medicare," "Expo '67: Montreal Welcomes the World," "Hippie Society: The Youth Rebellion," and "Going Underground: Canada's Subway and Montreal's Metro."

OUR LAND

Top: In 1999, Nunavut became the third territory in Canada. Its creation is based on the largest Aboriginal land claim agreement in Canadian history. Eighty-five percent of residents are Inuit. Below: Jeanne Sauvé set several firsts: first woman from Quebec to become a federal Cabinet minister, first female Speaker of the House of Commons, and first female governor general.

How do both of these stamps suggest Canada's coming of age?

Chapter Five: Canada Comes of Age: 1968–2005

Expectations

Overall Expectations:

By the end of this chapter, you will be able to

- demonstrate an understanding of the Canadian identity
- describe the demographic and social patterns in Canada since the 1960s
- describe how Canadian values have developed and changed
- explain the impact of social and political movements on Canadian society
- describe how individuals have contributed to Canada and its emerging identity
- describe some of the major forces and events that have influenced Canada's policies and Canadian identity since 1968

Specific Expectations:

By the end of this chapter, you will be able to

- identify some of the major effects of, and concerns arising from freer trade and globalization
- describe how Canadian immigration policies have changed over time and how such changes have affected patterns of immigration
- understand the advantages of multiculturalism, as well as some of its problems
- describe the changing relationship between the First Nations and the government after 1960

Word List

Apartheid	**Assimilate**
Boat people	**Constitution**
Debt	**Deficit**
Discrimination	**Economic recession**
Economic nationalists	**Motion of non-**
Patronage	**confidence**
Royalties	**Sovereignty**
Surplus	**Tariff**
Visible minorities	**Wage–price spiral**

①

① Pierre Trudeau first became Canada's prime minister in 1968. He promised that Canada would become a "just society." He fought hard for national unity. He supported people's rights. He earned respect on the world stage.

③ Brian Mulroney was Canada's prime minister from 1984 to 1993. He wanted to reduce the national debt. He made a free trade agreement with the United States. He appointed Stephen Lewis as ambassador to the United Nations.

Stephen Lewis

② Canada's immigration policies changed in the 1970s. Many people from other cultures wanted to come to Canada and make it their home. Canada is now a multicultural society.

1980	1990	2000	2010

③ ④ ⑤ ⑥

④ Great gains were made by Canada's Aboriginal peoples in the 1990s. Agreements on Aboriginal land claims were reached. Nunavut was put on the map. The fight for Aboriginal rights continues.

Flag of Nunavut

⑥ Since the 1970s, women have made progress in rights and in access to jobs. Kim Campbell became Canada's first female prime minister in 1993. Women are still fighting for equal pay and against poverty.

⑤ Jean Chrétien was Canada's prime minister from 1993 to 2003. He wanted to lower the deficit. He also wanted to defeat the separatist movement in Quebec. Separatists, such as Lucien Bouchard and Quebec Premier Jacques Parizeau, campaigned for Quebec to separate from Canada.

Lucien Bouchard

Trudeaumania

The election of Pierre Elliott Trudeau unleashed a wave of popular support that few Canadians had ever witnessed. The press called this rock star–like attention "Trudeaumania."

By 1968, Canadians believed that they could have anything they wanted. The national mood was optimism, hope, and excitement. Canadians wanted fresh faces to lead them into a new era. The best person to do that seemed to be Pierre Elliott Trudeau.

When Prime Minister Lester Pearson resigned, Trudeau was chosen as the new Liberal leader. He seemed ideal. At 48, Trudeau was single and much younger than most politicians. He was also handsome, witty, intelligent, and fully bilingual. He enjoyed sports and parties. People found him exciting to listen to. He projected the image of being a determined, forceful leader. Trudeau brought new ideas to politics. He had a strong sense of justice and a deep love for Canada. He immediately called an election.

People were impressed by Trudeau's clear vision of a just society. In this society, Trudeau said, the rights of all Canadians would be respected and everyone could enjoy the good things of life. Trudeau did not speak lightly. In 1949, he had supported the unions in the bitter Asbestos Strike in Quebec. He had strongly criticized the province's values.

Canadian voters were swept up in a fever of enthusiasm. "Trudeaumania" the press called it. The Liberal Party under Trudeau won the 1968 election and formed a majority government.

The Just Society

The Trudeau government faced many challenges, though. Canada's economy was slowing down. Unemployment rates were high. There was an international oil crisis. Inflation rates were on the rise. Tensions were rising between "old" Canadians and new immigrants. Canada's Aboriginal peoples wanted improved status. Women demanded equality with men. Quebec separatists were gaining support.

Having a prime minister with a beautiful young wife and young children was a new experience for Canadians.

Many people believed that Trudeau's "Just Society" election slogan was a promise for a better world. Canadians had high expectations of the changes that Trudeau and his government would make.

Arctic Sovereignty

In the summer of 1969, an American super-tanker, *Manhattan*, travelled through the Northwest Passage. The Americans were looking for a route they could use to transport Alaskan oil to the south. Canada had not given permission for the voyage.

Canada considered the mission a threat to its **sovereignty** in the North. The Trudeau government passed the Arctic Waters Pollution Prevention Act. The new law established a "100-mile pollution-prevention zone in Arctic waters adjacent to the mainland and the islands of the Arctic archipelago."

A Bilingual, Multicultural Canada

Trudeau wanted Canada to be bilingual. He wanted English- and French-speaking Canadians to have equal language rights. In 1969, the government passed Canada's Official Languages Act. The new law stated that the federal government would serve Canadians in both the French and English languages. It also made companies doing business in Canada label their products in both languages.

In 1971, Trudeau also passed the Multiculturalism Act. This Act stated that Canada was officially multicultural. (For more on bilingualism and multiculturalism, as well as the 1970 October Crisis, see Chapter 6.)

Under Trudeau, Canada overhauled its immigration policies. Canada welcomed new groups of immigrants and refugees. Among them were refugees from Czechoslovakia in 1968–69; from Tibet in 1970; from Uganda, especially South Asians, in 1972; from Chile 1973–74; and from Vietnam in 1978–80. The modern face of Canada was rapidly changing.

The USS Manhattan *and the Canadian icebreaker,* Louis St. Laurent, *crunch through the snow-covered ice of Northern Baffin Bay.* Should Canada actively promote its claim to the Arctic? Explain.

Important symbolic changes were also made during Trudeau's first term in office. These include

- Muriel McQueen Fergusson becoming the first woman Speaker of the Senate
- Bora Laskin becoming the first Jewish Chief Justice of the Supreme Court of Canada
- Pauline McGibbon becoming Ontario's first woman lieu-tenant governor (the Crown's representative in the province just as the governor general is the Crown's representative at the federal level)
- Len Marchand becoming the first Aboriginal Cabinet minister
- Jeanne Sauvé becoming the first woman Speaker of the House of Commons (and later, the first woman governor general of Canada)

Some Aboriginal groups and feminists (members of a movement concerned with equal rights for women) described these appointments as tokenism. The appointments, though, opened the door to future opportunities for minority groups and women in Canada.

Pierre Trudeau and Bora Laskin

Pauline McGibbon with her husband

Jeanne Sauvé

FOCUS

1. Why were Canadians so attracted to Trudeau in the late 1960s?
2. What did Trudeau mean by a "Just Society"?
3. Name two changes that Trudeau made as prime minister.

Canada in the 1970s: The Economy

The Canadian and world economies began to slow down in the early 1970s. Unemployment rose and the cost of living increased. Businesses, homeowners, and farmers borrowed money at interest rates up to 20 percent to pay for mortgages and new equipment.

The problem got worse as consumers and businesses paid more for gasoline and heating oil. In 1973, oil was a mere $8 a barrel. That changed when Middle Eastern producers formed the Organization of Petroleum Exporting Countries (OPEC). OPEC controlled world oil prices. By 1980, the price of oil was over $30 a barrel and rising. The high cost of oil and gas increased inflation.

No one knew how high prices would go. Business leaders did not want to invest in new ventures. Economic expansion was too risky. Companies cut back production. Many businesses went bankrupt. Workers were laid off. Consumer confidence in the economy fell.

In 1975, the Trudeau government passed a law to control wages and prices. It wanted to break the **wage–price spiral**. The new law limited increases in salaries and hourly wages. It also limited the price increases that

The NEP meant that Alberta could not charge higher oil prices, like the OPEC countries. Should the province have been allowed to benefit from them?

stores could charge for goods. Labour unions and business people criticized the government's interference; however, no one had a better idea. By 1979, Canada, like the rest of the world, was in an **economic recession**.

Meanwhile, Alberta, as an oil-producing province, wanted to benefit from higher world oil prices. The federal government said no. It introduced the National Energy Program (NEP). The policy reduced profits for Alberta oil producers and the **royalties** collected by the Alberta government. Westerners were furious. They accused Trudeau of protecting central Canada at the expense of the West.

As part of the NEP, the government purchased several smaller oil companies and created Petro-Canada. It wanted to strengthen Canadian ownership of resources. Petro-Canada took part in oil exploration and retail sales.

The Deficit Rises

During the 1960s, Ottawa usually spent less money than it collected in taxes. The country had a **surplus** budget. By the 1970s, though, the government was spending more money than it raised through taxes. It was creating a **deficit**. Money was needed to pay for unemployment insurance, job creation projects, and other social programs. Soon, the government had to borrow money in order to pay for programs—the country was being run on deficit budgets. In the 1970s, the deficit was above $12 billion; in the 1980s, it reached $38 billion. Each annual deficit meant an increase in the national **debt**. Canada paid much money in interest on the national debt. Trudeau's opponents said that the country could not survive if the national debt kept increasing at such a rate.

The Ties That Bind

Canadians were divided on the issue of American investment in Canadian companies. Some favoured it because it increased jobs. Others feared that it would endanger Canadian independence. Trudeau understood the benefits

Joe Clark represented change.

and dangers of Canada's close ties to the United States. His government created the Foreign Investment Review Agency (FIRA). In 1974, the agency began to screen takeover bids aimed at Canadian industrial or resource companies. Some Canadians supported FIRA's efforts; others did not.

Election 1979

By 1979, Canadians were ready for a change. Economic problems hurt the Liberals. As a result, the Progressive Conservatives won the election, and Joe Clark, from High River, Alberta, became prime minister. Clark headed a minority government. Eight months later, though, he was forced to call an election when his budget was defeated. In 1980, Trudeau and the Liberals returned to power.

FOCUS

1. **What economic problems did Canada face in the 1970s?**
2. **Why did Trudeau create FIRA and the NEP?**
3. **Why did Trudeau lose the election of 1979? Who won it?**

A New Constitution for Canada

Trudeau was a strong federalist. He believed that only a strong federal government could solve the problems facing Canada.

Many provincial leaders disagreed. They wanted more powers for the provinces. Premiers Brian Peckford of Newfoundland, Peter

Since 1976, the people of Quebec had elected René Lévesque, a strong and popular leader, as premier. Lévesque's party, the Parti Québécois, supported separation from Canada.

Lougheed of Alberta, and William Bennett of British Columbia joined Quebec in demanding more provincial powers. They wanted provincial control over the price of local oil and gas.

Trudeau disagreed. He believed someone had to stand up for the powers of the central government. These opposing views of Canada created friction between the provinces and the federal government. (The issue of Quebec and separatism is discussed at length in

Chapter 6; it played a major role in Trudeau's public life.)

Reforming the Constitution

Trudeau intended to renew and reform Canada's constitution. He wanted to better meet the needs of Canadians in the 1980s and to address the active concerns of Quebecers. Many Quebecers supported the goals of Premier René Lévesque and his Parti Québécois. Trudeau wanted to bring them more comfortably into the federal fold. He did not want to see Quebec stray out of Confederation and separate from Canada.

When it came to constitutional reform, Trudeau had three main goals:

1. **To patriate the Constitution:** Canada would bring the British North America Act home from Britain and revise it to better reflect Canadian realities. Canadians could thereby make their own changes without British approval.

2. **To develop an amending formula:** The premiers and the federal government would agree on a formula to change, or amend, the Constitution.

3. **To create a Charter of Rights and Freedoms:** A Charter would become a major part of the Constitution. It would list specific rights and freedoms that must be protected in Canada. All existing and all future laws would have to be consistent with this Charter.

Canada Comes of Age

Trudeau and his government faced a huge task. Although most people supported changes to Canada's Constitution, getting all provincial leaders to agree on them was another matter. Many meetings were held in 1980 and 1981. Finally, after much compromise and discussion, agreement was reached on 5 November 1981.

Quebec Stands Alone

Agreement was not total, though. Although the federal government and nine provincial premiers were satisfied, René Lévesque of Quebec was not. Still, there was enough agreement to move forward. The new Constitution Act was signed by Queen Elizabeth II and came into effect in 1982. It included the Canadian Charter of Rights and Freedoms.

Trudeau's dream of a new constitution had been achieved, but at a price. He had satisfied the wishes of nine premiers, but not succeeded in meeting the needs of Quebec.

Trudeau and Queen Elizabeth II signed the Constitution Act 17 April 1982.

Premier Lévesque and other officials rejected the new constitution. They felt angry that it had been imposed on them despite their opposition. Some Quebecers felt betrayed. Other Canadians felt that it was impossible to satisfy the province. Still, most Canadians were pleased to have full control of their constitution.

FOCUS

1. What were Trudeau's goals for Canada's constitution?
2. Who rejected the new constitution? Why?

Trudeau and International Affairs

Trudeau's ideas and efforts in foreign affairs gained him worldwide respect. Many people felt that the Canadian prime minister was more popular and respected in other countries than at home. His speeches and statements on international affairs were always well received and widely reported.

Trudeau was a respected world leader.

Trudeau's goal in international affairs was for Canada to reach out to the world. Doing this was one way to reduce heavy American influence over Canada. In addition, Trudeau's diplomatic trips resulted in new trade opportunities and more jobs for Canadians. Trudeau worked to develop new ties with Cuba and the rest of Latin America—this area had been largely ignored by Canadians. Trudeau visited Cuba and met with Fidel Castro, Cuba's long-time dictator. His trip angered U.S. President Richard Nixon and the Americans. Cuba and the United States did not "recognize" each other nor did they have diplomatic relations.

Canada became more open to communicating with communist countries. Under Trudeau, diplomatic relations were established with communist China. Canada was one of the first Western countries to do this. Trudeau felt that communicating and trading with countries such as China could pressure them into improving their people's civil and human rights.

In 1983, the Trudeau government finally allowed the United States to test the accuracy of the cruise missile (without warheads) over northern Alberta. This computer-guided bomb travels more than 2000 km at low altitudes, where it cannot be detected by radar. Aboriginal Canadians objected to the testing, arguing that it broke treaty agreements. Greenpeace and other Canadian environmentalists protested, too, and went to court to stop it. The courts ruled against them; the testing continued.

During his last years in office, Trudeau used his influence to work for world peace. He sought to bring about nuclear disarmament, especially between the two world superpowers. His goal was to reduce the threat of nuclear war. Though his efforts were praised, he was unsuccessful. Hostility between the United States and the Union of Soviet Socialist Republics persisted.

Cuban leader Fidel Castro and Pierre Trudeau share a moment.

Trudeau Retires

On 29 February 1984, Trudeau announced that he was retiring from politics and international affairs. He had dominated Canadian life, as had no other prime minister since John A. Macdonald, Canada's first national leader. Trudeau had been in office for 15 years. Only Macdonald and Mackenzie King had served longer.

Many Canadians felt the retirement was long overdue. Trudeau was unpopular in the West and among many business people across the country. His strong-willed leadership created a mood of conflict between the provinces and the federal government.

Yet, in 1987, when Trudeau came out of retirement to speak against the Meech Lake Accord (see Chapter 6), many Canadians listened. Trudeau's opinions, as sharp and forceful as ever, still mattered. Pierre Elliott Trudeau died on 28 September 2000.

FOCUS

1. Why was Trudeau interested in having Canada reach out to the world?
2. In your opinion, was Trudeau a "great" prime minister? Explain.

The Mulroney Years

In the 1984 election, John Turner, the Liberal who had replaced Trudeau, faced off against Brian Mulroney, leader of the Progressive Conservative Party.

Mulroney hailed from Baie Comeau, Quebec. A colourful speaker, he had been a successful lawyer and businessman before entering politics. Mulroney sensed that Canada was ready for change. He understood the mood of the country. Mulroney promised to provide Canadians with "jobs, jobs, jobs." He also pledged to

- reduce the annual deficit and encourage the growth of private industry
- reduce the conflict between the provinces and the federal government
- strengthen the armed forces
- improve relations with the United States

Voters liked what they heard. Mulroney's election victory was the greatest landslide in Canadian history. The Progressive Conservatives won 211 seats; the Liberals, 40 seats; the NDP, 30 seats; an Independent, 1 seat.

Soon, though, Mulroney encountered political problems. Eight of his Cabinet ministers were forced to resign within the first three years because of scandals. Many Canadians became critical of the Mulroney government, and the government was accused of widespread **patronage** appointments. Mulroney did not quit.

Economic Success

From 1984 to 1988, Canada's economy grew at a faster rate than any other Western nation. Industries expanded.

Brian Mulroney was a tireless political campaigner.

Hundreds of thousands of jobs were created faster than at any time in previous years. Unemployment rates dropped. Canada's annual deficit dropped from $38 billion per year to $28 billion a year. Nonetheless, the Progressive Conservatives remained a long way from their goal of deficit elimination.

Parliament passed laws to support business growth. It reduced taxes on corporations. FIRA, which had restricted American investment, was replaced with Investment Canada, which encouraged American investment. "Canada is open for business," declared Prime Minister Mulroney before an American audience. The government cancelled the NEP as Canada welcomed American investment in its oil industry.

Canada's **economic nationalists** strongly opposed these measures. They argued that Canada was selling out to the United States. Canada's sovereignty was at risk. Most Canadians saw only the increased number of jobs, new companies, and new development. The economy was booming. They were not worried about the increasing foreign investment in Canada.

A CLOSER LOOK AT THE GST

The Mulroney government introduced a dramatic change to the Canadian tax system on 1 January 1991. The Canadian federal sales tax (FST) on manufactured goods was replaced with a Goods and Services Tax (GST) of 7 percent on goods and services. It would be paid directly by Canadian consumers at time of purchase.

Most Canadians did not know about the FST, a tax built into the price of purchased goods. The advertised price already included FST of between 9 and 13.5 percent—consumers never saw the tax. The FST was applied to all manufactured goods, including those exported to other countries.

The Mulroney government believed that elimination of Canada's FST would lower the cost of Canadian exports. Canadian products would become more competitive—that is, cheaper—more exports would result, and more Canadian jobs would be created.

The GST was unpopular with Canadians. Consumer groups claimed it was unfair to poorer people because it was placed on many necessities of life. Toothpaste was taxable. So were car repairs. Small and single servings of snack foods became taxable, as did funerals, legal fees, and insurance.

In the late 1990s, under an initiative of the Chrétien government, Nova Scotia, New Brunswick, and Newfoundland and Labrador harmonized their provincial taxes with the GST. Consumers in those provinces now pay HST (harmonized sales tax) of 15 percent. However, not all provinces were interested in harmonizing, or blending, their sales tax with Ottawa's GST.

Elijah Harper

BORN: 1949, Red Sucker Lake, Manitoba

SIGNIFICANCE: As a member of the Manitoba legislature in 1990, Harper effectively blocked the approval vote of the Meech Lake Accord in Manitoba. He blocked the Accord because he believed that Aboriginal peoples had not had enough opportunity to take part in Canada's political process.

BRIEF BIOGRAPHY: Elijah Harper, a Cree from northeastern Manitoba, was raised by his grandparents until the age of six, when he was sent by his father to a residential school. He began attending the University of Manitoba in 1971, and afterwards served as a community development worker for the Manitoba Indian Brotherhood and a program analyst for the Department of Northern Affairs.

At age 29, he was elected chief of the Red Sucker Lake First Nation, serving from 1978 to 1981. Harper was elected to the Manitoba legislature in 1981. In 1986, he was appointed minister responsible for Native Affairs; a year later, he became minister of Northern Affairs for Manitoba.

Harper continues to work for Aboriginal rights. He has received many humanitarian awards, including the Stanley Knowles Humanitarian Award, the Aboriginal Achievement Award, the Order of Merit from St. Paul's University, and the Order of the Sash from the Manitoba Métis Federation.

For more on the Meech Lake Accord, see Chapter 6. Given Harper's background, do you think that his opposition to the Accord could have been predicted? Was it reasonable? Explain.

The Search for an Accord

Under the Liberals, the federal government and the provinces had not got along very well. Mulroney had campaigned on a promise to reduce this conflict. He had also pledged to find a compromise that would allow Quebec to willingly support the Canadian constitution.

In April 1987, the prime minister invited the 10 provincial premiers to a retreat in Meech Lake, Quebec. After much debate, an agreement was reached on constitutional change. Later called the Meech Lake Accord, it proposed to take away some power from the federal government and give more of it to the provinces. This process is called "decentralizing." It also recognized Quebec as a distinct society. The agreement did not pass in all provincial legislatures, though, so it was not adopted.

Mulroney made another attempt to change the Canadian Constitution. The proposed Charlottetown Accord was defeated by national vote, or referendum, on 26 October 1992. Once again, the nation was in the middle of a unity crisis. Many Canadians blamed Mulroney for moving too fast on an emotional and complex issue. (See Chapter 6 for more.)

MOVING AWAY FROM GOVERNMENT SERVICES

From about 1950 on, Canadian governments created programs to provide Canadians with a social safety net. Canada's safety net included old age pensions, universal health care, child welfare programs, and unemployment benefits. Mulroney, however, was concerned with their costs and reduced them to save money.

Mulroney also reduced government involvement in the economy. He did this by selling government-owned companies. Mulroney sold such companies as Petro-Canada, Air Canada, and CNCP Telecommunications.

These companies are examples of Crown corporations. Mulroney also promoted private retail businesses taking over more postal services. The process of transferring a business to private ownership is called "privatization." Between 1984 and 1992, the federal government privatized 39 Crown corporations and other corporate interests. Canada's business community—its private sector—began providing services that were once the responsibility of the federal government.

FOCUS

1. What did Mulroney promise Canadians?
2. What economic success did Canada enjoy?
3. Why was the GST introduced?
4. Explain the term *privatization*.

Foreign Policy Changes

The Mulroney government promised to improve and increase the strength of Canada's armed forces. In 1985, Canadian Forces personnel received newly designed, modern uniforms. New tanks, armoured vehicles, and guns were bought. Canada ordered 138 CF-18 fighter planes. St. John Shipbuilding began building HMCS *Halifax*, the first of several Halifax Class Canadian patrol frigates, which would cost $3.9 billion. Under Trudeau, the Canadian Forces had weakened.

Arctic Waters

In 1986, the United States sent the icebreaker *Polar Sea* through the Arctic northern passage. Permission had not been asked of the Canadian government. The United States claimed that the passage was an international waterway. Russian submarines were known to use Arctic waters, too, to escape NATO detection.

Canada considered the Arctic islands and waterway Canadian territory, but had done

Canada has long borders and coastlines that are difficult to defend. From smoky industrial ports to icy Arctic waters, Halifax Class patrol frigates help assert Canadian sovereignty and protect Canadian interests.

little to establish control of the area. The Progressive Conservatives said they were going to buy nuclear-powered submarines to patrol Canadian shores and the Arctic. The idea was well liked, but the $8 billion cost was not.

Still, Canadians agreed that something had to be done. Canada needed to assert Canadian rights to the northern coastal waters. When U.S. President Ronald Reagan visited Canada in 1988, he told Prime Minister Mulroney that his nation would notify Canada whenever an American submarine planned to use the Northwest Passage. Canada began air patrols and military exercises as far north as Ellesmere Island.

The United Nations

In 1984, Prime Minister Mulroney appointed Stephen Lewis Canadian ambassador to the United

Canadian Forces on manoeuvres in the Arctic.

In 2005, Canadian Forces asserted Canadian sovereignty on Hans Island, Nunavut, during a sovereignty patrol of the Arctic.

Nations. This move surprised many people because Lewis was a former leader of the Ontario NDP. Lewis turned out to be an excellent choice.

Lewis spoke out on issues relating to the needs of developing countries. He spoke with passion and strength. By 1989, Canada was again recognized as a leading middle power at the UN. Serving a fifth term on the United Nations Security Council confirmed this.

Later, in 1991, Canada was part of the UN's 32-nation contingent in Operation

Desert Storm. Iraq had attacked its neighbour, Kuwait. After Iraq refused to retreat, the United Nations' forces launched the operation to free Kuwait. The forces were led by the United States. Desert Storm was the first time that the United Nations made a declaration of war. It did so to protect one of its member nations.

Stephen Lewis was an eloquent spokesperson for Canada at the UN. He later became a strong advocate for African sufferers of HIV (human immunodeficiency virus). (See Chapter 8 for more.)

Apartheid and the Commonwealth

Most of the Commonwealth's 54 members are former British colonies, and Canada is an important member. The Commonwealth is dedicated to promoting world peace, social tolerance, racial equality, and economic growth. (See Chapter 8 for more.)

During the 1980s, the Commonwealth faced serious problems. Developing countries within it had a great need for economic aid. Beyond that, South Africa's racist policies concerned the Commonwealth. Although South Africa was no longer part of the organization, it still practised **apartheid**. Britain had failed to oppose a system that went against Commonwealth goals and ideals.

Prime Minister Mulroney spoke out strongly against apartheid. He urged all Commonwealth countries to put pressure on South Africa. Refusing to trade with the country was one effective way to do it. Not all Commonwealth countries agreed to stop trading with South Africa, though. Britain under Prime Minister Margaret Thatcher continued

A CLOSER LOOK AT APARTHEID

South Africa's apartheid policies became official in 1948. Apartheid rules kept Blacks apart from whites. They also denied Blacks basic rights of citizenship. Blacks did not have the right to vote, to own property, or to travel with freedom. Commonwealth members objected to this so much that South Africa was forced to withdraw from the Commonwealth in 1961. In 1991, apartheid was officially abandoned. The pressure many countries had put on South Africa came to good effect. In 1993, the first multiracial government was elected in South Africa, and in 1994, the country rejoined the Commonwealth.

to trade with the country. Canada's strong stand against apartheid created some friction there. Overall, Mulroney's leadership and attacks on South Africa's apartheid policies made him one of the most respected Commonwealth leaders of the late 1980s.

Canada's strong anti-apartheid stand would not be forgotten. Nelson Mandela spent 30 years in prison under the apartheid regime. After he became South Africa's first Black president, Mandela visited Canada in 1998. He paid tribute to Canada and Canadians for opposing apartheid. He noted that South Africa would not have given up apartheid and turned to democracy without the support and encouragement of countries such as Canada.

South African President Nelson Mandela thanked Canadians for their support of a free South Africa. Jean Chrétien, prime minister by 1998, stands at Mandela's left.

"I have fought against white domination, and have fought against black domination. I have cherished the ideal of a democratic and free society in which all persons live together in harmony and with equal opportunities. It is an ideal, which I hope to live for and to achieve. But if needs be, it is an ideal for which I am prepared to die."

FOCUS

1. Explain how Mulroney changed Canada's foreign policy regarding (a) Arctic defence, (b) the armed forces, and (c) the Commonwealth.
2. What is apartheid? Why did Canada oppose apartheid in South Africa?

The Chrétien Years

For many years, Jean Chrétien was one of Canada's most popular political figures. In 2005, though, the Gomery Commission Report accused him of carelessness with government money in the "sponsorship scandal."

Jean Chrétien became Canada's 20th prime minister in 1993. He defeated Kim Campbell, the new Progressive Conservative leader. She had briefly succeeded Brian Mulroney.

Chrétien was an experienced politician. He had served under Pearson and Trudeau. His reputation for honesty and toughness made him popular with voters. From a family of modest means, he became a wealthy lawyer and a respected Cabinet minister. Chrétien projected a popular, down-to-earth image as the "little guy from Shawinigan."

The new prime minister faced two major problems. He had to deal with a budget deficit of $46 billion, which was rising annu-ally, and a strong Quebec separatist movement (discussed more fully in Chapter 6). Chrétien himself came from Quebec.

Chrétien appointed Paul Martin as minister of finance and directed him to reduce government spending. Martin froze public service wages, cut defence and foreign aid spending, and reduced the number of government employees. By 1998, Martin announced a budget surplus. It was the first Canadian surplus in 25 years.

Expanding World Trade

The Chrétien government worked to improve Canada's economic ties throughout the world. It built upon the Free Trade Agreement that Mulroney's government had negotiated with the United States. (See Chapter 7.) NAFTA (North American Free Trade Agreement) came into effect in 1994. It brought Canada, the United States, and Mexico into a much closer trading relationship. Canada extended economic ties west to other Pacific Rim Countries through APEC (Asian-Pacific Economic Cooperation), too. As for the north, Canada became a founding member of the Arctic Council, an alliance of eight nations with lands in the Arctic.

As of 1994, Chrétien and the premiers formed "Team Canada." Their mission took them to many parts of the world. "Team

Canada Comes of Age

Canada" travelled to China, South America, Cuba, and Asia. It focused mainly on increasing trade and investment. Chrétien also urged other world leaders to support human rights for their citizens.

More Privatization
In the desire to make government run more efficiently, Chrétien and leaders such as Alberta's Ralph Klein and Ontario's Mike Harris privatized more government-owned corporations. For example, Alberta sold its retail liquor outlets and telephone company. Under Premier Harris, Ontario's Highway 407 became the country's first privately owned highway.

Social Union Agreement
Several times in the late 1990s, Canada's premiers met with federal officials to discuss social services. They wanted to determine how best to deliver such services as child care, health care, pensions, and education. In 1999, they signed the Social Union Agreement. Its purpose was to eliminate duplication of services between the federal

Jean Chrétien stands with APEC leaders at a conference held in British Columbia.

and provincial governments. The premiers also hoped that the agreement would increase co-operation and discussion between the federal and provincial governments. All provinces, except Quebec, agreed to the principles outlined in the agreement.

FOCUS
1. What two major problems did Chrétien's Liberals face when they first came to power?
2. What was Chrétien's "Team Canada"?

The Martin Minority

Once Paul Martin became prime minister, he had to contend with Auditor General Sheila Fraser's news that there had been uncontrolled spending during his time as finance minister.

Paul Martin's interest in Canadian politics began early. His father, Paul Martin Sr., served many years in the House of Commons. Martin was elected to the House of Commons as a Liberal in 1988; however, Mulroney's Progressive Conservatives formed a majority government.

This election marked John Turner's second loss to Mulroney, so he decided to step down as Liberal leader. Martin campaigned for the leadership of the Liberal Party in 1990, but lost to Jean Chrétien. In 1993, Chrétien guided the Liberals to the first of three majority governments: 1993, 1997, and 2000.

Martin as Minister of Finance

Martin served as minister of finance under Chrétien from 1993 to 2002. During this time, Canada faced huge yearly deficits. Making tough budget cuts, Martin reduced the national deficit and government spending, balanced the annual budget, and paid down Canada's debt. Some Canadians, though, felt that these goals had been achieved through deep cuts to spending in such areas as health care.

Martin's supporters openly organized for the day when he would become the new leader of the Liberal Party. In 2002, when Martin and Chrétien could not resolve a disagreement on spending, Martin left the Cabinet. When Chrétien retired, Martin was elected Liberal Party leader. In December 2003, Governor General Adrienne Clarkson swore in Paul Martin as prime minister.

Martin as Prime Minister

Sheila Fraser, Canada's auditor general, had previously reported disturbing news. She stated that there had been uncontrolled spending in the Public Works Department during Chrétien's term as prime minister. Fraser said that the government paid over $100 million to companies in Quebec for doing little or no work.

Martin appointed Justice Charles Gomery to investigate what became known as the "sponsorship scandal." A preliminary report in late 2005 cleared Martin, but not Chrétien. The Opposition blamed Martin because he had been minister of finance and, in their opinion, he should have known where the money was going.

Martin called an election for 24 June 2004, which the Liberal Party barely won. It had 135 seats (mostly from Ontario) while the Conservatives under Stephen Harper had 99. The Bloc Québécois won 54 Quebec seats, and the NDP and an independent took 20. The Liberals formed a minority government.

Martin needed the support of 20 Opposition members to govern. His government managed to pass the budget with support from the NDP. In return, NDP leader Jack Layton negotiated a change in spending. While in office, Martin established friendlier relations with U.S. President George W. Bush. However, the two countries disagreed on the issues of softwood lumber and the Canadian cattle trade.

The Martin government survived several more months after Conservative Belinda Stronach turned Liberal and the 2005 budget passed.

Under Martin, the Civil Marriage Act came into law in July 2005. Canada became one of only a few countries to legalize same-sex marriage. This Act represented a milestone for the Liberals and for Canada.

In November 2005, a straight **motion of non-confidence** defeated Martin's government. In the January 2006 election that followed, the Liberals lost to Stephen Harper and the Conservatives.

FOCUS

1. **What were Martin's achievements as minister of finance?**
2. **What changes did Martin make as prime minister?**

Conservative Politics: 1993–2006

After two consecutive terms in power, Brian Mulroney resigned in 1993. Kim Campbell, a member of his Cabinet, became Canada's first female prime minister and first female leader of the Progressive Conservative Party.

Campbell called a quick election and on October 1993 her party suffered a crushing defeat. The PC party managed to win only two seats in all of Canada. In contrast, the new Reform Party, under the leadership of Albertan Preston Manning, won 52 seats. With only two seats, the Progressive Conservative Party had become almost invisible in Parliament.

The Bloc Québécois and Reform Party dominated Opposition benches. Jean Charest was elected leader of the PC party and increased its representation to 20 seats in the 1997 election. The western-based Reform Party, still led by Manning, became the Official Opposition with 60 seats.

The fortunes of the Progressive Conservatives and the Reform Party seemed to be connected. Both parties were fighting for the support of the same conservative-minded voters. Both parties struggled to establish a party platform that would attract Canadians from coast to coast. Both experienced frequent leadership changes. Both depended on regional support and lacked stability. Neither could win a majority.

After Charest left for Quebec provincial politics in 1998, Joe Clark, a former prime minister, returned to public life as leader of the Progressive Conservatives. In March 2000, the Reform Party of Canada disbanded and reinvented itself as the Canadian Reform Conservative Alliance Party. It hoped to broaden its Western Canada focus and attract new conservative voters from Ontario to Atlantic Canada. It was known as the

Stephen Harper and his family on election night, 23 January 2006.

Alliance Party under the brief leadership of Stockwell Day.

By 2003, both parties had new leaders. Nova Scotian Peter MacKay led the Progressive Conservatives and Stephen Harper led the Canadian Alliance. Both Harper and MacKay understood that the two parties could not win elections by competing for the same voters. There was talk of a merger.

In 2003, Harper, MacKay, and their party members agreed to merge the two parties. After yet another leadership convention, Stephen Harper was elected the leader of the new party in March 2004. This party was called the Conservative Party.

In the federal election of 2004, Harper's Conservatives almost toppled the Liberal Party, now led by Paul Martin. The Liberals clung to power with a minority.

In late 2005, the Liberals were defeated in the House of Commons, and an election was called for 23 January 2006. Harper promised an open and accountable government and criticized the Liberals for the "sponsorship scandal." Conservative policies now included

- a promise to give Canadian parents $100 a month for daycare for children under 6 and tax credits for community child care
- a tougher and more efficient criminal justice system
- a free vote on the definition of same-sex marriage
- more money invested in hiring regular soldiers and reserves
- a promise to cut the $975 immigration fee in half

Results of 2006 Election

Conservatives	124 seats
Liberals	103 seats
Bloc	51 seats
NDP	29 seats
Independent	1 seat

The Liberals seemed tired and confused. When the ballots were cast, Harper had won a minority and Paul Martin announced he would retire from politics.

FOCUS

1. Why did the Progressive Conservative Party and Reform Party find it difficult to win elections in the 1990s?
2. What policies helped Harper win the election of 2006?

New People
for a New Society

Who should be allowed to come to Canada? Until the Second World War, the federal government made it difficult for Asians, Jews, and eastern Europeans to immigrate to Canada. It did not believe they would "fit in" with Canadian society. In 1914, 376 Sikhs

As lieutenant governor of Ontario, James Bartleman, centre, sits next to 100 000 books to be sent to Native communities in Northern Ontario. Bartleman is the first member of a First Nation in this role. Before that, he had a distinguished career in the Canadian foreign service.

from India were turned away from Vancouver. They had waited onboard the *Komagata Maru* for two months before being rejected. A few refugees from Europe were accepted

into the country after the Second World War as a humanitarian gesture. Canada's basic immigration policy remained the same, though. White people from the Commonwealth, the United States, and France were preferred. Other Europeans came next. Non-whites were not welcomed.

New Policies

By the 1970s, many Canadians felt the immigration policy needed to be changed. They believed that Canada should choose immigrants based on the need for workers with specific skills. It should not matter what country people were from. In 1976, the Canadian government announced a new immigration policy. Immigrants would be judged by a point system. Points were

Kim Phuc, shown in happier times, immigrated to Canada from Vietnam. A 1972 photograph of 12-year-old Kim and her family fleeing the horrors of napalm attack during the Vietnam War still haunts the world conscience.

awarded for education, job skills, and knowledge of English or French.

Many Asians, Africans, and Caribbean people now came to find a new life in Canada. By the end of the 1980s, over 60 000 **boat people**, primarily refugees from South Vietnam, had come to Canada. During the 1990s, Canada accepted displaced Romas, thousands of Kosovars, Somalians, Rwandans, and Chinese refugees.

Lincoln Alexander was Ontario's lieutenant governor from 1986 to 1991. He was the first Black Canadian to hold this post. Born in Canada, he became a symbol of Canadian diversity.

THE HUTTERITES: A PEOPLE APART

One community within Canada that has little interest in "fitting in" is the Hutterites. Many Hutterites arrived in Canada from the United States in 1918. Their refusal to fight in the First World War brought them persecution for their religious beliefs. Hutterites oppose war and reject military service. Earlier, many had fled Eastern Europe due to religious persecution there. In Canada, Hutterite immigrants found freedom to live according to early Christian teachings.

Today, they live much as they did before. They follow strictly a communal form of life, where members live in colonies of about 125 and share property together. Many operate well-managed farms. They speak in a German dialect, dress modestly, and live simply. Committed to growing in love for others, they respond to the larger world by supporting various aid and relief projects. Since the Second World War, they have been granted conscientious objector status in Canada. That means their refusal to give military service due to their beliefs is recognized and respected here.

Like other nations, Canada sometimes updates its immigration policies. In 2005, the government announced that immigration numbers would be increased from 245 000 to 345 000 per year. Canada decided to accept more people for several reasons:

- The national birth rate had declined since the 1960s.
- The population was getting older.
- There was a shortage of skilled workers.

Individuals wishing to live in Canada can apply under three different categories. The government provides a Web site so that potential immigrants can learn about the process.

Canadian institutions such as the Royal Canadian Mounted Police (RCMP) have made adjustments for the traditions and values of a broad range of Canadians.

New Faces

By 2000, the immigration policy had changed the face of Canada. The change was obvious because many of the new immigrants looked different. Different in colour, dress, and customs, they made up **visible minorities**. Children born in Canada found their new classmates were from Uganda, India, South America, or Trinidad.

A line-up in the supermarket might include people from all over the world. Many Canadians found this interesting and exciting. Others found it frightening. People often fear what they do not understand. Sometimes, fear can turn to prejudice and hate.

Integration

Today, it is generally believed that Canada is a richer society due to the presence of immigrants from all over the world. New Canadians are free to keep much of their original culture, such as customs, beliefs, and traditions, while adapting to Canadian ways.

New Canadians gradually integrate into a Canadian identity. Some have jobs in the RCMP, local police, and firefighting forces. Some work in law, medicine, and other professions. Radio and TV stations have reporters of different racial and ethnic backgrounds.

Canadians celebrate their multicultural heritage. Toronto's CHIN International picnic and Caribana festival are two of the many multicultural or multiracial celebrations held each year in Ontario. The face of Canada has indeed changed.

BELOW RIGHT: *Jarome Iginla, NHL and Team Canada hockey player*
BELOW: *Ujjal Dosanijh, former B.C. premier*
FAR RIGHT, LARGE IMAGE : *Daniel Igali, freestyle wrestling champion*

ABOVE: *Michael Lee-Chin, founder of AIC Limited, a large mutual fund company*
RIGHT: *Vivienne Poy, senator*
FAR RIGHT: *Anil Thapa, radio voice of Nepalese Canadians*

FOCUS

1. **Which groups of people found it difficult to immigrate to Canada before the 1970s? Why?**
2. **How did Canada's immigration policy change during the 1970s?**
3. **What does the term *visible minority* mean?**
4. **How does immigration benefit Canada?**

Prejudice and Racism

These Toronto students wrote prize-winning essays on how to deal with racial bullying. Their common message was that students should get involved when they see others being bullied or harassed—they should not rely on teachers or other adults to help. The essay competition, in which 4000 students took part, was part of celebrations for the 2006 International Day for the Elimination of Racial Discrimination, which is celebrated annually in Canada.

Individuals sometimes prejudge other people before they get to know them. They show prejudice, and sometimes prejudices result in acts of **discrimination**. Over the years, many Canadian immigrants have suffered from prejudice. They could not get good jobs.

Some employers demanded "Canadian experience." Some immigrants had trouble finding a place to live. Immigrants found themselves the target of racial attacks.

In racial acts, people mistreat other people because of race or culture. Racism is a form of stereotyping. Racists believe that people of one race are smarter and superior to people of another race or culture. They seek power over others. Canada has not been immune to racism. Its treatment of African Canadians is one of many examples.

Overcoming Racism

Deep-seated racism against Blacks persisted after the Second World War. Many of these people were native-born, descendants of Blacks who had sought freedom in Canada in the last century. African Canadians, like their American counterparts, fought discrimination. In 1946, the Nova Scotia Association for the Advancement of Coloured People raised money to help Viola Desmond fight segregation in movie theatres. Desmond was a Halifax beautician. She was arrested in a New Glasgow theatre for sitting downstairs. Blacks were supposed to sit on the balcony. The case was

thrown out on a technicality. The incident brought a lot of negative publicity. Slowly, discriminatory laws like that one were abandoned.

Discrimination on the basis of race was common elsewhere, too. For example, in Dresden, Ontario, Blacks made up 17 percent of the town's population in 1950. Restaurants, poolrooms, barber and beauty shops, however, refused to serve non-whites.

The plight of Blacks in Nova Scotia received international attention when the city of Halifax decided to demolish Africville. Halifax's Black population had lived in the tightly knit community since the mid-19th century. The community had been greatly neglected by city authorities, though. The city did not provide water, sewage facilities, or garbage collection. It had built the municipal dump nearby. In 1961, the city council focused on Africville. It decided to remove the 400 citizens because it wanted their land for an industrial development. Residents protested the action. Eventually, many were compensated for their property and offered other housing; however, a loss of community resulted from the relocation.

For audiovisual information about Africville, visit the CBC Digital Archives at www.cbc.ca/archives and open the file "Africville: Expropriating Nova Scotia's Blacks."

Oscar Peterson

BORN: 1925, Montreal, Quebec

SIGNIFICANCE: Some people consider Peterson to be the greatest jazz musician in the world. He has recorded more than 100 albums.

BRIEF BIOGRAPHY: When he was 14, Peterson won a national CBC piano contest. He soon had his own weekly radio show. He played at local clubs in and around Montreal. He debuted at Carnegie Hall in 1949, where, at the age of 24, he outshone more prominent performers. Peterson has had a long and successful career as a jazz pianist. He has played with Ella Fitzgerald, Dizzy Gillespie, and Lester Young. He has won Grammy Awards, a Juno, and the Glenn Gould Prize.

Unlike many Canadian musicians, Peterson has remained in Canada rather than pursue his career in the United States. He moved to Toronto in 1958. Here, he briefly operated a world-famous jazz school during the 1960s. In 1986, he began teaching music part-time at York University in Toronto. In 1991, he became chancellor of the university. Peterson's many honours include becoming a Companion of the Order of Canada. **For more information, visit the CBC Digital Archives at www.cbc.ca/archives and open the file "Oscar Peterson: A Jazz Giant."**

CANADIAN LIVES

By the 1960s, African Canadians, like Americans in the Black Power movement, began to assert their rights. Black leaders refused to accept second-class citizenship. Many of these leaders were recent immigrants from the West Indies and Africa.

Over time, West Indian immigration to Canada had increased. From 1955 to 1961, only about 4000 Caribbean immigrants were allowed to enter the country; between 1971 and 1981, though, 140 000 West Indians came to Canada. Two-thirds settled in southern Ontario, where they could maintain their cultures, newspapers, Caribana festival, and anti-racist organizations. Trudeau's Liberal government welcomed visible minorities.

Canada now acts against racism. The federal government promotes the hiring and education of visible minority members. Initiatives such as the 2006 creation of www.blackhistorycanada.ca also help. As Black activist Rosemary Sadler said, "African

Canadian students need to feel affirmed, be aware of the contributions made by other blacks in Canada, have role models …"
Since 1989, Canada has celebrated the International Day for the Elimination of Racial Discrimination by promoting respect, equality and diversity. Still, discrimination and even hate crimes occur. Even the Canadian Charter of Rights and Freedoms cannot end this. People have to learn to respect one another, and that takes time.

HATE CRIMES

Hate crimes are acts of violence directed against people because of racial, religious, ethnic, or other differences. According to one Canadian poll, about 60 000 hate crimes are committed in Canada's major urban centres every year. Hate crimes need not be violent to be defined as criminal offences. Slurs, threats, and vandalism can all be hate crimes.

Two Canadians have received much media attention for their hate crimes. James Keegstra, an Alberta teacher, was fired for giving anti-Semitic lectures. Ernst Zundel was prosecuted for expressing racist ideas. Both were charged under Canada's criminal code. Canada's criminal code states that anyone "who, by communicating statements, other than in private communication, wilfully promotes hatred against an identifiable group is guilty of an indictable offence and is liable to imprisonment."

FOCUS

1. Define (a) prejudice, (b) discrimination, and (c) racism.
2. How did Halifax authorities discriminate against residents of Africville?
3. What are hate crimes?

Canada's Aboriginal Peoples

Aboriginal Canadians were the first Canadians. Before Europeans came to Canada, they lived a life in harmony with nature. Most Aboriginal Canadians did not have a system of private property. The bounty of nature was shared by everyone.

Over time, contact with Europeans destroyed the Aboriginal way of life. Traders brought guns, whisky, and disease. Aboriginal peoples began to depend on Europeans for a living. Beaver, mink, and other animals were hunted for their fur.

European Settlements and Treaties

As Europeans established settlements, they took Aboriginal lands. Sometimes, a treaty was made between the Aboriginal peoples and the government. Aboriginal peoples lost land that they regarded as their heritage. They were usually allowed small areas of land, called "reserves," a few tools, and an annual pension. Today, First Nations leaders argue that their ancestors did not understand that they were giving up their land by signing treaties with the government.

The government offered Aboriginal peoples little help. It expected them to become productive farmers, even though the land they got was usually unsuitable for farming. Most Aboriginal peoples lost the customs and values they cherished. If they left the reserves to seek work, they faced discrimination. They often lived in poverty. They were trapped in a lifestyle that robbed them of their self-respect.

First Nations Lobby Groups

Canadian Aboriginal groups struggled against poverty, poor health care, poor housing, and lack of education opportunities. Lobbying for government help would be useful, but at times, federal governments passed laws that stopped them from forming lobby groups.

During the late 1940s, several representatives from Canada's Aboriginal peoples came together. They formed the North American Indian Brotherhood (NAIB). Not all First

Nations supported its efforts, and the government prevented its growth. In 1969, the National Indian Brotherhood (NIB) was created. Many Aboriginal organizations supported this new lobby group. It successfully fought the Liberal government's 1969 White Paper on how to **assimilate** Aboriginal peoples into white society.

In 1982, the NIB became the Assembly of First Nations (AFN). It consisted of chiefs and elders who represented most Aboriginal groups in Canada. They wanted self-determination, or self-government, for First Nations peoples. Dedicated Aboriginal chiefs, such as Georges Erasmus, Ovide Mercredi, Phil Fontaine, and Matthew Coon Come, led the AFN. The AFN has pressed successfully for improvements in Aboriginal education, business opportunities, and family support.

Phil Fontaine, in a ceremonial blanket, receives applause on being elected national chief for the Assembly of First Nations. His term began in 2003.

Matthew Coon Come has represented Aboriginal peoples in the United Nations and at other meetings, such as the Earth Summit in Brazil. He was named Chief of the Mistassini Cree from 1981 to 1986. In 1987, he was elected Grand Chief of the Grand Council of the Crees for the first of four terms. From 2000 to 2003, he served as AFN Grand Chief. He is widely known for asserting the rights of the Crees of Northern Quebec. Their challenges have included hydro-electric megaprojects.

CONFRONTATION AT KANESATAKE

In March 1990, Mohawk warriors from the Kanesatake Reserve outside Montreal blocked a road leading to Oka, Quebec. They were protesting the development of a golf course on an ancient Mohawk burial ground. The police were called in when the warriors refused to leave. One officer died in the shootout.

For 11 weeks, Mohawk protesters faced Canadian soldiers in a tense standoff. Finally, the protesters surrendered. The disputed lands were ultimately turned over to the Mohawk nation.

THE INDIAN ACT

In 1876, the Canadian Parliament passed the Indian Act. The Act defined "Indian" in the legal sense. The Act was changed a number of times from 1876 to 1985. Inuit and Métis are included under the Act.

Today, the government of Canada keeps a list, or register, of all Aboriginals who fall under the authority of the Indian Act.

- *Status Indians* are Aboriginals who are registered under the terms of the Indian Act. They have different rights from Métis and non-status Indians. For example, they have housing benefits on reserves and some exemption from federal and provincial taxes. Status Indians or their ancestors have signed a treaty with the government.
- *Registered Indians* are status Indians whose ancestors have not signed treaties with the government. They also come under the regulations of the Indian Act. Most registered Indians live in British

Ovide Mercredi, lawyer and Aboriginal rights activist, as well as AFN chief 1991–97

Columbia, parts of Quebec, the Northwest Territories, Nunavut, and the Yukon.

- *Non-status Indians* are members of the First Nations who are not registered under the terms of the Indian Act. Their ancestors may not have been registered.
- Métis are Canadians of mixed blood. They are descended from both Indians and Europeans.
- *Inuit* are part of the Eskimo-Aleutian linguistic family. Most of the more than 51 000 Inuit live in the James Bay area of Quebec, northern Quebec, Labrador, and Nunavut.

Women and the Indian Act

The Indian Act stripped Aboriginal women of their Indian status when they married non-Indian men. Loss of Indian status meant that these women could not live on reserves and they lost their benefits. Indian men who married non-Indian women did not lose Indian status.

In 1981, a Maliseet woman from New Brunswick, Sandra Lovelace, asked the United Nations' Human Rights Committee to review her case. The Committee agreed that the Indian Act discriminated against Aboriginal women. The Indian Act was changed in 1985 to allow Aboriginal women and men who had lost Indian status prior to 1985 to regain it. The Indian Act remains in effect today.

FOCUS

1. How did contact with Europeans change the Aboriginal way of life?
2. How might the European view of treaties differ from the Aboriginal view?
3. What was the purpose of the Indian Act?
4. How did the Indian Act discriminate against women?

Towards Aboriginal Self-Government

"Like the Thunderbird of old I shall rise again out of the sea; I shall grab the instruments of the white man's success—his education, his skills, and with these new tools I shall build my race into the proudest segment of your society.

Chief Dan George in 1967
Lament for Confederation

Canada's Aboriginal peoples want an adequate standard of living like other Canadians. They also want to regain or assert control over their ancestral lands and their lives. The legal issues concern two questions.

- Do Aboriginal peoples still have a legal right to their ancestors' original lands?
- Do Aboriginal peoples have the right to live off the land (hunt, fish) as their ancestors did?

Canada's Aboriginal peoples sought to win the principle of Aboriginal land claim and the right to use the land as their forefathers had. Canadian and provincial governments maintained that Aboriginals gave up their right to the land. Canada's Aboriginals argued that the land had been stolen from them. They took their cases to court.

Land Claims in Quebec

In the 1970s, the Quebec government was planning to build a series of dams on James Bay. The dams would have flooded huge sections of land occupied by the Cree and Inuit peoples of Quebec. The Crees went to court. They claimed Aboriginal title to the land. The project was stopped. In 1975, the Aboriginal groups received 170 000 square km, a measure of self-government, relocation costs, and $225 million over 20 years. Quebec got the right to build the huge hydro project. This agreement is known as the James Bay Agreement. (See Chapter 6 for more.)

Land Claims in British Columbia

Lawyers representing British Columbia Aboriginals argued that their clients had not given up ownership of the land (Aboriginal title). They had not signed treaties with either the provincial or federal government. The province argued that there was no such thing as Aboriginal title.

A turning point came in 1973. The Nisga'a nation lived in the Nass Valley of British Columbia. They had lived there long before the first Europeans came to Canada. For more than 100 years, they had been trying to have their ownership of the land recognized. The Nisga'a people claimed Aboriginal title to 24 000 square km near the Nass River in northern British Columbia. Their case finally reached the Supreme Court of Canada in 1971.

In 1973, the Court made its decision. Three judges ruled in favour of the Aboriginal viewpoint and three against. One judge said that proper process was not followed. The Court, however, recognized that Aboriginal title existed.

The Canadian government heeded that decision. It set out to negotiate settlements for land claims in areas where treaties did not exist. All agreements since 1973 have included some degree of self-government for Aboriginal communities.

The Nisga'a Treaty

The Nisga'a Final Agreement of 2000 gave the Nisga'a people the right to self-government and the right to manage lands and resources. The Nisga'a won the power to set local taxes and also received $196.1 million. They could now administer a

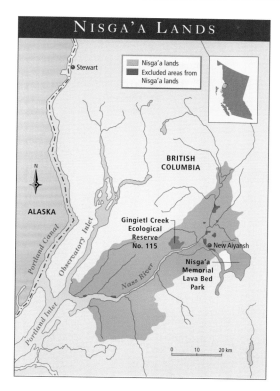

NISGA'A LANDS

Nisga'a lands
Excluded areas from Nisga'a lands

Stewart
BRITISH COLUMBIA
ALASKA
Portland Canal
Observatory Inlet
Gingietl Creek Ecological Reserve No. 115
New Aiyansh
Nisga'a Memorial Lava Bed Park
Nass River
Portland Inlet
0　10　20 km

territory of 2020 square km. They had gained a form of self-government within Canada.

Chief Joseph Gosnell, of the Nisga'a Tribal Council, helped negotiate the Nisga'a Treaty. Just before the B.C. legislature approved it in 1998, he spoke.

"We have worked for justice for more than a century. Now, it is time to ratify the Nisga'a Treaty, for Aboriginal and non-Aboriginal people to come together and write a new chapter in the history of our Nation, our province, our country, and indeed, the world.

"The world is our witness. Be strong. Be steadfast. Be true."

FOCUS

1. **Why is self-government important for Aboriginal Canadians?**
2. **In your view, are Aboriginal Canadians treated equally today? Explain.**

Nunavut: Our Land

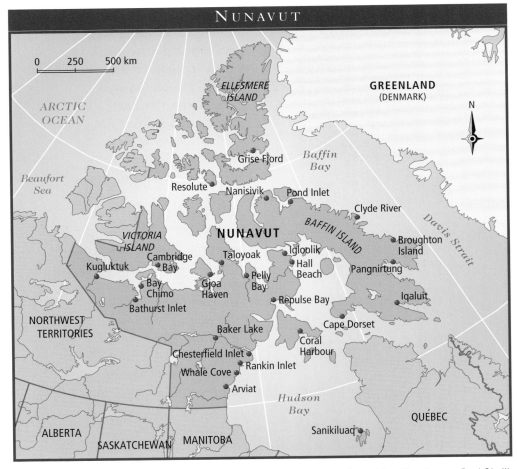

NUNAVUT

0   250   500 km

ARCTIC
OCEAN

ELLESMERE
ISLAND

GREENLAND
(DENMARK)

N

Baffin
Bay

Grise Fjord

Beaufort
Sea

Resolute   Nanisivik   Pond Inlet

Clyde River

Davis Strait

VICTORIA
ISLAND

NUNAVUT

BAFFIN ISLAND

Broughton
Island

Kugluktuk

Cambridge
Bay

Taloyoak

Igloolik

Hall
Beach

Pangnirtung

Bay
Chimo

Gjoa
Haven

Pelly
Bay

Bathurst Inlet

Repulse Bay

Iqaluit

NORTHWEST
TERRITORIES

Baker Lake

Cape Dorset

Chesterfield Inlet

Coral
Harbour

Whale Cove

Rankin Inlet

Arviat

Hudson
Bay

QUÉBEC

ALBERTA

SASKATCHEWAN

MANITOBA

Sanikiluaq

In Nunavut, everyone over the age of 16 can vote or run for public office. Lawyer Paul Okalik (right) was 34 years old when elected as Nunavut's first territorial leader.

km. It makes up one-fifth of Canada, or an area larger than Saskatchewan and Alberta combined.

Despite its size, Nunavut is home to only about 25 000 people. About 85 percent are Inuit—the word "Inuit" means people. The territory has four official languages: Inuktitut, Inuinnaqtum, French, and English. Eighty percent of the Inuit speak Inuktitut very well. The Inuit promote their culture through the Department of Culture, Language, Elders, and Youth.

The creation of the territory gave the Inuit greater decision-making power and control. The Inuit Tapirisat of Canada, the Ungavik Federation of Nunavut, and the Canadian government had negotiated for more than 15 years. The Inuit

Nunavut grew out of the largest Aboriginal land claims agreement in Canadian history. On 1 April 1999, the map of Canada changed due to the creation of this territory. Formerly part of the Northwest Territories, this frozen land above the treeline is two million square

sought title to the Arctic lands and self-government. Earlier, in 1982, people in the Northwest Territories had agreed to split the territory in two through a vote. The eastern part would become Nunavut. The boundaries of Nunavut were decided by another popular election in 1992. In 1993, the Nunavut Land Claims Agreement was made. In choosing to create a territory, though, the Inuit chose a public government structure that would serve Inuit and non-Inuit alike.

Iqaluit, formerly known as Frobisher Bay, was chosen as the capital. Snowmobiles, dogsleds, and airplanes are the major methods of transportation. There are no road links to areas outside the territory and only one road within it. The road connects the communities between Arctic Bay and Nanisivik. The majority of Inuit families continue to depend on hunting and fishing for their food. The territory's oil, gas, and mineral riches have become increasingly important to the region's economy. The Department of Sustainable Development promotes eco-

Paul Okalik

The Inuit have traditionally used stone inukshuks to guide travellers and offer welcome and comfort. This inukshuk (right) is embedded with images of Nunavut's people and is used by the Nunavut Literacy Council.

nomic development, while working to preserve the environment. Nunavut's vast resource wealth is likely to be of great benefit to the citizens of Nunavut and Canada.

Canadian Vision

Aboriginal and Inuit Cultures

Canada's Aboriginal and Inuit peoples have a rich heritage of oral and written literature and artistic tradition. Fine examples are modern poets Daniel David Moses and Jeanette Armstrong. They write about Aboriginal identity, culture, the natural world, conflict, and change. Novelist Thomas King describes Aboriginal struggle and triumph with painful reality. His novel, *Green Grass, Running Water*, tells the story of five Blackfoot characters in modern-day Canada.

Buffy Sainte-Marie

Susan Aglukark

Popular singers like Susan Aglukark and Buffy Sainte-Marie contribute through their music. Ojibway playwright Drew Hayden Taylor brings Aboriginal concerns to the stage. Aboriginal and Inuit prints, sculpture, and wall hangings are exhibited and collected around the world. Painter Norval Morriseau pioneered the style known as Woodland Indian Art, which blends Aboriginal and Euro Canadian ideals. Daphne Odjig is one of the many Woodland Indian artists in Canada today. Her paintings deal with human relationships within Aboriginal culture. Inuit printmaker Kenojuak Ashevak's drawing, "The Enchanted Owl," was used on the stamp celebrating the 100th anniversary of the Northwest Territories. She was the first Aboriginal artist to be awarded the Order of Canada. Pitseolak Ashoona's book, *Pitseolak: Pictures out of My Life*, published in 1971, was made into a National Film Board documentary. **To learn more about Aboriginal and Inuit cultures, visit the CBC Digital Archives and investigate the file "An Inuit Education: Honouring a Past, Creating a Future."**

In the 1950s, James Houston, first civil administrator at Cape Dorset, encouraged the Inuit to carve, sew, and draw to earn extra money. Pitseolak was one of them. She began with socks and parkas, which Houston sold for her. Then he gave her pens, pencils, and paper to draw. The concept of expressing herself on paper intrigued Pitseolak. She produced thousands of drawings depicting monsters and spirits, early Inuit life, and other things close to her heart.

In Their Own Words

When I was small
I used to help my father
Make ax handles.
Coming home from the wood
with a bundle
of maskwi, snawey, aqamoq,
My father would chip away,
Carving with a crooked knife,
Until a well-made handle appeared,
Ready to be sand-papered
By my brother.

When it was finished
We started another,
Sometimes working through the night
With me holding a lighted shaving
To light their way
When our kerosene lamp ran dry.
Then in the morning
My mother would be happy
That there would be food today
When my father sold our work.
                              Rita Joe

Reprinted with permission from
Poems of Rita Joe Abanaki Press, 1978

ABOVE: *"Seal Hunting," a felt- tip drawing by Labrador artist Josephina Kalleo.*

LEFT: *Although most people think Aboriginal art is painting and sculpture, Aboriginals have also made substantial contributions in other artistic areas, such as weaving and textiles.*

FOCUS

1. **What social and economic challenges face Nunavut?**
2. **Choose any five Inuit or Aboriginal artists and summarize their contributions to Canadian culture.**

Seeking Justice

For Aboriginal Canadians, the struggle to win an equal footing in Canadian society is ongoing. This struggle takes place on many fronts. Aboriginal Canadians seek economic, political, social, and cultural equality. Old wrongs need to be righted. New rights need to be gained. Aboriginal peoples are now making important strides.

Residential Schools— Healing the Wounds

In 1998, the government of Canada apologized to Canada's Aboriginal peoples for the abuse many individuals had suffered in residential, or boarding, schools. More important, it recognized that a healing process was needed to resolve what had happened over time.

Before 1867, churches operated residential schools for Aboriginal children. Late in the 1890s, the federal Department of Indian Affairs began to provide money to run such schools. About 130 schools, located in most provinces of Canada, came to serve Aboriginal children between the ages of 5 to 16. More than 80 000 students attended these schools.

Thomas Moore before and after his entrance into the Regina Indian Residential School in Saskatchewan in 1874. What are your impressions of these two pictures?

At a residential school.

The Department wanted to provide a "general and moral" education for First Nations peoples. Officials believed that the children should be removed from their families and from life on reserves. Away from family and tribal influences, children would be assimilated into European culture. The government felt that First Nations peoples should learn to farm or ranch, not keep their hunting and gathering way of life. It did not understand the nature of the Aboriginal heritage, nor did it consider that its policies might cause harm.

Residential schools were not given much

money. They were often poorly equipped, poorly monitored, and lacking in good-quality teaching. Many Aboriginal students suffered emotionally, spiritually, and mentally. Some experienced physical and sexual abuse. Many were scarred for life. In 1996, the last residential school was phased out. By that time, though, much damage had been done. Generations of Aboriginal peoples had lost family ties, personal pride, and much of their history.

First Nations groups and the federal government agreed they must address the issue and do it in a way that would avoid the emotional pain of court litigation. The government would offer out-of-court settlements to former students. A speedy process was promised.

Between 2001 and 2005, First Nations groups, church organizations, and government negotiated heavily. In 2005, an agreement in principle was reached. The government set aside almost $2 billion to compensate residential school students.

Relocation—Solution or Mistake?

Most smaller reserve communities are in isolated northern areas of Canada. Many lack road access. They depend on diesel generators for electricity. Construction supplies and fuel are usually brought in by barges. Food

Matthew Coon Come, of the Mistassini Cree, is known internationally for his work on behalf of Aboriginal rights.

supplies are brought in by air, making their cost expensive. Air link is the only way for some people to get medical care.

Traditionally, Inuit lived along the northern coast of Quebec and Labrador. They were a nomadic people whose livelihood depended on hunting and fishing. In 1967, Canada and Newfoundland established the village of Utshimassits. It was located at Davis Inlet on an island off the Labrador coast. Five hundred Inuit settled in the new community. They gave up their nomadic lifestyle.

The move had tragic consequences. The new community did not have enough drinking water and sanitation was poor. Living conditions were like those of a developing country. Poverty, despair, isolation, and poor housing hurt everyone.

Métis These Canadians are of mixed Aboriginal and European descent, especially French or Scottish descent. The Métis began as Canadian settlers and fur trappers of dual heritage. Many settled in communities in the Red River area of Rupert's Land, now Manitoba. Most Métis were Roman Catholic. Their culture was a unique combination of traditions from their European and Aboriginal parents.

In 1869, Canada purchased Rupert's Land from the Hudson's Bay Company. The Métis who lived there wanted their land and cultural rights recognized. They sought to keep their way of life and their prairie hunting grounds. They were independent.

The Métis chose Louis Riel as their leader. When the Canadian government sent surveyors to divide up the land, the Métis set up their own government. They negotiated a place for themselves within Confederation. As a result, the province of Manitoba was established in 1870.

Their problems were far from solved, though. As more Europeans moved west to farm, the Métis struggled to preserve their hunting way of life. Their right to the land was not respected. They got deeply frustrated. Eventually, in 1885, the Métis fought against the Canadian government. Louis Riel and Gabriel Dumont led the doomed uprising. Riel was put to death for treason. Dumont fled to the United States. Many Métis left.

Today, Métis people live throughout North America. They have formed several organizations to help preserve their culture and history. These include the Manitoba Métis Federation, Métis Association of Alberta, the Ontario Métis Aboriginal Association, and the Canadian Métis Society.

Some notable Métis include John Norquay, former Manitoba premier; poet Pauline Johnson; and Douglas Cardinal, award-winning architect. **What was the source of the major conflict between the Métis and the government of Canada? For more current information about the Métis community in Canada, visit www.metisnation.ca.**

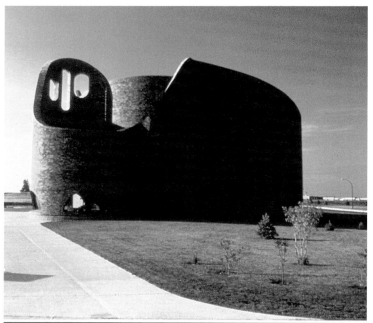

St. Mary's Church in Red Deer, Alberta, was designed by architect Douglas Cardinal of Métis descent. Cardinal's style is based on nature's curves. The curved walls are gentle and look as if sculpted by the wind.

Inuit children were affected the most. When six young Inuit tried to commit suicide in 1993, the problems of Davis Inlet became world news.

In 1996, the people of Utshimassits signed an agreement with the government to relocate. They went to a new 200-hectare settlement, Little Sango Pond (Natuashish), on the Labrador mainland.

In 2005, another Aboriginal community made the news due to its social and health problems. Most of the 1900 members of the Kashechewan First Nation reserve in Northern Ontario were evacuated. Their water contained E-coli bacteria. Unsafe, it was causing rashes and illnesses. The community was one of over 50 reserves in Ontario on a "boil water advisory." The federal government promised new housing, a safe water supply, and a new community school. Once again, there was talk of relocating a community.

Self-Reliance in Business

Not all Aboriginal communities and individuals have fared so poorly. Many Aboriginal Canadians have completed post-secondary education. Some are self-employed in the professions or trades. Others have managed successful small businesses, both as individuals and in partnerships. Aboriginal Business Canada (part of Industry Canada) helps First Nations, Métis, and Inuit entre-preneurs with business financing.

Some First Nations groups own their business enterprises collectively. The majority employ Aboriginal workers, especially Aboriginal youth. Having these jobs strengthens self-reliance.

Just over 25 years ago, the Tsuu T'ina First Nation opened Redwood Meadows Golf and Country Club, an 18-hole course, just outside Calgary, Alberta. The venture has been so successful that the First Nation opened a smaller 9-hole course, Buffalo Run. The Osoyoos Band, also known as the Okanagan Nation, operates some businesses in the Okanagan Valley in British Columbia. Among its ventures are vineyards and a winery, campgrounds, concrete ready mix, and a construction company.

After signing the James Bay Agreement, the Cree Nation invested in the regional airline industry. With a partner, Air Creebec was created in the early 1980s. By 1988, the airline was owned 100 percent by the Cree Nation. This airline serves the James Bay area of Ontario and Quebec.

FOCUS

1. What were residential schools? What was their impact on Aboriginal youth?
2. In your view, what would be the hardest thing about attending a residential school? Why?
3. What can governments and Aboriginal groups do to improve life on reserves?

Canada's Business Community

In the last century, business interests in Canada were an interesting mix of private and government money. Private investors were interested in companies that served the country's needs only if they could expect to make a profit. The government's concerns were different. It created publicly owned institutions to help keep the country together. Trans-Canada Airlines, the Canadian Broadcasting Corporation, and the National Film Board are examples of Crown corporations that the federal government has created.

The roots of a few major private corporations are deeper than 1900. The Hudson's Bay Company was established in 1670. It has evolved from a fur-trading company into a giant department store chain. The Canadian Pacific Railway (CPR) dates from 1881. As the country's first transcontinental railway, it helped connect Canada. In 2005, the CPR had a vast network of rails in Canada, as well as in the American Midwest and northeastern states.

Other corporations have become multinationals in the last half century. For example, the Power Corporation of Canada is an international management company that handles finances, insurance, and investment. Its business ventures are measured in billions of dollars. Quebecor began as a small Quebec company and now operates in North America and in Europe. Its interests include commercial printing, cable and Internet services, newspapers, broadcasting, and telecommunications.

The success of many private corporations has grown out of the skills and ambitions of individuals, even three generations ago. An entrepreneur is a person who starts an enterprise or business, often taking financial risk.

Some Successful Canadian Entrepreneurs

Samuel Bronfman was born in 1889, in Eastern Europe. Bronfman opened a distillery in Montreal. In the mid-1920s, his company merged with the Seagram distillery of Ontario. Under Bronfman, Canadian whisky became highly popular worldwide. In 1952, business profits were used to set up the Samuel and Saidye Bronfman Family Foundation. The foundation supports such causes as medicine, education, and the arts. In 1967, Bronfman was named a Companion of the Order of Canada.

K. C. Irving was the most important industrialist in the Maritimes. Kenneth Colin Irving was born in New Brunswick in 1899. As a boy, Irving showed interest in automotive mechanics. He

Canadian Tire is a well-known retail store chain in Canada. Established in Toronto in 1922, it now operates more than 400 stores across the country. It is known for its "money" and innovative tire guarantees.

served in the Royal Flying Corps during the First World War. He then returned home and opened a gas station. In 1925, he moved to St. John to run the first Ford dealership. Irving soon bought several transportation-related companies. He later purchased shipbuilding companies, railroads, and paper mills. He built tankers for oil transportation. K. C. Irving died in 1992. Today, his three sons manage the Irving Group, which includes newspapers.

George Weston was a baker's apprentice. The small family business he started in 1884 has evolved into George Weston Limited. Loblaws, Fortinos, No Frills, and The Great Canadian Superstore are well-known parts of it. After 1924, Weston's son Garfield focused on food processing and distribution. Today, his son, Galen, oversees the largest food-processing and distribution corporation in Canada.

Magna's Frank Stronach mounted a "model of relief" for victims of Hurricane Katrina in 2005. Should the wealthy help others?

Frank Stronach arrived in Canada from Austria in 1957. At first, he and a partner specialized in the tool and die business. They got a contract to make sun visor brackets for General Motors of Canada. This break helped Stronach's small business evolve into Magna International. Today, Magna International supplies major companies with auto parts. The corporation earns more than $6 billion in sales annually.

Thomas Bata learned the shoe business from his father in Czechoslovakia. In 1939, he left his homeland and settled in Ontario. He began a shoe manufacturing company, Bata Shoes. Bata turned his small business into a huge empire. By the 1990s, Bata Shoes had production facilities in more than 65 countries. There is a related museum in Toronto.

Canada's entrepreneurs have proven that they can compete worldwide in productivity, creativity, and quality of products.

FOCUS

1. **What is a Crown corporation?**
2. **Briefly explain how Bronfman, Irving, and Stronach have contributed to the economic development of Canada.**

Canada's Hi-Tech Youth

The young people of the 21st century belong to the satellite and computer age. By the year 2000, theirs was a world of MP3s, MP4s, video I-pods, and memory sticks. The popular "pagers" of the 1990s had become obsolete. So had audiocassettes.

Bulky cellphones, once considered amazing, had been miniaturized. Phones would vibrate instead of "ring." The vibrating was a discreet way of telling owners that they were getting calls. "Text messaging" became a quiet way to answer calls. Video cellphones and voice messages were quickly adopted by this tech-savvy generation.

Improvements in the microchip technology in the 1990s reduced the cost of computers. By 2000, computers were so powerful that they offered DVD copying and fast interactive multimedia capability.

New wireless modems allowed computers to be used in any room in the house. The computer and the Internet turned the world into a huge library for students. If they wished, they could gain access to most university and government databases.

The Internet met other needs, too. It served as a business tool, allowing people to shop online, receive and pay bills, and even send income tax returns to the federal government in Ottawa. Many young Canadians were more interested in chat rooms and e-mail, though. A whole new way of communicating with friends had been created.

This communication aspect of the Internet opened new dangers. Pedophiles used the Internet to lure young people into threatening situations. Many concerned parents bought their children special phones that could reveal their location.

Two girls enjoy text-messaging side by side.

Identity theft became more sophisticated. Computer hackers had success in getting personal information, such as credit card numbers and bank account numbers. Some hackers destroyed business and personal files by spreading computer viruses.

Canada's youth held jobs in all segments of the economy. The fast-food industry, retail sales, and sporting goods stores depended on teens and young adults for workers. Most young people got paid a minimum wage. Some earned money to finance a trendy lifestyle.

As their parents had, young people developed their own style and culture. Some males and females sported multiple body piercings. Ear, nose, tongue, belly button, and eyebrow rings were popular. Tattoos of all sizes and colours were also in fashion. Many people saw piercings and tattoos as a form of self-expression.

What do you and your friends look like? How do you compare with the young people described here?

Children born in the baby boom now confronted the demands and desires of their own children. Adults who might once have been viewed as rebellious youth were seen as conservative old-timers. The generation gap continued.

FOCUS

1. **How has technology affected the lives of young people in the new century?**
2. **What problems has the high-tech era created?**

Women's Rights by the 21st Century

In 1948, the United Nations passed the Universal Declaration of Human Rights. This document made a strong statement against discrimination based on race, colour, language, religion, and gender. Canada accepted the

This Canadian, a member of HMCS Regina, gets ready to fire her light machine gun in the Gulf of Oman. She is part of NATO forces campaigning against terrorism.

principles of this document. Doing so provided a huge boost for women's rights.

In 1967, Prime Minister Lester Pearson established the Royal Commission on the Status of Women. It was chaired by Ottawa journalist Florence Bird. After listening to women's groups across the country, the Commission released its conclusions in 1970. The Commission's recommendations increased women's rights in the workforce.

The 1982 Canadian Charter of Rights and Freedoms also improved women's rights. Jobs and professions that were once dominated by men now opened to women. Today, Canadian women have equal access to such jobs as firefighters and law enforcement officers. Women can comfortably attend Canada's military, business, law, and medical schools.

In the Canadian Forces, women can now take combat roles, such as that of fighter pilot. The Canadian warship, HMCS *Nipigon*, became the first to have a mixed-gender crew. In 2005, Canada's active forces in Afghanistan included male and female soldiers.

Some Outstanding Canadian Women

Adrienne Clarkson and her family first came to Canada as refugees from Hong Kong in 1942. From 1965 until 1982, Clarkson worked as a host, writer, and producer for several CBC television programs. She then served as the agent-general of Ontario in Paris, France. In 1987, she returned to Canada. She became president and publisher of McClelland & Stewart. In 1998, Clarkson chaired the Board of Trustees of the Canadian Museum of Civilization in Hull, Quebec. From 1999 to 2005, she served as governor general of Canada.

Judy Darcy has been a dedicated union leader. She held many positions within the Canadian Union of Public Employees (CUPE). She was both shop steward and national president. Darcy represented more than half a million working men and women. Vancouver City Council appointed her to the Vancouver Economic Development Commission. In 2003, the Council of Canadians gave her the Activist of the Year Award.

Ursula Franklin became a senior scientist for the Ontario Research Foundation. She has taught and researched in the field of materials science and in the area of the social impact of technology. In 1967, Franklin was appointed as a professor at the University of Toronto. After her retirement in 1989, she wrote *The Real World of Technology*. Her book looks at the impact of technology on society.

Celia Franca was invited to found a classi-

Ursula Franklin

Celia Franca

cal ballet company after a group of Toronto ballet lovers became aware of the British-born artist's creative and organizational skills. Franca established the National Ballet of Canada in 1951 and served as artistic director until 1974. Under her strong leadership, the company gained an international reputation, and the art of ballet developed further in Canada. Franca danced, taught, choreographed, and directed ballet productions. Her honours include the Order of Canada and the Governor General's Performing Arts Award (1994).

Beverly Mascoll was the president of Mascoll Beauty Supply. The company she started in 1970 specialized in making and selling beauty and hair-care products for Black consumers. The Beverley Mascoll Foundation has offered scholarships to Canadian youth. In 1998, Mascoll was appointed a Member of the Order of Canada for outstanding entrepreneurship and for assisting Canada's youth.

Doris Anderson

Doris Anderson has long been a spokesperson for women's rights in Canada. Within seven years of taking a job at *Chatelaine*, she was running the magazine. The Alberta-born writer, editor, and journalist revamped *Chatelaine* completely. She introduced a feminist slant to her editorials and the stories she commissioned. In 1982, Anderson was appointed to the Canadian Advisory Council on the Status of Women. She also served as president of the National Action Committee on the Status of Women.

Heather Reisman is an example of a woman who has done well in the private sector. She is in the ranks of women who have become executives and managers in large corporations, banks, and unions. Reisman is the president and chief executive officer of Indigo Books & Music. She also was a governor of the Toronto Stock Exchange and of McGill University.

Luan Mitchell-Halter managed a large meat packing plant in Saskatchewan. When her husband died, she carried on the family business. Her hard work resulted in a partnership and a $44 million expansion, which created many jobs for the local community. Mitchell-Halter's efforts were honoured in 2003 when she received the McGill Management Achievement Award.

Roberta Jamieson has earned national and international acclaim for her promotion of non-adversarial methods of conflict resolution. She has had a career of firsts.

Roberta Jamieson

Jamieson was the first Aboriginal woman in Canada to obtain a law degree (1976). She helped found the Native Law Students Association of Canada. She became the first Aboriginal commissioner of the Indian Commission of Ontario. In 1989, she was the first woman to be appointed Ombudsman for Ontario. For her work in mediation and conflict resolution, Jamieson was awarded the University of Toronto's Goodman Fellowship in 1991. In 1998, she received a National Aboriginal Achievement Award, the Aboriginal community's highest honour, for her outstanding contributions to public service.

Women in Politics

Women also made important political advances. Audrey McLaughlin became leader of the federal NDP in 1989. She was followed by Alexa McDonough in 1995. In 1993, Kim Campbell became the first female prime minister in Canadian history. Of the 391 women candidates in the 2004 general election, 65 were elected to Parliament; that compares with only one woman being elected to Ottawa from 1968 to 1972.

Provincially and municipally, the number of women elected to serve increased, too. Hazel McCallion, the mayor of Mississauga, was first elected in 1978 and has been re-elected ever since. She is one of hundreds of women elected to city councils throughout Canada.

Rosemary Brown was the first Black woman to be elected to a legislature in Canada. She won a seat as an MLA in British Columbia in 1972. In 1975, she ran for the leadership of the NDP, but lost. Brown's political career and influence provided young Canadian women of colour with a valuable role model. Rosemary Brown was inducted as an Officer in the Order of Canada in 1996.

Hazel McCallion, long-time mayor

Women and Poverty

Despite all these improvements, many women live well below the poverty line. There are many reasons for this. One is the national divorce rate, which was 38 percent in 2003. Divorce leaves many women struggling to raise families on their own. Most provinces are still trying to track "deadbeat dads" and make them pay child support. Finding affordable daycare remains a challenge, too.

Immigrant women have a particularly hard time. Many of them depend on non-unionized jobs in the fast-food industry, retail sector, and garment industry sweatshops. They work in care-giving facilities, such as nursing homes and daycare. The struggle for a better life for the non-professional woman is ongoing.

FOCUS

1. What was the purpose of the Royal Commission on the Status of Women? What was its importance?
2. How did the women's rights movement of the 1960s and 1970s change the lives of women in the 1990s?
3. What are some problems faced by women today?

Canadian Icons and Identity

Identity has always been fragile in Canada. Canada's population is so much smaller than that of the United States that many talented Canadians go south to further their careers.

Christopher Plummer is as internationally known for his acting in more than 50 films as he is for his work on stage. An early star of the Stratford Festival, he returned in the theatre's 50th season, earning acclaim as King Lear.

Singer Céline Dion, who draws huge crowds to her Las Vegas shows, is one. When hockey player Wayne Gretzky was traded to Los Angeles in 1988, *The Globe and Mail* described the move as the "defection of national treasure." Some Canadians, though, manage to be identified with Canada whether at home or abroad.

What makes something Canadian? That issue is harder to resolve than the space here to discuss it; simply put, if something is done by a Canadian, it is Canadian.

The federal government has done much to support the development of a distinctive Canadian culture. Chapter 2 describes how it created the Canadian Broadcasting Corporation and the National Film Board. Chapter 7 identifies other federal efforts, such as encouraging Canadian content on radio and on TV.

The Canada Council for the Arts plays an important part in promoting the arts. Beyond offering its well-known Literary Awards, it gives funds to Canadian artists and arts organizations. It encourages work in media arts, music, theatre, visual arts, writing, and publishing. In 2003–04, it awarded almost $140 million.

Canada presents many faces to the world. Some of these "faces" have become icons, or easily recognized representatives of all Canadians. They may come from any walk of life. They may be musicians, hockey players, authors, individuals with a mission, even politicians. What they have in common is their Canadian experience and their importance as presenters of Canada's cultural identity. They are Canadians that other Canadians admire.

Wayne Gretzky

BORN: 1961, Brantford, Ontario

SIGNIFICANCE: Many people feel that Wayne Gretzky is Canada's greatest hockey player and ambassador for the game.

BRIEF BIOGRAPHY: Gretzky's passion for hockey began early. When he was four, his father built a rink in the backyard. He put in lights so the rink could be used at night. Gretzky's father, Walter, encouraged him to play hard, but always in a gentlemanly way. Gretzky developed exceptional skills, while rejecting the "obstruct and grab" form of hockey.

Gretzky signed with the World Hockey League's Edmonton Oilers at age 19. When the Oilers joined the NHL the following year, he won the Most Valuable Player award. Gretzky led the Edmonton Oilers to four Stanley Cups during the 1980s.

Gretzky was traded to the Los Angeles Kings in 1988. Many Canadians were stunned. They saw the trade as a symbol of U.S. political, economic, and cultural control over Canada. Gretzky played for the Kings, the St. Louis Blues, and the New York Rangers. He retired from playing in 1999. Gretzky holds 59 NHL records. These include most regular-season goals (894) and most goals in a single season (92). After 20 years, Gretzky ended his reign with the most shocking record of all: 2857 career points—more than 1000 points above the record of Gordie Howe, his personal hero and previous holder of the record. It took Howe 26 years to score 1850 points; it took Gretzky only 10.

In November 2000, Gretzky became executive director of Team Canada. His job has been to select top players for Canada's Olympic men's hockey teams. Team Canada won the gold medal during the 2002 winter Olympics. In 2005, Gretzky became head coach of the Phoenix Coyotes. He co-owns this team. **Is Wayne Gretzky a good role model for young Canadians? Explain. For an audiovisual profile, visit the CBC Digital Archives at www.cbc.ca/archives and review the file "The Great Wayne Gretzky."**

CANADIAN LIVES

Terry Fox

Born: 1958, Winnipeg, Manitoba

Died: 1981, New Westminster, British Columbia

Significance: Terry Fox began a run across Canada to raise money and generate publicity for cancer research. His "Marathon of Hope" succeeded beyond all expectations. He drew nationwide and international attention to cancer research. Fox is one of Canada's most inspiring figures.

Brief Biography: At 19, Terry Fox lost his right leg to osteogenic sarcoma, a rare form of bone cancer. After receiving an artificial leg, Fox learned how to walk again. He ran regularly to build his physical and emotional strength, and returned to university. Fox was young and idealistic. He decided to run across Canada to raise money for cancer research. Many people wondered about a one-legged man running coast to coast.

On 12 April 1980, Fox dipped his artificial leg into the Atlantic Ocean in Newfoundland and set out for Victoria, B.C., on his "Marathon of Hope." At first, he received little media attention. By the time he

reached Ontario, however, Fox was a media sensation. His run raised thousands of dollars for cancer research. When he reached Toronto, tens of thousands of people cheered him on. A few weeks later, in Thunder Bay, Ontario, Fox's run was cut short.

Doctors found cancer in his lungs. Fox returned to British Columbia for treatments. On 19 September 1980, he became the youngest Companion of the Order of Canada. Support from Canadians was overwhelming. Millions of dollars were pledged to the "Marathon of Hope," but the money did not help him. On 29 June 1981, Terry Fox died.

Fox's legacy lives on in the Terry Fox Foundation. It has raised more than $360 million, and of this money, over 85 percent goes to research. Fox inspired people worldwide. The Terry Fox Run is held in 50 countries annually. **Why do Canadians consider Terry Fox to be a hero? Visit the CBC Digital Archives at www.cbc.ca/archives and explore "Terry Fox's Marathon of Hope" and "Terry Fox 25: Reliving the Marathon of Hope."**

CANADIAN LIVES

Karen Kain

K-OS

Toller Cranston

Michael Ondaatje

Tomson Highway

Nelly Furtado

TOP LEFT: **Karen Kain**, *principal dancer in the National Ballet of Canada (1969–1997) artistic director as of 2005*

ABOVE: **Michael Ondaatje**, *award-winning author of* The English Patient *and more.*

TOP CENTRE: **K-OS**, *rap artist with a social conscience.*

ABOVE CENTRE: **Tomson Highway**, *Canada's best-known Aboriginal playwright.*

TOP RIGHT: **Toller Cranston**, *Bronze medal figure skater, 1967 Olympics*

ABOVE RIGHT: **Nelly Furtado**, *performer with a unique brand of music*

FOCUS

1. Define *national identity*.
2. How has government tried to promote a sense of Canadian identity?
3. Why is Wayne Gretzky called "The Great One"?
4. What other Canadian icons can you think of?

Sharpening Your Skills

Why Study the Past?

THE SKILL

Understanding the importance of history for society and for individuals

THE IMPORTANCE

The need for everyone to know their own history

- History prepares us to understand the problems of our world and broadens our outlook. History sheds light on the present. It is difficult for Canadians to understand their own country unless they know something of its past. French–English antagonisms in Canada had their beginnings in the British Conquest of 1759, the Riel rebellions, and the conscription crisis of the First World War. Aboriginal land claims are based on their historical roots.

- History enables leaders to plan rational policies. People make decisions based upon their knowledge of what happened previously. Sensible children will put their hands in the fire only once. Likewise, our leaders would be wise to make important decisions only after first examining how past generations dealt with similar problems.

- History is to society what memory is to the individual. History is society's memory. It enables us to answer the following questions: Who are we? How did we get here? What is our purpose? Where are we going? *Individual scenario:* The hockey player hustled into the corner after the puck and was crunched against the boards. His helmet saved him from serious injury, but when the player shakily regained his feet, he had lost his memory. As a result, when a teammate passed him the puck, he allowed an opponent to take it away and score. Because of his amnesia, the defenceman had forgotten who he was, and what he was supposed to be doing. Without his memory, he was lost. *Society scenario:* One of the strongest bonds uniting large groups of people is their awareness of having a common past. *Seven Generations: A History of the Kanien-kehaka*, for example, states "that unless Mohawk people fast become familiar with the chronology of events that have shaped their past, the very survival of the Mohawk Nation is at stake."

- History prepares people to be productive and happy citizens. As you progress through this book, you will improve your ability to think, write, debate, discuss, research, analyse, distinguish between fact and opinion, read, take notes, evaluate different points of view, identify biases, organize information, and reach reasoned conclusions. Democracy needs such citizens. So, too, do employers.

Maclean's magazine asked company executives what qualities they were looking for in hiring new employees. The executives identified 10 skills and personal qualities as high in demand. They said they looked for people who were literate, creative, motivated, analytical, willing to learn, able to learn, able to generalize from the specific, able to think without help, able to communicate, and able to work with others.

Company presidents, lawyers, doctors, farmers, bankers—virtually everyone—must know how to
- locate the best information in their fields
- determine the accuracy of this information
- select the best choice among different options
- devise a plan based on this information
- convince others of the soundness of this plan

These are the skills used in the study of history.

Career Choices for Individuals with Historical Training

Teacher	Genealogist
Journalist	Interpreter, historic sites
Writer	Museum curator
Lawyer	Architect
Librarian	Archaeologist
Archivist	Heritage consultant
Researcher	Parks Canada staff
Tour guide	Editor
Consultant	Business

Application

People base the decisions they make on history. Baseball managers research how well certain batters have hit against that night's opposing pitcher. Judges make decisions based on the results of past court cases. Doctors keep records of their patients. Halls of Fame, monuments, stamps, museums, and holidays honour past events or individuals. What do you or your family do that involves knowing something about your own past? Reflect on this question and record your thoughts.

Questions & Activities

Questions and Activities

Test Yourself
Match the person or item in column A with the description in column B.

A	B
1. Rosemary Brown	**a)** Civil Marriage Act
2. Wayne Gretzky	**b)** Manitoba politician who prevented vote for approval of the Meech Lake Accord
3. Oscar Peterson	**c)** first woman prime minister of Canada
4. Joseph Gosnell	**d)** tax introduced by Brian Mulroney
5. Elijah Harper	**e)** role model for young women of colour
6. Kim Campbell	**f)** policy that involves selling Crown corporations to private businesses
7. NEP	**g)** outstanding hockey player
8. GST	**h)** energy program introduced by Trudeau in the 1970s
9. Paul Martin	**i)** world-renowned jazz piano great
10. Privatization	**j)** Nisga'a Chief who helped negotiate land claim treaty

Discuss and Debate

1. Compare the ideas and policies of Pierre Trudeau and Brian Mulroney. Use at least five of the following headings as organizers for your comparison:
   - Relations with Provincial Leaders
   - Energy Policy
   - Attitudes to the National Debt
   - Attitude About Powers of the Federal and Provincial Governments
   - Attitudes to French–English Relations
   - Attitudes Towards the Meech Lake Accord
   - Attitudes Towards the United States
   - Belief in the Role of Government in the Economy

2. Prepare one side of the argument for a class debate: Resolved that some privatization of health care will benefit Canadians.

3. "There is no Canadian identity." Brainstorm arguments for and against this idea.

4. Name jobs that, before the 1970s, might have been considered "for men" or "for women" in the following areas: (a) offices, (b) factories, (c) farms, (d) hospitals, (e) schools, (f) home, (g) the military. How do you feel about that?

5. Some people claim that feminism is no longer a necessary social movement. Women and men, they say, are now considered equal. Women have access to jobs traditionally considered men's, and the responsibilities of raising a family are now equally distributed between men and women. Do you think that a focus on women's rights and issues is still needed? Explain.

6. Identify the advantages and disadvantages of minority and majority governments.

Do Some Research

1. Do some research on one of your favourite Canadian sports or entertainment personalities. Write a Canadian Lives biocard. Pass the cards around the class and then assemble them in a class folder.

2. At times, there is prejudice in Canada, not only against immigrants, but also against groups that people perceive as "different." Find out more about one of these groups. What can you do to help members of that group become fully accepted as part of Canadian society?

3. Perform a Google search on one of these Canadian entrepreneurs: Frank Stronach, Beverly Mascoll, or Samuel Bronfman. Write a one-page biography that notes that person's birth, business, problems overcome, workers employed, accomplishments, and value of assets.

4. Research the Web site identified below and report to the class on one Aboriginal Economic Development Success Story: http://www.ainc-inac.gc.ca/nr/ecd/srch_e.html.

Be Creative

1. Write a letter to a local newspaper outlining your ideas on one of the following themes: (a) gender equality, (b) native rights, (c) Canadian culture, and (d) immigration policy.

2. Organize a radio or television program to re-enact a famous Canadian sporting event of the 1970–2000 period. Present your program to the rest of the class.

3. Present a visual or sound collage on one of Canada's most famous musicians, singers, artists, actors, dancers, or writers.

4. Organize a multicultural "caravan" or pageant in your class or school.

5. Research the music of such Canadian folk music icons as Neil Young, Joni Mitchell, Ian and Sylvia, and Gordon Lightfoot.

Web Watch

The CBC Digital Archives at www.cbc.ca/archives has many useful files. See, for example, "Jean Chrétien: From Pool Hall to Parliament Hill," "Georges Erasmus: Native Rights Crusader," "Trudeaumania: A Swinger for Prime Minister," "A Lost Heritage: Canada's Residential Schools," and "Phil Fontaine: Native Diplomat and Dealmaker."

FOR THE GOOD OF ALL

THÉRÈSE CASGRAIN

LE BIEN COMMUN

THE COMMON GOOD

32

CANADA

This 1985 stamp honours reformer Thérèse Casgrain, who led the campaign that resulted in the women of Quebec gaining the right to vote in 1940. She campaigned for women's rights, for human rights, and against the nuclear threat, helping to found various citizen groups. In 1970, she was appointed to the Senate.

Why do you think Casgrain might be a good role model for Canadian women?

Chapter Six
My Country,
Mons Pays

Expectations

Overall Expectations:
By the end of this chapter, you will be able to
- explain the significance of some key individuals and events in the evolution of French–English relations in Canada since 1914

Specific Expectations:
By the end of this chapter, you will be able to
- identify the contributions made by regional, provincial, linguistic, ethnic, and religious communities to Canada's multicultural society
- explain how conscription divided English Canada and Quebec during the First and Second World Wars
- identify major events that contributed to the growth of Quebec nationalism and the rise of the separatist movement in Quebec from 1945 on
- describe responses by Canadians and their political leaders to the Quebec separatist movement
- identify the major groups of French Canadians outside Quebec—Franco-Ontarians and Acadians
- describe the effects of selected scientific and technological innovations developed by Canadians, including Joseph-Armand Bombardier
- compare the different beliefs and values of parties that emerged out of political movements (e.g., Union Nationale, Parti Québécois, Bloc Québécois)
- describe how selected significant individuals and artists have contributed to a sense of the Canadian identity

Word List

Anglophone	**Bloc Québécois**
Distinct society	**Federalists**
Francophone	**Nationalists**
October Crisis	**Parti Québécois**
Patriate	**Quiet Revolution**
Separatism	**Surrealists**
Sovereignty-association	**Urbanization**
Unilateral independence	

❶ In 1604, French people settled in New France. In 1763, the British took control of Quebec. The French felt threatened by the English settling in what became the province of Quebec. In 1867, Confederation guaranteed French culture in Quebec.

Arrival of ships from France

❷ In 1960, the Quiet Revolution began in Quebec. This was a time of modernization. The province built many hydro projects. One was near James Bay. At that time, it was the largest in the world. Many Quebecers felt they could now hope for equality with other Canadians.

The massive dams of the James Bay project were a source of pride and confidence for many in Quebec.

❸ In 1970, the Quiet Revolution became louder. A terrorist group, the FLQ, kidnapped two people and murdered one Quebecer. The War Measures Act was imposed. Separatists saw that change must come through peaceful means.

1965	1970	1975	1980	1985	1990	1995	2000	2005	2010

❸ ❹ ❺ ❻

❹ René Lévesque was the first Parti Québécois leader. In 1976 he was elected premier of Quebec. He promised to separate Quebec from Canada. He was unsuccessful. His party is still powerful, though.

Premier Lévesque holds a Quebec Nordiques jersey with a symbol of the Rebellion of 1837 on it.

❻ A separatist government in Quebec tried to separate Quebec from Canada. A special vote, or referendum, was held in 1995. Quebec voted narrowly to stay within Canada. Separatists continue to be a strong force in Quebec.

❺ In 1987, Brian Mulroney suggested that Quebec be recognized as a distinct society. This was part of the Meech Lake Accord. Elijah Harper, a provincial politician, prevented Manitoba from giving its needed approval of the Accord. He felt Aboriginal communities should also be seen as distinct.

The French in Early Canada

Each spring the arrival of ships from France was eagerly awaited by the Canadiens in New France.

Christopher Columbus's voyage to the Caribbean in 1492 launched European exploration of the Americas. France, England, Holland, and Spain sent men to explore this new world. In 1604, Sieur de Monts and Samuel de Champlain established a colony at Port Royal on the Bay of Fundy. It was the first permanent European settlement in North America. Champlain established a second colony on the St. Lawrence River, at Quebec.

Residents of what was called New France soon thought of themselves as Canadien,

rather than *français*. Many had been born in North America. They developed a lifestyle and identity suitable to their environment. The new colonists established Roman Catholic schools, a university, churches, hospitals, missions, forges, breweries, and entertainment, such as horse racing.

The Conquest of New France

By the 18th century, France and England had worldwide empires. The two rivals competed for furs and trading routes. French forces in

New France were outnumbered and out-gunned. During the Seven Years' War, one by one, French outposts surrendered to the British. Louisbourg fell in 1758, Quebec in 1759, and Montreal in 1760. Much of the French colony lay in ruins. Farms and villages had been burned to the ground. Canadiens were placed under British military rule until the British government took formal control of the colony in 1763. The Canadiens faced the challenge of surviving as an isolated French-speaking, Roman Catholic population, under the rule of English-speaking Protestants.

French–English Relations: 1763–1867

Getting along would prove to be difficult. England's first policy, the British Proclamation Act of 1763, sought to assimilate French Canadians by encouraging British immigration. It was hoped that English residents would outnumber the French. The French would then find it more practical to adopt English language, religion, and customs.

The British policy of assimilation did not work. It was replaced by the Quebec Act in 1774. This new law tried to win the loyalty of the French-speaking colonists by honouring and preserving their language and customs. At the same time, though, English-speaking settlers flooded into Nova Scotia, New Brunswick, and Quebec. They were fleeing from the political unrest in the "American"

colonies to the south. The new settlers, or Loyalists as they became known, had no interest in maintaining the Canadiens' lifestyle. It was not long before these new immigrants began to make demands for British laws and British traditions.

To address the complaints from these new English-speaking settlers, Britain passed the Constitutional Act in 1791. It divided the colony of Quebec into Upper Canada (later Ontario and mostly English-speaking) and Lower Canada (later Quebec, and mostly French-speaking). Under the new law, each colony had its own government. Aboriginal needs were largely ignored by both French and English Canadians.

Forty-six years later, the Rebellions of 1837 clearly signalled that citizens were unhappy. People in both Upper and Lower Canada objected to being ruled by privileged minorities. After armed uprisings in both colonies, the British government sent John George Lambton, Earl of Durham, to investigate and report on the colonists' concerns. Durham granted amnesty to most of the rebels. His report to the British Parliament recommended more self-government for the colonies. Durham hoped to assimilate Canadiens by reuniting the two colonies and by again encouraging British immigration. He wanted to increase English-speaking immigration to Canada so that French-speaking citizens would be outnumbered. French Canadians resented Durham's conclusions.

At Durham's suggestion, the British united Upper and Lower Canada in 1841. The arrangement did not work. By the 1860s, the Canadian government was in a stalemate. French and English were evenly balanced in the government. Neither group was able to

Louis Riel became an early symbol of the divisions between French and English Canada. He is also considered the "Father of Manitoba."

maintain a dominant position. Some politicians believed that a strong central government would better manage common services, while local affairs would benefit from local administration.

George-Étienne Cartier, leader of the largest political party in Lower Canada, worked with John A. Macdonald, a leader in Upper Canada. Their efforts led to a confederation, or federal union, of three British North American colonies—Nova Scotia, New Brunswick, and the United Province of Canada—in 1867. Each province received control over religion and education within its borders. The new federal government controlled national defence, transportation, money, inter-provincial communications, and more.

French–English Relations: 1867–1934

The Confederation partnership was not an easy one. Several problems tested the new Canadian unity:

- Manitoba joined Confederation in 1870 as a bilingual province. Louis Riel, the fiery leader of the Métis (mixed European and Aboriginal blood) used armed resistance and negotiation to protect the property and culture of the mainly French-speaking people in the North West Territory. Riel led two armed rebellions against the Canadian government, the first in Manitoba in 1870 and the second in Saskatchewan in 1885. He and his supporters wanted self-government and the preservation of their unique heritage. Riel was captured, tried for treason, and executed. English Canada believed Riel was a traitor and supported the government's action. French Canada was outraged by the execution of a hero who had been trying to protect the mainly French-speaking, Roman Catholic Métis.

- Manitoba's English-speaking majority abolished the use of French language instruction in schools with the passage of the Manitoba Schools Act of 1890. Ontario did the same in 1912 by passing Regulation 17. French Canadians began to feel that their language and culture were safe only in Quebec.

- During the First World War, the issue of conscription seriously split French and English Canadians. English Canadians favoured making men fight. French Canadians felt that the war was a European conflict and should not involve Canada. When conscription became law, French Canadians felt betrayed by Canada's English-language majority. Conscription became a unity issue again in the Second World War.

- The Depression (1929–1939) emphasized the fears and insecurities of French Canadians. It was easy to believe that Quebec's problems had been caused by "foreign control." Many French Canadians believed that their culture would disappear under the English domination of the province. They voted for change.

Born in St. Hilaire, Quebec, in 1864, Ozias Leduc was renowned for his church murals. Thirty-one churches in Quebec and eastern Canada are decorated with Leduc's religious images. This painting, "L'Enfant au Pain" (1899), is one of Leduc's most famous. Though he sold few paintings while alive, Leduc holds a prominent position in the artistic communities of Quebec and Canada today. His paintings hang in the National Gallery of Canada and the Museum of Modern Art.

FOCUS

1. What is the evidence that French Canada has deep roots in North America?
2. Why did the British propose assimilation for the French after the Conquest?
3. List the major issues that divided English and French Canadians after Confederation.

The Duplessis Era in Quebec: 1936–1959

The Union Nationale, a new political party led by Maurice Duplessis, swept into power in Quebec in 1936. Maurice Duplessis was the premier of Quebec from 1936 to 1939, and again from 1944 to 1959. Many people viewed Duplessis as a champion of French-Canadian

Duplessis (left of centre) often worked closely with the Roman Catholic Church in Quebec. The Church encouraged people to vote for him.

nationalism. He promised to fight Ottawa for more power for Quebec. He assured French Canadians that decisions about Quebec's industry and resources would be made in Quebec. Duplessis pledged to preserve the French language, religion, and culture. His Union Nationale party worked closely with the Roman Catholic Church, which operated hospitals, schools, and colleges in Quebec.

The Catholic Church worried that Quebec youth would become less religious as they left their traditional rural communities for factory jobs in towns and cities. They feared **urbanization**. Duplessis encouraged young people in the province to revere their past, to respect traditional values, and to maintain their Roman Catholic religion. The government discouraged modern influences. As a result, a generation of French Canadians reached adulthood with little background in business, science, and technology.

Quebec, like the rest of Canada, lived through a period of intense industrial growth before and after the Second World War. Industrialization brought new developments. Many of these economic developments were funded by English-owned businesses. Hydroelectric power and mining were such sectors.

Quebec's growing industrial economy and urbanization contributed to the rise of trade unions. Workers united in the hopes of increasing wages and of improving working conditions. Duplessis was anti-union, though. He believed that unions were communist inspired. Large corporations—largely English-speaking—supported Union Nationale policies and helped finance the Party's election campaigns. The Quebec government, the Roman Catholic Church, and many large corporations worked together to prevent the growth of trade unions in Quebec. With weak unions, corporations did not have to improve wages or working conditions.

Miners in Quebec's asbestos industry went on strike in 1949. They wanted higher wages and better working conditions. Duplessis ordered the provincial police to break up the strike and arrest its leaders. Violence resulted. The workers stood firm. When the strike ended three months later, they had gained little.

Nevertheless, the Asbestos Strike was an important milestone in Quebec history. Many workers objected to Duplessis's tactics and to his support of large English-owned corporations. Many workers were union members. They saw the need for laws to protect workers and unions. Some church leaders began to question Duplessis's policies.

While in office, Duplessis increased the Quebec government's power in education and social services. The Church's involvement in Quebec's education and social services was reduced. Education in the skilled career trades was made more important. The Duplessis government introduced compulsory school attendance for children ages 6 to 14 to ensure the success of educational reforms.

The Duplessis government increased Quebec's minimum wage and created many new jobs. The government built hospitals

Many strikers were injured in clashes with police during the Asbestos Strike.

and highways. It also provided hydro development in rural areas as a means of modernizing Quebec. The most symbolic project undertaken by Duplessis was the adoption of Quebec's flag, the fleur-de-lis. It helped strengthen and symbolize Quebec unity.

Despite these improvements, serious social and educational problems were apparent within the province. The following quote reveals some of them:

In 1946, teachers were underpaid and teaching was still considered a vocation. Despite the construction of many new schools in 1951, more than 70 percent of the 8780 schools in the province still had only one classroom, 60 percent had no electricity and 40 percent no running water or indoor toilets. The level of schooling among francophones was still low. In the late 1950s, only 63 percent of students who started elementary school would finish the seventh grade. Under-funded and poorly organized, the education system was still undemocratic, elitist and sexist. (From the Province of Quebec Web site: www.meq.gouv.qc.ca)

Canadian Vision

Cité libre

Cité libre was a magazine of ideas created in 1950 to defend freedom of expression and put an end to the "Great Darkness" of the Duplessis regime. *Cité libre* opposed the Catholic Church's stronghold on all aspects of social life in Quebec. Pierre Trudeau wrote for the magazine.

Opposition to Duplessis

Duplessis held power for a long time because political opposition to his party was weak. He was a skilled speaker. He could energize his audiences as well as appeal to their sense of nationalism. The Roman Catholic Church, an important influence in Quebec society, strongly supported him.

Politics were corrupt under Duplessis's rule. Political ridings voting for the Union Nationale received favours in the form of new roads, hospitals, or other services. Ridings that voted Liberal did not. English, British, and American corporations soon discovered that the way to do business in Quebec was to support Duplessis. Sparsely populated rural regions elected more people than the densely populated cities. Labour unions and political opponents were ruthlessly restricted.

Some religious leaders and many intellectuals in the province opposed Duplessis's corrupt political machine. Several prominent writers, artists, professors, and lawyers spoke out openly against the government, and even against the powers of the Church. Pierre Trudeau, Gérard Pelletier, and others realized that politics in Quebec needed to become more open and democratic. They believed that everyone should share in the benefits of industrialism. Maurice Duplessis died on 7 September 1959. The old Quebec died with him. A new era in the province's history was about to begin.

Here, hockey legend Maurice "Rocket" Richard holds the Stanley Cup in 1957. Richard's record of 82 goals in Stanley Cup play stood until 1986. On 17 March 1955, though, NHL President Clarence Campbell suspended the Canadien for the rest of the year. Angry fans erupted from the Montreal Forum, looting and rioting. They felt that Campbell was trying to spoil Quebec's chances of winning the Stanley Cup. Richard was a symbol of French-Canadian nationalism. When he died in 2000, all Quebec mourned.

Canadian Vision

Paul-Emile Borduas

Borduas was born in St. Hilaire, Quebec, in 1905. He wanted to paint church murals like his teacher, Ozias Leduc. Over time, Borduas shifted away from the religious tradition of Leduc. He took on the modern approach of the **Surrealists**. His work began to reflect the art for art's-sake philosophy so celebrated by such Surrealist artists as Miro and Dali. Borduas became leader of the Mouvement Automatistes in Montreal. They celebrated colour, light, line, and mass as subjects of painting. They prized spontaneity in art above all else.

In 1942, Borduas published a manifesto, *Refus Global*. Though mainly about art, *Refus Global* challenged the traditional values of French-Canadian society. Borduas wanted to minimize the influence of the Roman Catholic Church and of the Duplessis government. Since Duplessis believed that modern art was communist inspired, he fired Borduas from his teaching post. He black-balled Borduas from Quebec society. Unable to support himself in Quebec, Borduas fled to New York, and later to Paris. Lonely and homesick for his native Quebec, he died in his Paris studio in 1960.

HISTOR!CA *Minutes*

What was the importance of *Refus Global*? To learn more about *Refus Global* and Borduas, visit the CBC Digital Archives at www.cbc.ca/archives and view the audiovisual file "Le Refus Global: Revolution in the Arts."

FOCUS

1. How did the Union Nationale influence life in Quebec?
2. List the positive and negative results of the Duplessis years.
3. Who opposed Duplessis, and why?

The Quiet Revolution

When Duplessis died, the Union Nationale Party was in a state of collapse. The people of Quebec were ready to redefine their province's role in the world. In 1960, the Liberals, led by Jean Lesage, won their first Quebec election since 1939. *La Revolution Tranquille* (the Quiet Revolution) began. A period of dramatic change was about to unfold.

The **Quiet Revolution** had several goals. It was time for Québécois to be *maîtres chez nous* (masters in our own house), as one of Lesage's most popular Cabinet ministers, René Lévesque, put it. The phrase became a rallying point. All policy during the six years of Lesage's government was designed to fulfil this goal.

Premier Lesage's most pressing problem was the erosion of social and economic conditions. **Francophones** felt like second-class citizens in their own province. French Canadians made less money than many immigrant groups did. Most of the higher paying jobs in the province went to **anglophones**. The vast majority of immigrants to Quebec learned English, not French. The province had one of the highest infant death rates in Canada. Very few francophone students majored in math, science, or engineering. Most of the largest corporations in the province were

Jean Lesage introduced the Quiet Revolution in Quebec.

owned by English Canadians or Americans. English was the language of business. People who spoke English were more likely to be promoted; those who spoke French were not. French Canadians wanted political and financial control over their own affairs. Quebec needed to modernize.

The power of the Church in the province's education system was reduced with the creation of the Quebec Department of Education. A new curriculum placed emphasis on technical skills, business, math, and science. The government provided more hospitals and better health-care services. It reduced the Church's control of the province's health system.

Lesage's government passed laws to protect the use of the French language and to ensure the survival of French-Canadian culture. Other laws guaranteed the rights of labour unions and provided social benefits. The Quebec Pension Plan (QPP) was introduced in 1966 to provide pensions to Quebec workers.

The Lesage government took a more active role in developing provincial resources. In 1969, Quebec bought all the hydroelectric companies in the province. It then made more electricity available to rural areas. During the 1970s, the province built the

GILLES VIGNEAULT AND QUEBEC

One of Quebec's most influential singers, Gilles Vigneault was born in 1928, just outside Montreal. Vigneault's Québécois ballads captured the character, isolation, and landscape of rural Quebec. In 1965, Vigneault's collection of poetry won the Governor General's Award. But it is for his music that Vigneault is most famous. "Mon Pays," a ballad about winter, is almost a national anthem in Quebec.

In 1970, Vigneault became an outspoken supporter of the Parti Québécois.

world's largest hydroelectric project near James Bay. The project was one of several in Quebec. These projects symbolized political and economic control for the province. However, the James Bay project created major hardships for the Cree and Inuit of the area.

On the cultural front, Quebec developed a more vibrant and self-confident society. Hundreds of musicians, writers, painters, and filmmakers began to use their talents to celebrate the new Quebec. People gained a new pride in their province. They began to call themselves Québécois (Quebecers) rather than French Canadians.

Jean Lesage and his Liberals lost the 1966 election. Some voters were unhappy with the many changes introduced during their six years in power. Others were concerned about the increasing provincial debt. The Union Nationale Party, led by Daniel Johnson Sr., returned to power.

New Goals

Most French Canadians agreed with the goals of the Quiet Revolution. Some, however, had different ideas about modernization. One group—which included Jean Marchand, Pierre Trudeau, and Jean Chrétien—wanted Quebec to have more influence in the federal government in Ottawa. Another group felt Quebec would be better off with fewer ties to the rest of Canada. It believed Quebec's culture and interests were separate from those of other Canadians. These people wanted Quebec to be politically independent. René Lévesque, the former Liberal, became a symbol and a leader for many people who felt this way.

A smaller group believed that Quebec would be freed only through violent revolution. This group, the Front de Libération du Québec (FLQ), pledged to fight a war of liberation. The first stage in this war was terrorism.

The Cree in Quebec

When the Quebec government proposed the James Bay hydroelectric project in 1971, the Aboriginal people who lived there were outraged. The project would flood over 176 000 square km of forest and tundra in Northern Quebec. This land belonged to the Cree. The Cree had never given up their rights to this vast territory because they believed their way of life would be destroyed. The Grand Council of the Cree took the case to court. In 1975, after intense negotiations, the Council and the Quebec government signed the James Bay and Northern Quebec Agreement. The Cree and many Inuit peoples in the area gave up their claim to large portions of Northern Quebec in return for a cash payment, land reserves, and hunting and trapping rights.

In 1986, the Quebec government proposed a new series of hydroelectric projects in the area. These would flood an additional 800 square km of Cree land. The Grand Council of the Cree went to court again. It argued that the Quebec government was in breach of its James Bay Agreement. The Council felt the new projects would cause an environmental catastrophe. By 1994 the projects were shelved.

Today, the Grand Council of the Cree is a powerful international voice. The Cree have experience in Canadian and international law. Their campaign for Aboriginal rights has increased awareness of this issue in Canada and around the world.

The Cree are worried about Quebec separation. Like the Québécois, the Cree say they are a distinct people, with the right to protect and promote their culture and identity. The Cree assert Aboriginal title to their land. They claim the right to use their land as their ancestors did. They believe Quebec does not have the right either to speak for them or to take or control their land. They maintain that if Quebec becomes independent, the Cree nation should be allowed to have its own referendum.

Why were the massive dams of the James Bay project a source of pride and confidence? How did the Cree feel?

VIVE LE QUEBEC LIBRE!

It was 1967, and Confederation in Canada was 100 years strong. All across the country, communities celebrated. The largest Centennial event was the world fair hosted by Montreal—Expo '67.

Charles de Gaulle, president of France, represented his country at the opening ceremonies. He gave a rousing speech from the balcony of Montreal City Hall. "Vive Montréal, vive Québec, vive le Québec libre, vive le Canada français, vive la France." His words were greeted with a roar of applause from the crowd. De Gaulle had appealed to the deepest feelings of many Quebecers—"Vive le Québec libre" was a separatist slogan.

In Ottawa, the reaction was very different. By encouraging Quebec's independence in this way,

Charles de Gaulle

the French president had "interfered" with Canada's internal affairs. Canadian Prime Minister Lester Pearson protested the interference. At the request of the Canadian government, de Gaulle returned promptly to France. **Was the Canadian government correct to send Charles de Gaulle home? What would you have done? Why?**

FOCUS

1. What was the major goal of the Quiet Revolution?
2. List three changes made by the Lesage government.
3. How did the Cree fight against Quebec's hydroelectric industry?
4. Why do you think some people of Quebec preferred to call themselves Québécois rather than French Canadians?

Bilingualism

The Quiet Revolution forced the federal government to rethink the relationship between Canada's two main cultures. During the 1960s and 1970s, Canadian Confederation was studied and examined several times by various government-appointed committees or commissions. Their task was to suggest ways to modernize the political, economic, and social relationships between the provinces and the federal government.

Each committee made recommendations

This unique photograph shows four Liberal prime ministers: Pierre Trudeau, John Turner, Jean Chrétien, and Lester Pearson. Much of the French–English debate has been led by Canada's Liberal Party.

for constitutional change. Few of the recommendations were adopted. Agreement among the 10 provincial governments on any change to Canada's Constitution was almost impossible.

In 1967, the Commission on Bilingualism and Biculturalism warned that unless "an equal partnership" between French and English Canada was formed, the country was likely to break up. It recommended that Canada be formally declared bilingual and that French and English be given equal status in the courts, Parliament, and government services.

Trudeau wanted to extend the rights of French-speaking Canadians in other parts of Canada. He believed that French Canadians would be isolated in Quebec if the law did not protect the French language outside Quebec.

Prime Minister Trudeau envisioned Canada as a bilingual country. He wanted English- and French-speaking Canadians to share equal language rights. In 1969, the government passed Canada's Official Languages Act. The new law required that Canadians be served in either French or English when dealing with the federal government. It required companies doing business in Canada to label their products in both languages.

Trudeau was disappointed that he could not persuade Canada's provinces to follow the federal lead. Some Western Canadians felt it was a waste of money. Even some French Canadians objected. Many English Canadians felt that there were not enough French-speaking people outside Quebec to justify the costs of bilingualism. They believed that

This sign below the Peace Tower, reflects the federal governments vision of a bilingual Canada.

French Canadians already held favoured status when applying for government jobs and promotions. Anglophones in government positions objected to learning French. Many people had mixed feelings about the policy. They wanted to promote the French-Canadian culture outside Quebec, not just the French language. A few felt it was too late to solve problems with laws.

The importance of the French language in Canada increased dramatically. French Canadians also had greater opportunities for jobs within the federal civil service. The Official Languages Act was also good for francophones outside Quebec. Acadians in the Atlantic provinces and francophones in Ontario and Manitoba all benefited.

FOCUS

1. What did the Commission on Bilingualism and Biculturalism say would happen if Quebec did not receive equal partnership with English Canada?
2. What is the Official Languages Act? Why were many people unhappy with it?

The October Crisis

Not all Quebecers were satisfied with the amount or pace of change during the Quiet Revolution. In the 1960s, a small group of radical separatists used bombs to achieve their goals. These people were members of the Front de Libération du Québec (FLQ).

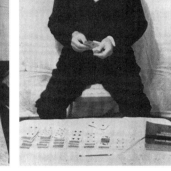

LEFT: *The FLQ set off several bombs in Montreal.* RIGHT: Why do you think the FLQ kidnapped James Cross, a British citizen?

They wanted to gain attention by bombing federal government property. The FLQ was organized into cells, or small groups of people. Communication between cells was by secret code. Members of one cell did not know who was in another cell. If one cell was captured by police, it could not betray others. Despite these precautions, the police were able to arrest, try, and imprison several FLQ members.

On the morning of 5 October 1970, FLQ members kidnapped James Cross, a British diplomat, from his Montreal home. They demanded a ransom of $500 000, plus TV and radio time to broadcast FLQ views to the Quebec people. They also wanted safe passage out of Canada for themselves, and for imprisoned FLQ members. They warned that Cross would be executed if their demands were not met. The FLQ hoped the Cross kidnapping would spark a wave of violence that would result in the separation of Quebec from Canada.

French and English Canadians were numb with shock. Terrorism might happen in unstable countries, but surely not in safe, quiet Canada. The police could find no clues to the Cross kidnapping.

Five days later, on October 10, the terrorists struck again. Pierre Laporte, the Quebec minister of labour, was kidnapped at gunpoint while playing football outside his home. This second kidnapping drove many people in Quebec into near panic.

The War Measures Act

Quebec police were frustrated by their inability to solve the two kidnappings. People feared the FLQ would strike again. Quebec Premier Robert Bourassa asked the federal government for help. Prime Minister Trudeau responded by asking Parliament to proclaim the War Measures Act, which suspended legal rights and freedoms. The Act was designed for emergency use when Canada was at war. It had been used during both world wars, but never during peace. The Act gave police special powers to search, question, and arrest

Parts of Montreal looked like a war zone during the FLQ crisis. Do you think soldiers should have been sent in to help solve the crisis? Explain.

suspects without cause. A curfew was declared in Montreal. The army was called in to assist the police.

On October 17, police received a tip about an abandoned car. The body of Pierre Laporte was found in its trunk. He had been strangled with the chain from his own religious medal. Quebecers were shocked that one of their own had been killed so brutally by the FLQ.

On November 6, one of the Laporte kidnappers was found in a closet during a search of a Montreal apartment. Police did not realize until later that the terrorists were hiding behind a partition in the same closet. These people were found on December 28 in an abandoned farmhouse 30 km southeast of Montreal.

In the end, it was routine police investigation that finally led to the discovery of James Cross. On December 3, police and soldiers surrounded the house where Cross was being held. He had been there for nearly nine weeks. All of Canada watched as the deal for his release was negotiated.

Pierre Laporte's funeral at Montreal's Church of Notre Dame was a day of mourning for many Canadians. For more on this tragedy, visit www.cbc.ca/archives and view the file "The October Crisis: Civil Liberties Suspended."

Television crews in helicopters followed the kidnappers' car as it raced through downtown Montreal to "Man and His World," the site of Expo '67. There, Cross was released into the custody of the Cuban Consul. The kidnappers were flown to Cuba.

The results of the **October Crisis** were far-reaching. Under the War Measures Act, about 500 people were arrested and held in custody for up to three weeks. They had been imprisoned merely on suspicion. Most were released without charge. Many people lost faith in the government's ability to protect society and their civil rights. Any sympathy most Québécois might have had for the FLQ was wiped out. The Front was in ruins. Quebecers who believed in **separatism** were firmly convinced that their goals should be achieved through peaceful means. For the first time, other Canadians, both French and English, became fully aware of the feelings dividing the country. They resolved to work even harder at co-operation and understanding. Everyone realized that Canada, too, was vulnerable to violence and terror.

Robert Bourassa had just become premier of Quebec when the FLQ crisis exploded. Laporte was not only a colleague, but was once a rival for the leadership of the Quebec Liberal Party. Bourassa spent much of his political life combatting separatism and promoting a changed, but united Canada.

FOCUS

1. **What was the goal of the FLQ?**
2. **Why did the government proclaim the War Measures Act? How did it use the powers the Act gave it?**
3. **What were the results of the October Crisis?**

René Lévesque and the Parti Québécois

The end of the FLQ crisis in 1970 did not mean the end of separatism. Many Québécois leaders still believed in achieving independence—but by lawful means.

René Lévesque was one such person. Lévesque was a popular journalist and an

government was corrupt. PQ support increased dramatically.

The PQ pledged to end corruption in Quebec politics, to protect the French language, and to aid the weaker groups in society. The PQ eased fears that independence might

Lévesque was a forceful, passionate speaker.

Trudeau (left) and Lévesque (right) were powerful champions for the federalist and separatist causes.

influential minister in the Lesage government of the 1960s. He became frustrated with the Liberal federalist policies. He resigned from the party to found the Mouvement Souveraineté Association in 1967. It joined forces with another separatist party in 1968 to form the **Parti Québécois**, or PQ. Lévesque was elected party leader.

The popularity of the PQ rose as the popularity of the Bourassa Liberals fell. Quebec was plagued with strikes between 1973 and 1976. Unemployment rose, as did the cost of living. People began to believe the Bourassa

bring a loss of money and jobs. Lévesque stressed that an independent Quebec would have close economic ties with Canada. During the election campaign of 1976, the PQ promised good government. To attract voters who were uneasy about voting for a separatist party, the PQ announced that the question of separation would be decided in a future referendum.

Lévesque and the PQ won 69 out of 110 seats on election day. The Liberals won 28. Many Canadians were stunned. Even PQ members were surprised by the size of the victory. Quebec separatists were ecstatic. The world viewed the PQ victory with unease. What did it mean for Canada?

Pierre Elliott Trudeau, a strong Québécois federalist, was Canada's prime minister. Canadian **federalists** looked to Trudeau for leadership in fighting the Quebec separatist movement.

In 1979, the Parti Québécois announced it would hold a referendum in May 1980. Quebecers would vote on the idea of leaving Confederation.

PQ leaders worked hard on the wording of the question they would put to voters. They knew many were afraid of separatism. To reduce voters' alarm, they softened the question. Quebecers were asked to vote *oui* (yes) or *non* (no) on whether they wished to give the Quebec government the "mandate (or right) to negotiate **sovereignty-association** with Canada."

Both the *oui* and the *non* campaigns were hard fought. The province was bombarded with rallies, speeches, pamphlets, and radio and TV ads. Lévesque and his followers

Hockey was used in the referendum of 1970. Here, Lévesque holds a Quebec Nordiques jersey with a symbol of the 1837 Rebellion on it.

claimed a *oui* vote was needed to protect the French language and the culture of Quebec. They urged Québécois to remember their history and pride in their homeland. They claimed that a strong *oui* vote would give the province more political clout when dealing with Ottawa.

The *non* campaign was headed by the new Quebec Liberal leader, Claude Ryan, a political rookie. Ryan attacked the wording of the question. He argued that the PQ was trying to disguise separatism by calling it sovereignty-association. His speeches were passionate. Ryan began to impress the voters as a sincere and dedicated man.

Members of all three federal parties supported the *non* side. Pierre Trudeau used his personal popularity in the province to help persuade Quebecers to remain in Canada. One million Canadians signed a petition to tell the people of Quebec they wanted them to remain in Canada.

The turning point of the 1980 Quebec referendum came when Lise Payette, a PQ Cabinet minister, unintentionally mobilized Quebec women into the debate. Payette delivered a speech in which she called Claude Ryan's wife an "Yvette" and accused all women who voted against the PQ of being "Yvettes." Yvette was the name of the girl in a grade 2 reader used in Quebec schools. The reader showed Yvette staying at home to cook and sew while her brother had exciting adventures. Payette was implying that all women who were against sovereignty-association were submissive and could not think for themselves.

Enraged women in Quebec started an Yvette movement. Within a week of Payette's comments, the Yvettes held a rally of 15 000 women. This rally was the first serious setback for the PQ. From that point on, the federalist campaign gathered momentum.

On Referendum Day, 85 percent of eligible Quebec voters cast their ballots. When the polls closed, people across the nation waited in suspense as the results trickled in.

Within an hour, the outcome was clear. As expected, the English-speaking vote was solidly opposed to separation. Almost 60 percent of the province voted to stay in Canada. Referring to the majority of women who voted *non* to sovereignty-association, one PQ organizer commented: "The Yvettes killed us."

Lévesque and the PQ had suffered defeat, but the people of Quebec believed that they had provided good government. Both were re-elected in 1981. Ryan resigned, and Robert Bourassa returned as the Liberal leader.

Canadians understood that Quebec's voice would be heard again. Political or constitutional change would be needed to avoid the future breakup of the country. But would the Québécois ever be satisfied within a Canadian framework? A delicate balance would be difficult to achieve.

A CLOSER LOOK AT SOVEREIGNTY-ASSOCIATION

Sovereignty meant that Quebec would be politically independent. Only the Quebec government could collect taxes, and Quebec would run its own foreign affairs. *Association* meant that Quebec would still be tied to Canada economically. The two countries would use the same money. They would have the same tariffs on imports. A mandate to negotiate the question would give the PQ government the authority to try to work out a deal with the rest of Canada. A *oui* vote would not necessarily mean that Quebec would leave Canada. If and after any agreement was reached, a second vote would be called.

Prime Minister Trudeau was determined to keep Quebec in Canada. To do this, he decided to **patriate** and revise the Canadian Constitution. Doing so meant a long and often bitter struggle. There was considerable debate and compromise before Canada's Constitution Act, 1982, was finally complete. A major problem was convincing all 10 provinces to agree to the new constitution. Eventually, all but one province agreed—Lévesque and the PQ opposed it. Rather than providing a binding tie, Canada's Constitution Act, 1982, further divided Quebec from the rest of the country.

When Réne Lévesque resigned from the Parti Québécois in 1985, support for the party declined. Lévesque died in 1987. Although most Québécois did not accept his ideas on separatism, they loved him. He was thought of as the man with the giant heart who had dedicated his life to them and to the survival of Québécois culture.

Canadian Vision

Mon Oncle Antoine

The film *Mon Oncle Antoine* was first screened in 1971. It is said by many to be the best film Canada has ever produced. Its creator was Claude Jutra, who earned international fame because of it. Jutra was born in Montreal in 1930 to a family of doctors. His film-making talent became obvious when he was only 18. Halfway through medical school, Jutra directed an award-winning short film called *Perpetual Motion*.

It caught the attention of the National Film Board. Jutra's first feature-length film, *A Tout Prendre*, was financed privately because the NFB was unwilling to fund it. It won a number of international awards and marked the first wave of Quebec filmmaking. In 1969, Jutra began work on *Mon Oncle Antoine*. It got more attention in English-speaking Canada and in the United States than it did in French Canada. Furthermore, American critics loved it.

FOCUS

1. What did René Lévesque do before entering politics?
2. Why did he leave the Liberal Party?
3. Who were the "Yvettes"? Why did they rally against the separatist cause?
4. What was the result of the 1980 referendum?
5. How did Trudeau attempt to bind Canada together?

Language in Quebec

In 1977, the Lévesque government revolutionized Quebec's language practices with the passage of Bill 101. This bill made French the language of business and government. French was now the official language of Quebec. All communication from the Quebec government would be only in French.

The Commission de Surveillance was established to enforce Bill 101. Consumers had the right to be served in French. Workers had the right to work in French. All signs and billboards had to be written and displayed in French. French was the language of instruction in school. Immigrant children would learn French in the school system, not English. Only children whose parents had been educated in English would be sent to English-language schools.

Many anglophones and immigrants in the province were horrified

In April 2000, the Quebec courts ruled that signs showing English and French words in the same size were illegal. What challenge does this earlier sign point to?

by the legislation. They claimed that Bill 101 violated bilingualism. Some people formed Alliance Quebec. They took their case to court. Others simply left the province.

One hotly contested issue was the use of English-language signs in Quebec stores. Anglophones were upset at the idea of French-only signs in their stores. In 1982, the Quebec Supreme Court ruled that store signs must be in French, but that they could also be bilingual.

Robert Bourassa, who had retired in the late 1970s, returned to Quebec politics in 1985 as leader of the Liberal Party. His Liberals defeated the Parti Québécois in the 1985 election. Like Lévesque, Bourassa believed that Quebec should have the power to control its language law.

The store signage issue was raised again in 1988 on appeal to the Supreme Court of Canada. The Supreme Court ruled that although the government of Quebec had the right to require all signs to be in French, it did not have the right to prevent the use of other languages on the signs.

The Quebec government promptly passed a new law. Bill 178 required French-only signs on the outside of buildings, but permitted bilingual signs on the inside of buildings—as long as French dominated. Francophones within the province strongly supported Bourassa. Anglophones, most of whom were long-time Liberals, denounced him. They began to abandon the party.

The tri-colour iris emblem now symbolizes Quebec cultural diversity.

Some anglophones took their case to the United Nations Committee on Human Rights. In 1993, the Committee ruled against Bill 178. Bourassa's government passed Bill 86 in response. Bill 86 said that commercial signs in Quebec could be bilingual, as long as the French language is dominant.

The debate over Quebec's language laws continues. Even the Internet is subject to the dispute. The Commission de Surveillance investigates when people complain about English-only Internet communication. This issue has not yet been heard in the courts.

A CLOSER LOOK AT THE CANADIAN CHARTER OF RIGHTS AND FREEDOMS

The Charter is part of the Constitution Act, 1982. It guarantees the rights and freedoms of all Canadians. All Canadian laws (present and future) must follow the terms of the Charter and allow freedom of speech, of thought, and of expression. However, the Charter places "reasonable limits" on the rights and freedoms that Canadians enjoy.

Section 33 gives Canadian provinces the right to pass laws that ignore or override certain Charter rights. Section 33 was added to give Canadian provinces flexibility when dealing with their respective citizens. Quebec has used this clause to maintain its language laws.

Canadian Vision

O Canada!

In 1880, the song that would become Canada's national anthem was written by Adolphe-Basile Routhier and Calixa Lavallée. It was composed to help celebrate French Canada's national day, St. Jean Baptiste Day. The song was an instant hit.

In 1908, Stanley Weir wrote English words to Lavallée's famous tune in celebration of the 300th anniversary of the founding of Quebec. His version became popular in English Canada. In 1980, Parliament recognized "O Canada!" as the national anthem. Minor changes were made to the English words, but the French version remains exactly as Routhier and Lavallée wrote it.

French Version:
O Canada!

O Canada!
Terre de nos aïeux,
(Land of our forefathers)
Ton front est ceint de fleurons glorieux!
(Thy brow is wreathed with a glorious garland of flowers!)
Car ton bras sait porter l'épée il sait porter la croix!
(As your arm is ready to wield a sword so is it ready to carry the cross)
Ton histoire est une épopée
(Thy history is an epic)
Des plus brillants exploits
(of the most brilliant exploits)
Et ta valeur, de foi trempée,
(Thy value, steeped in faith)
Protégera nos foyers et nos droits
(Will protect our homes and our rights)
Protégera nos foyers et nos droits.
(Will protect our homes and our rights)

English Version:
O Canada!

O Canada!
Our home and native land!
True patriot love in all thy sons' command.
With glowing hearts we see thee rise,
The True North strong and free!
From far and wide,
O Canada,
We stand on guard for thee.
God keep our land, glorious and free!
O Canada,
We stand on guard for thee!
O Canada,
We stand on guard for thee!

Read both versions of "O Canada!" and carefully note the differences.

HISTOR!CA
Minutes

Bombardier Snowmobiles The snowmobile was invented by Quebec mechanic Joseph-Armand Bombardier (1907–1964).

HISTOR!CA

Minutes

Bombardier built everything himself. In 1936, he invented the first vehicle steered by skis. Later, he invented a tank-like all-terrain vehicle with room for up to 12 people. Until the Quebec government announced it would keep roads clear of snow, the vehicle was a common sight on snowy Quebec roads.

Then, in 1959, Bombardier introduced the Ski-Doo. Modelled more on a motorcycle than a bus, the Ski-Doo was an instant success in Canada. For the first time ever, remote Arctic communities were accessible by land. The Ski-Doo transformed social life there. By the 1990s, more than 2 million Ski-Doos had been sold worldwide.

From this base, Bombardier Inc. came to enter the rail, aerospace, and defence sectors, serving the global market. Working in several world languages, it now has manufacturing plants in Montreal, Austria, Iceland, and the United

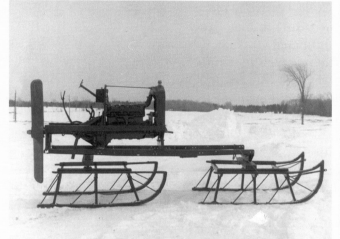

This vehicle evolved into the popular Ski-Doo. From that invention, Bombardier Inc. went on to produce trains, ships, and planes. RIGHT: *Joseph-Armand Bombardier.*

States. Like Quebecor and Power Corporation, its home remains Quebec.

To see more of Bombardier's projects, go to www.bombardier.com or visit the CBC Digital Archives at www.cbc.ca/archives ***and view the file "Bombardier: The Snowmobile Legacy."***

FOCUS

1. **What is Bill 101? How did it affect Quebec's language laws?**
2. **How has Quebec used the Charter of Rights and Freedoms to uphold its language laws?**
3. **What evidence is there that language continues to be a divisive issue in Quebec?**
4. **Why is language both a bridge and a wall in Canada?**

Failed Accords

Meech Lake Accord

Progressive Conservative leader Brian Mulroney became prime minister in 1984. Mulroney was a bilingual Quebecer. He was determined to resolve the conflict between Quebec and the rest of Canada. Mulroney had campaigned on a promise to reduce this conflict. He had also promised to find a compromise that would allow Quebec to support the Constitution.

Although the Constitution Act, 1982, was legally binding on Quebec, Mulroney found it unacceptable that Quebec had not agreed to it. He believed that if the Constitution gave Quebec special status, it would bring the province into constitutional agreement with the rest of Canada.

Brian Mulroney

In April 1987, the prime minister invited the 10 provincial premiers to the government's private retreat in Meech Lake, Quebec. After much debate, an agreement was reached on constitutional change (later called the Meech Lake Accord). The agreement proposed to give more power to the provinces. It also recognized the province of Quebec as a **distinct society**. It had the approval of all three federal parties, and was soon approved by 8 of the 10 provinces. Only Newfoundland and Manitoba held out. Their agreement was necessary for the Accord to take effect.

Opponents of Meech Lake felt that the Accord weakened federal government powers and gave too much power to the provincial governments. They also felt that the price paid to bring Quebec into the Constitution was too great and that the phrase "distinct society," which lacked a precise legal meaning, might give rise to future legal and constitutional disputes.

Aboriginal Canadians opposed Meech Lake. They argued that Aboriginal communities should also be recognized as distinct. They saw the survival of their communities

---

MEECH LAKE ACCORD

The Meech Lake Accord specified the following:

- Quebec would be recognized as a distinct society within the Constitution.
- All provinces would have the right to recommend the appointment of senators and Supreme Court justices.
- Changes to federal institutions (the number of members in the House of Commons, Senate, and Supreme Court, for example), as well as changes from territories to provinces, would require approval by all Canadian provinces, as well as the Canadian Parliament.
- Provinces could opt out of the newly created national social programs and receive federal revenues for their own social programs, as long as these met national objectives.

Which of the above would you have supported or not supported? Explain.

within Canada as no less important than the survival of Quebec.

On 23 June 1990, Elijah Harper, of Manitoba, spoke on behalf of Aboriginal Canadians to the Manitoba legislature. He effectively prevented the Meech Lake vote from taking place there. The deadline for agreement thus expired without unanimous approval. Prime Minister Mulroney's first attempt to bring Quebec into the Constitution had failed.

Charlottetown Accord

Mulroney attempted constitutional change a second time. Constitutional committees were established to canvass the country and to report back. Bourassa's government threatened to hold a vote on separatism if the country did not address Quebec's demands. Tension mounted.

Finally, after months of discussion, an agreement was reached in Charlottetown, Prince Edward Island. This site was symbolic because the Confederation discussions of 1864 had taken place there.

In October 1992, the Charlottetown Accord was presented to Canadian voters for

Elijah Harper

approval in a national referendum. The vote was 55 percent No to 45 percent Yes.

Once more, Canada was caught in a unity crisis. Regionalism in western Canada blossomed, as did Quebec separatism. Some Quebec members of Parliament left their parties to create the Bloc Québécois. Many people blamed Prime Minister Mulroney for his timing of the constitutional discussions. Others blamed Quebec and the other provinces.

CHARLOTTETOWN ACCORD

The 1992 Charlottetown Accord consisted of several points:

- Quebec was recognized as a distinct society with its own traditions.
- The idea of Aboriginal government was put on a par with federal and provincial governments.
- The Canadian Senate would be elected, not appointed.
- Canadian provinces would have extended powers, including power over social and health programs, as long as these were within "national standards."

Which of the above would you have supported or not supported? Explain.

FOCUS

1. Why were some people against the Meech Lake Accord?
2. How did Elijah Harper prevent the Accord from taking place? Why did he do it?
3. Why did the Charlottetown Accord fail?

Referendum 1995

Mulroney's minister of the environment, Lucien Bouchard, became disillusioned with both federalism and the Progressive Conservative Party after the Meech Lake Accord. In 1990, he quit the party and sat as an independent member of the House of Commons. Soon, Bouchard was joined by several more Conservative MPs from Quebec. Together, they formed the Bloc Québécois.

Lucien Bouchard

The Bloc vowed to represent the interests of Québécois in the federal Parliament. In the 1993 federal election, the Bloc won 54 seats to form the official Opposition.

In 1994, Jacques Parizeau, leader of the Parti Québécois, became premier of Quebec. Parizeau won the election in part because he promised voters an early referendum on separation, using clear, plain wording. Parizeau moved immediately to unite the Québécois separatist movement. In June 1995, he invited Bouchard and other politicians from Quebec to create a document outlining how separation could be achieved.

On 27 October 1995, a huge national unity rally took place in Montreal. Do you think this show of support would help or hurt the federalist cause?

My Country, Mons Pays

The referendum was set for 30 October 1995. The Quebec government sought permission to negotiate a new agreement with the rest of Canada. It wanted Quebec to gain political independence, but maintain economic ties with Canada. Yes voters would also be giving the Parti Québécois permission to declare **unilateral independence** within one year of the referendum date, if negotiations failed.

Daniel Johnson Jr., leader of the Quebec Liberals, Jean Charest, federal Conservative leader, and federal Liberal Cabinet ministers led the campaign for the No vote. At first, momentum seemed to be with the No side. The federalists underestimated the opposition, however. As voting day approached, separatists received more and more support. The referendum looked to be a very close race. Thousands of English Canadians from all over Canada gathered in Montreal for a huge rally on October 27. The rally was an extraordinary display of Canadian nationalism.

THE REFERENDUM QUESTION

Federalists believed that the wording of the 1995 Quebec referendum question was unclear and that most Quebecers did not know exactly what they were voting on. Read the question below. Is the wording clear or ambiguous? Explain.

Do you agree that Quebec should become sovereign after having made a formal offer to Canada for a new economic and political partnership, within the scope of the Bill respecting the future of Quebec, and the agreement signed on June 12, 1995?

Voter turnout was high on Referendum Day. Canadians everywhere waited anxiously for the results. Everyone knew the decision would be close, but no one predicted just how close: 49.4 percent in favour of the question, 50.6 percent against it. The federalists had won, but by a very narrow margin.

Jacques Parizeau blamed the separatist loss on big business money and "the ethnic vote." He resigned and the popular Lucien Bouchard replaced him.

FOCUS

1. Why did Lucien Bouchard quit the Progressive Conservative Party?
2. What is the Bloc Québécois?
3. Why was the referendum result so close in 1995?

Separatism and the Supreme Court

Jean Chrétien, then prime minister, vowed that federalist Canada would never be caught unprepared again. He appointed Stéphane Dion, intergovernmental affairs minister, to ensure that Ottawa would be ready for the separatists' next move. This federalist strategy was referred to as Plan B.

The Judges' bench in the main courtroom of the Supreme Court of Canada.

Dion decided to ask the Supreme Court of Canada to rule on the legality of separation. This approach was risky. The Supreme Court would make an independent judgment. It would apply the law, not emotion. Many Canadians feared the decision would help the separatist cause. The Quebec government believed that the Supreme Court had no business ruling on the future destiny of Quebec. It boycotted the hearings.

In August 1988, the Supreme Court ruled that the voters of Quebec could determine the future of their province in a democratic manner. Both federalists and separatists claimed victory. Separatists were happy because if Quebec voters approved a separation referendum, Canada would have to nego-tiate separation. Federalists liked the ruling because the Court specified a need for a clear referendum question and a clear majority vote in favour of separation. Both Bouchard and Charest defined a clear majority vote as 50 percent plus one. Prime Minister Chrétien and Stéphane Dion, however, maintained that a vote of 50 percent plus one was too small a majority to decide the fate of the nation. In 2005, a new Parti Québécois leader, André Boisclair, declared that a future vote on separation would not need to accept any federal guidelines.

The Supreme Court of Canada ruled as follows:

- Under Canadian and international law, it would be illegal for Quebec to declare unilateral separation from Canada.
- If the Quebec people voted to separate from Canada through the democratic process of a provincial referendum, the Canadian government could voluntarily negotiate separation terms with the new Quebec. (This process would ensure minimal disruption to Canada and to Quebec.)
- A referendum vote must be a clear majority, and the vote must be made on a clear question. (The Court did not define either term.)

Clarity Act

In December 1999, Chrétien's government surprised many Canadians when it introduced the Clarity Act, Bill C-20, to the House of Commons. Based on the Supreme Court ruling on Quebec separation, the Bill outlined the conditions under which the federal government would negotiate separation of a province. The proposed law stated that negotiations would be carried out in accordance with the Supreme Court ruling. Borders, assets, liabilities, Aboriginal and minority rights would be negotiable.

The Clarity Bill marks the first time that a federal government had publicly set conditions under which it would negotiate the secession of any province.

A CLOSER LOOK AT FRENCH IN CANADA

According to an article in *The New York Times* (28 October 1999): "The French language has entered a period of slow but steady decline in Canada in face of a wave of Asian immigration and a growing number of so-called allophones in Quebec, according to two studies published this week. Allophones speak neither French nor English, Canada's official languages, at home.

The studies, undertaken by the Association for Canadian Studies in Montreal and the Conseil de la Langue Française in Quebec, predicted that Chinese would soon be spoken more than French in English-speaking Canada, while French would continue to decline slowly in Quebec, where it is predominant.

The studies said the number of French speakers had been eroded by three years of rising immigration to Ontario and British Columbia.

The study by the Conseil de la Langue Française also indicated that the French language in Quebec, a province of 7.3 million people, is threatened.

Marc Termote, who wrote the study, said the number of francophones in the province could drop by 2 percentage points, to 81 percent, in 20 years, with allophones accounting for 9.5 percent."

How would a Quebec separatist likely react to this article? Why?

FOCUS

1. **Why did the Quebec government denounce Plan B?**
2. **What is the Clarity Bill? Why is it so significant?**
3. **In your view, should any province be allowed to separate from the nation? Explain.**

Quebec's Changing Faces

As Canada celebrated the outset of the 21st century, there was general happiness over the prosperous nation that Canada had become since 1867. Yet, national unity was still an issue. Some Canadians in the west, east, and north felt that they were not equal partners in Confederation. Some threatened to leave or try to alter the terms of the Confederation agreement. The most serious threat to Canadian unity came from the separatist forces in Quebec. Although they had been beaten in referenda in 1980 and 1995, they had not given up hope. Two powerful and popular political forces were fighting for the separatist cause: the Bloc Québécois and the Parti Québécois.

Here, outgoing PQ leader Bernard Landry, right, joins hands with respected Bloc Québécois leader Gilles Duceppe at the June 2005 PQ convention in Quebec City. Both the Bloc and the PQ support separation.

The Bloc Québécois

The Bloc Québécois was formed by Lucien Bouchard after the failure of the Meech Lake Accord. The federal party runs candidates only in the province of Quebec. It has won many seats and votes since its birth. The Bloc stands as the voice of Quebec separatism in the House of Commons. After Lucien Bouchard left Ottawa to serve as leader of the Parti Québécois and premier of Quebec (1995–2001), Gilles Duceppe took over as Bloc leader.

The Parti Québécois

After the bitter failure of the 1995 referendum, Jacques Parizeau resigned as premier. The popular Lucien Bouchard replaced him as leader of the Parti Québécois. Bouchard went on to lead the Parti Québécois to two electoral victories in Quebec, but did not introduce another referendum on separation.

My Country, Mons Pays

Federalists, Separatists, and Nationalists in Quebec

Quebec separatists see themselves as citizens of Quebec—they do not see themselves as citizens of Canada. They want Quebec to leave Confederation and to establish itself as an independent country.

Separatists believe that independence is the only way for Quebec to control its own affairs. They think that independence will protect the uniqueness of the Québécois culture. Separatists want to keep strong economic ties to the rest of Canada.

On the other hand, Quebec federalists believe that Quebec has prospered as part of the Canadian Confederation. Federalists acknowledge that the Québécois suffered injustices and discrimination in earlier times. They also believe that the French language and culture are well protected today within Confederation. Federalists believe that Confederation strengthens Quebec. They feel that the province can realize its fullest potential within Canada.

Many Québécois often fall between these two groups. They are neither fully separatist, nor fully federalist. These people are sometimes referred to as soft separatists or **nationalists**. They want a strong Quebec, but within

The controversial André Boisclair became leader of the Parti Québécois in 2005.

a united Canada. They are often central in the battles for the hearts and minds of Quebecers. Some Quebecers shift from federalist to separatist to nationalist depending on political or personal events.

New immigrants to Quebec will likely play a bigger role in any future political battles or referenda. Many immigrants feel that they have entered Canada, not just Quebec. They have supported Canada in the two Quebec referenda. They also hope to have all Canada open to their children in the future. Many have neither English nor French as their first language. The old French–English struggles have less meaning for them.

Thérèse Casgrain

BORN: 1896, Montreal, Quebec

DIED: 1981, Montreal, Quebec

SIGNIFICANCE: Casgrain was the first francophone woman appointed to the Senate.

BRIEF BIOGRAPHY: Thérèse Casgrain was a suffragette, humanist, radio personality, and reformer. She played a leading role in Quebec's social and political culture during the 20th century. She campaigned ceaselessly for women's rights. Casgrain was a founding member of the Provincial Franchise Committee for women's suffrage in 1921. During the 1930s, she hosted a radio show, *Fémina*, in which she discussed the role of women in Quebec society. In the 1940s, she joined the CCF. This movement helped mobilize opposition to Duplessis's government. In the 1960s, she founded the League of Human Rights and the Quebec branch of the Voice of Women. Her purpose was to protest the nuclear threat. Casgrain has been a role model for many Quebec women. She symbolizes the active political role that women can play in the province. **In your view, what is Casgrain's most important achievement?**

CANADIAN LIVES

Women and Quebec

The voting preferences of Quebec women have had a powerful, but underestimated impact on the province's politics. Although eligible to vote federally since 1917, Quebec women received the right to vote in provincial elections only in 1940. Quebec suffragettes, led by Thérèse Casgrain and Marie Gérin-Lajoie, were opposed by the Roman Catholic Church. Francophone nationalists considered the suffrage movement to be an Anglo-Saxon and anti-Quebec idea.

Quebec women largely support a united Canada. They tend to see separatism as an economic risk to the

Gabrielle Roy

province and therefore to their personal well-being. According to Statistics Canada in 1997, women over 15 years of age made up 44 percent of the workforce in Quebec. However, 68 percent were in low-paying, part-time jobs. They believe a united Canada provides them and their children with greater stability, security, and opportunity.

Quebec women have enjoyed great success in the arts. Céline Dion, world-famous singer and celebrity, recorded her songs only in French until 1990. Authors Anne Hébert, Gabrielle Roy, and Marie-Claire Blais wrote books that won Governor General's Awards.

Julie Payette represents a new breed of Quebec women. Born in 1963, she speaks five languages and holds a multi-engine commercial pilot licence. She has also sung with the Montreal Symphonic Orchestra Chamber Choir, the Piacere Vocali in Switzerland, and the Tafelmusik Baroque Orchestra in Toronto. In May 1999, Payette flew on the space shuttle *Discovery* to the International Space Station. She was the first Canadian to visit the Space Station. In September 1999, Payette accompanied Prime Minister Jean Chrétien and Quebec Premier Lucien Bouchard to Japan for trade discussions.

FOCUS

1. How do the Bloc Québécois and Parti Québécois differ?
2. Define a Quebec separatist, federalist, and nationalist.
3. What role have women played in the separatism debate?
4. Do you think that the separatists will ever win a referendum? Explain.

French Canada Today

A Multicultural Community

Bill 101, the Quebec language law, passed in 1977. It forced all immigrants to send their children to French language schools. By 2000, a whole generation of immigrant children in Quebec had been educated as francophones. West Indians, Koreans, Filipinos, Chinese, and Latin Americans all spoke fluent French. Many of these young men and women became fully bilingual as they learned English at home or by watching TV. Some spoke three languages by maintaining the cultural heritage of their parents or grandparents. This multicultural, multiracial, multilingual population has developed in a Québécois culture. They are also aware of a much wider world outside the boundaries of the province.

Traditionally, immigrants in Quebec have preferred federalism to separatism. Jacques Parizeau, Quebec's premier during the 1995 Referendum, blamed the separatist defeat on "money and the ethnic vote."

Today's youth, though, have grown up in a separatist political climate. Québécois born since 1977 have lived through two sovereignty votes and several separatist governments. They have heard Quebec leaders claim that Canada rejected Quebec by not passing the Meech Lake and Charlottetown Accords. Quebec's young voters grew up in an environment that saw successive Quebec governments demand more powers for Quebec. It is no surprise that many Quebec youth appear to prefer the separatist option—these young voters will likely chart Canada's future.

In September 2005, Prime Minister Paul Martin appointed Michaëlle Jean as governor general of Canada. In many ways, she represents the new Quebec—and the new Canada.

In Their Own Words

When Michaëlle Jean was installed as governor general, she gave a forceful speech. Part of it appears below.

"The time of the 'two solitudes' that for too long described the character of this country is past. The narrow notion of 'every person for himself' does not belong in today's world, which demands that we learn to see beyond our wounds, beyond our differences for the good of all.

Quite the contrary: We must eliminate the spectre of all the solitudes and promote solidarity among all the citizens who make up the Canada of today. As well, we must make good use of our prosperity and our influence wherever the hope that we represent offers the world an extra measure of harmony."

What do you think Jean meant when she spoke of the "two solitudes"?

Michaëlle Jean

BORN: Haiti

SIGNIFICANCE: Jean is the first Black woman to be appointed governor general.

BRIEF BIOGRAPHY: Michaëlle Jean was born in 1957 in Haiti, one of the world's poorest and most violent countries. In 1968, political thugs attacked her father. Jean's family fled to Canada. She attended school in rural Quebec. She later earned a degree in modern languages. Jean speaks five languages fluently—Creole, French, English, Italian, and Spanish.

She worked as a television journalist for Radio-Canada and the CBC in Quebec. She was appointed governor general in 2005, replacing the popular, but

Governor General Michaëlle Jean receives the symbolic first poppy of the 2005 Poppy and Remembrance campaign at her residence, Rideau Hall. The governor general is a patron of the Royal Canadian Legion, which runs the campaign.

somewhat controversial Adrienne Clarkson.

Jean is an immigrant woman of colour. She represents Canadians who are not descended from English or French settlers. When she was first selected, a small group of separatists claimed that she was for an independent Quebec. Jean forcefully stated her loyalty to Canada. **Do you think Michaëlle Jean is a good choice as Canada's governor general? Explain. For more information about the work and activities of the governor general, visit the official Web site at www.gg.ca.**

CANADIAN LIVES

Acadians The francophones in the Atlantic provinces have a proud heritage. They are different from their Quebec neighbours. They have a different history, different memories, a different culture, and a slightly different language. At the same time, they look to the larger French-speaking population of Quebec as allies in the struggle to maintain their identity.

The Acadian presence dates back to the original settlements along the Bay of Fundy. Often ignored by France, Acadians created an agricultural community. They dyked and improved the rich farmlands. They traded with the Aboriginal peoples and the English colonies to the south for the things they could not produce themselves.

Acadia was soon caught up in the strife between Britain and France. After 1713, much of Acadia was under British rule. Acadians tried to remain neutral, but the British did not trust them. In 1755, as tensions grew, the British decided to deport the

Expulsion of the Acadians

Acadians from British North America and send them to English colonies farther south. This was called *Le Grand Dérangement*.

Very few Acadians escaped this deportation. Others slowly made their way back to their homeland. Eventually, many settled in what is now northern New Brunswick. Some Acadians remained in the American colonies and adapted to their new country. Today, Americans of Acadian ancestry are found in Louisiana, Maine, Vermont, and other U.S. states. Their modern name in Louisiana is "Cajun," an Americanization of Acadien.

The Acadian community is strong and vibrant. Many Acadians have achieved national and international acclaim. Roméo LeBlanc, Canada's governor general from 1995 to 1999, was the first Acadian to fill this post. Antonine Maillet, a prominent Acadian writer, won France's Prix Goncourt in 1979 for her novel *Pélagie-la-charrette*. It was the first time in the prize's history that an author living outside of France won it. Acadians celebrated the 400th anniversary of their presence in North America in 2005.

For more information about Acadia and Acadians, visit the official Web site of the Société Nationale de l'Acadie at www.acadie400.ca.

COMMUNITY SNAPSHOT

Franco-Ontarians There have been French settlers in Ontario almost as long as there have been French people in Canada. The first known French voyageur to arrive in what would later be Ontario was Étienne Brûlé. In 1610, he was sent on a survey mission for Champlain. By 1840, the rapidly growing population of French Canada began to spill into Ontario, particularly near the Ottawa River and the Sudbury regions.

Most Franco-Ontarians tried to preserve their culture, language, and religion in the predominantly English-speaking, Protestant world of Ontario. In 1910, they established the Association Canadienne-française de l'Ontario (ACFO). In 1913, the first French-language newspaper in Ontario, *Le Droit*, was published. It was based in Ottawa and published daily.

A major concern for Franco-Ontarians during the early part of the 20th century was French-language education. By 1890, English became the compulsory language of instruction. French language instruction was mostly

Many Franco-Ontarians settled along the Ottawa River where they found employment in the forestry industry.

abolished. In 1912, the provincial government passed Regulation 17 in an attempt to assimilate French-speaking Ontarians into the predominantly English-speaking culture.

This bill limited French instruction in schools to the first two years of elementary school.

All French-speaking children would receive English-language instruction after grade 2. Although amended in 1913 to allow for one hour of French study per day, Regulation 17 caused a massive outcry among Franco-Ontarians. Rallies, marches, and protests opposed the regulation.

By the time of the conscription crisis of the First World War, Ontario's language issue had become a national debate. Regulation 17 was abolished in 1927. Before it was, though, it shaped a whole generation of Franco-Ontarians, who were not allowed to receive an education in their first language. Now, Franco-Ontarians from all over the province thrive. They are proud of their culture, their language, and their heritage. **For more information about Franco-Ontarians, visit the Web site of ACFO: www.acfo.ca.**

FOCUS

1. **In what ways does Michaëlle Jean represent the new face of Quebec?**
2. **What evidence is there that French Canada is more than the province of Quebec?**
3. **How important is it to speak French as well as English? Explain.**

Taking Research Notes

THE SKILL
Paraphrasing and making proper research notes

THE IMPORTANCE
Used in many aspects of life and for historical research

Everyone makes notes. These range from telephone messages, to minutes of meetings, to lecture notes, to travel directions, to historical research. The ability to take detailed, yet concise notes is essential to good writing and shows an organized mind. Summarizing is an important life skill.

An excellent way to take notes is to use 7.5 cm x 12.5 cm recipe cards (or paper cut to size). This technique is superior to taking notes in a notebook. Cards can be arranged chronologically or grouped into topics according to your essay's organization. Notebooks must be constantly leafed through. Cards can be grouped and regrouped.

Record the source of the information (and the page number) at the top of each card. Write on only one side. Limit each card to one idea, topic, or quotation—the better for organizing. Except for direct quotes, take notes in point form. Express the important information in your own words—paraphrasing will prevent accidental plagiarism. If you download information from the Internet, do so in a special font (such as italics, capital letters, or Arial black) to avoid plagiarism. Use abbreviations to save time. Keep a notebook handy to record your own thoughts about the assignment, perhaps other areas or sources to explore, a possible opening sentence, a method of organizing.

What information should be recorded? Most beginners worry about not finding enough information, but they almost always end up with too much. Finding the proper balance between too much and too little information comes with practice.

The secret is narrowing your topic.

Plagiarism: An Academic Sin

Type "plagiarism" in Microsoft's thesaurus and up pops the following words: stealing, copying, illegal use, breach of copyright, bootlegging. The dictionary defines plagiarism as "copying what somebody else has written or taking somebody else's ideas and trying to pass it off as original."

Don't write an essay on the topic "the Quiet Revolution in Quebec." It is too large and undefined. Instead, ask a question you would like to know the answer to. There are different kinds of questions. Here are a few examples:

- a factual question: What were the goals of the Quiet Revolution?
- a causal question: Why did the Quiet Revolution take place?
- a comparative question: What were the major differences between the Quiet Revolution and the Duplessis era?

Such questions will help you narrow the topic and assist in deciding what information to take down.

For example, if you took notes from this textbook for the essay topic The Quiet Revolution in Quebec: What Did They Want?, the notes might look like this.

> Don Bogle, Eugene D'Orazio, Don Quinlan, *Canada: Continuity and Change* (Markham: Fitzhenry & Whiteside, 2006), pp. 328–29
> − Que. attempt to examine and define its place; to modernize
> − attempt to become "masters in our own house"— wanted more money and better jobs
> − wanted Fr. to be the prov's working language
> − w. better scientific, business, and technical ed.
> − w. to control the major businesses in prov.
> − w. better health care, hospitals, pensions, labour unions, rural electrification
> − control own prov.

By selecting only the relevant facts and ideas, by summarizing in your own words, and by using point form, the original 500 words in the text have been reduced to 66 words.

Other useful ways of making notes include placing your information on timelines or using mind-mapping techniques. The above research information would look like this if mind mapped.

Application

Using the material in this chapter, prepare notes (using both methods described here) for the general topic of French–English relations in Canada. Before taking notes, be sure to refine the topic by selecting a factual, causal, or comparative question.

Questions & Activities

Questions and Activities

Match the people in column A with the descriptions in column B.

A	B
1. Maurice Duplessis	**a)** first leader of the Parti Québécois
2. James Cross	**b)** first Black governor general of Canada
3. Jacques Parizeau	**c)** leader of the Union Nationale
4. Michaëlle Jean	**d)** founder of the Bloc Québécois
5. Thérèse Casgrain	**e)** premier responsible for the 1995 Quebec referendum
6. Réne Lévesque	**f)** kidnap victim of the FLQ
7. Lucien Bouchard	**g)** first French-Canadian woman elected to the Senate

Quick Recall
Identify the following in two sentences each.

1. FLQ
2. Quiet Revolution
3. Yvette movement
4. Federalist
5. Meech Lake Accord
6. Clarity Bill
7. Franco-Ontarians
8. War Measures Act
9. Plan B
10. Acadians

Do Some Research

1. Find out more about the expulsion of the Acadians. Using computer-based resources, discover why the Acadians were deported. How many were forcibly removed from their homes and lands? Where were they sent? How many returned to their homeland? What problems do Acadians have in trying to protect their language and culture in North America?

2. Use the Internet to research the circumstances that led to the use of the War Measures Act in 1970. What powers did this give the authorities? How did this law affect the people? Was its use really necessary? At what other times in Canadian history was the War Measures Act used? Compare these circumstances to those of 1970.

3. Separatists in Quebec claim that the Quebec government should have the right to represent the province in foreign countries. They want offices similar to Canadian embassies. Should Quebec have this right? What are the advantages for Quebec and for Canada? What are the disadvantages? Check the Quebec government Web site for more information supporting or rejecting this claim. Research the Parti Québécois Web site for more information about its goals (www.pq.org).

4. Research the events leading up to the Quebec Referendum in 1995. What was the separatist strategy? What was the federalist strategy? Who were the major figures? Who organized the massive rally held in Montreal in October 1995? What was the outcome of this demonstration? Did it achieve its goals? How did separatists view this event? How did federalists view it?

Instant Analysis
Some statements can be labelled true or false. Others may depend on a variety of facts, opinions, and special situations. Place these statements in three categories: True, False, or It Depends. Explain your answer.

1. Quebec wants to separate from Canada.
2. English and French Canadians rarely co-operate.
3. Like other provincial governments, governments of Quebec are usually prepared to defend their provincial rights and responsibilities.
4. The Quiet Revolution was a period of tremendous change for Quebec.

362 MY COUNTRY, MONS PAYS

5. Confederation has generally been a bad deal for French Canadians.
6. Language rights will always be an issue in Quebec and Canada.
7. Many Canadians are tired of the whole French–English debate and want to move on.

Discuss and Debate

1. What does the term *official bilingualism* mean? Do you support this policy? How do French-speaking Canadians benefit from this policy? How do English-speaking Canadians benefit from bilingualism? What are the disadvantages for English-speaking Canadians? Take a vote to find out your class's opinion on official bilingualism.

2. Do you think it is right for governments to make decisions about Canada without the consent of all the provinces? Explain.

3. What do you think would have happened if René Lévesque and the *oui* supporters had won the Quebec referendum in 1980?

4. Organize a class discussion on the use of the War Measures Act during the October Crisis. You might debate this motion—Resolved: That the War Measures Act was an unnecessary threat to civil liberties and should not have been used.

Be Creative

1. Make a bilingual poster advertising the benefits of living in a nation with two official languages.

2. Listen to some of the music of French Canada. Perhaps your teacher can help you translate some of the lyrics.

Web Watch

Government of Quebec: www.gouv.qc.ca

Cité Libre: www.citelibre.com

Bombardier Inc.: www.bombardier.com

CBC Digital Archives: www.cbc.ca/archives. There are many audiovisual sources here. Consider some of these files: "Maurice Duplessis," "René Lévesque's Separatist Fight," "The October Crisis: Liberties Suspended," "Constitutional Discord: Meech Lake," "James Bay Project and the Cree" and "Maurice 'Rocket' Richard."

THE SPIRIT OF HAIDA GWAII

ART CANADA

The Spirit of Haida Gwaii
L'Esprit de Haida Gwaii, 1986-1991
Bill Reid

90

Haida artist Bill Reid was commissioned to create "The Spirit of Haida Gwaii" for the Canadian Embassy in Washington, DC (1991). Reid, who did much to revive Northwest Coast Indian arts, suggested that the five-ton sculpture could serve as a symbolic bridge between cultures. The work reflects his fascination with Haida art and life and status as an internationally acclaimed artist.

Why is this art an appropriate way to represent Canada in the United States?

Chapter Seven
Canadian–
American Relations

Expectations

Overall Expectations:
By the end of this chapter, you will be able to
- describe how individual Canadians have contributed to the development of Canada and its sense of identity
- describe major local, national, and global events that have influenced Canada's policies and identity since 1914

Specific Expectations:
By the end of this chapter, you will be able to
- summarize Canada's changing relationship with the United States
- identify some of the ways in which the United States has influenced Canadian foreign policy
- assess the advantages and disadvantages of American participation in the Canadian economy
- identify major effects of freer trade and globalization (e.g., creation of the North American Free Trade Agreement)
- explain how American culture and lifestyles (e.g., music, dance, clothing, speech, movies, television, Internet) have influenced Canada
- describe how the work of selected individuals has reflected Canadian identity
- identify how the federal government has used the media to promote a common Canadian identity

Word List

Acid rain	Auto Pact
CRTC	Embassy
Free trade	Global warming
Icon	International Boundary
International Joint	Commission
Commission	NAFTA
Split run magazine	Suez Crisis
Trade sanctions	

1 Canada's closest neighbour is the United States. The two countries are partners on many levels. Still, the people of the two countries do not know one another well. Many old and wrong ideas persist.

2 The United States greatly affects Canada's entertainment industry. Canadians find this a constant challenge. Canada has several organizations that work hard to develop and preserve Canadian culture.

SCTV cast

3 The United States is Canada's most important trading partner. They share many economic interests. The two nations are friends and allies. They also deal with divisive issues.

Canadian fishers blockaded an American ferry during the salmon wars.

Canadian–American Relations

① ② ③ ④ ⑤

④ Canada and the United States have shared the world's longest undefended border. The border was almost invisible until 2001. After the World Trade Center bombing, though, security was tightened.

Waterton Glacier International Peace Park spans the U.S.– Canada international border between Montana and Alberta.

Fergie Jenkins was the first Canadian baseball player to make it into the Hall of Fame.

⑤ Hockey, football, baseball, and basketball are played across the continent. United States citizens can play on Canadian teams. Canadians can play on American teams. The Olympic Games are an exception.

Canada's Gold medal–winning Olympic Hockey team, 2006

ADVANCE ORGANIZER **367**

The Geographic Link

"Geography has made us neighbors. History has made us friends. Economics has made us partners. And necessity has made us allies."

U.S. President John F. Kennedy addressing Canada's Parliament, 1961

Waterton Glacier International Peace Park is in both Montana and Alberta. It is also a UNESCO World Heritage site.

Canada and the United States share the world's longest border. It is 9000 km long. We have similar immigration patterns, settlement histories, and livelihoods. Often in the past, we have acted in the same way when dealing with the rest of the world. Americans and Canadians have worked together since Canada became a country in 1867. Our two nations have closer economic, social, and political ties than any other two nations in the Western world. Canada's population is only one-tenth that of the United States, though. Canadians must work hard to preserve a special character. Close association with the United States enriches Canada; however, it is important that it not swallow us up. Canadians have always wanted to resist the American presence, yet gain from it at the same time.

Northwest Angle is a small corner of land in Minnesota. It borders Manitoba's Lake of the Woods. Visitors to Northwest Angle must travel through Canada to get there—unless they come by boat. Northwest Angle's citizens were unhappy with the condition of their roads and with American fishing regulations. In 1998, the people said they wanted to leave the United States and join Canada. There was no Canadian response.

Canadian–American Relations

1945 1950 1955 1960 1965 1970 1975 1980 1985 1990 1995 2000 2005 2010

BORDER CROSSINGS

Most of the Can–Am border is unfenced. We rely on lakes, rivers, and roadways to define where one country ends and the other begins. There are 140 land crossings along the Can–Am border. Fifty of these are in remote areas. Often, these are not even staffed at night. Some border crossings are busy, though. These include the Ambassador Bridge linking Windsor, Ontario, with Detroit, Michigan; the Peace Bridge connecting Fort Erie, Ontario, with Buffalo, New York; and the Blue Water Bridge linking Sarnia, Ontario, with Port Huron, Michigan. More than 300 000 Canadians and Americans cross the border every day for business and pleasure.

When seen from the air, the border in wooded areas looks like a 6 m–wide strip of clear-cut. To cross the border from Detroit to Windsor, people drive due south into Canada. The border passes between two small islands in the Thousand Islands in the St. Lawrence River near Gananoque, Ontario—the very short bridge that connects them is the world's shortest international bridge. Sometimes, the border runs through the middle of a town. Sometimes, it runs through the middle of a house. It even cuts through the main reading room of the Haskell Library in Derby Line, Vermont.

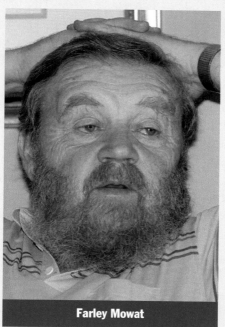

Farley Mowat

Many Canadians and Americans are used to crossing the border without fuss. During the Vietnam War, 20 000 American draft-dodgers entered Canada. The United States was not pleased.

Not all border crossings are routine. In 1985, well-known Canadian author and naturalist Farley Mowat was not allowed into the United States. He was going there to give a series of lectures. He was popular, but outspoken in his views, so had been put on an American list of "undesirables." American officials turned him back at the border. Canadians were outraged. Mowat's rejection was later overturned, but he refused to travel to the United States again. *My Discovery of America* is his account of the event.

The terrorist attacks on 11 September 2001 have increased security at Can–Am border crossings. Border alerts have sometimes caused long backups. Now, Canadian and American immigration officials check citizens' papers. In 2005, the United States said that Canadians would likely need passports for entry. The border is now more guarded and defended. The targets are international terrorists, *not* Canadians and Americans.

International Peace Arch at Douglas, B.C., and Blaine, Washington.

The border is a visible sign that separates Canada and the United States. It also plays a symbolic role. Peter C. Newman, a Canadian author, said: "The boundary is the most important fact about this country. It defines not only our citizenship but also how we behave collectively and what we think individually. It determines who we are."

A 1999 *Maclean's* magazine survey suggested that a borderless North America was only a matter of time. The survey showed that most Canadians wanted to remain different. About 25 percent said that they would become Americans. A similar *Maclean's* poll in 2002 showed that the desire for American citizenship had dropped. There was also less support for a common North American form of money. Only 38 percent of Canadians thought that both countries shared a common set of values and beliefs.

TIMELINE

1783 The Treaty of Paris established the border from the Atlantic to the Prairies, along a series of rivers and what is now the St. Lawrence system, and the 49th parallel.

1842 The Webster-Ashburton Treaty added more precise definition, especially in the Maritimes.

1846 The Oregon Treaty continued the border along the 49th parallel from the Prairies to the Pacific, and through the Straits of Georgia and Juan de Fuca.

1908 The **International Boundary Commission** was established. This commission, with one commissioner from each country, looks after the border and any related issues.

At the Canadian–American border between British Columbia and Washington State: Besides the two markers, a long line of clear-cut vegetation marks this portion of the world's longest, undefended border.

FOCUS

1. **What are some concerns that Canadians feel about living so close to the United States?**
2. **Do you think that eventually Canada and the United States will become one nation? Explain.**

The Political Link

Canada and the United States usually have a warm and friendly relationship. In 1938, U.S. President Franklin D. Roosevelt received an honorary degree from Queen's University, Kingston. In sharing his "Good Neighbour Policy," he noted that Canadians and Americans did not see one another as "foreigners." He promised that the people of the United States "would not stand idly by" if Canadian soil were threatened by another nation.

Foreign Affairs

Canada and the United States often agree on how issues with other countries should be handled. The two neighbours share many interests. They have many "friends" in common. They belong to many of the same military and political alliances. These include APEC (Asia-Pacific Economic Cooperation), NATO (North Atlantic Treaty Organization), OAS (Organization of American States), and NORAD (North American Aerospace Defence Command). Meetings and telephone conversations between the two leaders are quite common. The United States has an **embassy** in Ottawa and consulates across Canada. Canada has an embassy in Washington and consulates in several American cities.

In 1956, Prime Minister Lester Pearson worked closely with the United States to end the **Suez Crisis**. Neither country wanted the Soviet Union to become part of the Arab–Israeli hostilities. In 1991, both countries took part in the Gulf War. The United Nations sponsored the military action because Iraq had invaded oil-rich Kuwait. In 1999, both Canada and the United States served NATO forces in Kosovo, Yugoslavia, to prevent mass slaughter.

From time to time, the two nations disagree about how to handle a situation. Moments of tension arise. Canada did not approve of American policy towards Cuba, the Vietnam War, and the 2003 Iraq War. The United States did not want Canada to

Canadian troops receive medals for their work in the Afghanistan campaign in 2005.

Canadian–American Relations

establish diplomatic relations with communist governments in Cuba and China.

Sometimes, friendship develops between the leaders. A highlight was the 1985 Shamrock Summit. "Irishmen" President Ronald Reagan and Prime Minister Brian Mulroney got along well.

Sometimes, though, the two leaders hold different opinions. During the Vietnam War, Prime Minister Lester Pearson called for a suspension of air strikes against North Vietnam. He hoped to restore peace talks—U.S. President Johnson was furious. Earlier, the United States disapproved of John Diefenbaker's nationalist policies. The Americans were displeased when Canada exported wheat to communist China. In 2005, Prime Minister Paul Martin openly disagreed with President George W. Bush. He did not like his policies about global warming and softwood lumber exports to the United States.

A FRIEND IN NEED

In 1979, the staff of the American embassy in Iran was taken hostage. Six American diplomats escaped. They hid in the homes of Canadian embassy officials. No one knew the Americans were even alive. Two months later, in January 1980, the Americans left Iran secretly. They got out by using fake Canadian passports. The Royal Canadian Mounted Police and the American Central Intelligence Agency worked together to prepare the documents. Overnight, Canadian ambassador Ken Taylor became a hero. The wives of the Canadian officials also showed courage. They lived in fear that the Iranians would discover their "guests." It was up to these women to act as if everything was normal at home. They did.

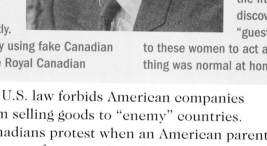

U.S. law forbids American companies from selling goods to "enemy" countries. Canadians protest when an American parent company forces its Canadian branch to cancel a sale.

FOCUS

1. What are some of the international organizations and alliances that Canada and the United States both belong to?
2. What are some common interests between the countries?
3. What disagreements have existed between Canada and the United States?
4. Who is Ken Taylor? How did he become a hero?

Environmental Links

The Space Link

Canada and the United States have worked closely together in the area of space exploration. In 1962, NASA (National Aeronautics and Space Administration) helped Canada launch Canadian satellites into the earth's outer atmosphere. By 1976, Canada, working with NASA, launched a telecommunications satellite. It broadcast radio and TV programs directly into Canadian homes. Several Canadian astronauts, such as Marc Garneau, have taken part in NASA-sponsored space flights.

The co-operative effort between Canada and the United States to explore and use the space environment is long-standing and ongoing.

In 1982, NASA contracted with Canadian scientists to develop and purchase the remote manipulation device, Canadarm. It has proved invaluable during NASA's manned space flights. New remote manipulation devices are a major Canadian contribution to space exploration. Here, the Canadarm is installing a docking module.

The Water Link

In 1909, Canada and the United States set up the **International Joint Commission** (IJC). Three representatives from each country serve on it. The IJC's role is to protect lakes and river systems along the border. When communities or industries pollute these waters, both countries suffer. The IJC investigates pollution problems. The Commission also considers applications for dams or canals in these waters. If it approves a project, it can set conditions limiting water levels and water flow. It may also monitor how the structure is run. Shore properties, wetlands, and the interests of farmers, shippers, and others must be protected.

The Great Lakes— A Chemical Hot Spot

Over 360 chemical compounds have been identified in the Great Lakes.

Many, such as lead, DDT, and mercury, are dangerous to humans and aquatic ecosystems. For example, various species of fish now suffer from tumours. Their capacity to reproduce is decreasing. Populations of fish-eating birds and mammals also seem to be on the decline. Of the 10 most highly valued species of fish in Lake Ontario, 7 have now almost vanished. As of 1987, both governments were required to report publicly to the IJC on how well they were cleaning up the Great Lakes.

Canadian fishers blockaded an American ferry during the salmon wars.

Salmon Quotas

Proper management of Pacific salmon has long been a matter of concern. In 1985, after many years of negotiation, the Pacific Salmon Treaty set long-term goals for the benefit of the salmon and the two countries. The treaty set up equal distribution of the Pacific salmon catch. Each country would limit its catch to specific quotas. By 1993, it was obvious that the treaty was not working.

Canadian fishers felt that the Americans were catching too many fish. The salmon population was declining. The dispute dragged on. In 1997, Canadians blockaded an Alaskan ferry off the coast of British Columbia. It was not until June 1999 that Canada and the United States signed a new treaty setting salmon quotas. These quotas are in effect until 2009.

FOCUS

1. What is the purpose of the International Joint Commission?
2. How is the Great Lakes a chemical hot spot?
3. How did Canada and the United States resolve the salmon war?

Environmental Issues

The environment is a source of friction between Canada and the United States. Areas include acid rain, air pollution, greenhouse gas emissions, and waste management. Various groups have brought pressure on both governments to resolve environmental con-

Unlike the obvious effects of oil pollution, acid rain makes water clear.

cerns. Greenpeace is one of them. Independently funded, it works to protect the environment. Members have done things like climb smokestacks around the world to focus attention on air pollution.

Acid Rain

In 1979, the first major report on **acid rain** in Canada stated that acid rain came not only from smokestacks, but from cars and trucks. Canadian politicians realized sooner than Americans that acid rain was becoming a serious problem to address.

During the 1980s, acid rain affected much of eastern Canada. Many of the water and soil systems in the region lost the ability to neutralize acid. They soon lost all plant and fish life. The clearness of the water often meant that lakes were in serious trouble. Many lakes died. The salmon habitat in the Maritimes is gone. Large forests in eastern Canada have been damaged. Quebec's maple syrup production has dropped greatly.

In 1991, Prime Minister Brian Mulroney and President George Bush signed an Air Quality Agreement. This ended a 10-year cross-border struggle about acid rain. Each country must now provide reports to prove that it is living up to the clean air legislation. One example of this is the vehicle emissions test every two years. Between 1980 and 1996, American emissions dropped 27 percent. It is projected that by 2010 they will be down by 40 percent. In Canada, sulphur emissions were 54 percent lower in 1994 than they were in 1980. The struggle over acid rain continues.

Waste Management

One problem is the hauling of Ontario garbage to landfill sites in Michigan. Local landfill sites have filled up in recent years. Environmentalists and residents in Canada have been fighting the opening of new local garbage sites.

Canadian–American Relations

The situation became critical in the Toronto area in 2002. Its primary landfill site closed and nearby Ontario sites were unavailable. A deal to allow Ontario garbage to be shipped to sites near Detroit was made. Up to 200 large trucks haul garbage every day from Ontario to Michigan. This makes up about 12 percent of Michigan's annual waste total. Americans are unhappy about Canadian garbage coming into their country.

Canadian garbage is being dumped at a Michigan site.

Example of industrial pollution.

Global Warming

In 1997, Canada and more than 160 countries met in Kyoto, Japan, to discuss **global warming**. In 2001, President George W. Bush stated, "Kyoto is dead." He feared that this agreement would hurt the American economy. The United States is responsible for 25 percent of all greenhouse gas emissions. The Kyoto Accord was officially ratified in 2002. Countries pledged to reduce greenhouse gas emissions. The United States was not one of them. In 2005, Canada hosted the UN Framework Convention on Climate Change.

FOCUS

1. What is Greenpeace? What role does it play in environmental issues?
2. How have Canada and the United States differed on environmental issues?
3. Do you think Canada has done enough to deal with acid rain, waste management, and global warming? Explain.

The Economic Link

Canada lives next door to the world's largest economic power. The American economy produces nearly $2 trillion of wealth a year. Canadians and Americans are joined together in a deep economic relationship. This relationship supports more than two million jobs

Much trade flows across the Ambassador Bridge between Windsor and Detroit.

in each country. Two-way trade more than doubled from 1990 to 2005. We are each other's largest trading partner—more than $1.5 billion crosses the border each day. More than 81 percent of Canadian exports go to the United States ($350 billion in 2004).

Nearly 70 percent of our imports come from the United States ($250 billion in 2004). The United States sells twice as many goods to Canada's market of 32.5 million people than it does to its next biggest trading partner, Japan, which has 130 million people. Canada buys more American goods than do all 15 countries in the European Union combined.

Canada and the United States are not equal economic partners, however. The American population is about 10 times greater.

Many Canadians feel that Canada is tied too tightly to the United States. Our economic well-being tends to rise and fall with decisions made south of the border. This makes it difficult for Canada to act independently of the United States.

The Question of Ownership

Foreigners own more than half of Canada's 500 largest corporations. Some people say Canadians are tenants rather than landlords in their own country.

American-owned companies such as these now have a strong presence in Canada.

Millions of dollars in profits and resources leave Canada each year for the United States. Many multinationals have branch plants or stores throughout Canada. These include General Motors, IBM, Coca-Cola, Microsoft, Allstate Insurance, and McDonald's. Although they have stores in Canada, their head offices are in the United States.

Some of Canada's most respected companies have been sold to the Americans. Lumber giant MacMillan Bloedel, for example, went to Weyerhaeuser in 1999. Gulf Canada and Future Shop were bought out by American companies in 2001. The Molson Brewing Company, which was established in 1786, merged with Coors, a larger American company, in early 2005.

THE HUDSON'S BAY COMPANY

And in 2006, even the Hudson's Bay Company (HBC) was sold to American investors. HBC has been an **icon** in Canadian history and business. Founded in 1670, it was Canada's largest department store retailer. Its stores included The Bay, Zellers, and Home Outfitters. About 70 000 people worked for it at over 500 locations across Canada. The company had roots in the fur trade and in the travels of explorers. Two centuries before Confederation, King Charles II of England granted the company the lands of the Hudson Bay watershed. For some, the sale of such an important part of Canadian history is troubling. **Do you think it matters that Canadian companies are being sold to foreign interests? Explain.**

In an annual survey conducted by *Maclean's* magazine, 83 percent of Canadians felt that greater Canadian control of

FOREIGN INVESTMENT REVIEW AGENCY AND INVESTMENT CANADA

In 1974, the Liberals under Pierre Trudeau introduced the Foreign Investment Review Agency (FIRA). FIRA's job was to screen the efforts of foreign companies to purchase Canadian companies. The purpose was to slow down U.S. control of Canadian industries and natural resources. FIRA was to act as a "watchdog" to protect Canada's best economic interests. Some Canadian business owners worried it might take away their right to control their own companies. The United States saw FIRA as so unfriendly that it considered economic sanctions against Canada.

From 1971 to 1981, American ownership of Canadian corporations remained at about 25 percent. By 1982, FIRA appeared to be little more than a "paper tiger." It approved 9 out of every 10 applications for foreign takeovers.

Shortly after taking office in 1984, Brian Mulroney replaced FIRA with Investment Canada. His government wanted to increase prosperity and create jobs through industrial growth—it did not worry about the source of investment in Canada. **Are you worried about the source of investment in Canada? Explain.**

businesses operating in Canada was important. They felt control was needed to maintain a strong Canadian identity in the 21st century. Yet between 1997 and 2002, foreign (non-American) companies bought 345 Canadian companies, worth $144 billion; Canadian companies purchased 447 foreign companies, including American ones. The value was $124 billion.

Many economists state that American money has helped Canada grow strong and wealthy. Canadians have benefited from American technology. American

British Columbia forest.

investments have created thousands of jobs here. The close economic link has helped strengthen political and military relations, too.

Economic Disputes Since 2000

By 2000, nearly 60 percent of American wood and paper imports came from Canada. In 2002, the U.S. put a 27 percent tax on imports of Canadian spruce, pine, and fir. A long dispute erupted. As of 2006, dispute resolution committees for NAFTA (North American Free Trade Agreement) decided twice in Canada's favour. Negotiations continue.

Another source of conflict was the so-called "mad cow" issue. In May 2003, the United States stopped importing Canadian beef. A single Alberta cow had the "mad cow" virus. Canada's 90 000 beef producers lost $11 million a day. More than 5000 jobs were lost. In July 2005, the United States began to ease the ban.

A CLOSER LOOK AT THE AUTO PACT

In 1904, Henry Ford built a car plant in Windsor, Ontario. Over the next 60 years, American branch plants for Chrysler, Ford, and General Motors were set up in Canada. Still, most car manufacturing occurred in the United States. By the early 1960s, Canada had a huge auto–trade deficit with the United States. On 16 January 1965, the Canada–U.S. Automotive Products Agreement (the **Auto Pact**) was signed. Its purpose was to deal with that problem.

The Auto Pact removed tariffs on cars, trucks, buses, tires, and automotive parts. A single North American manufacturing market was created. Chrysler, Ford, and General Motors could form a single integrated production and marketing system. Larger, more efficient car plants were built in both countries. Higher levels of integration and better access to the world's largest auto market helped Canada. Canada was able to develop an internationally competitive auto industry.

The agreement stated that for every car sold in Canada, one had to be built in Canada. Each vehicle built in Canada also had to have at least 60 percent Canadian content in both parts and labour. Tariffs were applied if these conditions were not met.

In 1970, Canada registered a small auto trade surplus with the United States for the first time. Between 1965 and 2002, the number of people employed in the automobile industry rose from 75 000 to 491 000. Also, the number of vehicles made in Canada jumped from 846 000 to over 2.6 million.

In 2000, however, the World Trade Organization, which governs world international trade, ruled that the Auto Pact was unfair to foreign dealers. In 2001, the Pact was formally dissolved. As a direct result, Canada, which had been the world's 4th largest auto producer in 1999, slipped to 8th place by 2005.

FOCUS

1. Why do many Canadians think that Canada is too dependent on the American economy?
2. What is FIRA and why did Trudeau introduce it?
3. What effects did the Auto Pact have on Canada's automotive industry?
4. What are some current Canadian–American economic issues?

The Free Trade Agreement

During the early 1980s, the American and Canadian economies suffered a hard recession. Many Canadian business people wanted to sell their products and resources duty-free to the huge American market. They felt Canada should have a free trade agreement with the United States. That would give Americans greater access to Canadian markets and resources, too.

Canadians and Americans watched as European nations forged a successful economic union, the "Common Market." Brian Mulroney, now prime minister, and his Conservatives began to support **free trade**. Mulroney worried that U.S. duties and tariffs would slow the flow of Canadian goods and services to the United States. Free trade would allow unrestricted passage of goods across the border. It seemed like the answer.

Not all Canadians wanted free trade—many spoke out against it. In 1988, Mulroney called an election. He asked Canadian voters to decide the issue.

Mulroney and his Progressive Conservatives won the election, so Canada began to negotiate with the United States. The Free Trade Agreement between Canada and the United States came into effect in January 1989. President Ronald Reagan called the FTA a new economic constitution for North America.

The FTA gave Canada and the United States access to each other's markets for most goods. From 1989 to 2004, Canadian exports to the United States increased from $101 billion to $350 billion plus. About 25 percent of this growth was due to free trade.

In 1994, the FTA was expanded to

THE FREE TRADE DEBATE

Supporters of free trade said that it would benefit Canada because

- Canadian producers would gain access to a market 10 times larger than Canada's
- increased Canadian exports would allow Canadian companies to make longer and more economical production runs
- more Canadian jobs would be created
- foreign investors would be attracted to Canada
- consumers would pay lower prices
- economic prosperity would mean that Canadians could spend more on research and development

Opponents of free trade said that it would hurt Canada because

- the nation would lose its political sovereignty
- the poorer areas of the country would get poorer
- Canadians would become more Americanized
- unemployment would increase
- Canada would send too many natural resources out of the country
- Canada's service industries would be threatened by their larger American competitors

include Mexico. It was renamed the North American Free Trade Agreement (NAFTA). NAFTA links 440 million people in three countries. About 30 percent of the world's wealth lies in one trade region, the world's largest free trade bloc. Canadian companies now compete with Mexican companies, though. As a general rule, Mexican workers receive lower wages and fewer benefits than Canadian workers.

In 1999, The *Toronto Star* assessed free trade in this way: "In a decade in which the U.S. has been the primary engine of world economic growth, hitching our wagon to the 50 American stars appears to make a great deal of sense. If the U.S. economy falters, though, we may come to regret just how dependent we have become on a single export market."

Canada is becoming deeply integrated into the American economy. This reality may

THE CANADIAN AUTO WORKERS

Many labour leaders still claim that free trade was not good for Canadian workers. Certainly, it was not something that Canadian auto workers favoured. Bob White, first president of the Canadian Auto Workers, was outspoken in his criticism of free trade. Four years before the FTA, in 1985, White led the Canadian workers at Ford, GM, and Chrysler plants out of the American United Auto Workers and into an independent Canadian union. That meant Canadian workers could negotiate with the Big 3 on their own terms. White served three terms as president. In 1992, he stepped down to become president of the Canadian Labour Congress.

have enormous political, cultural, and economic effects. Will there be a common currency, a customs union, the creation of common institutions? Canada has been walking a tightrope with the United States for at least half a century. The key question seems to be—what price are Canadians willing to pay for Canadian distinctiveness?

FOCUS

1. What is free trade?
2. What are its advantages and disadvantages for Canada?
3. Define the word "tariff."
4. Why did some Canadians feel free trade was important to Canada's economy?

The Cultural Divide

How well do Americans and Canadians really know one another? Are they neighbours or strangers? Are they friends or foes?

Canadians think they know a lot about Americans. They get information about the United States from American movies, television, magazines, music, and sports. Many Canadian students study American history, literature, or geography in school.

Americans receive little, if any, information about Canada in school. As a columnist for *The Boston Globe* wrote: "Canada is like Belgium or Ecuador—a nice enough place, but not very important."

Americans near the border see Canadians when they come to Canada for their vacations or purchase cottages here. There are also many cross-border shoppers on both sides. Some Americans meet "snowbirds." Snowbirds are retired Canadians who spend winters in warmer Florida and in other southern states. Some American movie fans are familiar with Canadian talent. The American music industry has a sincere appreciation for the songs of Shania Twain, Avril Lavigne, and Céline Dion.

When Canadians travel to Europe or Asia, a strange thing happens. They don't like to be mistaken for Americans. They put Canadian flags on their bags or lapels so people see that they are Canadian. Suddenly, they are proud of their country and their heritage.

So What's the Difference?
Anyone comparing Canada and the United States will find real differences in these areas:

- the political systems
- the Canadian duality (French and English)
- speech and language patterns
- pronunciation of the English language
- regional accents
- traditions of multiculturalism—the Canadian cultural mosaic is different from the unity of the American melting pot.
- Canada's peaceful separation and continuing ties with Great Britain—these were rejected by the United States.
- Canada's conservative tradition, one in which civil war and revolution have played no part
- attitudes towards social welfare programs—Canadians expect them; Americans do not.

Perhaps the greatest difference between Canadians and Americans is Canada's perpetual quest for a national identity. Americans don't seem to look for one. They always seem to have one.

Canadian–American Relations

Avril Lavigne

Shania Twain

Céline Dion

Bryan Adams

Nickelback

Canadian performers enjoy great success both north and south of the border.

Canadian English and American English are not always the same.
Canadian English reflects both British and American patterns of speech. Here are a few examples:

CANADIAN	AMERICAN
chesterfield	sofa
serviette	napkin
blinds	shades
eh?	what?
schedule (pronounced *shed ule*)	schedule (pronounced *sked ule*)
highway	interstate
z (pronounced *zed*)	z (pronounced *zee*)
(Native) reserve	(Native) reservation

What other differences can you think of?

CANADIAN STEREOTYPES OF AMERICANS

1 Everyone in the U.S. owns a gun, or would like to.

2 Americans all live in cities in big apartment buildings.

3 Americans just care about money and big business. They have big homes and fast cars.

4 I can name you five thousand times when the Americans raced to the help of other people in trouble. Can you name me even one time when someone else raced to the Americans in trouble?

—Gordon Sinclair in a 1973 CFRB radio broadcast

5 Americans get their foreign policy from John Wayne movies: "Shoot first and ask questions later."

6 The major threat to Canadian survival today is American control of the Canadian economy.

7 Americans know almost nothing about Canada. What they think they know is usually wrong.

8 Americans are loud and pushy.

Is Canada just the United States moved north? Is there something about Canadian culture that is unique? In 1999, *Maclean's* magazine took its annual poll of Canadian attitudes. It discovered that 90 percent of those polled felt that Canada had a unique identity. About 77 percent felt that this identity is based on a strong sense of Canadian history.

Culture also contributes to identity. The Canadian government believes that strong support of cultural activities strengthens Canadian identity. By 1949, the federal government worried about the impact of American mass media on Canadian culture. It launched a Royal Commission to investigate Canadian culture, education, and communication. Chaired by Vincent Massey, the Massey–Lévesque Commission released its report in 1951.

The five commissioners noted that their task was "concerned with nothing less than the spiritual foundations of our national life." Their recommendations led to the creation of the National Library of Canada in 1953 and the Canada Council in 1957. The Commission also recommended federal funding for the arts. The government established the Canada Council for that purpose. Today, some 700 000 Canadians earn their living in the cultural sector. Government assistance to the arts has increased. The Heritage Canada portfolio was created "to insure access to Canadian voices and Canadian spaces, to protect Canada's heritage and to enhance pride in Canada."

AMERICAN STEREOTYPES OF CANADIANS

1 Mountains. Wilderness. Polar Bears. Snow. Mounties. French speaking.

2 Canadians are healthier than we are because they have to fight the elements to survive.

3 Canadians are nice and polite, not rude and noisy like some Americans you see. 'Course, I've only met two Canadians I know of.

4 Canada will always be remembered by my generation as the nation that stood for peace, whether in the Middle East or Vietnam or Cyprus. If I were a Canadian, I'd rather have that said about me than anything else.

5 Canadians are generally indistinguishable from Americans, and the surest way of telling the two apart is to make this observation to a Canadian.

6 Canadian drivers are crazy. I'm sorry, but there's no other word for it. They put their foot on the gas and their hand on the horn and look out, here I come. I wonder if it's got anything to do with their religion. —Tour guide, Williamsburg, Virginia

7 Canadians don't have any heroes, and not much history. —History student, U. of Rochester, New York

Pierre Berton, in his book, *Hollywood's Canada*, states that between 1907 and 1975, 575 American motion pictures had their stories set in Canada. These movies showed Canada as a land of mountains, pine trees, and snow! Canada was a wilderness without any cities or towns. "Anybody introduced to Canada entirely through motion pictures—and that includes hundreds of thousands of people around the world," Berton wrote, "would find it impossible to believe that since the mid-1920s this has been predominantly an urban country." No wonder visitors to Canada bring heavy sweaters in July. They believe Hollywood's image of Canada.

FOCUS

1. In your view, how well do Canadians and Americans really know one another?
2. In your opinion, how are Canadians and Americans different? How are they similar?
3. What was the Massey–Lévesque Commission? What did it recommend?

Canada in the Mirror

Canadian Content

Radio and television have had significant impact on Canadian culture and identity. Canadians spend an average of 22.7 hours a week watching TV. That adds up to 49 days a year. Only about 40 percent of that originates in Canada. Canadian shows such as *Corner Gas* and *Air Farce* are popular. Most of what is watched, though, comes from the United States.

SCTV *was one of the most successful comedy shows. Here, the cast, who all achieved success south of the border, are reunited.* How many do you recognize?

CANADIAN BROADCASTING REGULATIONS

1968 The federal government sets up the Canadian Radio-Television Commission (CRTC) to regulate broadcasting.

1970 **CRTC** content rulings are created.

1972 CRTC's Canadian content requirement rises. It becomes 60 percent of prime-time broadcast hours for the CBC and 50 percent for privately owned stations. (The CRTC defines *prime time* as 6 p.m. to 12 p.m.)

1976 In response to the way the nature of broadcasting and telecommunications is expanding in Canada, the CRTC develops into the Canadian Radio-television and Telecommunications Commission.

2000 CRTC's Canadian Television policy is revised. Canadian content requirements apply to peak time, or 7 p.m. to 11 p.m., for the largest Canadian television groups.

Can you think of a development in what is available on television that would hurt the CRTC's efforts to protect Canadian content?

A goal of the CRTC is to protect Canadian culture in the broadcasting industry. The Commission rules that Canadian-owned radio stations play "Canadian" music at least 35 percent of their "on air" time. Canadian content requires that at least two of these three conditions are met:

- The composer or performer is Canadian.
- The song is performed or recorded in Canada.
- The lyrics are by a Canadian.

Canadian-owned television stations must have 60 percent Canadian content overall. Between 6 p.m. and midnight, Canadian content must be 50 percent of all broadcasting.

Some critics call the CRTC's requirements a form of censorship. However, in a 2004 survey, 84 percent of Canadians felt that content rules were needed to protect Canadian culture and identity. They help make Canadian entertainment available to Canadian audiences.

Michael J. Fox is one of Canada's best-known actors. Born in British Columbia, Fox became famous as Alex Keating on the successful U.S. sitcom, Family Ties, *and went on to star in* Spin City *and the* Back to the Future *movies.*

ROGERS COMMUNICATIONS

One of the largest cable-television companies in the world is Canadian owned and operated. Rogers Communications made $4.6 billion Canadian in 2004. It owns 43 radio stations, several TV channels, cable TV stations, and more than 300 video rental stores. It also owns 70 magazines, including *Maclean's* and *Chatelaine*. Other assets are the Toronto Blue Jays baseball team and the Rogers Centre in Toronto. Rogers has over 6 million voice and data subscribers and more than 18 000 employees.

Hollywood North

Many American films and TV shows are produced in Canada. Toronto, Montreal, Halifax, and Vancouver have become major film-producing centres. Movie producers take advantage of the lower Canadian dollar. Many films are made in the Toronto area. Some people call it "Hollywood North."

Canadian film-makers often have a hard time competing against the American film industry. Barely one in 20 films on Canadian screens is Canadian. Some Canadian movies have achieved international acclaim, though.

ABOVE: *Atom Egoyan, the successful director of* The Sweet Hereafter, Ararat *and* Where The Truth Lies*, has remained in Canada despite being pursued by Hollywood studios.* TOP RIGHT: *Neve Campbell enjoys a successful career in films and movies on both sides of the border.*

Atom Egoyan's *The Sweet Hereafter*, for example, or Bruce Beresford's *Black Robe*, or Thom Fitzgerald's *The Hanging Garden*, are well known. But, for the most part, American-based distributors control about 85 per-

cent of the Canadian film market and movie theatres. Canadians spend some $180 million going to the movies every year, yet few American distributors are eager to invest in Canadian feature films. As noted Canadian film-maker Claude Jutra (*Mon Oncle Antoine*) commented, "Not making the films you want to make is awful, but making them and not having them shown is worse."

Promoting Canadian Films

In 1967, the Canadian Film Development Corporation was established to help promote the Canadian feature film industry. It fostered films with significant Canadian creative, artistic, and technical content. This organization was later replaced by Telefilm Canada. This Crown corporation invested $2 billion in Canada's film industry between 1989 and 2005.

In 2001, the Canada Feature Film Fund (CFFF), under Telefilm Canada, had an annual budget of $100 million. In 2005–2006, the CFFF financed 12 Canadian feature films. Canadian Norman Jewison is a well-known film director. In 1988, he established the Canadian Centre for Advanced Film Studies in Toronto. Its aim was to further the film careers of Canadians. Jewison envisioned a thriving Canadian film industry.

Canadian films are featured at a variety of film festivals across the country. Many people regard the Toronto International Film Festival as one of the world's most important. Canada has a rich tradition of regional and national film events, too. By 2005, more than 80 000 Canadians were employed in the film industry. While the leading stars are often American, more than 90 percent of the pro-

Mike Myers moved to the United States to make movies. He is well known for his Austin Powers character.

A CLOSER LOOK AT THE NATIONAL FILM BOARD

In 1939, the Canadian government established the National Film Board (NFB). The NFB was to make films that reflected and interpreted Canada's social and cultural life. Since that time, the NFB has created more than 9000 original films. Many have been widely praised. Many have received international awards. In 1989, Hollywood gave an honorary Oscar to the NFB, "in recognition of its 50th anniversary and its dedicated commitment to original artistic, creative and technological activity and excellence in every area of film making." **Why was the NFB created? For more information about current NFB projects, visit www.nfb.ca.**

duction crew is Canadian. The film industry is thriving in Canada today. Still, Canadian-made films make up less than 5 percent of the Canadian film market.

FOCUS

1. What is the CRTC?
2. What qualifies as "Canadian content"?
3. Why is Toronto called Hollywood North?
4. What Canadian stars can you name?
5. Why do some Canadian actors go south?

Publishing Voices

Some of the world's great writers are Canadian. Robertson Davies, Margaret Laurence, Austin Clarke, Rohinton Mistry, Nino Ricci, Lisa Moore, Dionne Brand, Anne Hébert, Michael Ondaatje, Margaret Atwood, Mordecai Richler, Carol Shields, Alice Munro, W. O. Mitchell, Roch Carrier, Farley Mowat, Pierre Berton, and Michel Tremblay are just some of them. Our world-class literature is, in part, due to the success of a public policy that supports Canadian publishing.

The Canadian Authors Association was founded in 1921. Its goal was to promote nationalism and to convince Canadians to buy Canadian, rather than American, books. Some critics wanted American magazines banned from Canada. In the 1930s, *Maclean's* magazine promised to print only Canadian non-fiction writing and to use Canadian spellings. Other Canadian magazines followed suit.

More than 300 book-publishing houses are Canadian owned. They produce 80 percent of new Canadian-authored books. Many are small and have to compete against huge global and U.S. publishers. Canadian books account for 30 percent of the total book market in this country. Many Canadian publishers have close relationships with American, British, and French publishers. They help distribute their books to Canadian readers.

Heritage Canada helps Canadian publishers and gives money for market research and development. The Canada Council for the Arts, the Social Sciences and Humanities Research Council (SSHRC), and provincial arts councils provide help to publishers and writers.

Canada produces over 1400 different magazines. The total circulation is about 500 million copies. Canadian publishers have about a 30 percent share of the Canadian market. Still, foreign magazines, mainly from the United States, pose an ongoing threat.

Canada's federal and

SPLIT RUN MAGAZINES

In 1993, Time Warner produced a split run version of one issue of *Sports Illustrated*. It printed the regular *Sports Illustrated* and *Sports Illustrated Canada*. To most readers, the American and Canadian editions were the same. The standard for determining whether a magazine was foreign or domestic was based on where it had been printed. Time Warner now argued that its magazine was Canadian. Most of its advertisements were Canadian.

In 1999, a parliamentary task force estimated that more than 100 U.S. magazines might establish split run editions. It predicted that the loss of advertising revenue would force many Canadian periodicals out of business. Since Canadians make up a large part of the market for these magazines, the American government was not pleased. It warned that if the bill passed it would hit back with **trade sanctions**. This problem was solved when an agreement was reached.

provincial governments believe that most Canadians want to retain a unique identity. They work to support the arts. The CBC, the National Film Board, the Canada Council, the CRTC, and Telefilm Canada all grew out of the federal government's concern.

Titles by award-winning author Margaret Atwood include *A Handmaid's Tale* and *The Blind Assassin*.

Many provinces fund arts councils to support regional and local cultural activities. Also, private corporations sponsor concerts,

Dionne Brand is a poet, novelist, essayist, film-maker, and Black activist.

theatre and dance companies, and art shows. All this allows Canadian artists to be heard and seen in their own country.

The real decision about the future of Canadian culture lies with average Canadians. Only they—only we—can decide how much being different from Americans matters. Only Canadians can develop their own authors, publishers, musicians, and more. If it means something special to be Canadian, Canadians must work to discover and preserve that identity.

FOCUS

1. What are split run magazines?
2. What is Heritage Canada, and how does it help Canadian publishers?
3. Name three Canadian books that you have read.

The Sports Link

The United States has had a significant impact on Canadian sports. Television has moved sports off the playing fields and into living rooms around the world.

Hockey

In May 1994, Parliament declared hockey Canada's national winter sport, and lacrosse Canada's national summer sport. There is little doubt, however, that hockey is our most beloved sport.

The National Hockey League (NHL) was formed in 1917. There were only four teams then: two in Montreal, and one each in Toronto and Ottawa. Boston was the first American team to join the NHL (1924). In the next two years, teams in Detroit, Chicago, and two teams in New York joined. All the players on these teams were Canadian.

By 2006, the NHL had 30 teams, only 6 Canadian. Canadians make up only 52 percent of the player roster. League headquarters is now in New York City, not Montreal. The NHL president is an American. U.S. TV networks often make up schedules and game times. Nonetheless, Canadians still

Canada's Olympic women's hockey team celebrates its gold medal win in the 2006 winter games.

dominate the ranks of outstanding hockey players. Think of Gordie Howe, Maurice Richard, Bobby Orr, Wayne Gretzky, Mario Lemieux, and more.

Canada dominated hockey at the Olympic Games for many years. In

HISTOR!CA
Minutes

2006, the Canadian women's team won gold against Sweden in Turin. In 2002, both the women's and men's teams won Olympic gold. The national women's hockey team has won virtually every world championship open to it. Its success reflects the growth of hockey since the National Women's Hockey League began in Canada in 1989. The League had seven teams by 2005. In Ontario alone, more than 20 000 women now play organized hockey. Hayley Wickenheiser, Cassie Campbell, Danielle Goyette and Gillian Apps are among Canada's women hockey "greats."

Canadian Football

The Canadian Football League (CFL) got its name in 1958, but its roots go back to the Canadian Rugby Football Union in 1884. In 1909, Earl Grey, a popular governor general of Canada, donated the Grey Cup trophy. In the Grey Cup final, two Canadian teams face off against each other. The first time the East and West met in a Grey Cup game was 1921.

The Edmonton Eskimos beat the Montreal Alouettes to win the Grey Cup in overtime at the 2005 game in Vancouver.

The game has been played in snow, fog, wind, and mud.

Although often financially troubled, the League offers an exciting brand of football. It can also claim to be uniquely Canadian. More and more, it has sought to protect Canadian football. In 1936, the League placed a limit of five American players per team. By 1996, "imports" were set at 19 out of 36 players per team.

In 2005, a former CFL commissioner, John Tory, talked about the Grey Cup. "In our country, hockey has clearly been the most important. But if you look at the one event that draws everyone together, it's the Grey Cup." As of 2006, the CFL had nine teams, with East and West divisions. Although it glories in regional contests, the Grey Cup truly unites the country. As Peter C. Newman wrote in *The Canadian Revolution*, "Confederation worked one day a year—the afternoon of the Grey Cup."

Baseball

This sport has a long tradition in Canada. Some people suggest it was being played here before it was "invented" by Abner Doubleday in the United States. Babe Ruth hit his first professional home run in Toronto. Jackie Robinson, an African-American, broke the "colour barrier" when he played for the Montreal Royals. The Royals were the Brooklyn Dodgers' top farm team.

Canada now has one team in the major baseball league. The Toronto Blue Jays are in the American League. The Montreal Expos were transferred to Washington

in 2005 due to poor attendance. Many Americans were shocked when Toronto won the World Series in 1992, and again in 1993. It was unthinkable that America's "national pastime" could be dominated by a "foreign" country.

Many Canadians have played in the major leagues. Ferguson Jenkins was from Chatham, Ontario. He pitched for the Chicago Cubs and the Philadelphia Phillies. Throughout the 1990s until his retirement in 2005, Larry Walker of Maple Ridge, B.C., was one of the most dominant players in the game. Canadian Eric Gagné was the top reliever in 2004.

On the non-professional level, there are many baseball, fastball, and softball leagues for both males and females. Baseball ranks along with soccer as a popular summer sport.

Canadian Larry Walker won the Most Valuable Player Award for the National League, 1997.

Basketball

A Canadian invented basketball. James Naismith of Almonte, Ontario, was teaching in Springfield, Massachusetts, in 1891 at the time. It was not until 1994, though, that Canada had teams—the Vancouver Grizzlies and the Toronto Raptors—in the National Basketball Association (NBA). As new teams in a well-established league, they struggled to win. In 2001, the Vancouver team moved to Memphis.

Canadian Steve Nash, a player for the Phoenix Suns, won the NBA's Most Valuable Player Award in 2005. Seventeen Canadians have played in the NBA. These players include Todd MacCulloch, Jamaal Magloire, Rick Fox, Brian Heaney, and Leo Rautins. Fox won three NBA Championship rings as a member of the Los Angeles Lakers.

Challenges in Professional Sports

Canada has one-tenth the population of the United States. It has achieved much fame, however, in professional sports, especially hockey. Sports scholarships, available throughout American colleges and universities, are not usually allowed in Canada. As a result, many of Canada's best athletes go to the United States for their post-secondary education. That means that the level of Canadian college sports has seriously eroded. The drain probably affects professional sports in Canada, as well.

Strikes, escalating salaries, and drug scandals in sports have affected the public's opinion of professional sports. This reality, plus the huge influence of the United States, poses a genuine challenge for the preservation of Canadian spectator sports.

Point guard Steve Nash is the first Canadian and second non-U.S. player to win the NBA's Most Valuable Player Award.

FOCUS

1. How has the United States influenced Canadian sports?
2. Identify five Canadian sport heroes from different sports.
3. Who is your favourite Canadian sports figure of all time? Why?

Sharpening Your Skills

Organizing and Making Sense of Research Notes

THE SKILL
Arranging data so that it makes sense and tells an accurate story

THE IMPORTANCE
Accuracy and proper organization are important skills in both the work
world and in everyday life.

You have just landed a job as a reporter at a local newspaper. The first day is hardly an hour old when your boss comes bustling into your small cubicle. "Jones," she reports, "died over the weekend." She wants you to write his obituary. A paragraph will do, she figures, but it must be finished in time for tomorrow's edition.

The newspaper's guidelines state that all such obituaries must
- be free of factual errors
- be written with proper grammar
- give proper emphasis to the more important facts
- support all interpretations and conclusions with reasonable evidence
- indicate what is interpretation and what is fact

A half-day of research reveals the following information.

RESEARCH NOTES ON JONES

a) Court records show that Jones and his spouse were granted a divorce in March 1911.
b) Several newspaper articles and letters from Liberal Party leaders indicate that during the 1906 election, Jones was regarded as a rising politician.
c) A letter dated 9 December 1909 from the prime minister to Jones stated that "although the world has not yet had the chance to appreciate your invaluable work, I shall always remember that you, my dear Jones, were the true author of the [two illegible words] Act."

d) County records give Jones's date of birth as 20 August 1873.

e) A letter from Jones to his spouse on 15 November 1909 indicates that Jones was working closely with the prime minister on an Environment Protection Act.

f) Jones's household records show that over a 15-year period, the household purchased an average of 15 bottles of brandy per week.

g) Jones's marriage certificate is dated 3 May 1903.

h) Several history books indicate that Jones never won an election and that he faded out of politics during the First World War.

With the paper's guidelines in mind, you organize your notes, think about Jones, and write the following three obituaries. (See samples 1, 2, and 3.)

As you have been taught, you ask a friend to proofread your work. Based on the newspaper's guidelines, what would be your comments on each obituary? For example: Sample 1 has several factual errors. Jones was not born in 1875, nor was he 30 when he married. We don't know for certain that "he ran for office" in 1906, nor do we know that "personal information" about Jones being an alcoholic was ever revealed. We don't know that he was an alcoholic, nor that his wife "divorced him." Since these were interpretations, not facts, the author should have used such words as "perhaps," "may have," and "it is probable." Finally, Jones's most important contribution to the country has been ignored. There are no grammatical mistakes, and the obituary is chronologically correct.

Application

Write your own accurate obituary for Jones.

SAMPLE 1: Jones was born on August 20, 1875. He was 30 when he got married. In 1906, he ran for office and according to the media he was regarded as a rising politician. Unfortunately, personal information about Jones circulated at the time and people found out that he had been an alcoholic for 15 years. He never achieved office. In March 1911 his wife divorced him and during the First World War he was out of politics for good.

SAMPLE 2: Born in 1873, Jones got married at the age of 31. Shortly after his mariage, he was thought to be a very promising poltican, and was well-liked by the Canadian Prime Minisiter. Unfortunately, a drinking problem led to the end of his marriage and the eventual end of his political carrreer.

SAMPLE 3: Jones, according to the Prime Minister, was "the true author of the Act." His household accounts suggest that he was a heavy drinker. In 1906, he was regarded as a rising politician. He was married in 1903 and divorced in 1911. He never achieved office and faded out of politics during the First World War. He was born in 1873.

Questions and Activities

Match the words in column A with the descriptions in column B.

A	B
1. Ronald Reagan	a) Canadian film industry
2. Lyndon Johnson	b) Mulroney–Reagan meeting
3. Ken Taylor	c) watchdog on broadcasting
4. Hollywood North	d) talent loss to south
5. Shamrock Summit	e) clash with Lester Pearson
6. Massey–Lévesque Commission	f) watchdog on foreign investment
7. CRTC	g) blockades
8. sports scholarships	h) American president in 1980s
9. FIRA	i) Canadian ambassador in Iran
10. Pacific Salmon Treaty	j) report on Canadian culture

Identify and state the importance or impact of each of the following:

1. NAFTA
2. Ferguson Jenkins
3. James Naismith
4. "Good Neighbour Policy"
5. IJC
6. NFB
7. Hayley Wickenheiser
8. acid rain
9. Telefilm Canada
10. Investment Canada

Discuss and Debate

1. Hold a debate on this topic: "Canadians are Americans in everything but name."

2. Draw up two lists showing the positive and negative results of Canada's close relationship with the United States.

3. Is there any value in having a Canadian identity separate from an American one? Explain.

4. What is Canadian culture? American culture? Describe the major similarities and differences.

5. Is Canada a partner or puppet in North American culture and economy? Discuss.

6. What do you feel are the important issues facing Canada in its relationship with the United States?

7. How is your lifestyle set by patterns "born in the U.S.A."? How much of this influence do you resent? How much do you welcome?

8. What efforts have been made in the cultural and economic fields by the federal government and other agencies to promote a distinctive Canadian culture and economy? How effective have they been? What other steps should be taken, if any?

9. Name as many past and current Canadian musicians, actors, and television programs as you can. Which of these reflect something distinctly Canadian?

10. Listen to your favourite radio station for one hour between 4 p.m. and 10 p.m. Write down the title of the song, the performer(s), and the nationality for each song. Determine percentages for Canadian, American, and other. Which do you like most? Should nationality matter?

Do Some Research

1. What roles did each of these prime ministers play in shaping Canadian foreign policy with the United States? (See chapters 4 and 5.)

a) Lester Pearson   **b)** Pierre Trudeau
c) Brian Mulroney   **d)** Jean Chrétien
e) Paul Martin

2. Should foreign ownership of Canadian resources be limited? Explore.

3. What impact has the United States had on each of the following cultural areas in Canada?

a) mass media—radio, television, movies
b) the arts—music, theatre
c) publishing—books, magazines, newspapers
d) sports—NHL, CFL, NBA, baseball, amateur sports
e) education—textbook authors, nationality of teachers/professors
f) the Internet

4. Draw a chart to show areas where Canadians and Americans are both similar and different. Headings might include

a) Political Structure
b) Geography
c) Language Characteristics (e.g., accents, use of certain words)
d) Lifestyle and Standard of Living
e) Basic Beliefs
f) Social Attitudes

5. The International Joint Commission was set up between Canada and the United States to resolve areas of dispute. What have some of these areas been? What are current areas of tension?

6. What are the different views that the Canadian and American governments take on global warming? Which government do you think has the more correct view? Why?

Web Watch

The CBC: www.cbc.ca

The CFL: www.cfl.ca

The CRTC: www.crtc.gc.ca

IJC: http://www.ijc.org

Government of Canada: http://canada.gc.ca

Government of United States Portal: www.us.gov

Greenpeace Canada: www.greenpeace.ca

NAFTA: http://www.dfait-maeci.gc.ca/nafta-alena

The NFB: www.nfb.ca

The NHL: www.nhl.com

American President in the Whitehouse: www.whitehouse.gov

Statistics Canada: www.statcan.ca/start.html

The CBC Digital Archives at www.cbc.ca/archives has excellent audiovisual files on themes important to this chapter. For example: "Seeking Sanctuary: Draftdodgers," "Ruling the Airwaves: The CRTC and Canadian Content," "The Auto Pact: En Route to Free Trade," "At Loggerheads: The Canada–U.S. Softwood Lumber Dispute," "Canada–U.S. Free Trade Agreement," "The Saint Lawrence Seaway: Gateway to the World," "Acid Rain: Pollution and Politics," "Canadarm: A Technology Star," "Troubled Waters, Pollution in the Great Lakes," and "The Spirit of Hockey."

HUMAN RIGHTS

CANADA 45

JOHN PETERS HUMPHREY

Here, Canadian lawyer John Peters Humphrey is recognized for his role in drafting the Universal Declaration of Human Rights. The Declaration is a major achievement of the United Nations. Humphrey served as director of human rights for the UN from 1944 to 1966; he consistently worked to protect human rights.

HISTOR!CA
Minutes

Why do you think the Declaration is considered so important?

Chapter Eight
Hands Around the World

Expectations

Overall Expectations:
By the end of this chapter, you will be able to
- describe major global forces and events that have influenced Canada's policies and Canadian identity
- evaluate Canada's participation in war and contributions to peacekeeping and world security

Specific Expectations:
By the end of this chapter, you will be able to
- describe how Canada's participation in selected world events and international organizations and agreements has contributed to an evolving sense of national identity
- identify some of the ways in which foreign powers have influenced Canadian foreign policy
- summarize Canada's role in some key Cold War activities, 1945 to 1989
- assess the roles played by the Canadian armed forces since 1945, including peacekeeping, peace-making, and maintaining security
- describe the importance of selected scientific and technological innovations developed by Canadians
- identify changes in Canada's international status since the First World War
- describe Canada's responses to some of the major human tragedies that have occurred since the First World War.
- describe the development of Canada's role as a world leader in defending human rights since the Second World War

Word List
Avian flu	**Boycott**
Ethnic cleansing	**GNP**
Genocide	**Human rights**
Indigenous	**Isolationism**
Pandemics	**Peacekeeping**
Peacemaking	**Prisoners of**
SARS	**conscience**
Veto	

Advance Organizer

❶ The way Canada deals with other countries is its foreign policy. This policy changes over time. What happens in the world and how Canada relates to other nations affects it.

Fidel Castro and Jean Chrétien

❷ The United Nations (UN) promotes human rights and world co-operation. As a member, Canada believes strongly in the role of the UN. Canadian soldiers have served in many peacekeeping and peacemaking operations.

Cold War Diefenbunker

❸ The Cold War began after the Second World War and lasted until 1990. It was a war of nerves between the Soviet Union and the United States. The superpowers threatened each other with shows of military strength rather than outright warfare.

Hands Around the World

1965   1970   1975   1980   1985   1990   1995   2000   2005   2010

4 Canada is part of two major alliances: NATO and NORAD. Canada supports NATO to help protect Europe and the North Atlantic. It supports NORAD to help protect North America against attack. Membership could involve Canada in war.

5 The Commonwealth is a free association of countries that were once part of the British Empire. La Francophonie is a free association of French-speaking nations. Canada belongs to both and enjoys friendships all over the globe.

6 Canada sends money, supplies, and advisers to poor, troubled nations. The Canadian International Development Agency looks after aid that Canada gives. Sometimes, too, Canada sends Canadian Forces workers to provide disaster relief.

What Is Foreign Policy?

Foreign policy is the plan on which a nation bases its relations with the rest of the world. A nation that does not make such relations still has a foreign policy. It is known as **isolationism.**

Foreign policy usually involves both objectives and methods. Objectives are the goals that the nation hopes to achieve through its relations with other nations. Methods are the ways in which the nation pursues those goals.

Foreign policies can differ greatly. In general, foreign policy helps nations do well in trade and commerce. It also helps them keep peace or look for revenge. Foreign policy may also reflect a desire to do good in the world. Some goals may be idealistic. An example is a commitment to send aid to poor countries. Foreign policy is shaped by a country's geographical position. Military and economic power, as well as ethnic and religious ties, also affect how policy develops.

As the chart outlines, Canada's foreign policy has evolved over time. It reflects Canada's growing independence and changing view of the world.

South Africa's Nelson Mandela

DEVELOPMENT OF CANADA'S FOREIGN POLICY

1914 Canada enters the First World War as part of the British Empire.

1919 Canada signs the Treaty of Versailles as a separate country. It becomes a charter, or original, member of the League of Nations.

1922 In the Chanak Affair, Canada refuses to send troops to Turkey as Britain requested.

1923 Canada signs the Halibut Fisheries Treaty without an accompanying British signature.

1925 Canada House is established in London, England. It is the office of the Canadian High Commissioner.

1926 Vincent Massey becomes the first Canadian minister in Washington; Canada and the United States begin full diplomatic relations.

1931 The Statute of Westminster gives Canada full control over its foreign affairs.

1939 On its own, the Canadian Parliament declares war on Germany at the start of the Second World War.

1945 Canada becomes a charter member of the United Nations.

1949 Canada joins NATO.

1950 Canada takes part in the Korean War within UN forces.

1961 Canadian Prime Minister John Diefenbaker opposes South Africa renewing membership in the Commonwealth. He is the only white leader to do so.

1991 Canada fights in the war against Iraq.

2001 Canada joins the war against the Taliban, an Islamic movement, in Afghanistan after events of 9/11.

Hands Around the World

The Department of Foreign Affairs and International Trade is responsible for foreign policy. Its role is to

- conduct all diplomatic relations on behalf of Canada
- foster the expansion of Canada's international trade
- manage the Canadian Foreign Service

Prime Minister Stephen Harper asserts his government's strong support of the Canadian mission in Afghanistan by visiting and encouraging troops there.

A Canadian soldier watches for threats above a ground-breaking ceremony for a new police station in Kandahar in 2006. He is part of a Canadian team of diplomats, aid workers, police, and soldiers helping Afghanistan.

CIDA President Hugette Labelle and the Chinese vice-minister of foreign trade sign a memorandum of co-operation in Beijing, China, as Jean Chrétien applauds.

FOCUS

1. What is foreign policy?
2. List three reasons why countries have foreign policies.
3. List two objectives of the Department of Foreign Affairs.
4. In your view, what should be the most important goal of Canadian foreign policy? Why?

Canada and the United Nations

In 1945, Canada and 50 other countries joined together to establish the United Nations (UN). In the wake of war, they recognized the great need for an organization dedicated to keeping peace and promoting friendly relations among nations. The UN champions peace and human rights around the world. It serves as a centre of international co-operation and works to resolve economic, cultural, social, and humanitarian issues.

Many member nations have contributed to the design and materials found in the UN headquarters. Canada's gift was the nickel-bronze doors that lead to the General Assembly. These doors represent the four themes of the United Nations: peace, justice, truth, and brotherhood.

The UN is composed of independent, sovereign nations. Unlike a national parliament or congress, it does not pass laws. Instead, it shapes the policies of the international community. Member countries can be large or small, rich or poor. Political views and social systems vary.

The UN is based in New York City, but UN offices are in countries all over the world. Discussions are held in six official languages: Arabic, Chinese, English, French, Russian, and Spanish. Instantaneous translations are offered during UN debates.

UN Structure

The General Assembly, sometimes seen as a world parliament, is the UN's main body. All 191 member states are represented in it. Each has one vote. Decisions on ordinary matters are taken by simple majority. Important questions need a two-thirds majority.

Every year, the Assembly holds its regular meeting to make recommendations on matters within the UN Charter. The Charter is the organization's founding document. The General Assembly does not have the power to force action. Its strength comes from the united opinion it expresses. The *General Assembly*

- sets policies and determines programs for the UN Secretariat

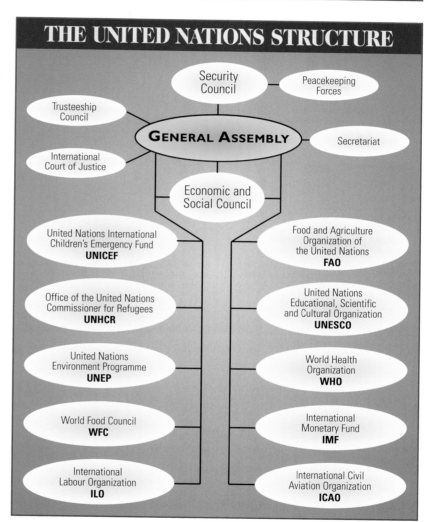

THE UNITED NATIONS STRUCTURE

Security Council

Peacekeeping Forces

Trusteeship Council

GENERAL ASSEMBLY

Secretariat

International Court of Justice

Economic and Social Council

United Nations International Children's Emergency Fund
UNICEF

Food and Agriculture Organization of the United Nations
FAO

Office of the United Nations Commissioner for Refugees
UNHCR

United Nations Educational, Scientific and Cultural Organization
UNESCO

United Nations Environment Programme
UNEP

World Health Organization
WHO

World Food Council
WFC

International Monetary Fund
IMF

International Labour Organization
ILO

International Civil Aviation Organization
ICAO

To learn more about the UN, visit its official Web site: www.un.org.

- directs activities for development
- approves the UN budget, including peace-keeping operations

The president of Nigeria addresses the UN General Assembly about financing for development.

Any decision taken by the Council must be carried out by UN member countries. The five permanent Security Council members have the right of **veto.** Should any of them use that right, a resolution is defeated.

The Security Council mediates international disputes. It asks opposing parties to reach agreement by peaceful means. Should that fail, the UN can act to bring about a settlement in other ways.

- It may place economic sanctions on a country that threatens peace. Doing this involves nations refusing to sell or buy goods to or from that country. For example, not so long ago, Iraq did not want the UN to inspect its armaments, or military weapons; the UN responded by bringing a **boycott** against the country.
- The UN may send in **peacekeeping** forces to keep opposing forces apart, or put a peace agreement into effect.
- Military action is another way to deal with a conflict. The UN has taken this choice several times, responding to invasion in South Korea in 1950 and to Iraq's invasion of Kuwait in 1990. The UN calls such action **peacemaking**.

- admits new members
- appoints the UN Secretary-General

The *Security Council* meets whenever it needs to, whenever peace is threatened. It works to maintain peace and security. The Security Council has 15 members. The 5 permanent members are China, France, the Russian Federation, the United Kingdom, and the United States. The remaining 10 members are elected by the Assembly for two-year terms. Canada has been elected to the Security Council several times.

The *Secretariat* works for all branches of the UN. With a staff of about 8900, it carries out the UN's day-to-day work. Its head is the Secretary-General.

The *Economic and Social Council* coordinates the economic and social work of the UN and its related specialized agencies. The Council has 54 members. It meets for a one-month session each year. The meetings alternate between New York and Geneva. The

Here, the powerful UN Security Council votes to ask the Prosecutor of the International Criminal Court to review events in Darfur, Sudan, since 2002. The Prosecutor investigates crimes against humanity.

Council oversees the way the UN supports economic growth in developing countries. It administers development projects. It promotes human rights. It fosters co-operation in areas such as housing, family planning, environmental protection, and crime prevention.

The *Trusteeship Council* was established to assist territories with self-government or independence. The council has aided several countries that are now members of the UN. The Trust Territory of the Pacific Islands, now known as Palau, joined the UN in 1994. At present, the Trusteeship Council has suspended operations because there are no trust territories.

The *International Court of Justice* is the main judicial branch of the UN. Fifteen judges, elected by the General Assembly and the Security Council, form the World Court. The Court settles legal disputes between member states. It also deals with such issues as soldiers accused of committing atrocities in what was once Yugoslavia.

FOCUS

1. Why was the United Nations founded in 1945?
2. What type of work does the United Nations do?
3. Which UN responsibility do you think is the most important? Why?

Peacekeeping and Peacemaking

Keeping global peace is one of the UN's most important goals. It is also one of the most difficult.

Since 1948, the UN has led more than 45 peacekeeping operations. A majority of them have taken place in the last 20 years. About 800 000 military personnel have served with UN forces. More than 2000 peacekeepers have lost their lives.

Canada has played a vital role in peacekeeping. In 1956, Lester Pearson was president of the UN General Assembly. He suggested a peace plan to end Arab–Israeli conflict over the Suez Canal. The plan involved sending a UN peacekeeping force. A year later, Pearson became the first Canadian to receive the Nobel Peace Prize.

Canadian soldiers have served as peacekeepers in Cyprus, Somalia, Kashmir, the Congo, Iran, Iraq, Somalia, Bosnia, Afghanistan, Kuwait, and more.

Somalia: Operation Restore Hope

Not all missions end well. Somalia is one of the poorest nations in the world. In the 1990s, warlords ruled it. They fought brutal battles against one another. Millions of people starved. The warlords seized most of the food

In 1988, UN peacekeepers as a whole earned the Nobel Peace Prize. There were seven missions in operation at the time.

aid that the UN tried to deliver to the people.

In 1992, the UN sent a peacekeeping force. The force was largely made up of American troops, but many Canadians took part, as well. The mission was called "Operation Restore Hope."

The UN peacekeepers ended up fighting local warlords. There was great slaughter of Pakistani and American forces. The UN withdrew. Canadian forces were shamed by the murder of a Somali prisoner by his Canadian captors. The mission ended in failure, and today Somalia remains torn apart by internal rivalries and poverty.

Massacre in Rwanda

Canadian armed forces served under the UN flag in Rwanda from 1993 to 1996. They were trying to protect the capital city of Kigali during the Rwandan Civil War. These troops brought food and medical supplies to starving Rwandans. Canadian troops worked with others to maintain UN cease-fire orders. Despite these efforts, this peacekeeping mission ended tragically.

The UN commander was Canadian General Roméo Dallaire. He predicted a massacre of Rwanda's Tutsi population by the Hutu people. He warned his UN superiors, but they did not listen. When a massacre began, his tiny force was unable to stop the **genocide**.

A million Tutsis died in the massacre. Some Belgian peacekeepers were also slaughtered.

Later, questions were raised. People were concerned about the UN's effectiveness. The UN was humiliated and discredited for lack of action. Some claimed that because the mission took place in Black Africa, the UN chose not to risk troops to control the situation. UN troops were withdrawn in 1996.

Rwanda is now trying to deal with its ugly past. Those accused of committing genocide have been put on trial.

What happened in Rwanda and Somalia exposed the weakness of the UN. The UN cannot

UN PEACEKEEPING PERSONNEL, AS OF OCTOBER 2005	
Military personnel and civilian police serving in peacekeeping operations	66 921
Countries contributing personnel	105
International civilian personnel	4 475
Local civilian personnel	7 996
UN volunteers	1 762
Total number of personnel serving in peacekeeping operations	81 154
Total number of fatalities in peacekeeping operations since 1948	2 004

Rwandan refugees show ID documents to Canadian and West African peacekeepers trying to help displaced persons. The peacekeepers are controlling the gate of a camp.

RIGHT: *Iraqi dictator Saddam Hussein ordered the torching of Kuwaiti oil wells when UN peacemakers drove his forces from Kuwait. Canadian oilmen helped bring the fires under control.*

Roméo Dallaire

BORN: 1946; Holland; born to a Canadian soldier and a Dutch nurse

SIGNIFICANCE: Roméo Dallaire experienced the massacres of Rwanda. He alerted the world to the UN's weakness. The depression he later suffered showed that post-traumatic stress syndrome can even affect generals.

BRIEF BIOGRAPHY: Dallaire became Force Commander of the United Nations mission to Rwanda in 1993. The small UN force was there to supervise the peace process after years of civil war in Rwanda. When it was clear that extremist Hutus were bent on murdering the Tutsi minority, Dallaire pleaded for reinforcements. His plea was turned down. Somalia had made the UN fearful of another failure in Africa. Nearly a million people died in the Rwandan geno-

cide. Not until the scale of the massacre was revealed did the UN send in a larger force.

For a time, the experience shattered Dallaire. It pushed him to the edge of suicide. He wrote a bestselling book, *Shake Hands with the Devil: The Failure of Humanity in Rwanda,* about his terrible experience. In 2004, the book won the Governor General's Literary Award for Non-Fiction. In March 2005, Prime Minister Paul Martin appointed Dallaire to the Senate. Dallaire continues to study conflict resolution. He talks about the personal and political lessons he learned in Rwanda to audiences all over the world. **In your opinion, should Roméo Dallaire be considered a hero? Explain. To learn more** about Dallaire and his current work, go to **www.romeodallaire.com.**

C A N A D I A N   L I V E S

readily respond to rapidly changing violent situations. It is better at "keeping peace." Many countries have become reluctant to take part in UN missions. They are afraid of losing troops.

When there is no peace to keep, the UN has used its forces to "make" peace. Canada has taken part in these more difficult and dangerous missions. These are UN peacemaking efforts.

- In June 1950, North Korea invaded South Korea. North Korea was backed by the Soviet Union and South Korea was friends with the United States. The United Nations declared this invasion an act of aggression. It asked for support from UN members to resist the invasion. Forces from over 30 countries fought to stop the North Koreans. More than 20 000 Canadian soldiers fought in Korea—312 were killed in action.
- On 18 January 1991, UN forces from 32 countries launched Operation Desert Storm against Iraq. They did so because Iraq had invaded Kuwait. The war lasted only 41 days. Iraq soon abandoned the invasion. It was only the second time that the UN had used military action to stop aggression. Canada contributed land, sea, and air forces to this successful mission.

The UN has often been criticized for its failure to prevent the outbreak of war and for

UN Secretary-General Boutros Boutros-Ghali stands before a shed that contains the remains of hundreds massacred a year earlier at a Rwandan church. UN peacekeepers were too few to stop the slaughter.

its inability to achieve world peace. Today, the world remains a hotbed of hostilities. Many of these conflicts could lead to war.

As the 21st century unfolds, nations still dream of peace, but many countries endure violence, terrorism, and civil war. The world is still a dangerous place. Both peacemaking and peacekeeping forces are needed.

FOCUS

1. **What is the difference between peacekeeping and peacemaking?**
2. **Compare the UN experience in Rwanda and Somalia.**
3. **Would you consider serving in a UN peacekeeping operation? Explain.**

Human Rights and Freedoms

From its beginning, the United Nations has worked to protect **human rights**. Members set this goal in response to the horrors of the Holocaust and the Second World War. The United Nations Charter, signed in 1945, stated that its main objective was "to save succeeding generations from the scourge of war" and "to reaffirm faith in fundamental human rights." The Charter promotes and encourages "respect for human rights and for fundamental freedoms for all without distinction as to race, sex, language or religion."

In 1946, the UN established the Commission on Human Rights. Canadian John Humphrey, director of Human Rights at the UN Secretariat, drafted much of the 1948 Universal Declaration of Human Rights.

UN work on human rights continues. UN groups and missions look into claims that human rights have been violated. The UN sends advisers to help nations build modern societies that respect the rule of law and human rights. It has helped wartorn Iraq and Afghanistan draft constitutions that respect human rights and freedom.

HISTOR!CA
Minutes

AMNESTY INTERNATIONAL

Amnesty International (AI) is the world's largest human rights organization. More than 70 000 of its two million members live in Canada. All AI members are committed to the universal protection of human rights.

AI works to abolish the death penalty worldwide. It also campaigns against torture and mutilation. It promotes religious freedoms, tries to protect the rights of refugees, and acts to free **prisoners of conscience**, people who hold beliefs that their government does not tolerate or respect.

AI remains independent and impartial. It does not accept government funding. Its work is supported by financial donations. In 1977, AI was awarded the Nobel Peace Prize. In 2004, it launched a campaign to stop violence against women. **Do you support the work of Amnesty International? Explain. For more information about Amnesty International in Canada, see www.amnesty.ca.**

amnesty international
JUSTICE | EQUALITY | FREEDOM

Hands Around the World

UNIVERSAL DECLARATION OF HUMAN RIGHTS

- All human beings are born free. They have equal dignity and rights.
- Everyone is entitled to all the rights and freedoms, without distinction of any kind.
- Everyone has the right to life, liberty and security of person.
- No one shall be held in slavery.
- No one shall be subjected to torture or degrading treatment.
- Everyone has the right to recognition as a person before the law.
- All people are equal before the law.
- Everyone has a right to effective legal remedy for actions which violate fundamental rights.
- No one shall be subjected to arbitrary arrest, detention or exile.
- Every person is entitled to a fair hearing by an impartial jury.
- Anyone charged with a penal offence will be presumed innocent until proven guilty according to law in a public trial.
- Every person is entitled to privacy of family, home and correspondence.
- Everyone has the right to freedom of movement, and the right to leave his or her country, and to return.
- Everyone has the right to seek and to find asylum from persecution.
- Everyone has the right to a nationality.
- Men and women, of full age, have the right to marry and have a family.
- Everyone has the right to own property.
- Everyone has the freedom of thought, conscience and religion.
- Everyone has the right of opinion and of expression.
- Everyone has the right to freedom of peaceful assembly and association.
- Every person has the right to take part in the government of one's country. The will of the people shall be the basis of the government's authority.
- Everyone has the right to social security.
- Everyone has the right to work, to free choice of employment, to just and favourable conditions of work and to protection against unemployment.
- Everyone has the right to equal pay for equal work.
- Everyone has the right to form and join trade unions for the protection of worker interests.
- Everyone has the right to rest and leisure. This includes reasonable limitation of working hours and periodic holidays with pay.
- Everyone has the right to a standard of living adequate for individual health and well-being, and for that of one's family.
- Everyone has the right to education, which shall be free at the earliest levels.
- Elementary education shall be compulsory.
- Every person has the right to participate freely in the cultural life of his or her community.
- Every person is entitled to a social and international order in which the rights and freedoms set forth in this declaration can be fully realized.

Louise Arbour

BORN: 1947, Montreal, Quebec

SIGNIFICANCE: Louise Arbour was chief prosecutor for the UN International Criminal Tribunal. She was responsible for prosecuting war crimes in the former Yugoslavia and Rwanda.

BRIEF BIOGRAPHY: Louise Arbour was born and educated in Quebec. She received her law degree in 1970. In 1987, Arbour was appointed to the Ontario Supreme Court's High Court of Justice. In 1990, she joined the Ontario Court of Appeal.

Arbour has stood up for human rights in Canada. She was vice-president of the Canadian Civil Liberties Association. She campaigned for prisoners to gain the right to vote. She published articles on human rights, criminal law, gender issues, and civil liberties.

In 1996, the UN Security Council appointed Arbour as prosecutor for the International Criminal Tribunal. For the first time since the Nuremberg and Tokyo trials after the Second World War, trials for war crimes would be held. The focus was on the former

Yugoslavia and Rwanda. Arbour's job was to investigate and lay charges against individuals for war crimes and crimes against humanity, such as genocide. She worked tirelessly. She even observed the excavation of a mass grave site near Vukovar, Croatia. "... these bodies were thrown together indiscriminately in a hole ... They were young men.... I watched the bodies come out of the ground and it was like they were coming alive again. They were demanding to be identified. They were demanding that their mothers be told."

In May 1999, Arbour called for the arrest of Slobodan Milosevic, former Yugoslav president, and four other political and military leaders. They were charged with committing crimes against humanity.

Arbour's work brought her international and national praise. In 1999, she was appointed to the Supreme Court of Canada. She served until 2004. She then became the UN High Commissioner for Human Rights. **Do you think Arbour was a strong choice for this UN role? Explain.**

Human Rights in Canada

As the international community began to see human rights as basic and important, so did Canada. Canadian society considers human rights fundamental to human dignity. Over time, this belief has been reflected on paper. Ontario introduced its Human Rights Code in 1962. The Code was the first of its kind in Canada. By 1975, every province had a human rights code.

In 1976, Canada accepted the International Bill of Rights, which goes beyond the UN's 1948 Universal Declaration. The Bill is based on two UN documents that cover civil, political, economic, social, and cultural rights. It binds Canada to take a strong stand on human rights issues. In 1977, the federal government created the Canadian Human Rights Act and Commission. It has also passed other international treaties

Donald Marshall is an Aboriginal Canadian who was wrongly convicted of murder. Marshall spent years in prison before being cleared. Many thought that bias and racial prejudice were at the heart of his imprisonment. Other Aboriginal Canadians have been wrongly imprisoned, too. Aboriginal Canadians tend to feel that when it comes to the police and justice system, they are denied full human rights. The UN has indicated that Aboriginal Canadians are not treated as full citizens.

related to human rights.

Despite all that, pressure mounted for Canada to improve its legal protection of human rights. Under Trudeau, the Canadian Charter of Rights and Freedoms passed in 1982. The Charter became a key part of the Canadian Constitution. It covers a wide range of fields, including mobility rights, equality rights, and language rights. Every law in Canada is subject to this Charter.

To ensure that human rights are protected, several groups act as watchdogs. Prison reform, for example, has been an issue for Canada's human rights activists. The Elizabeth Fry Society (www.elizabethfry.ca) and the John Howard Society (www.johnhoward.ca) are two international organizations. They work to better the conditions of prisoners and ex-convicts. Both try to make sure that the human rights of prisoners are respected.

FOCUS

1. **What is the goal of the United Nations Charter?**
2. **In your opinion, what are five rights that everyone should have?**
3. **Do all Canadians share equal human rights? Discuss.**

Children's Rights

Craig Kielburger

BORN: 1982, Thornhill, Ontario

SIGNIFICANCE: Kielburger is an activist against child labour. He is also the founder of Free the Children, an international youth movement. It seeks to change laws that affect child labour and exploitation.

BRIEF BIOGRAPHY: When he was 12, Craig Kielburger read the story of Iqbal Masih. Iqbal was a young boy from Pakistan. He was sold into slavery at age four. He was later freed, but was murdered at age 12. Craig was horrified. He became interested in worldwide injustice against children—there are at least 250 million child labourers in the world today. Most of these children work long hours under hazardous conditions. Many are abused.

In 1995, Kielburger and his friends founded Free the Children. This non-profit organization focuses on fighting the abuses of child labour. Kielburger began to

speak out for the rights of children. When members of the Ontario Federation of Labour heard him talk, they donated $100 000. This money went to build a rehabilitation/education centre in Alwar, India, for young children. Kielburger has travelled to over 30 countries on behalf of Free the Children. His organization has written thousands of letters to raise the issue of children's rights in Canada and around the world. In 1998, he spoke in Calcutta as part of the "Global March to End Child Labour." Tens of thousands of people all over the world took part in the march. They carried the message "that the time has come to guarantee every child a childhood, that no child should lose his or her chance to learn and develop by being forced to work all day long." **Do you think that Canadian youth can make a difference in the world today? To learn more about Kielburger's work and organization, visit www.kielprojects.com.**

CANADIAN LIVES

UNICEF and Children's Rights

The United Nations International Children's Emergency Fund (UNICEF) was founded in 1946. UNICEF was created to provide emergency relief for children in postwar Europe, China, and the Middle East. Canada was one of the first countries to establish a national committee to raise non-government funds for UNICEF. In 1965, UNICEF received the Nobel Peace Prize for its work.

All over the world, children are denied human rights. Because they are dependent on adults, children can be easily mistreated.

The year 1979 was the International Year of the Child. It focused global attention on the issue of children's rights. UNICEF co-ordinated the year's activities. In November 1989, the UN adopted the Convention on the Rights of the Child, an international human rights treaty. Among other rights, the treaty recognizes these ones:

- the inherent right to life
- the right to a name, an identity, and a nationality
- protection from physical and mental violence, exploitation, and abuse
- the right to be cared for by one's parents, if possible
- primary education
- access to information
- freedom of thought, conscience, and religion
- the right to express one's views
- the right to the highest attainable standard of health

These ideas are accepted in Canada. They may be accepted in poorer countries, too, but are harder to act on there. Even in Canada, many children live in poverty. Some face various forms of abuse. UNICEF remains a crucial element in the cause of children's rights. In 2005, it reported that hundreds of millions of children were being exploited around the world. The protection of children's rights has been a top priority of Canada's domestic and foreign policies for many years.

FOCUS

1. List five rights specified in the UN's Convention on the Rights of the Child that you feel are most important. Be prepared to explain your choices.
2. List three ways in which children's rights are violated around the world.
3. Why is Craig Kielburger important?

The Cold War

The Cold War dominated the world from 1946 to 1990. The Soviet Union and the United States were the world's two superpowers. They tried to keep each other in check. The Soviet Union controlled the areas in Eastern Europe that it had occupied during the Second World War. Soviet forces remained in Romania, Hungary, Bulgaria, Czechoslovakia, Poland, and East Germany. Rigged elections were held in these countries. Only Soviet-sponsored candidates could run for office. The United States and its allies protested. Unless they were prepared to go to war, they could do nothing.

In the words of Winston Churchill, "From Danzig on the Baltic, to Trieste on the Adriatic, an Iron Curtain has descended on Europe."

The Soviet Union began to build up its strength. From 1945 to 1990, fearful governments spent more money on the military than on food, housing, or medicine.

The Cold War was a struggle between opposing values. The Western bloc nations, led by the United States, believed in a multi-party democracy with a free market economy. The Eastern bloc, led by the Soviet Union, favoured a one-party communist dictatorship with strong economic controls.

The Cuban Missile Crisis

Many people believe the Cold War was at its worst in October 1962. The Soviet Union had built nuclear missile sites in communist Cuba. American U-2 spy planes photographed the sites. U.S. President John F. Kennedy spoke to his country on television.

A CLOSER LOOK AT THE ATOMIC BOMB

During the Second World War, a team of scientists worked on a top-secret mission. Its code name was "The Manhattan Project." J. Robert Oppenheimer led the team. Their mission was to make the world's first atomic bomb. They succeeded. On 16 July 1945, the United States tested the world's first atomic bomb. The atomic age had begun. Atomic bombs were used against Japan in August 1945. The destruction of Hiroshima and Nagasaki ended the Second World War in the Pacific.

Russian scientists were not far behind the Americans. The first Russian atomic bomb was detonated in 1949. The Soviet Union exploded its first hydrogen bomb in 1953. The explosion happened seven months after the United States exploded its own bomb.

By the 1980s, each of these superpowers had built thousands of nuclear warheads. These warheads had incredibly destructive firepower. During the height of the Cold War, it was said that each side had enough nuclear firepower to kill everyone in the world 40 times over.

In spite of the expansion of nuclear weapons, there were several attempts to reduce tensions. In 1973, U.S. President Richard Nixon and Russian Premier Leonid Brezhnev signed the Strategic Arms Limitation Treaty, or SALT. The treaty was intended to limit nuclear armaments. Later agreements dramatically reduced the world's nuclear arsenal.

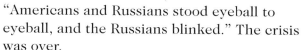

Hands Around the World

He said that American warships would blockade Cuba until the Russian missile sites were taken down.

For two weeks the world hung on the brink of nuclear war. Then, to the world's relief, the Soviets dismantled their missiles. One commentator noted, "Americans and Russians stood eyeball to eyeball, and the Russians blinked." The crisis was over.

Even now, much of the world is an armed camp.

Beyond the Cold War

By the late 1980s, the Soviet Union was in trouble on both political and economic fronts. Soviet leader Mikhail Gorbachev moved to Westernize the U.S.S.R. The Soviet military alliance, the Warsaw Pact—Bulgaria, Czechoslovakia, East Germany, Hungary, Poland, Romania and the U.S.S.R.—was dissolved. Slowly, some of the former Iron Curtain countries turned to democratic values.

By December 1991, the Soviet Union had dissolved into 15 countries. Russia was the largest of the former Soviet republics. The collapse of the once-mighty Soviet Union was the final chapter in the 45-year-old Cold War.

War was not over, though. Ethnic groups within Eastern Europe struggled to assert their independence from central governments. In the Balkan region of the former Yugoslavia, clashes erupted. In 1999, NATO forces attacked Serbia. They tried to prevent Serbia from its **ethnic cleansing**. The Serbian campaign against Albanians brought back memories of Nazi racism.

Czechoslovakia, however, divided peacefully. The Czech Republic and Slovakia were formed. Today much of Eastern Europe and the former territories of the Soviet Union are making political and economic progress. Still, the Cold War casts a long shadow.

FOCUS

1. **How was the Cold War different from other kinds of war?**
2. **What was the Warsaw Pact?**
3. **Why were people so fearful of the Cold War?**

Competition and Co-operation in Space

When the world first turned to exploration in space, there was far more competition than co-operation. In 1957, the Soviet Union launched the world's first space satellite, Sputnik. The communists then proclaimed that this proved their system was better than the American. In April 1961, Soviet astronaut Yuri Gagarin became the first human to orbit the earth. American John Glenn did the same a month later.

Exploring space was seen as a race, and U.S. President John Kennedy worried that his country would lose it. In 1962, he said that a major goal for the United States was to put a person on the moon "before the decade is out." In July 1969, the American space mission Apollo 11 landed on the moon.

In 1981, the Americans developed a series of space shuttles to carry astronauts and equipment into space. Marc Garneau became the first Canadian astronaut in space. He flew on the American space shuttle Challenger in 1984. Roberta Bondar and Stephen MacLean, a physicist and astronaut, were the next Canadians in space. They flew in two separate flights on the shuttle Discovery in 1992.

Astronaut and medical doctor Roberta Bondar was the first Canadian woman in space.

The Russians launched the Mir Space Station in 1986. It became a symbol of the Russian space program. Mir orbited the earth every 90 minutes. It allowed scientists to study living in space over long periods of time. Some astronauts remained in space for as long as three months. Astronauts from many countries, including Canada, have lived on Mir. Chris Hadfield was the first Canadian astronaut to visit it (1995). By 1996, Canadians had taken part in six space missions.

In November 1998, a huge non-military space project got under way. Russians launched Zarya, the first piece in the building of the International Space Station (ISS). Sixteen countries, including Canada, co-operated to build this highly complex structure. In December 1998, the Americans launched the Unity module. It linked up to Zarya. These two modules have orbited the earth well over 8000 times. In May 1999, astronaut Julie Payette became the first Canadian aboard the ISS. In 2001 astronaut Chris Hadfield helped deliver the 17.6 m Canadarm 2, Canada's contribution to the space station.

Completed in 2004, the station measures 110 m. It has a pressurized living and working space. There are seven science labs. It is larger than the cabin and cargo hold of a Boeing 747 aircraft.

Canada in Space

Canada's efforts in space go back to 1962, when Canada launched its first space satellite—the Alouette. Its success resulted in the launch of Anik A in 1972. Anik A beamed radio, telephone, and television signals across Canada. In 1982, Anik D became the first Canadian satellite made in Canada.

The Canadarm is Canada's major contribution to space exploration. Under the direction of the National Research Council, it was designed to work much like a giant 15 m "arm" outside a space shuttle. The first Canadarm was completed in 1981 at a cost of $100 million. Canada built five Canadarms for the United States. (See Chapter 7.) The latest Canadarm is so flexible that astronauts can photograph the underside of the space shuttle to detect

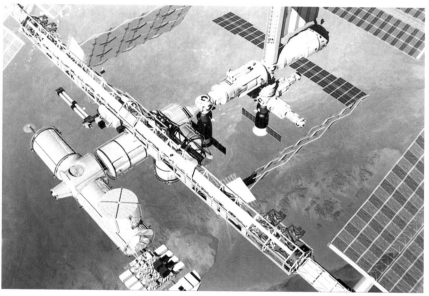

The International Space Station—an example of international co-operation.

broken or missing heat-resisting tiles.

In 2005, China put "taikonauts" (astronauts) in space. The Canadian Space Agency quickly signed agreements to have Canadian technology involved in future manned flights. As the world looks towards the stars, it is clear that Canadian technology and personnel have much to contribute.

FOCUS

1. **Should Canada take part in space exploration? Explain.**
2. **Would you be interested in going into space? Why or why not?**

Canada's Military Alliances

Alliances with other nations are an important part of Canada's foreign policy. An alliance is formed when two or more nations agree to help one another. Canada is a member of several alliances. Some of these are military and are for defence purposes. Others are political. Some are cultural, and others economic. Each alliance strengthens our ties to other nations. Alliances encourage co-operation and peaceful solutions to the world's problems.

North Atlantic Treaty Organization (NATO)

Canada was a founding member of the North Atlantic Treaty Organization in 1949. Canada's prime minister, Louis St. Laurent, was the first Western leader to suggest that such an organization be formed. NATO was created in response to Soviet aggression after the Second World War. Soviet leader Joseph Stalin refused to remove Russian troops from the occupied

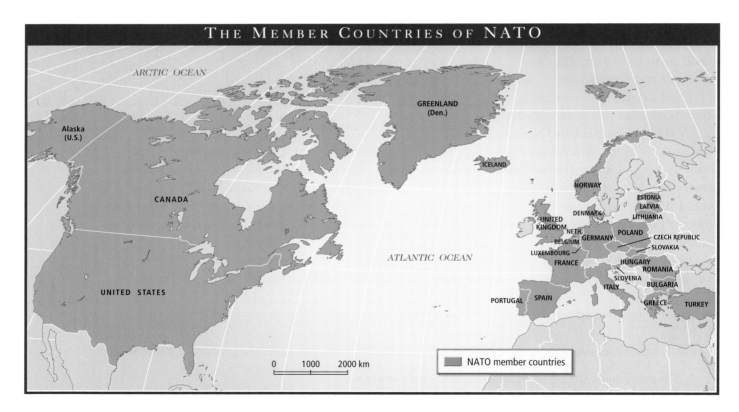

THE MEMBER COUNTRIES OF NATO

ARCTIC OCEAN

GREENLAND (Den.)

Alaska (U.S.)

ICELAND

NORWAY

CANADA

ESTONIA
LATVIA
DENMARK
LITHUANIA

UNITED KINGDOM
NETH.
BELGIUM
LUXEMBOURG
FRANCE
GERMANY
POLAND
CZECH REPUBLIC
SLOVAKIA
HUNGARY
ROMANIA
SLOVENIA
ITALY
BULGARIA

ATLANTIC OCEAN

UNITED STATES

PORTUGAL SPAIN
GREECE TURKEY

0   1000   2000 km

NATO member countries

countries of Eastern Europe. There was growing concern that the Soviet Union would invade the rest of Europe. In the early years, 16 countries signed the NATO charter. Belgium, Canada, Denmark, France, Germany, Greece, Iceland, Italy, Luxembourg, Netherlands, Norway, Portugal, Spain, Turkey, the United Kingdom, and the United States were among them. One of NATO's goals was to bring about peace and stability in Europe. Another was to limit the growth of the Soviet Union and its Warsaw Pact allies.

NATO's headquarters is in Brussels, Belgium. The Supreme Military Commander of NATO is always an American. The political leader, or Secretary-General, is elected by member nations. Beginning in 1999, former communist countries joined NATO. In 2005 NATO was composed of 29 nations.

Members pledge to support one another in the event of attack. Each member contributes to the defence of Western Europe and the North Atlantic. Thousands of Canadian troops have been stationed in Europe, the Middle East, and Africa in support of NATO. During the Cold War, Canadian naval destroyers and frigates patrolled for Soviet submarines.

Canadian soldiers are greeted by happy Kosovars at the Canadian base in Urosevec, Kosovo. Not all military situations are so pleasant for Canadian forces.

In 1999, the objectives of NATO were put to a severe test. Acting on their own, without UN support, NATO forces attacked Yugoslavia. Their main intent was to protect ethnic Albanians in the province of Kosovo. The human cost was high, and NATO's actions remain a source of controversy.

NATO in Afghanistan

NATO has made a long journey from an alliance originally based in Europe and directed at the U.S.S.R. After the 9/11

Canadians are expected to serve in Afghanistan for some time to come. Here, members of Canadian Forces troops celebrate Christmas 2005 in Kandahar, where Canada is focusing its efforts to help make the region stable.

terrorist attack on the World Trade Center towers in New York, the United States built a "grand alliance" against the Taliban regime in Afghanistan. The Taliban were helping Osama Bin Laden. He was the leader of the Al-Qaeda terrorist network that destroyed the World Trade Center. Within a day, NATO had applied Article 5 of the alliance: an attack against any member of the alliance was an attack against all members. For the first time in the history of NATO, a military force served beyond Europe's borders. In a short, but hard-hitting campaign, the Taliban were forced out of power and the leader of Al-Qaeda fled.

Canada is deeply involved in this mission. In the initial fighting, Canada sent its largest military force overseas since the Korean War. As of March 2006, 10 Canadians had died in Afghanistan. Some died from enemy fire and some from "friendly," or accidental, fire. Canada's elite commando unit, the JTF2 (Joint Task Force 2), has fought in top-secret combat missions. Early in 2006, Canada led a NATO brigade of the International Security Assistance Force. NATO is working in co-operation with other groups that also involve Canadians, such as the United Nations, and non-government organizations, including Care Canada.

Canada is committed to the long-term rebuilding of Afghanistan, among the very poorest countries in the world. Canadian military personnel, diplomats, aid workers, and civilian police are all working together to help reinforce the country's fragile democracy, make the region stable, and improve people's quality of life so that terrorism will no longer breed there. Some observers feel that Canadians will be risking their lives and helping for at least a decade to come.

North American Aerospace Defence Command

Canada and the United States established the North American Air Defence Agreement (NORAD) in 1958. It was designed to protect North America from attack by the Soviet Union. One measure taken was to build three radar lines in Canada. These DEW, or Distant Early Warning, lines were known as the Far Arctic Line, the Mid-Canada Line, and the Pine Tree Line. Their purpose was to detect and intercept Russian bombers or missile attacks. The NORAD radar stations were used from the 1960s into the 1970s. Hundreds of NORAD missiles were aimed at targets in the Soviet Union. The missiles could respond instantly to an attack. American and Canadian bombers and fighters were in the air or at the ready at all times.

Over the years, NORAD's focus has changed, along with its name. It is now the North American Aerospace Defence Command. NORAD focuses on human-made objects in space. It is guarding North America from attack by aircraft, missiles, and space weapons.

In 2000, the United States invited Canada to take part in a new military venture. It wanted Canada's help to create a missile defence system. Canada refused to participate in "the weaponization of space." Canada's alliance with the United States is close, but the countries often take different positions on major issues.

Military Alliances Today

Canada's membership in NATO and NORAD is expensive. Many Canadians feel that these alliances are dominated by the United States. They believe that Canada may not be consulted before action is taken. Some argue that Canada should not make alliances solely for military purposes. Others believe that with the decline of the Soviet Union and the end of the Warsaw Pact, NATO and NORAD are no longer important. Yet, as this chapter describes, NATO, especially, is active in world events.

FOCUS

1. Why are alliances with other countries important for Canada?
2. What is NATO's purpose?
3. What is NORAD?
4. Do you think that membership in NATO and NORAD is necessary? Explain.

Economic and Political Alliances

Many of Canada's alliances are not military. Canada has economic ties with countries from all over the globe. Canada's multicultural diversity and history support strong cultural ties to other countries.

The Organization of American States (OAS)

The OAS is the world's oldest regional organization. First called the International Union of American Republics, it was founded in 1890. All 35 independent countries in the Western hemisphere are now members.

Canada joined in 1990. It decided that membership would help it to gain more influence within its own hemisphere and to promote trade. Concerns about the natural environment and the illegal drug trade also encouraged it to join. The OAS is working to create a free trade area of the Americas. It hopes that freer trade will help get rid of the poverty and discrimination within member countries.

The Arctic Council

Canada's Arctic region contains 40 percent of Canada's land mass and 66 percent of its marine coastline. Founded in 1996, the Arctic Council is an alliance of eight polar countries: Canada, the United States, Denmark/Greenland, Finland, Iceland, Norway, Russia, and Sweden. It is dedicated to preserving Arctic environments and to protecting the plants and animals of the region. The Council monitors the ecological health of the Arctic. It also works to improve the economic, social, and cultural well-being of northern peoples. The Arctic Council gives permanent participation to delegations from northern **indigenous** peoples. Canada hosted the first Arctic Council meeting in Iqaluit in 1998.

Jack Anawak is Canadian ambassador for circumpolar affairs representing Canada at the Arctic Council. The Inuit earlier helped negotiate the Nunavut land claim; as a federal MP, he sometimes spoke Inuktitut in the House of Commons.

The G8 Economic Summit

A summit is a high-level meeting between the leaders of different countries. The G8 has its roots in the 1973 oil crisis and the global economic recession that followed. These problems led the United States to form the Library Group, a gathering of senior financial officials from the United States, Europe, and Japan, to discuss economic issues. In 1975, with the addition of the United Kingdom, France, West Germany, and Italy, the Group of Six (G6) was created.

At the suggestion of U.S. President Gerald Ford, Canada joined the following year and the organization became the G7. In 1991, at the end of the Cold War, Russia began attending some of the meetings, and in 1998 the G8 was created. Russia was excluded from the financial ministers' meetings, though, because it was not a major economic power. Early in 2005, several American politicians demanded that Russia be suspended from the G8 until it provided more democratic and political freedoms for its people. In 2006, though, Russia hosted the G8 Summit.

The G8 meets each year to discuss trade matters and relations with developing countries. The agenda often includes employment, the information highway, the environment, crime and drugs, human rights and arms control. These meetings allow political leaders to discuss complex issues. They also

Prime Minister Paul Martin (top right) fits into the official APEC group photo at the 2004 Summit in Santiago, Chile.

provide opportunities for leaders to get along and trust one another, something that could help in times of world crisis. By 2006, the G8 had met four times in Canada.

Asia-Pacific Economic Cooperation (APEC)

APEC was founded in 1994. It is an association of 24 Pacific Rim nations, or nations that border the Pacific Ocean. APEC promotes free trade and economic development in the Pacific Rim region. The region is home to over two billion people. It accounts for more than half of the world's pollution, energy, and food consumption. APEC meets annually. In 1997, when it was Canada's turn to host, the meeting was controversial. Outside the Vancouver summit, protesters marched. They believed that Indonesia should not be present at APEC talks. Indonesia was a dictatorship.

The Commonwealth and La Francophonie

Canada is a member of two multiracial and multicultural associations. One is the Commonwealth; the other is La Francophonie. These two worldwide organizations have helped Canadians establish friendly ties with many countries. Canada's official bilingual nature gives it two windows on the world.

At the 2002 Commonwealth Games, Canadian athletes Simon Whitfield and Carol Montgomery both won gold in the Triathlon event on the same day.

The Commonwealth flag consists of the Commonwealth symbol in gold on a blue background centred on a rectangle.

The flag developed from the car pennants flown at the Ottawa Commonwealth Heads of Government Meeting in 1973.

The "C" represents the word "Commonwealth" and the radiating spears represent the many ways in which members co-operate.

The Commonwealth of Nations

Britain once controlled colonies all over the world. As these colonies gained their independence, the Empire evolved into the British Commonwealth in 1931. The word "British" was dropped in 1946.

The Commonwealth is a loose economic and cultural organization. Members assist one another by encouraging mutual trade. The Colombo Plan was organized in 1950 so that richer Commonwealth nations, such as Great Britain, Canada, Australia, and New Zealand, could give aid and technology to developing Commonwealth members. Canada made great contributions through this plan. It provided technical assistance, resources, financial assistance, and scholarships to developing nations especially in South and Southeast Asia.

During the 1960s, South Africa's racist polices were a major concern. South Africa was asked to leave the Commonwealth. It was not allowed to return until its apartheid policy ended in 1994.

By 2006, 53 nations were part of the Commonwealth. They represented 30 percent of the world's population. Over time, Britain seemed to lose interest in leading the Commonwealth. Different Commonwealth countries provided leaders instead. For example, Canada's Brian Mulroney led the Commonwealth in 1986 and 1988. Most members believe that the Commonwealth helps the rich nations and the poor nations of this world to work together.

La Francophonie

French is one of Canada's two official languages. After Paris, Montreal is the largest French-speaking city in the world. It is natural that Canada should be a leading member of La Francophonie. Canada is one of 51 French-speaking states and governments within the voluntary association. La Francophonie was founded in 1970. The Canadian federal government, the province of Quebec, and the province of New Brunswick, with its Acadian population, are all members.

La Francophonie is similar to the

When Quebec announced that it could compete under its own flag at the 2001 "Jeux de la Francophonie," this performer twirled a flaming stick. The Games are as much a cultural as a sports event.

Commonwealth. Most of the participating nations were once part of the French Empire. Canada has had no direct political links with France for over 250 years. Still, the ties of language and culture remain deep. La Francophonie promotes cultural, scientific, technological, and legal ties among its members. The economic connection is less well developed. The cultural ties of La Francophonie are probably stronger than they are in the Commonwealth.

The symbol of La Francophonie was developed for the second Summit. This took place in Quebec City in 1987. It became the distinctive logo of future Summits. The five colours represent the different colours of the flags of the states and governments that took part in the Quebec City Summit. They also represent the five continents that are home to the various partners of La Francophonie.

FOCUS

1. Briefly explain why Canada is involved in the following organizations: OAS, Arctic Council, G8, APEC, Commonwealth, and La Francophonie.
2. In your opinion, which organization is most important? Why?
3. What is the Colombo Plan?

Canada's Aid to the Developing World

Over half of the world's six billion people are hungry. Home is often a crowded shack with a dirt floor. Fresh water, sewers, and plumbing are only dreams. Many people never have the chance to learn to read and write. Children grow up without basic health care.

Construction engineers with the Canadian Forces Disaster Assistance Response Team help villagers in Pakistan rebuild a water pump after the 2005 earthquake. The engineers are helping villagers restore the vital water supply.

Often, they fend for themselves in local garbage dumps. They become children of the streets, battered and abused, living short lives. Many countries lack funds to deal with disasters. There is no money to help in times of war, famine, flood, or earthquake. Some developing nations are run by dictators who ignore human rights.

Canada chooses to help the nations of the developing world.

There are several types of reasons.

HISTOR!CA

Minutes

Humanitarian reasons: Canadians believe that people have the right to live in freedom, without want and without suffering.

Military and political reasons: People in great poverty can sometimes turn to violence. Poverty is often a lure for terrorists. It is in Canada's interest to support a world without violence. Canadians do not want developing nations to be enemies of Canada.

Economic reasons: Canada may benefit by helping developing countries. These countries may become richer because of Canadian aid programs. They may then buy Canadian products and technology.

Social and cultural reasons: Canada is multicultural. Many of our citizens have close ties to people in other countries. Relatives and friends living in difficult situations encourage Canadians to be more generous.

In 1968, Canada established CIDA—the Canadian International Development Agency. CIDA administers aid to developing nations. CIDA's contribution is never paid in cash. It is provided in the form of programs and projects that are developed cooperatively with the receiving country. CIDA has given aid to nations in Africa, the Middle East, Asia, the former Soviet Union, and Central Europe. Canada gives aid through many UN aid programs, too.

In 1970, Canada agreed that richer nations should pledge 0.7 percent of their gross national product (**GNP**) to international aid. Lester Pearson, working for the World Bank, had recommended this to the world community. In 2006, though, Canadian aid was at about 0.23 percent of GNP. Few countries had met the target.

CUSO is the leading non-government Canadian agency that has sent more than 10 000 skilled Canadians overseas. CUSO provides international aid in education, technology, agriculture, business, and health. Workers serve two-year terms at minimal salary. Many Canadians call their CUSO experiences unforgettable.

Removing land mines is another form of aid. The land mine, still deadly after wars are over, is one of the world's most barbaric

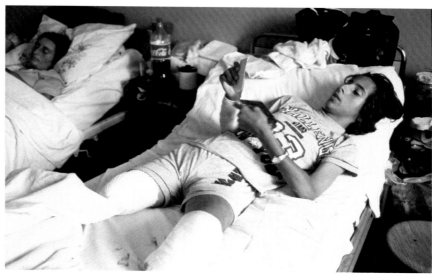

This 13-year-old lost both legs to a booby-trapped mine in Kosovo. Seventy percent of land mine victims there are under 24. CIDA provides leadership in removing land mines across the world.

weapons. The device explodes on contact. It is estimated that 110 million land mines are hidden in 64 countries. Victims are most often women and children.

In 1996, Canada sponsored a conference to explore ways to ban land mines. Seventy-four nations agreed that land mines should be banned worldwide. The International Campaign to Ban Land Mines was launched, and the UN General Assembly passed a resolution urging the ban. By 1997, 122 nations, including Canada, signed the Mine Ban Treaty. By 2006, 140 had signed, but 40 countries, including the United States, had not.

Cardinal Paul-Emile Léger

BORN: 1904; Valleyfield (Salaberry-de-Valleyfield), Quebec

DIED: 1991; Montreal, Quebec

SIGNIFICANCE: Cardinal Léger was one of Canada's great humanitarians. He worked hard to help the sick, the weak, and the poor, especially in Canada and in Africa.

BRIEF BIOGRAPHY: Cardinal Paul-Emile Léger was the oldest son of a Quebec grocer. As a young boy, he spent hours listening to his father's friends argue about political issues. At age 12, he went to study at the Minor Seminary of Saint Thérèse. By 1923, he believed he was intended to become a priest. Léger was ordained as a priest six years later. He left for France to serve as a teacher with the Sulpician Order. In 1933, he went to serve in Japan. When the Second World War broke out, he returned to Valleyfield. In 1947, Léger was appointed rector of the Canadian Pontifical College in Rome. He saw that the city was devastated by war. The new rector worked hard raising funds in Canada to help the city's poor. In 1950, Pope Pius II chose Léger to be archbishop of Montreal. The city's social problems became Léger's immediate concern. He spoke out boldly against the provincial government of Maurice Duplessis. In 1953, Léger became a cardinal, a key leader within the Roman Catholic Church. He admitted, "to be a Cardinal is very convenient in a certain way, it gives you a little bit of authority."

From 1962 to 1965, the Roman Catholic Church was in the midst of much change. The Second Vatican Council was at work. Léger argued for reform. He believed that the Church needed to be more relevant to the modern world. In 1963, Léger visited Africa. He set up Fame Pereo (the I am Dying of Hunger organization) to help people suffering from leprosy.

Cardinal Léger stepped down as archbishop of Montreal in 1967. He travelled to Cameroon, Africa, and set up the Centre for the Rehabilitation of the Handicapped. In 1979, at age 75, he returned to Montreal. With Roland Michener, he was named co-chair of the Canadian Foundation for Refugees. The Foundation's role was to help Vietnamese boat people fleeing to Canada. **In your opinion, what was Léger's greatest achievement? Why?**

Disaster Relief

Canadians respond to many disasters and emergencies, and not all of them so far away. In 2005, even New Orleans in the United States needed aid. It suffered greatly from Hurricane Katrina. When disaster has struck far away, Canadians have responded quickly and generously.

The Indian Ocean Tsunami: In December 2004, a giant tsunami rolled across the Indian Ocean. It wiped out cities, towns, and villages. Within hours, 250 000 people were killed. Entire communities were swept away. The hardest hit areas were in Indonesia, Thailand, and Sri Lanka. Millions of survivors faced starvation and disease.

Canadian soldier on an earlier DART mission in Honduras.

The world responded with the greatest outpouring of aid in history. Billions of dollars, thousands of aid workers, and hundreds of agencies went to the region. Canada pledged almost $1 billion in aid relief. The Canadian Disaster Assistance Response Team, or DART, was sent to Sri Lanka's battered province of Ampara to provide fresh water and medical care.

The Kashmir Earthquake: On 9 October 2005, Pakistan was rocked by a powerful earthquake. The greatest damage and loss of life happened in isolated communities in Kashmir and Pakistan's North West Frontier Province. About 80 000 died in the first days. Millions more faced death from disease, starvation, and the cold of the oncoming winter. One thousand hospitals and 4000 schools were crushed. The Canadian government pledged $79 million and DART to help provide fresh water and medical care.

World climate experts predict that global warming will lead to more disasters, droughts, and hurricanes. Canadians will be called upon to provide disaster relief again and again.

FOCUS

1. List two reasons why Canada should help developing nations.
2. What is CIDA? What does it do?
3. Should Canada provide disaster relief to other nations? Explain.

The New World Order

At the turn of the 21st century, most people faced the future with optimism. A bright new century had dawned. Increasing wealth, great leaps in technological progress, and the end of the Cold War all promised that peace and prosperity were on the way.

9/11: Terror in New York

On 11 September 2001, just as most North American students were heading to school, something truly terrible happened. Two airplanes smashed into the tall twin towers of the World Trade Center in New York. As millions of horrified people watched, the twin towers burned and crumbled into dust. People from more than 70 nations died.

The terror was not yet over. Moments later, another plane crashed into the Pentagon, the U.S. military headquarters in Washington.

Workers hang from a crane inspecting the debris from the World Trade Center. This photo was taken a few days after the 9/11 attack.

Yet another plane, perhaps targeting the White House, plunged into a field in Pennsylvania.

The world would never be the same. Feelings of fear and anger ran high. Desires for justice and revenge took hold. Optimism fled.

The Fog of War

The United States had been the target of a carefully planned terrorist attack. Terrorists from the Middle East had hijacked four planes. Their purpose was to cause widespread death and destruction in the United States, and they succeeded. The United States and most of the world vowed to bring the people who had caused such tragedy to justice. U.S. President George W. Bush and many other world leaders announced war on all terrorists and any nations that harboured them.

Closing Ranks

The assault on the World Trade Center brought Canadians and Americans closer together. Most Canadians were shocked and horrified by the attack. Dozens of Canadians had perished. The vast majority of Canadians closed ranks with their neighbours to the south. Money, supplies, blood, medicine, and muscle power were committed to the recovery effort in New York. Huge memorials and demonstrations of support took place all across Canada. Many Canadians even placed American flags in their windows or on their lawns.

The War Against Terrorism

The Canadian government moved quickly to instill confidence among Canadians and to combat terrorism.

- An elite Canadian anti-terrorist force, the JTF2 (Joint Task Force Two) was dispatched to the war zone in Afghanistan. The terrorists who plotted the attacks on the World Trade Center were living in Afghanistan and were protected by its government. Joint Task Force Two was later expanded. As of 2006, this secretive force was still in Afghanistan conducting high-risk missions.
- As of 2006, 2400 Canadian Forces personnel served in Afghanistan on a highly dangerous, but important mission.
- Security at border crossings and airports was increased.

Helping Afghanistan rebuild means danger for Canadians serving near Kandahar. In this roadside bomb attack, three were only injured; others are not so lucky.

- The government committed billions of dollars to fighting terrorism and increasing security. Its measures included expanding the armed forces, hiring air marshals for Canadian flights, purchasing new high-tech security equipment and increasing security at border crossings and airports.

War on Another Front—Fighting Disease

Diseases that start in a village on a continent far from Canada may pose a dangerous threat to Canadians. One negative result of a smaller, more interconnected world is that disease travels more easily and rapidly. What happens outside Canadian borders has an impact on the health and well-being of Canadians.

Stephen Lewis

BORN: 1937; Ottawa, Ontario

SIGNIFICANCE: Stephen Lewis is committed to fighting for human rights, especially for people far less fortunate than most Canadians. He speaks out for reform in Canada and around the globe.

BRIEF BIOGRAPHY:
Stephen Lewis was born into a very political family with an active social conscience. His father, David, helped found the CCF and later served as an NDP leader. Lewis entered politics while still a university student. He was elected as an NDP member of the Ontario legislature in 1963. Here, he fought for the rights of women and workers. Lewis served as Ontario NDP leader from 1970 to 1978.

In 1984, Lewis was appointed as Canada's ambassador to the UN. He served until 1988. He then worked as deputy executive director of UNICEF from 1995 to 1999.

In 2001, Lewis became the UN Secretary-General's special envoy for HIV/AIDS in Africa. He now fights this pandemic problem with much energy. Lewis has argued that although drugs to combat AIDS are available in rich countries, they are unavailable to the world's poor. By 2006, HIV/AIDS had already claimed 17 million African lives.

Lewis's 2006 book, *Race Against Time*, opens with these words: "I have spent the last four years watching people die." For some Canadians he has become a moral compass. He reminds people of their responsibility to help others across the world. *Maclean's* magazine named Lewis "Canadian of the Year" in 2003. *Time* magazine listed him as one of the 100 most influential people in the world in 2005. **Should Canadians do more for those suffering from AIDS in other countries? Explain. To learn more about Stephen Lewis's work to combat AIDS, visit www.stephenlewisfoundation .org or www.unaids.org.**

CANADIAN LIVES

One of the world's most difficult challenges now is the outbreak of global **pandemics**. A pandemic disease can threaten the lives of millions of people. It can affect a whole country, or even the world. In recent years, HIV/AIDs, **SARS**, and the **Avian flu** have become or have threatened to become pandemic.

Canada has worked especially hard to help control the spread of HIV/AIDS. It has committed money to pay for drugs needed in African countries, where HIV/AIDS threatens millions. Canadian Stephen Lewis is in the forefront of the battle to stop the rapid spread of AIDS on this continent.

Canada is dealing with the threat of possible pandemics at home. SARS arrived in 2003. It killed 44 Canadians before being brought under control. In 2006, the world was struggling to track Avian flu. This virus transmits a deadly flu bug from birds to humans. Canada is playing an active role in researching, tracking, and preparing for a possible outbreak.

These Canadian doctors are in Kashmir to provide care for earthquake victims. They are part of the DART relief effort.

New Century, Old Problems

Like the early 20th century, this century opened with acts of terrorism. After the attack in New York, terrorists bombed trains in London and Madrid. After the American military victory in Iraq and the collapse of Saddam Hussein's government, suicide bombings, kidnappings, and other terrorist acts continued. Canadians were sometimes victims in these events.

As this new century unfolds, Canadians will have to balance fear with optimism. Young Canadians have yet to make their mark on Canada and the world. They will write the next chapters of this new century. You will be a part of it.

HISTOR!CA
Minutes

FOCUS

1. What is Canada's role in the fight against terrorism?
2. Which diseases threatened the world at the beginning of the 21st century?
3. What types of good works do Canadians perform in the world today?
4. How do you see this new century unfolding? What might your role in it be like?

Sharpening Your Skills

Public Speaking

THE SKILL
Presenting ideas orally before a large group of people

THE IMPORTANCE
The need for good presentation skills in job interviews, class presentations, and many occupations

Similar to an essay, an oral presentation should have a focus or major argument, an introduction, information to prove your argument, and a conclusion that restates your argument and summarizes the major points made in developing your idea.

Do your best to present oral presentations in an interesting manner. If you only read a speech, you run the risk of boring your audience. Instead, be sure to write your key points on cue cards. Sound enthusiastic.

Rehearse. If possible, tape-record your speech and listen to it critically. You may find that you need to pronounce some of your words more clearly, or that you're speaking too fast or too slowly. Or, you could practise in front of a mirror, paying attention to your posture and gestures. Ask someone to watch as you rehearse and give an honest opinion. Your audience may be able to spot distracting mannerisms, such as touching your hair or shuffling your feet.

Focus on your voice. The way you use your voice adds to the impression you make. Obviously, you will want to speak loudly enough so that the audience can hear you easily. Consider such factors as the size of the room and whether there are outside noises you must speak over (such as the hum of a machine). Speak more loudly to emphasize an important point. At other times, you might gain attention by speaking more softly, making the audience listen more carefully. Avoid speaking in a flat voice with little range.

Do not speak so fast that you become difficult to understand. If you have a time limit, pace yourself so that you can finish your speech without having to hurry at the end. Varying your speed from time to time can make your speech more effective. Slow down to emphasize a point. Think of taking a dramatic pause at the end of a particularly important statement.

Consider how you look. Your appearance and the way you use your body can be almost as important as your voice. Dress in clothing that is appropriate to your audience and the occasion. Avoid wearing unusual clothes or jewellery that might distract the audience or get in the way as you speak. Stand up straight, but in a relaxed manner. Keep a pleasant expression on your face.

Make eye contact. As much as you can, keep eye contact with your audience; however, avoid looking up and down so quickly that you get motion sickness. Using point-form cue cards helps to avoid these problems.

Make gestures. Gestures can help emphasize important parts of your speech. Don't overdo them, though. If you gesture constantly, you will lessen the effect and make the audience more aware of your gestures than your words.

Use audio-visual aids. These can enliven your presentation. PowerPoint, slides, maps, graphs, models, chalkboards, films, tape recordings, and videotapes add welcome variety to your speech and help hold the audience's attention.

Avoid stage fright. Take a deep breath or two to stay calm. Act confident. Remember that your audience is rooting for you to do well. Walk briskly to your place and look directly at the audience. Make sure that you gain the group's attention. You might first introduce yourself. Once you begin speaking, you'll find that your nervousness will decrease. Conclude your talk on an upbeat note—not, "well, that's about it"—and thank the audience.

Key Points in Using an Audiovisual Aid

- Have the aid ready to use before your speech. If an aid is particularly interesting or unusual, it may be a good idea to have it hidden until the appropriate time in your speech. Otherwise, your audience may be too distracted to pay close attention to the earlier parts of your speech.
- Mount illustrations and set them up on an easel, rather than trying to hold them while speaking.
- If you are going to write on a chalkboard, remember to keep turning back to your listeners. Talk to the audience, not to the aid. Keep eye contact.
- Don't pass a visual aid around during your speech—it would be too distracting.
- Be sure not to block your audience's view.
- Ensure that your visual aid is large enough to be seen at the back of the room.
- Rehearse with your aid so you can incorporate it smoothly into your speech.

Application

Play the word whisker game. *Word whiskers* are distracting phrases or words that people insert too often in their speech. Avoid saying "er" or "um" between words or phrases, or overusing such words as "like" and "you know." The word whisker game is an excellent way to eliminate these habits that other people find so annoying. Two or more can play. One person picks a topic, perhaps dogs as good pets or an issue from this chapter. After a five-second break, another student talks on that topic for 30 seconds, aiming not to make any word whiskers.

Questions & Activities

Questions and Activities

Match the names or items in column A with the descriptions in column B.

A	B
1. Lester Pearson	**a)** person responsible for day-to-day activities of UN
2. NATO	**b)** Canadian–American alliance
3. Security Council	**c)** winner of Nobel Peace Prize
4. NORAD	**d)** UN Commander in Rwanda
5. Secretary-General	**e)** alliance to defend Europe
6. La Francophonie	**f)** body of UN responsible for maintaining peace
7. Stephen Lewis	**g)** UN agency for children's welfare
8. UNICEF	**h)** association of French-speaking nations
9. Cardinal Léger	**i)** crusader for AIDS relief
10. Roméo Dallaire	**j)** supporter of the poor in Africa and in Canada

Unscramble the letters to form words introduced in this chapter.

1. INTUDE STONIAN   **2.** DHIRT RODWL

3. LCMTENOMAHWM   **4.** ZSEU RSCISI

5. LDCO RWA   **6.** ERGNIFO IDA

7. NAPMECID   **8.** ERORTMSIR

9. EPEAC   **10.** WRDNAA

Discuss and Debate

1. Canada has taken part in nearly every UN peacekeeping mission. Do you think Canada should continue to volunteer for these activities? Why or why not?

2. There are still more than 10 000 nuclear weapons in the world, enough to kill everyone on the planet many times. In small groups, discuss the chances of world nuclear disarmament.

3. To what extent do you feel that the United Nations is an effective organization to preserve and maintain world peace?

4. Create lists outlining the good and bad points of Canada's membership in NATO and in NORAD. If Canada believes itself to be a peace-loving country, should it continue to belong to these military alliances? Explain.

5. Debate these topics:
a) The Commonwealth of Nations is an outdated organization. It should be dissolved.
b) La Francophonie, indirectly, helps Quebec separatism as it supports the participation of Quebec as a "nation."

6. J. S. Woodsworth, one of the founders of the CCF, once stated that the 19th century "made the world a neighbourhood: this century [20th] must make it a brotherhood." To what extent did it succeed? Will the 21st century become a true global neighbourhood? Explain.

7. Prime Minister Trudeau once said that he considered himself to be "a citizen of the world." What do you think he meant? To what extent do you consider yourself to be a citizen of the world?

Do Some Research

1. Learn more about the Nobel Peace Prize. Your report should answer these questions:
   a) What were the origins of the prize?
   b) Besides Lester Pearson, who has won the prize?
   c) Why were they awarded it?
   d) Is there anyone you think should be awarded the prize? Why do you think so?
   e) What other Canadians have won a Nobel Prize? What did they do to earn it?

2. Since 1945, more than 100 wars involving 80 countries have broken out. Over 25 million people have been injured or killed as a result. Examine the causes, events, and results of one of these wars.

3. Research one agency that tries to help people in developing countries. Gather as much information as you can about the projects that this agency undertakes. Some agencies you might study include these:

   a) Canadian Save the Children Fund
   b) Red Cross
   c) Oxfam
   d) Canada World Youth

4. Research a developing country in the news. Use some of the following headings as organizers: Population; Type of Government; Resources; Industries; Per Capita Income; Trade; National Debt; Obstacles to Development.

Be Creative

1. If you were creating a list of foreign policy objectives for Canada, what would they be and why?

2. Develop a list of what you consider to be the world's most important concerns. What should be Canada's responses to each of them?

Web Watch

Arctic Council: www.arctic-council.org

The Commonwealth: www.commonwealth.org

La Francophonie: www.francophonie.org

Canadian Department of Foreign Affairs:
www.dfait-maeci.gc.ca/menu-e.asp

NATO: www.nato.int

Organization of American States: www.oas.org

United Nations: www.un.org

The CBC Digital Archives, at www.cbc.ca/archives, has many audiovisual files on themes relevant to this chapter. For example: "Cold War Culture: The Nuclear Fear of the 1950s and 1960s," "Peacekeepers and Peacemakers: Canada's Diplomatic Contribution," "The Early Years of the AIDS Crisis," "Launching the Digital Age: Canada's Satellites," "Marc Garneau: Canadian Space Pioneer," "Witness to Evil: Roméo Dallaire and Rwanda," "One for All: The North Atlantic Treaty Organization," "Influenza: Battling the Last Great Virus," and "Canadarm—A Technology Star."

Glossary

Glossary

Acid rain rain that has become an acid because it has absorbed chemicals in polluted air

Alberta Five Five women who won the famous Persons Case in 1929; they established that women were persons under the law and thereby eligible to hold public office, such as being a senator.

Anglophone a person whose native tongue is English; an English-speaking person

Anti-Semitic showing a hatred or dislike of Jews or other Middle Eastern people

Armistice a truce; an agreement to stop shooting in a war

Assembly line a way to organize workers so that each person specializes in one job along a line of jobs. This method is efficient, but often repetitive for the workers.

Assimilate the process or policy whereby a group of people, for example, new immigrants or Aboriginal people, quickly adopts the way of life and language of the majority, thereby ignoring their original culture and language

Auto Pact a 1965 trade agreement between Canada and the United States to establish free trade in the automobile industry

Avian flu a virulent form of influenza, originally found in birds, that some fear may lead to a terrible pandemic like the Spanish flu of 1918

Baby boom temporary increase in the birth rate

Black market unofficial, often illegal, system of buying and selling goods

Blitzkrieg "lightning war"; Germany's conquest of Denmark, Norway, the Netherlands, Belgium, and France in 1940

Bloc Québécois a federal separatist party founded by Lucien Bouchard

Boat people a term originally used to describe people from South Vietnam who fled to Canada; generally, they would be people who leave their country by boat and hope to land in another nation and be accepted as refugees.

Bootleggers people who illegally make and sell alcohol

Boycott the strategic withdrawal of commercial or social relations; for example, refusing to trade with apartheid South Africa

Canadian Expeditionary Force the armed force that Canada sent to fight in the First World War

CANDU short for CANada Deuterium Uranium; (deuterium oxide is heavy water; uranium is a natural fuel). CANDU is a nuclear-powered reactor that uses pressurized heavy water and natural uranium to generate electrical power.

Capitalism an economic system that emphasizes the making of profit for business owners or shareholders; businesses are owned by private individuals or shareholders, not governments.

Censorship the review of information or images by government or military agencies with a view to whether it will be approved or not allowed to be passed on

Closure a rule in Parliament that lets the government cut off or limit debate on an issue and bring it to a vote

Cold War hostility between nations without actual fighting—a war of political ideas; after the Second World War, the United States encouraged democratic, capitalist governments in Europe while the Soviet Union encouraged communist ideas.

Collective bargaining a process where workers are represented by unions at meetings with employers to bargain for improved wages and working conditions

Communism an economic system promoting state ownership and an equal sharing of wealth and resources; it may be preceded by a revolution.

Commuter age a time when people lived a fair distance from their work and had to drive or take the train or bus to work and back; this period began in the 1950s with the growth of suburbs.

Concentration camp a camp to hold large numbers of people as political prisoners or to exterminate them; most associated with camps run by Nazi Germany

Conscription compulsory military service

Constitution the main or foundational laws of the land; the Canadian Constitution sets out the powers of the federal and provincial governments and includes the Charter of Rights and Freedoms.

Convoy a group of ships travelling together, often with armed escort for protection

CRTC Canadian Radio-television and Telecommunications Commission, set up by the Canadian government in 1968 to regulate and protect Canadian broadcasting

Death camps prison camps, such as those of Nazi Germany, where many prisoners die or are put to death

Debt a sum of money that is owed to someone else; when nations owe money to citizens or other countries, interest must be paid on their debt.

Deficit usually calculated on a yearly basis, this is what is created when people or governments spend more money than they have.

Depression a period of weak economic activity with high unemployment

Dictator a person who rules a country, holding all power, and often using force to stay in power

Discrimination unfavourable treatment of a person or group based on race, country of origin, or gender

Distinct society a term recognizing Quebec as a unique part of Canada; it was a key element in the Meech Lake and Charlottetown Accord negotiations; some of Canada's First Nations also claim this status.

Democratic socialism a system where socialism is achieved in a democratic way by having citizens vote for such a government; socialism itself is a political and economic system in which property and businesses are owned by the community instead of individuals with the idea that people would share business profits.

Dogfights air battles between fighter planes in the First World War

Eastern Front the battle line between German forces and Russian forces in Eastern Europe in the First World War

Economic nationalists people who believe that the economic life and resources of a nation should be owned and controlled by the residents or citizens of that nation

Economic recession a period of temporary business decline, which results in higher unemployment; a recession is less severe than an economic depression.

Embassy a branch of government in a foreign country, such as the Canadian embassy in Washington acting as Canada's voice through the ambassador

Enemy aliens in the First World War the name given to people living in Canada, but originally from enemy countries

Ethnic cleansing a form of genocide, or mass killing, that was attempted in the Balkan wars of the late 20th century

Fascism a form of dictatorship backed up by secret police and the army, based on nationalistic and racist theories

Federalists in terms of the people of Quebec, those Quebecers in favour of a united Canada and opposed to separation

Francophone a French-speaking person; a person whose native tongue is French

Free trade buying and selling between countries without tariffs, customs duties, or other government forms of intervening in the flow of trade

General strike a withdrawal of labour by a number of unions and workers co-ordinating their efforts

Genocide the deliberate destruction of a people or nation

Gestapo Nazi secret police

Ghettos parts of a city inhabited by a racial, national, or religious minority

Global warming an increase in the earth's temperature that is causing flooding as a result of polar icecaps melting and other environmental concerns—a current issue

GNP Gross National Product, or the sum value of all the goods and services produced in a nation, usually within one year

Gulag a labour camp, created by Joseph Stalin, where political prisoners were sent to serve their sentences; gulags were located in remote areas of the U.S.S.R.

Holocaust total destruction, especially the Nazis' mass killing of Jews, gypsies, homosexuals, and others in the Second World War

Human rights the basic rights that every human being should have and enjoy

Icon a solid historical image or presence in a country, such as the quick recognition of the Hudson's Bay Company throughout Canada's history; can also be a person who represents something admirable, such as Terry Fox

Indigenous referring to the original inhabitants of a region

Inflation a general increase in prices and the cost of living

International Boundary Commission a commission that is responsible for maintaining the boundary line and markers between Canada and the United States; there is one Canadian and one American commissioner.

International Joint Commission a Canadian–American group of six members who look at issues affecting both countries and make recommendations to the two governments; focuses especially on water resources

Internment camps a type of camp where people are held against their will, for example, camps for Japanese Canadians during the Second World War

Isolationism a policy of withdrawal from external events or global affairs

"Juno" the code name for the Canadian landing in Normandy, France, on D-Day, 6 June 1944; named after the beach

Kristallnacht "the night of broken glass"; a night in 1938 when Hitler's Nazis destroyed Jewish homes and businesses as revenge for the shooting death of a German diplomat by a Jewish student; it marked an increase in the persecution of Jews.

League of Nations an association of countries, formed in 1919, to promote international peace; the failed organization was later replaced by the United Nations.

Minority government government in Parliament or in a provincial legislature in which the ruling party has less than half of the seats in the Parliament or legislative assembly

Motion of non-confidence a specific vote in Parliament or in a provincial legislature when all members vote to express their approval or disapproval of the party in power

NAFTA North American Free Trade Agreement; created in 1994 as an agreement to promote free trade between Canada, the United States, and Mexico

Nationalists in terms of Quebec, Quebecers who wish to remain in Canada, but firmly support their province

Naturalized immigrants immigrants who have chosen to become citizens of a nation; they would then have the same rights as individuals born in that country.

Nazi a member of the National Socialist German Worker's Party, led by Adolf Hitler, from 1933 to 1945; a person belonging to an organization that holds similar extreme racist and fascist beliefs

No man's land the land between two lines of trenches in the First World War—usually very dangerous, muddy, and difficult to cross

Nuclear age a period in history that saw the use of nuclear energy for the first time; it is generally agreed that the age began with the dropping of the first atomic bomb on Hiroshima in 1945.

Nuclear arms race a desire or goal of two or more nations to build the most powerful nuclear weapons

October Crisis also known as the FLQ Crisis, a time in 1970 when the FLQ, a terrorist organization, kidnapped James Cross and Pierre Laporte

Order of Canada a way of honouring Canadians who have demonstrated exceptional service to their community or nation, or who have made an outstanding contribution in a particular field of Canadian life; there are three levels of Honour: Member, Officer, and Companion.

Over the top in the First World War, leaving the safety of a trench in order to attack the enemy

Pacifist a person who rejects war and violence

Pandemics outbreaks of disease on a global scale

Parti Québécois a Quebec political party that puts Quebec's interests first; founded by René Lévesque, it is dedicated to Quebec separating from Canada and becoming a sovereign nation.

Patriate to bring something—in this case, a constitution—to the country in which it applies; a uniquely Canadian word

Patronage providing a job or favour to someone, especially a political job given to an individual for work done on behalf of the political party

Peacekeeping the UN policy of supervising and enforcing peace after a negotiated end to conflict

Peacemaking the UN policy of using force to bring a conflict to an end or forcing an intruder to withdraw

Pogrom organized, government-approved killing of members of a community, notably the Jews in Russia

Prisoners of conscience people imprisoned for their ideas, values, and personal beliefs

Profiteering taking advantage of the crisis and confusion of wartime in order to make windfall profits

Prohibition a ban on the making and selling of alcohol; it is also the name of a time period in the 1920s and 1930s in North America.

Propaganda information that is presented in a one-sided, often untruthful manner in order to meet a specific political objective and to control public opinion

Public transit a system of transporting people by the use of vehicles owned by governments or government organizations, for example, trains and subways

Quiet Revolution a period of dramatic social, economic, and political change in Quebec during the 1960s

Ration books books that entitled Canadians to purchase restricted everyday goods, such as sugar, butter, meat, and gasoline, during the Second World War

Referendum a vote by all citizens to accept or reject a specific proposal

Refugee a person who has had to leave another country to escape cruel treatment because of political, religious, or other disagreement with the home government

Recession a period when economic growth weakens and recedes, often with a rise in unemployment

Royal Canadian Legion an association of present and past members of the Canadian armed services; it organizes many Remembrance Day activities.

Royalties in this case, a percentage of an amount of money (or fee) paid to a government in return for being allowed to drill for a natural resource, such as oil or natural gas, or mine for a mineral, such as gold

SARS Severe Acute Respiratory Syndrome; an infection that can lead to death. An outbreak hit Canada in May 2003.

Self-determination the right of a people to choose its own government

Separatism the movement to make Quebec an independent nation

Shell shock a form of nervous breakdown after exposure to battle conditions

Socialism a political and economic system where property, profits, and resources are shared more equally and may be owned by the state

Sovereignty another word for independence; for example, Quebec separatists seek sovereignty, or independence, for what they see as their nation.

Sovereignty-association one of the terms used by separatists to describe a future relationship between Canada and an independent Quebec

Specialization of labour a system whereby work is divided into highly specialized and unique jobs usually as part of a factory assembly line

Split run magazines a magazine publishing dispute between Canada and the United States about advertising and Canadian content

Statute of Westminster the British law that

declared that the Acts of the British Parliament do not apply to Canada; it formally recognized Canada's independence.

Suez Crisis Arab–Israeli boundary dispute in 1956; settled by Canadian Lester Pearson, who won the Nobel Peace Prize for his role

Suburbia populated outlying districts or outskirts of large cities

Surplus an economic term that means a nation or province has spent less money than it collected in taxes; it has money left over after all services have been paid for.

Surrealists an art and literature movement in the early 20th century that focused on symbols and dreams to express the subconscious

Tariff taxes, or duties, on goods imported from other countries

Trade sanctions an economic technique used by countries when they are unhappy with their economic relations with another country; for example, a U.S. trade sanction in the form of taxes has prevented Canadian softwood lumber from entering the United States.

Treaty of Versailles the treaty that ended the First World War and served as one of the causes for the Second World War

Triple Alliance an alliance of Germany, Austria-Hungary, and Italy made before the First World War

Triple Entente an alliance of Great Britain, France, and Russia made before the First World War

Ultimatum a final statement or demand that must be accepted or severe consequences will follow

Unilateral independence a declaration of independence without any negotiation; some Quebec separatists hoped to win a referendum and then declare Quebec independent right away.

Universal welfare program a government program that provides a minimum standard of living for all people in a country, regardless of wealth—in this case "universal" means all people. Programs can include health care, pensions, education, employment insurance, and workers' compensation due to injury at work.

Urbanization the movement of people from the countryside to the cities

Veto the power to overrule a decision; in the United Nations, some nations can overrule decisions of the Security Council.

Visible minorities groups within the population of a country, province, or city that are identified as being visibly different because of colour, race, or country of origin

Wage–price spiral a period when the prices of goods go up and workers demand that their wages go up to keep pace with the cost of living; as one part of the spiral rises, the other follows.

War bride a woman who marries a soldier while he is actively engaged in war service

War Measures Act the Act passed during the First World War that gave the Canadian government sweeping powers to arrest and detain enemy aliens; it was later used during the October Crisis of 1970 against the FLQ and alleged supporters.

Western Front the battle line separating Allied and German forces in Western Europe during the First World War

Wolf packs a term used to describe groups of German submarines that attacked and preyed on Allied shipping during the Second World War, especially in the Atlantic

Index

Acknowledgments

Pg. 6 Sopwith F1 Camel stamp, 1999 © Canada Post Corporation. Reproduced with Permission, John McCrae & poem stamp, 1968 © Canada Post Corporation. Reproduced with Permission; pg. 8 (left) Toronto Reference Library, T-12870, (top right) City of Toronto Archives, James Collection, (bottom right) W.I. Castle / Canada. Dept. of National Defence / Library and Archives Canada / PA-001326; pg. 9 LAC PA-11824; pg. 11 Saskatchewan Archives; pg. 12 (top) Glenbow Archives NA263-1, (bottom) City of Toronto Archives, James Collection; pg. 13 LAC PA-29788; pg. 15 (top) HMS Dreadnaught (British battleship, 1906). Heaving in the anchor, 1906. From the collections of the Naval Historical Center, (bottom) Colliers Photographic History of the War in Europe,; pg. 19 (top) LAC PA-66815, (bottom) City of Toronto Archives, JC8280; pg. 20 (top right) City of Toronto Archives, James Collection, (top right) City of Toronto Archives, James Collection, (bottom) Ontario Archives; pg. 21 LAC C-002468; pg. 22 W.I. Castle / Canada. Dept. of National Defence / Library and Archives Canada / PA-001326; pg. 22-23 LAC C-PA648; pg. 24 RCMI, Canada. Dept. of National Defence/Library and Archives Canada; pg. 26 LAC C-00167; pg. 26-27 LAC; pg. 27 LAC PA-05001; pg. 28 LAC PA-03737; pg. 30 LAC C-26340; pg. 31 Glenbow Archives, NA-1258-2; pg. 32 LAC PA-01654; pg. 33 (top) LAC PA-11824, (bottom) LAC; pg. 34-35 LAC C-19948; pg. 36 (top) City of Toronto Archives SC-244-2456, (bottom) LAC C-19952; pg. 37 LAC PA-042869; pg. 38 City of Toronto Archives, James Collection, 45554; pg. 39 City of Toronto Archives, SC244-654; pg. 40 LAC PA-4422, pg. 41 City of Toronto Archives, James Collection; pg. 42 NAC PA-11264; pg. 43 LAC C-18733; pg. 44 (top) National Museum of Canada, (bottom) National Museum of Canada; pg. 45 PANL; pg. 48 LAC C-26340; pg. 50 (top) RCMI, (bottom) LAC PA-3538; pg. 51 (top) LAC, (bottom) LAC PA-2890; pg. 52 LAC C-24963; pg. 55 LAC PA-25942; pg. F.H. Varley, "For What?," AN19710261-0770, Beaverbrook Collection of War Art © Canadian War Museum (CWM); pg. 58 photo courtesy of Don Bogle; pg. 59 courtesy of Colchester Historical Society Archives; pg. 61 Library and Archives Canada / PA-025025; pg. 66 Superman stamp, 1995 © Canada Post Corporation. Reproduced with Permission; pg. 68 (top) City of Toronto Archives, James Collection SC 244-903, (bottom right) Provincial Archives of Manitoba N 1888; pg. 69 (top) Stellerton Museum, (bottom) Glenbow Archives NA 12955D; pg. 70 City of Toronto Archives, James Collection SC 244-903; pg. 71 LAC; pg. 72 Provincial Archives of Manito-ba; pg. 74 LAC C-32857; pg. Provincial Archives of Manitoba 2762; pg. 76 LAC C-34443; pg. 77 Cape Breton Archives; pg. 78 LAC C-54523; pg. 79 John Mardon; pg. 80 LAC PA-127295; pg. 81 John Mardon; pg. 82 Courtesy of Canada's Sports Hall of Fame; pg. 83 Glenbow Archives; pg. LAC PA-139429; pg. 85 LAC PA-42652; pg. 87 Rogers Communications Inc.; pg. 88 Rogers Communications Inc.; pg. 89 Provincial Archives of Manitoba N 1888; pg. 90 (top) Ontario Archives, (bottom) LAC PA-55051; pg. 91 LAC; pg. 92 LAC C-37756; pg. 94 Provincial Archives of Manitoba; pg. Stellerton Museum; pg. 97 (top) LAC C-820594, (bottom) Glenbow Archives NA 12955D; pg. 98 Provincial Archives of Manitoba N 11765; pg. 99 Glenbow Archives NA 2308-1; pg. 101 ANC; pg. 102 LAC C-29461; pg. 103 LAC C-29461; pg. LAC/Communist Party of Canada PA-93922; pg. 106 LAC C-7731; pg. 107 LAC C-387; pg. 110 LAC C-29298; pg.112 LAC C-9339; pg. 114 Ontario Archives 9977; pg. 116 (top) Glenbow Archives NA-1019-168, (bottom) Hockey Hall of Fame; pg. 117 Ontario Archives; pg. 119 AirCanada Archives; pg. 120 J.E.H. MacDonald (1873-1932) Thomson's Rapids, Magnetawan River 1910, oil on paperboard, 15.2 x 23.4 cm, McMichael Canadian Art Collection, 1981.38; pg. 130 (top) LAC PA-25942, (bottom) LAC C-16792; pg. 131 (top) LAC, (bottom) LAC/DND; pg. 133 LAC PA-11471; pg. 135 Canadian Jewish Congress Archives; pg. 136 LAC; pg. 137 LAC C-16792; pg. 138 Photograph attributed to Heinrich Hoffmann / Library and Archives Canada / PA-164757; pg. 140 League of Nations Archives, UNOG Library; pg. 142 LAC; pg. 143 LAC; pg. 145 (top) RCAF Archives PL3053, (bottom) LAC/DND; pg. 146 LAC PA-6478; pg. 148 photo courtesy of Lou Ann Barnett; pg. 149 Friends of the HMCS Haida; pg. 150 DND; pg. 151 National Gallery of Canada; pg. 152 LAC; pg. 153 Library and Archives Canada / C-014160; pg. 154 Bank of Canada Archives / PC 305-460; pg. 155 (top) LAC PA-108332, (bottom) LAC; pg. 156 LAC C-31186; pg. 157 Vancouver Public Library; pg. 158 NAC C-81430; pg. 159 courtesy of Norman Killian, Camp X Historical Society; pg. 160 CP; pg. 161 © Hulton-Deutsch Collections/CORBIS; pg.162 © BETTMANN/CORBIS SYGMA; pg. 163 Vancouver Public Library, Special Collections, VPL 12851; pg. 164 CBC Still Photography; pg. 165 LAC C-47402; pg. 166 (left) LAC-49744, (right) AP; pg. 168 LAC/DND PA-107904; pg. 169 DND; pg. 170 National Gallery of Canada; pg. 171 private collection; pg. 172 LAC C-29452; pg. 173 (top) Toronto Transit Commission, (bottom) The Gazette; pg. 174 LAC; pg. 175 (left) LAC C-